The Random House Book of
TWENTIETH-CENTURY
FRENCH POETRY

The Random House Book of

# TWENTIETH-CENTURY FRENCH POETRY

with Translations
by American and British Poets

Edited by Paul Auster

Vintage Books  A Division of Random House  New York

First Vintage Books Edition, January 1984
Copyright © 1982 by Paul Auster
All rights reserved under International and Pan-American
Copyright Conventions. Published in the United States by
Random House, Inc., New York, and simultaneously in
Canada by Random House of Canada Limited, Toronto.
Originally published by Random House, Inc., in 1982.

*Since this page cannot legibly accommodate all acknowledgments
for permission to reproduce previously published material, they
appear at the back of the book, starting on page 621.*

Library of Congress Cataloging in Publication Data
Main entry under title:
The Random House book of twentieth-century
French poetry.
English and French.
Includes bibliographical references and index.
1. French poetry—20th century. 2. French poetry—20th
century—Translations into English. 3. English poetry—
Translations from French. I. Auster, Paul, 1947–    II. Title:
Random House book of 20th century French poetry
PQ1170.E6R36   1983   841'.91'08   82–17324
ISBN 0–394–71748–1 (pbk.)

Manufactured in the United States of America

9

# Contents

# PHILIPPE JACCOTTET

# ROBERT MARTEAU

# JACQUES DUPIN

# Introduction

I

*French and English constitute a single language.*

—WALLACE STEVENS

This much is certain: If not for the arrival of William and his armies on English soil in 1066, the English language as we know it would never have come into being. For the next three hundred years French was the language spoken at the English court, and it was not until the end of the Hundred Years' War that it became clear, once and for all, that France and England were not to become a single country. Even John Gower, one of the first to write in the English vernacular, composed a large portion of his work in French, and Chaucer, the greatest of the early English poets, devoted much of his creative energy to a translation of *Le Roman de la rose* and found his first models in the work of the Frenchman Guillaume de Machaut. It is not simply that French must be considered an "influence" on the development of English language and literature; French is a part of English, an irreducible element of its genetic make-up.

Early English literature is replete with evidence of this symbiosis, and it would not be difficult to compile a lengthy catalogue of borrowings, homages and thefts. William Caxton, for instance, who introduced the printing press in England in 1477, was an amateur translator of medieval French works, and many of the first books printed in Britain were English versions of French

romances and tales of chivalry. For the printers who worked under Caxton, translation was a normal and accepted part of their duties, and even the most popular English work to be published by Caxton, Thomas Malory's *Morte d'Arthur*, was itself a ransacking of Arthurian legends from French sources: Malory warns the reader no less than fifty-six times during the course of his narrative that the "French book" is his guide.

In the next century, when English came fully into its own as a language and a literature, both Wyatt and Surrey—two of the most brilliant pioneers of English verse—found inspiration in the work of Clément Marot, and Spenser, the major poet of the next generation, not only took the title of his *Shepheardes Calender* from Marot, but two sections of the work are direct imitations of that same poet. More importantly, Spenser's attempt at the age of seventeen to translate Joachim du Bellay (*The Visions of Bellay*) is the first sonnet sequence to be produced in English. His later revision of that work and translation of another Du Bellay sequence, *Ruines of Rome*, were published in 1591 and stand among the great works of the period. Spenser, however, is not alone in showing the mark of the French. Nearly all the Elizabethan sonnet writers took sustenance from the Pléiade poets, and some of them—Daniel, Lodge, Chapman—went so far as to pass off translations of French poets as their own work. Outside the realm of poetry, the impact of Florio's translation of Montaigne's essays on Shakespeare has been well documented, and a good case could be made for establishing the link between Rabelais and Thomas Nashe, whose 1594 prose narrative, *The Unfortunate Traveler*, is generally considered to be the first novel written in the English language.

On the more familiar terrain of modern literature, French has continued to exert a powerful influence on English. In spite of the wonderfully ludicrous remark by Southey that poetry is as impossible in French as it is in Chinese, English and American poetry of the past hundred years would be inconceivable without the French. Beginning with Swinburne's 1862 article in *The Spectator* on Baudelaire's *Les Fleurs du Mal* and the first translations of Baudelaire's poetry into English in 1869 and 1870, modern British and American poets have continued to look to France for new ideas. Saintsbury's article in an 1875 issue of *The Fortnightly Review* is exemplary. "It was not merely admiration of Baudelaire which was to be persuaded to English readers," he wrote, "but also imitation of him which, at least with equal earnestness, was to be urged on English writers."

Throughout the 1870's and 1880's, largely inspired by Théodore de Banville, many English poets began experimenting with French verse forms (ballades, lays, virelays and rondeaux), and the "art for art's sake" ideas propounded by Gautier were an important source for the Pre-Raphaelite movement in England. By the 1890's, with the advent of *The Yellow Book* and the Decadents, the influence of the French Symbolists became widespread. In 1893, for example, Mallarmé was invited to lecture at Oxford, a sign of the esteem he commanded in English eyes.

It is also true that little of substance was produced in English as a result of French influences during this period, but the way was prepared for the discoveries of two young American poets, Pound and Eliot, in the first decade of the new century. Each came upon the French independently, and each was inspired to write a kind of poetry that had not been seen before in English. Eliot would later write that ". . . the kind of poetry I needed, to teach me the use of my own voice, did not exist in England at all, and was only to be found in France." As for Pound, he stated flatly that "practically the whole development of the English verse-art has been achieved by steals from the French."

The English and American poets who formed the Imagist group in the years just prior to World War I were the first to engage in a *critical* reading of French poetry, with the aim not so much of imitating the French as of rejuvenating poetry in English. More or less neglected poets in France, such as Corbière and Laforgue, were accorded major status. F. S. Flint's 1912 article in *The Poetry Review* (London) and Ezra Pound's 1913 article in *Poetry* (Chicago) did much to promote this new reading of the French. Independent of the Imagists, Wilfred Owen spent several years in France before the war and was in close contact with Laurent Tailhade, a poet admired by Pound and his circle. Eliot's reading of the French poets began as early as 1908, while he was still a student at Harvard. Just two years later he was in Paris, reading Claudel and Gide and attending Bergson's lectures at the Collège de France.

By the time of the Armory show in 1913, the most radical tendencies in French art and writing had made their way to New York, finding a home with Alfred Stieglitz and his gallery at 291 Fifth Avenue. Many of the names associated with American and European modernism became part of this Paris–New York connection: Joseph Stella, Marsden Hartley, Arthur Dove, Charles Demuth, William Carlos Williams, Man Ray, Alfred Kreymborg, Marius de Zayas, Walter C. Arensberg, Mina Loy, Francis Picabia and Marcel Duchamp. Under the influence of Cubism and Dada, of Apollinaire and the Futurism of Marinetti, numerous magazines carried the message of modernism to American readers: *291, The Blind Man, Rongwrong, Broom, New York Dada*, and *The Little Review*, which was born in Chicago in 1914, lived in New York from 1917 to 1927 and died in Paris in 1929. To read the list of *The Little Review*'s contributors is to understand the degree to which French poetry had permeated the American scene. In addition to work by Pound, Eliot, Yeats and Ford Madox Ford, as well as its most celebrated contribution, James Joyce's *Ulysses*, the magazine published Breton, Éluard, Tzara, Péret, Reverdy, Crevel, Aragon and Soupault.

Beginning with Gertrude Stein, who arrived in Paris well before World War I, the story of American writers in Paris during the twenties and thirties is almost identical to the story of American writing itself. Hemingway, Fitzgerald, Faulkner, Sherwood Anderson, Djuna Barnes, Kay Boyle, e e cummings, Hart Crane, Archibald MacLeish, Malcolm Cowley, John Dos Passos, Katherine Anne Porter, Laura Riding, Thornton Wilder, Williams, Pound,

Eliot, Glenway Wescott, Henry Miller, Harry Crosby, Langston Hughes, James T. Farrell, Anaïs Nin, Nathanael West, George Oppen—all of these and others either visited or lived in Paris. The experience of those years has so thoroughly saturated American consciousness that the image of the starving young writer serving his apprenticeship in Paris has become one of our enduring literary myths.

It would be absurd to assume that each of these writers was directly influenced by the French. But it would be just as absurd to assume that they went to Paris only because it was a cheap place to live. In the most serious and energetic of the magazines of the period, *transition*, American and French writers were published side by side, and the dynamics of this exchange led to what has probably been the most fruitful period in our literature. Nor does absence from Paris necessarily preclude an interest in things French. The most Francophilic of all our poets, Wallace Stevens, never set foot in France.

Since the twenties, American and British poets have been steadily translating their French counterparts—not simply as a literary exercise, but as an act of discovery and passion. Consider, for example, these words from John Dos Passos's preface to his translations of Cendrars in 1930: ". . . A young man just starting to read verse in the year 1930 would have a hard time finding out that this method of putting words together has only recently passed through a period of virility, intense experimentation and meaning in everyday life. . . . For the sake of this hypothetical young man and for the confusion of Humanists, stuffed shirts in editorial chairs, anthology compilers and prize poets, sonnet writers and readers of bookchats, I think it has been worth while to attempt to turn these alive informal personal everyday poems of Cendrars' into English . . ." Or T. S. Eliot, introducing his translation of *Anabasis* by Saint-John Perse that same year: "I believe that this is a piece of writing of the same importance as the later work of James Joyce, as valuable as *Anna Livia Plurabelle*. And this is a high estimate indeed." Or Kenneth Rexroth, in the preface to his translations of Reverdy in 1969: "Of all the modern poets in Western European languages Reverdy has certainly been the leading influence on my own work—incomparably more than anyone in English or American—and I have known and loved his work since I first read *Les Épaves du ciel* as a young boy."

As the list of translators included in this book shows, many of the most important contemporary American and British poets have tried their hand at translating the French, among them Pound, Williams, Eliot, Stevens, Beckett, MacNeice, Spender, Ashbery, Blackburn, Bly, Kinnell, Levertov, Merwin, Wright, Tomlinson, Wilbur—to mention just some of the most familiar names. It would be difficult to imagine their work had they not been touched in some way by the French. And it would be even more difficult to imagine the poetry of our own language if these poets had not been a part of it. In a sense, then, this anthology is as much about American and British poetry as it is about French poetry. Its purpose is not only to present the work of

French poets in French, but to offer translations of that work as our own poets have re-imagined and re-presented it. As such, it can be read as a chapter in our own poetic history.

II

*The French tradition and the English tradition in this epoch are at opposite poles to each other. French poetry is more radical, more total. In an absolute and exemplary way it has assumed the heritage of European Romanticism, a romanticism which begins with William Blake and the German romantics like Novalis, and via Baudelaire and the Symbolists culminates in twentieth-century French poetry, notably Surrealism. It is a poetry where the world becomes writing and language becomes the double of the world.*

—OCTAVIO PAZ

On the other hand, this much is also certain: If there has been a steady interest in French poetry for the past hundred years on the part of British and American poets, enthusiasm for the French has often been tempered by a certain wariness, even hostility, to literary and intellectual practices in France. This has been more true of the British than the Americans, but, nevertheless, the American literary establishment remains strongly Anglophilic in orientation. One has only to compare the dominant trends in philosophy, literary criticism or novel-writing, to realize the enormous gulf between the two cultures.

Many of these differences reside in the disparities between the two languages. Although English is in large part derived from French, it still holds fast to its Anglo-Saxon origins. Against the gravity and substantiality to be found in the work of our greatest poets (Milton, say, or Emily Dickinson), which embodies an awareness of the contrast between the thick emphasis of Anglo-Saxon and the nimble conceptuality of French/Latin—and to play one repeatedly against the other—French poetry often seems almost weightless to us, to be composed of ethereal puffs of lyricism and little else. French is necessarily a thinner medium than English. But that does not mean it is weaker. If English writing has staked out as its territory the world of tangibility, of concrete presence, of surface accident, French literary language has largely been a language of essences. Whereas Shakespeare, for example, names

more than five hundred flowers in his plays, Racine adheres to the single word "flower." In all, the French dramatist's vocabulary consists of roughly fifteen hundred words, while the word count in Shakespeare's plays runs upward of twenty-five thousand. The contrast, as Lytton Strachey noted, is between "comprehension" and "concentration." "Racine's great aim," Strachey wrote, "was to produce, not an extraordinary nor a complex work of art, but a flawless one; he wished to be all matter and no impertinency. His conception of a drama was of something swift, inevitable; an action taken at the crisis, with no redundancies however interesting, no complications however suggestive, no irrelevances however beautiful—but plain, intense, vigorous, and splendid with nothing but its own essential force." More recently, the poet Yves Bonnefoy has described English as a "mirror" and French as a "sphere," the one Aristotelian in its acceptance of the given, the other Platonic in its readiness to hypothesize "a different reality, a different realm."

Samuel Beckett, who has spent the greater part of his life writing in both languages, translating his own work from French into English and from English into French, is no doubt our most reliable witness to the capacities and limitations of the two languages. In one of his letters from the mid-fifties, he complained about the difficulty he was having in translating *Fin de partie* (*Endgame*) into English. The line Clov addresses to Hamm, "Il n'y a plus de roues de bicyclette" was a particular problem. In French, Beckett contended, the line conveyed the meaning that bicycle wheels as a category had ceased to exist, that there were no more bicycle wheels in the world. The English equivalent, however, "There are no more bicycle wheels," meant simply that there were no more bicycle wheels available, that no bicycle wheels could be found in the place where they happened to be. A world of difference is embedded here beneath apparent similarity. Just as the Eskimos have more than twenty words for snow (a frequently cited example), which means they are able to experience snow in ways far more nuanced and elaborate than we are—literally to see things we cannot see—the French live inside their language in ways that are somewhat at odds with the way we live inside English. There is no judgment of any kind attached to this remark. If bad French poetry tends to drift off into almost mechanical abstractions, bad English and American poetry has tended to be too earthbound and leaden, sinking into triviality and inconsequence. Between the two bads there is probably little to choose from. But it is helpful to remember that a good French poem is not necessarily the same thing as a good English poem.

The French have had their Academy for more than three hundred years. It is an institution that at once expresses and helps to perpetuate a notion of literature far more grandiose than anything we have ever known in England or America. As an official point of view, it has had the effect of removing the literary from the realm of the everyday, whereas English and American writers have generally been more at home in the flux of the quotidian. But because they have an established tradition to react against, French poets—

paradoxically—have tended to be more rebellious than their British and American counterparts. The pressures of conformity have had the net result of producing a vigorous anti-tradition, which in many ways has actually usurped the established tradition as the major current in French literature. Beginning with Villon and Rabelais, continuing on through Rousseau, Baudelaire, Rimbaud, and the cult of the *poète maudit*, and then on into the twentieth century with Apollinaire, the Dada movement and the Surrealists, the French have systematically and defiantly attacked the accepted notions of their own culture—primarily because they have been secure in their knowledge that this culture exists. The lessons of this anti-tradition have been so thoroughly assimilated that today they are more or less taken for granted.

By contrast, the great interest shown by Pound and Eliot in French poetry (and, in Pound's case, the poetry of other languages as well) can be read not so much as an attack on Anglo-American culture as an effort to create a tradition, to manufacture a past that would somehow fill the vacuum of American newness. The impulse was essentially conservative in nature. With Pound, it degenerated into Fascist rantings; with Eliot, into Anglican pieties and an obsession with the notion of Culture. It would be wrong, however, to set up a simple dichotomy between radicalism and conservatism, and to put all things French in the first category and all things English and American in the second. The most subversive and innovative elements of our literature have frequently surfaced in the unlikeliest places and have then been absorbed into the culture at large. Nursery rhymes, which form an essential part of every English-speaking child's early education, do not exist as such in France. Nor do the great works of Victorian children's literature (Lewis Carroll, George Macdonald) have any equivalent in French. As for America, it has always had its own, homegrown Dada spirit, which has continued to exist as a natural force, without any need of manifestoes or theoretical foundations. The films of Buster Keaton and W. C. Fields, the skits of Ring Lardner, the drawings of Rube Goldberg surely match the corrosive exuberance of anything done in France during the same period. As Man Ray (a native American) wrote to Tristan Tzara from New York in 1921 about spreading the Dada movement to America: "Cher Tzara—Dada cannot live in New York. All New York is Dada, and will not tolerate a rival . . ."

Nor should one assume that twentieth-century French poetry is sitting out there as a convenient, self-contained entity. Far from being a unified body of work that resides neatly within the borders of France, French poetry of this century is various, tumultuous and contradictory. There is no typical case—only a horde of exceptions. For the fact is, a great number of the most original and influential poets were either born in other countries or spent a substantial part of their lives abroad. Apollinaire was born in Rome of mixed Polish and Italian parentage; Milosz was Lithuanian; Segalen spent his most productive years in China; Cendrars was born in Switzerland, composed his first major poem in New York City and until he was over fifty rarely stayed in France

long enough to collect his mail; Saint-John Perse was born in Guadeloupe, worked for many years in Asia as a diplomat and lived almost exclusively in Washington D.C. from 1941 until his death in 1975; Supervielle was from Uruguay and for most of his life divided his time between Montevideo and Paris; Tzara was born in Rumania and came to Paris by way of the Dada adventures at the Cabaret Voltaire in Zurich, where he frequently played chess with Lenin; Jabès was born in Cairo and lived in Egypt until he was forty-five; Césaire is from Martinique; du Bouchet is part American and was educated at Amherst and Harvard; and nearly all the younger poets in this book have stayed for extended periods in either England or America. The stereotypical view of the French poet as a creature of Paris, as a xenophobic purveyor of French values, simply does not hold. The more intimately one becomes involved with the work of these poets, the more reluctant one becomes to make any generalizations about them. In the end, the only thing that can be said with any certainty is that they all write in French.

An anthology, therefore, is a kind of trap, tending to thwart our access to the poems even as it makes them available to us. By gathering the work of so many poets in one volume, the temptation is to consider the poets as a group, to drown them as individuals in the great pot of literature. Thus, even before it is read, the anthology becomes a kind of cultural dinner, a smattering of national dishes served up on a platter for popular consumption, as if to say, "Here is French poetry. Eat it. It's good for you." To approach poetry in that way is to miss the point entirely—for it allows one to avoid looking squarely at the poem on the page. And that, after all, is the reader's primary obligation. One must resist the notion of treating an anthology as the last word on its subject. It is no more than a first word, a threshold opening on to a new space.

III

*In the end you are weary of this ancient world.*

—GUILLAUME APOLLINAIRE

The logical place to begin this book is with Apollinaire. Although he is neither the first-born of the poets included nor the first to have written in a consciously modern idiom, he, more than any other artist of his time, seems to embody the aesthetic aspirations of the early part of the century. In his poetry, which ranges from graceful love lyrics to bold experiments, from rhyme to free verse to "shape" poems, he manifests a new sensibility, at once indebted to the forms of the past and enthusiastically at home in the world of automobiles, airplanes and movies. As the tireless promoter of the Cubist

painters, he was the figure around whom many of the best artists and writers gathered, and poets such as Jacob, Cendrars and Reverdy formed an important part of his circle. The work of these three, along with Apollinaire's, has frequently been described as Cubist. While there are vast differences among them, both in methods and tone, they nevertheless share a certain point of view, especially in the epistemological foundations of the work. Simultaneity, juxtaposition, an acute feeling for the jaggedness of the real—these are traits to be found in all four, and each exploits them to different poetic ends.

Cendrars, at once more abrasive and voluptuous than Apollinaire, observed that "everything around me moves," and his work oscillates between the two solutions implicit in this statement: on the one hand, the ebullient jangle of sensations in works such as *Nineteen Elastic Poems,* and on the other the snapshot realism of his travel poems (originally entitled *Kodak,* but changed, under pressure from the film company of the same name, to *Documentaires*) —as if each of these poems was the record of a single moment, lasting no longer than it takes to click the shutter of a camera. With Jacob, whose most enduring work is contained in his 1917 collection of prose poems, *The Dice Cup,* the impulse is toward an anti-lyrical comedy. His language is continually erupting into playfulness (puns, parody, satire) and takes its greatest delight in unmasking the deceptions of appearances: Nothing is ever what it seems to be, everything is subject to metamorphosis, and change always occurs unexpectedly, with lightning swiftness.

Reverdy, by contrast, uses many of these same principles, but with far more somber objectives. Here an accumulation of fragments is synthesized into an entirely new approach to the poetic image. "The image is a pure creation of the mind," wrote Reverdy in 1918. "It cannot be born from a comparison but from a juxtaposition of two more or less distant realities. The more the relationship between the two juxtaposed realities is both distant and true, the stronger the image will be—the greater its emotional power and poetic reality." Reverdy's strange landscapes, which combine an intense inwardness with a proliferation of sensual data, bear in them the signs of a continual search for an impossible totality. Almost mystical in their effect, his poems are nevertheless anchored in the minutiae of the everyday world; in their quiet, at times monotone music, the poet seems to evaporate, to vanish into the haunted country he has created. The result is at once beautiful and disquieting —as if Reverdy had emptied the space of the poem in order to let the reader inhabit it.

A similar atmosphere is sometimes produced by the prose poems of Fargue, whose work predates that of any other poet included here. Fargue is the supreme modern poet of Paris, and fully half his writings are about the city itself. In his delicate, lyrical configurations of memory and perception, which retain an echo of their Symbolist predecessors, there is an attentiveness to detail combined with a rigorous subjectivity that transforms the city into an immense interior landscape. The poem of witness is at the same time a poem

of remembrance, as if, in the solitary act of seeing, the world were reflected back to its solitary source and then, once more, reflected outward as vision. With Larbaud, a close friend of Fargue's, one also finds a hint of the late nineteenth century. A. O. Barnabooth, the supposed author of Larbaud's finest book of poems (in the first edition of 1908 Larbaud's name was intentionally left off the title page), is a rich South American of twenty-four, a naturalized citizen of New York, an orphan, a world traveler, a highly sensitive and melancholy young man—a more sympathetic and humorous version of the traditional dandy hero. As Larbaud later explained, he wanted to invent a poet "sensitive to the diversity of races, peoples, and countries; who could find the exotic everywhere . . . ; witty and 'international,' one, in a word, capable of writing like Whitman but in a light vein, and of supplying that note of comic, joyous irresponsibility which is lacking in Whitman." As in the poems of Apollinaire and Cendrars, Larbaud-Barnabooth expresses an almost euphoric delight in the sensations of travel: "I experienced for the first time all the joy of living / In a compartment of the Nord-Express . . ." Of Barnabooth André Gide wrote: "I love his haste, his cynicism, his gluttony. These poems, dated from here and there, and everywhere, are as thirst-making as a wine list . . . In this particular book, each picture of sensation, no matter how correct or dubious it may be, is made valid by the speed with which it is supplanted."

The work of Saint-John Perse also bears a definite resemblance to that of Whitman—both in the nature of his stanza and in the rolling, cumulative force of his long syntactic breaths. If Larbaud in some sense domesticates Whitman, Saint-John Perse carries him beyond universalism into a quest for great cosmic harmonies. The voice of the poet is mythical in its scope, as if, with its thunderous and sumptuous rhetoric, it had come into being for the sole purpose of conquering the world. Unlike most of the poets of his generation, who made their peace with temporality and used the notion of change as the premise of their work, Saint-John Perse's poems are quickened by an almost Platonic urge to seek out the eternal. In this respect, Milosz also stands to the side of his contemporaries. A student of the mystics and the alchemists, Milosz combines Catholicism and cabalism with what Kenneth Rexroth has described as "apocalyptic sensualism," and his work draws much of its inspiration from numerological treatment of names, transpositions of letters, anagrammatic and acronymic combinations, and other linguistic practices of the occult. But, as with the poems of Yeats, the poetry itself transcends the restrictions of its sources, displaying, as John Peck has commented, "an obsessive range of feeling, in which personal melancholy is also melancholy for a crepuscular era, that long hour before first light 'when the shadows decompose.' "

Another poet who resists categorization is Segalen. Like Larbaud, who wrote his poems through an invented persona; like Pound, whose translations stand curiously among his best and most personal works, Segalen carried this

impulse toward self-effacement one step further and wrote behind the mask of another culture. The poems to be found in *Stèles* are neither translations nor imitations, but French poems written by a French poet *as if he were Chinese*. There is no attempt to deceive on Segalen's part; he never pretended these poems were anything other than original works. What at first reading might appear to be a kind of literary exoticism on closer scrutiny holds up as a poetry of solid, universal interest. By freeing himself from the limitations of his own culture, by circumventing his own historical moment, Segalen was able to explore a much wider territory—to discover, in some sense, that part of himself that was a poet.

In many ways, the case of Jouve is no less unusual. A follower of the Symbolists as a young man, Jouve published a number of books of poetry between 1912 and 1923. What he described as a "moral, spiritual, and aesthetic crisis" in 1924 led him to break with all his early work, which he never allowed to be republished. Over the next forty years he produced a voluminous body of writing—his collected poems run well over a thousand pages. Deeply Christian in outlook, Jouve is primarily concerned with the question of sexuality, both as transgression and as creative force—"the beautiful power of human eroticism"—and his poetry is the first in France to have made use of the methods of Freudian psychoanalysis. It is a poetry without predecessors and without followers. If his work was somewhat forgotten during the period dominated by the Surrealists—which meant that recognition of Jouve's achievement was delayed for almost a generation—he is now widely considered to be one of the major poets of the half-century.

Supervielle was also influenced by the Symbolists as a young man, and of all the poets of his generation he is perhaps the most purely lyrical. A poet of space, of the natural world, Supervielle writes from a position of supreme innocence. "To dream is to forget the materiality of one's body," he wrote in 1951, "and to confuse to some degree the outer and the inner world . . . People are sometimes surprised over my marvelling at the world. This arises as much from the permanency of my dreams as from my bad memory. Both lead me from surprise to surprise, and force me to be amazed at everything."

It is this sense of amazement, perhaps, that best describes the work of these first eleven poets, all of whom began writing before World War I. The poets of the next generation, however, who came of age during the war itself, were denied the possibility of such innocent optimism. The war was not simply a conflict between armies, but a profound crisis of values that transformed European consciousness, and the younger poets, while having absorbed the lessons of Apollinaire and his contemporaries, were compelled to respond to this crisis in ways that were without precedent. As Hugo Ball, one of the founders of Dada, noted in his diary in 1917: "A thousand-year-old culture disintegrates. There are no columns and no supports, no foundations anymore —they have all been blown up . . . The meaning of the world has disappeared."

The Dada movement, which began in Zurich in 1916, was the most radical response to this sense of spiritual collapse. In the face of a discredited culture, the Dadaists challenged every assumption and ridiculed every belief of that culture. As artists, they attacked the notion of art itself, transforming their rage into a kind of subversive doubt, filled with caustic humor and willful self-contradiction. "The true Dadaists are against Dada," wrote Tzara in one of his manifestoes. The point was never to take anything at face value and never to take anything too seriously—especially oneself. The Socratic ironies of Marcel Duchamp's art are perhaps the purest expression of this attitude. In the realm of poetry, Tzara was no less sly or rambunctious. This is his recipe for writing a Dada poem: "Take a newspaper. Take a pair of scissors. Select an article as long as you want your poem to be. Cut out the article. Then carefully cut out each of the words that form this article and put them in a bag. Shake gently. Then take out each scrap, one after the other. Conscientiously copy them in the order they left the bag. The poem will resemble you. And there you are, an infinitely original writer, with a charming sensibility, beyond the understanding of the vulgar." If this is a poetry of chance, it should not be confused with the aesthetics of aleatory composition. Tzara's proposed method is an assault on the sanctity of Poetry, and it does not attempt to elevate itself to the status of an artistic ideal. Its function is purely negative. This is anti-art in its earliest incarnation, the "anti-philosophy of spontaneous acrobatics."

Tzara moved to Paris in 1919, introducing Dada to the French scene. Breton, Aragon, Éluard and Soupault all became participants in the movement. Inevitably, it did not last more than a few years. An art of total negation cannot survive, for its destructiveness must ultimately include itself. It was by drawing on the ideas and attitudes of Dada, however, that Surrealism became possible. "Surrealism is pure psychic automatism," Breton wrote in his first manifesto of 1924, "whose intention is to express, verbally, in writing, or by other means, the real process of thought and thought's dictation, in the absence of all control exercised by reason and outside all aesthetic or moral preoccupations. Surrealism rests on the belief in the superior reality of certain previously neglected forms of association; in the omnipotence of dream, and in the disinterested play of thought."

Like Dada, Surrealism did not offer itself as an aesthetic movement. Equating Rimbaud's cry to change life with Marx's injunction to change the world, the Surrealists sought to push poetry, in Walter Benjamin's phrase, "to the utmost limits of possibility." The attempt was to demystify art, to blur the distinctions between life and art, and to use the methods of art to explore the possibilities of human freedom. To quote Walter Benjamin again, from his prescient essay on the Surrealists published in 1929: "Since Bakunin, Europe has lacked a radical concept of freedom. The Surrealists have one. They are the first to liquidate the liberal-moral-humanistic ideal of freedom, because they are convinced that 'freedom, which on this earth can only be bought with

a thousand of the hardest sacrifices, must be enjoyed unrestrictedly in its fullness, without any kind of programmatic calculation, as long as it lasts.' " For this reason, Surrealism associated itself closely with the politics of revolution (one of its magazines was even entitled *Surrealism in the Service of the Revolution*), flirting continually with the Communist Party and playing the role of fellow traveler during the era of the Popular Front—although refusing to submerge its identity in that of pure politics. Constant disputes over principles marked the history of the Surrealists, with Breton holding the middle ground between the activist and aesthetic wings of the group, frequently shifting positions in an effort to maintain a consistent program for Surrealism. Of all the poets associated with the movement, only Péret remained faithful to Breton over the long term. Soupault, by nature averse to the notion of literary movements, lost interest by 1927. Both Artaud and Desnos were excommunicated in 1929—Artaud for opposing Surrealism's interest in politics and Desnos for supposedly compromising his integrity by working as a journalist. Aragon, Tzara and Éluard all joined the Communist Party in the thirties. Queneau and Prévert parted amicably after a brief association. Daumal, whose work was recognized by Breton as sharing the preoccupations of the Surrealists, declined an invitation to join the group. Char, ten or twelve years younger than most of the original members, was an early adherent but later broke with the movement and went on to do his best work during and after the war. Ponge's connection was peripheral, and Michaux, in some sense the most Surrealist of all French poets, never had anything to do with the group.

This same confusion exists when one examines the work of these poets. If "pure psychic automatism" is the underlying principle of Surrealist composition, only Péret seems to have stuck to it rigorously in the writing of his poems. Interestingly, his work is the least resonant of all the Surrealists— notable more for its comic effects than for any uncovering of the "convulsive beauty" that Breton envisaged as the goal of Surrealist writing. Even in Breton's poetry, with its abrupt shifts and unexpected associations, there is an undercurrent of consistent rhetoric that makes the poems cohere as densely reasoned objects of thought. With Tzara as well, automatism serves almost as a rhetorical device. It is a method of discovery, not an end in itself. In his best work—especially the long, multifaceted *Approximate Man*—a torrent of images organizes itself into a nearly systematic argument by means of repetition and variation, propelling itself forward in the manner of a musical composition.

Soupault, on the other hand, is clearly a conscious craftsman. While limited in range, his poetry displays a charm and a humility absent in the work of the other Surrealists. He is a poet of intimacy and pathos, at times strangely reminiscent of Verlaine, and if his poems have none of the flamboyance to be found in Tzara and Breton, they are more immediately accessible, more purely lyrical. By the same token, Desnos is a poet of plain speech, whose

work often achieves a stunning lyrical intensity. His output extends from early experiments with language (dexterous, often dazzling exercises in word play) to free-verse love poems of great poignancy to longer, narrative poems and works in traditional forms. In an essay published just one year before his death, Desnos described his work as an effort "to fuse popular language, even the most colloquial, with an inexpressible 'atmosphere'; with a vital use of imagery, so as to annex for ourselves those domains which . . . remain incompatible with that fiendish, plaguing poetic dignity which endlessly oozes from tongues . . ."

With Éluard, arguably the greatest of the Surrealist poets, the love poem is accorded metaphysical status. His language, as limpid as anything to be found in Ronsard, is built on syntactic structures of extreme simplicity. Éluard uses the idea of love in his work to mirror the poetic process itself— as a way both to escape the world and to understand it. It is that irrational part of man which weds the inner to the outer, rooted in the physical and yet transcending matter, creating that uniquely human place in which man can discover his freedom. These same themes are present in Éluard's later work, particularly the poems written during the German Occupation, in which this notion of freedom is carried from the realm of the individual to that of an entire people.

If Éluard's work can be read as a continuous whole, Aragon's career as a poet divides into two distinct periods. Perhaps the most militant and provocative of the French Dadaists, he also played a leading role in the development of Surrealism and, after Breton, was the group's most active theorist. Attacked by Breton in the early thirties for the increasingly propagandist tone of his poetry, Aragon withdrew from the movement and joined the Communist Party. It was not until the war that he returned to the writing of poetry— and in a manner that bears almost no relation to his earlier work. His Resistance poems brought him national fame, and they are distinguished by their force and eloquence, but in their methods they are highly traditional, composed for the most part in alexandrines and rhyming stanzas.

Although Artaud was an early participant in Surrealism (for a time he even headed The Central Bureau for Surrealist Research) and although a number of his most important works were written during that period, he is a writer who stands so defiantly outside the traditional norms of literature that it is useless to label his work in any way. Properly speaking, Artaud is not a poet at all, and yet he has probably had a greater influence on the poets who came after him than any other writer of his generation. "Where others present their works," he wrote, "I claim to do no more than show my mind." His aim as a writer was never to create aesthetic objects—works that could be detached from their creator—but to record the state of mental and physical struggle in which "words rot at the unconscious summons of the brain." There is no division in Artaud between life and writing—and life not in the sense of biography, of external events, but life as it is lived in the intimacy of the body,

of the blood that flows through one's veins. As such, Artaud is a kind of Ur-poet, whose work describes the processes of thought and feeling before the advent of language, before the possibility of speech. It is at once a cry of suffering and a challenge to all our assumptions about the purpose of literature.

In a totally different way from Artaud, Ponge also commands a unique place among the writers of his generation. He is a writer of supremely classical values, and his work—most of it has been written in prose—is pristine in its clarity, highly sensitive to nuance and the etymological origins of words, which Ponge has described as the "semantical thickness" of language. Ponge has invented a new kind of writing, a poetry of the object that is at the same time a method of contemplation. Minutely detailed in its descriptions, and everywhere infused with a fine ironic humor, his work proceeds as though the object being examined did not exist as a word. The primary act of the poet, therefore, becomes the act of seeing, as if no one had ever seen the thing before, so that the object might have "the good fortune to be born into words."

Like Ponge, who has frequently resisted the efforts of critics to classify him as a poet, Michaux is a writer whose work escapes the strictures of genre. Floating freely between prose and verse, his texts have a spontaneous, almost haphazard quality that sets them against the pretensions and platitudes of high art. No French writer has ever given greater rein to the play of his imagination. Much of his best writing is set in imaginary countries and reads as a bizarre kind of anthropology of inner states. Although often compared to Kafka, Michaux does not resemble the author of Kafka's novels and stories so much as the Kafka of the notebooks and parables. As with Artaud, there is an urgency of process in Michaux's writing, a sense of personal risk and necessity in the act of composition. In an early statement about his poetry, he declared: "I write with transport and for myself. a) sometimes to liberate myself from an intolerable tension or from a no less painful abandonment. b) sometimes for an imaginary companion, for a kind of alter ego whom I would honestly like to keep up-to-date on an extraordinary transition in me, or in the world, which I, ordinarily forgetful, all at once believe I rediscover in, so to speak, its virginity. c) deliberately to shake the congealed and established, to invent . . . Readers trouble me. I write, if you like, for the unknown reader."

An equal independence of approach is present in Daumal, a serious student of Eastern religions, whose poems deal obsessively with the rift between spiritual and physical life. "The Absurd is the purest and most basic form of metaphysical existence," he wrote, and in his dense, visionary work, the illusions of appearance fall away only to be transformed into further illusions. "The poems are haunted by a . . . consciousness of impending death," Michael Benedikt has commented, "seen as the poet's long-lost 'double'; and also by a personification of death as a sort of sinister mother, an exacting being,

avaricious in her search for beings to extinguish—but only so as to place upon them perversely the burden of further metamorphoses."

Daumal is considered one of the chief precursors of the "College of Pataphysics," a mock-secret literary organization inspired by Alfred Jarry that included both Queneau and Prévert among its members. Humor is the guiding principle in the work of these two poets. With Queneau, it is a linguistic humor, based on intricate word plays, parody, feigned stupidity and slang. In his well-known prose work of 1947, for example, *Exercices de style*, the same mundane event is given in ninety-nine different versions, each one written in a different style, each one presented from a different point of view. In discussing Queneau in *Writing Degree Zero*, Roland Barthes described this style as "white writing"—in which literature, for the first time, has openly become a problem and question of language. If Queneau is an intellectual poet, Prévert, who also adheres closely to the patterns of ordinary speech in his work, is without question a popular poet—even a populist poet. Since World War II, no one has had a wider audience in France, and many of Prévert's works have been turned into highly successful songs. Anticlerical, antimilitaristic, rebellious in political attitude and extolling a rather sentimentalized form of love between man and woman, Prévert represents one of the more felicitous marriages between poetry and mass culture, and beyond the charm of his work, it is valuable as an indicator of popular French taste.

Although Surrealism continues to exist as a literary movement, the period of its greatest influence and most important creations came to an end by the beginning of World War II. Of the second-generation Surrealists—or those poets who found inspiration in its methods—Césaire stands out as the most notable example. One of the first black writers to be recognized in France, founder of the *négritude* movement—which asserts the uniqueness and dignity of black culture and consciousness—Césaire, a native of Martinique, was championed by Breton, who discovered his work in the late thirties. As the South African poet Mazisi Kunene has written about Césaire: "Surrealism was for him a logical instrument with which to smash the restrictive forms of language which sanctified rationalized bourgeois values. The breaking up of language patterns coincided with his own desire to smash colonialism and all oppressive forms." More vividly perhaps than in the work of the Surrealists of France, Césaire's poetry embodies the twin aspirations of political and aesthetic revolution, and in such a way that they are inseparably joined.

For many of the poets who began writing in the thirties, however, Surrealism was never a temptation. Follain, for example, whose work has proved to be particularly amenable to American taste (of all recent French poets, he is the one who has been most frequently translated), is a poet of the everyday, and in his short, exquisitely crafted works one finds an examination of the object no less serious and challenging than Ponge's. At the same time, Follain is largely a poet of memory ("In the fields / of his eternal childhood / the poet wanders / wanting to forget nothing"), and his evocations of the world as

seen through a child's eyes bear within them a shimmering, epiphanic quality of psychological truth. A similar kind of realism and attention to surface detail is also to be found in Guillevic. Materialist in his approach to the world, unrhetorical in his methods, Guillevic has also created a world of objects— but one in which the object is nevertheless problematical, a reality to be penetrated, to be striven for, but which is not necessarily given. Frénaud, on the other hand, although often grouped together with Follain and Guillevic, is a far more romantic poet than his two contemporaries. Effusive in his language, metaphysical in his concerns, he has been compared at times to the Existentialists in his insistence that man's world is a creation of man himself. Despairing of certainty (*There Is No Paradise*, reads the title of one of his collections), Frénaud's work draws its force not so much from a recognition of the absurd as from the attempt to find a basis for positive values within the absurd itself.

If World War I was the crucial event that marked the poetry of the twenties and thirties, World War II was no less decisive in determining the kind of poetry written in France during the late forties and fifties. The military defeat of 1940 and the Nazi Occupation that followed were among the darkest moments in French history. The country had been devastated both emotionally and economically. In the context of this disarray, the mature poetry of René Char came as a revelation. Aphoristic, fragmented, closely allied to the thought of Heraclitus and the pre-Socratics, Char's poetry is at once a lyrical summoning of natural correspondences and a meditation on the poetic process itself. Austere in its settings (for the most part the landscape is that of Char's native Provence) and roughly textured in its language, this is a poetry that does not attempt to record or evoke feelings so much as it seeks to embody the ongoing struggle of words to ground themselves in the world. Char writes from a position of deep existential commitment (he was an important field leader in the Resistance), and his work is permeated with a sense of new beginnings, of a necessary search to rescue life from the ruins.

The best poets of the immediate postwar generation share many of these same preoccupations. Bonnefoy, du Bouchet, Jaccottet, Giroux and Dupin, all born within four years of each other, manifest in their work a vigilant hermeticism that is characterized by a consciously reduced range of imagery, great syntactical inventiveness and a refusal to ask anything but essential questions. Bonnefoy, the most classical and philosophically oriented of the five, has largely been concerned in his work with tracking the reality that haunts "the abyss of concealed appearances." "Poetry does not interest itself in the shape of the world itself," he once remarked, "but in the world that this universe will become. Poetry speaks only of presences—or absences." Du Bouchet, by contrast, is a poet who shuns every temptation toward abstraction. His work, which is perhaps the most radical adventure in recent French poetry, is based on a rigorous attentiveness to phenomenological detail. Stripped of metaphor, almost devoid of imagery, and generated by a language

of abrupt, paratactic brevity, his poems move through an almost barren land-scape, a speaking "I" continually in search of itself. A du Bouchet page is the mirror of this journey, each one dominated by white space, the few words present as if emerging from a silence that will inevitably claim them again.

Of these poets, it is undoubtedly Dupin whose work holds the greatest verbal richness. Tightly sprung, calling upon an imagery that seethes with hidden violence, his poems are dazzling in both their energy and their an-guish. "In this infinite, unanimous dissonance," he writes, in a poem entitled "Lichens," "each ear of corn, each drop of blood, speaks its language and goes its way. The torch, which lights the abyss, which seals its up, is itself an abyss." Far gentler in approach are both Jaccottet and Giroux. Jaccottet's short nature poems, which in certain ways adhere to the aesthetics of Imagism, have an Oriental stillness about them that can flare at any moment into the brightness of epiphany. "For us living more and more surrounded by intellectual sche-mas and masks," Jaccottet has written, "and suffocating in the prison they erect around us, the poet's eye is the battering ram that knocks down these walls and gives back to us, if only for an instant, the real; and with the real, *a possibility of life.*" Giroux, a poet of great lyrical gifts, died prematurely in 1973 and published only one book during his lifetime. The short poems in that volume are quiet, deeply meditated works about the nature of poetic reality, explorations of the space between the world and words, and they have had a considerable impact on the work of many of today's younger poets.

This hermeticism, however, is by no means present in the work of all the poets of the postwar period. Dadelsen, for example, is an effusive poet, mono-logic and varied in tone, who frequently launches into slang. There have been a number of distinguished Catholic poets in France during the twentieth century (La Tour du Pin, Emmanuel, Jean-Claude Renard and Mambrino are recent examples), but it is perhaps Dadelsen, less well known than the others, who in his tormented search for God best represents the limits and perils of religious consciousness. Marteau, on the other hand, draws much of his imag-ery from myth, and although his preoccupations often overlap with those of, say, Bonnefoy or Dupin, his work is less self-reflective than theirs, dwelling not so much on the struggles and paradoxes of expression as on uncovering the presence of archetypal forces in the world.

Of the new work that began to appear in the early sixties, the books of Jabès are the most notable. Since 1963, when *The Book of Questions* was published, Jabès has brought out ten volumes in a remarkable series of works, prompting comments such as Jacques Derrida's statement that "in the last ten years nothing has been written in France that does not have its precedent some-where in the texts of Jabès." Jabès, an Egyptian Jew who published a number of books of poetry in the forties and fifties, has emerged as a writer of the first rank with his more recent work—all of it written in France after his expulsion from Cairo during the Suez crisis. These books are almost impossible to define. Neither novels nor poems, neither essays nor plays, they are a combi-

nation of all these forms, a mosaic of fragments, aphorisms, dialogues, songs and commentaries that endlessly move around the central question posed by each book: How to speak what cannot be spoken. The question is the Holocaust, but it is also the question of literature itself. By a startling leap of the imagination, Jabès treats them as one and the same: "I have talked to you about the difficulty of being Jewish, which is the same as the difficulty of writing. For Judaism and writing are but the same waiting, the same hope, the same wearing out."

This determination to carry poetry into uncharted territory, to break down the standard distinctions between prose and verse, is perhaps the most striking characteristic of the younger generation of poets today. In Deguy, for example, poetry can be made from just about anything at all, and his work draws on a broad range of material: from the technical language of science to the abstractions of philosophy to elaborate play on linguistic constructions. In Roubaud, the quest for new forms has led to books of highly intricate structures (one of his volumes, $\Sigma$, is based on the permutations of the Japanese game of go), and these invented shapes are exploited with great deftness, serving not as ends in themselves but as a means of ordering the fragments they encompass, of putting the various pieces in a larger context and investing them with a coherence they would not possess on their own.

Pleynet and Roche, two poets closely connected with the well-known review *Tel Quel*, have each carried the notion of antipoetry to a position of extreme combativeness. Pleynet's jocular, and at the same time deadly serious, "Ars Poetica" of 1964 is a good example of this attitude. "I. ONE CANNOT KNOW HOW TO WRITE WITHOUT KNOWING WHY. II. THE AUTHOR OF THIS ARS POETICA DOES NOT KNOW HOW TO WRITE BUT HE WRITES. III. THE QUESTION 'HOW TO WRITE' ANSWERS THE QUESTION 'WHY WRITE' AND THE QUESTION 'WHAT IS WRITING.' IV. A QUESTION IS AN ANSWER." Roche's approach is perhaps even more disruptive of conventional assumptions about literature. "Poetry is inadmissible. Besides, it does not exist," he has written. And elsewhere: ". . . the logic of modern writing demands that one should take a vigorous hand in promoting the death agonies of [this] symbolist, outmoded ideology. Writing can only symbolize what it is in its functioning, in its 'society,' within the frame of its utilization. It must stick to that."

This is not to say, however, that short, lyric poems do not continue to be written in France. Delahaye and Denis, both still in their thirties, have created substantial bodies of work in this more familiar mode—mining a landscape that had first been mapped out by du Bouchet and Dupin. On the other hand, many of the younger poets, having absorbed and transmuted the questions raised by their predecessors, are now producing a kind of work that is both original and demanding in its insistence upon the textuality of the written word. Although there are significant differences among Albiach, Royet-Journoud, Daive, Hocquard and Veinstein, in one fundamental aspect of their work they share a common point of view. Their medium as writers is neither

the individual poem nor even the sequence of poems, but the book. As Royet-Journoud stated in a recent interview: "My books consist only of a single text, the genre of which cannot be defined. . . . It's a *book* that I write, and I feel that the notion of genre obscures the book as such." This is as true of Daive's highly charged, psycho-erotic work, Hocquard's graceful and ironic narratives of memory, and Veinstein's minimal theaters of the creative process as it is of Royet-Journoud's obsessive "detective stories" of language. Most strikingly, this approach to composition can be found in Albiach's 1971 volume, *État,* undoubtedly the major work to be published thus far by a member of this younger generation. As Keith Waldrop has written: "The poem—it is a single piece—does not progress by images . . . or by plot. . . . The argument, if it were given, might include the following propositions: 1) everyday language is dependent on logic, but 2) in fiction, there is no necessity that any particular word should follow any other, so 3) it is possible at least to imagine a free choice, a syntax generated by desire. *État* is the 'epic' . . . of this imagination. To state such an argument . . . would be to renounce the whole project. But what is presented is not a series of emotions . . . the poem is composed mindfully; and if Anne-Marie Albiach rejects rationality, she quite obviously writes with full intelligence . . ."


I V

*. . . with the conviction that, in the end, translating is madness.*

—MAURICE BLANCHOT


As I was about to embark on the project of editing this anthology, a friend gave me a piece of valuable advice. Jonathan Griffin, who served as British cultural attaché in Paris after the war, and has translated several books by De Gaulle, as well as poets ranging from Rimbaud to Pessoa, has been around long enough to know more about such things than I do. Every anthology, he said, has two types of readers: the critics, who judge the book by what is *not* included in it, and the general readers, who read the book for what it actually contains. He advised me to keep this second group uppermost in my thoughts. The critics, after all, are in business to criticize, and they are familiar with the material anyway. The important thing to remember is that most people will be reading the majority of these poets for the first time. They are the ones who will get the most out of the anthology.

During the two years it has taken for me to put this book together, I have often reminded myself of these words. Frequently, however, it has been

difficult to take them to heart, since I myself am all too aware of what has not been included. My original plan for the anthology was to represent the work of almost a hundred poets. In addition to more familiar kinds of writing, I had wanted to use a number of eccentric works, provide examples of concrete and sound poetry, include several collaborative poems and, in a few instances, offer variant translations when more than one good version of a poem was available. As work progressed, it became apparent that this would not be possible. I was faced with the unhappy situation of trying to fit an elephant into a cage designed for a fox. Reluctantly, I changed my approach to the book. If my choice was between offering a smattering of poems by many poets or substantial selections of work by a reduced number of poets, there did not seem to be much doubt that the second solution was wiser and more coherent. Instead of imagining everything I would like to see in the anthology, I tried to think of the poets it would be inconceivable *not* to include. In this way, I gradually whittled the list down to forty-eight. These were difficult decisions for me, and though I stand by my final selection, it is with regret for those I was not able to include.*

There are no doubt some who will also wonder about certain other exclusions. In order to keep the book focused on poetry of the twentieth century, I decided on a fixed cut-off point to determine where the anthology should begin. The crucial year for my purposes turned out to be 1876: Any poet born before that year would not be considered. This allowed me, in good conscience, to forgo the problem posed by poets such as Valéry, Claudel, Jammes and Péguy, all of whom began writing in the late nineteenth century and went on writing well into the twentieth. Although their work overlaps chronologically with many of the poets in the book, it seems to belong in spirit to an earlier time. By the same token, 1876 was a convenient date for allowing me to include certain poets whose work is essential to the project—Fargue, Jacob and Milosz in particular.

As for the English versions of the poems, I have used already existing translations whenever possible. My motive has been to underscore the involvement, over the past fifty years, of American and British poets in the work

---

*Among them are the following: Pierre Albert-Birot, Jean Cocteau, Raymond Roussel, Jean Arp, Francis Picabia, Arthur Cravan, Michel Leiris, Georges Bataille, Léopold Senghor, André Pieyre de Mandiargues, Jacques Audiberti, Jean Tardieu, Georges Schéhadé, Pierre Emmanuel, Joyce Mansour, Patrice de la Tour du Pin, René Guy Cadou, Henri Pichette, Christian Dotremont, Olivier Larronde, Henri Thomas, Jean Grosjean, Jean Tortel, Jean Laude, Pierre Torreilles, Jean-Claude Renard, Jean Joubert, Jacques Réda, Armen Lubin, Jean Pérol, Jude Stéfan, Marc Alyn, Jacqueline Risset, Michel Butor, Jean Pierre Faye, Alain Jouffroy, Georges Perros, Armand Robin, Boris Vian, Jean Mambrino, Lorand Gaspar, Georges Badin, Pierre Oster, Bernard Noël, Claude Vigée, Joseph Gugliemi, Daniel Blanchard, Michel Couturier, Claude Esteban, Alain Sueid, Mathieu Bénézet.

of their French counterparts, and since there is abundant material to choose from (some of it hidden away in old magazines and out-of-print books, some of it readily available), there seemed to be no need to begin my search elsewhere. My greatest pleasure in putting this book together has been in rescuing a number of superb translations from the obscurity of library shelves and microfilm rooms: Nancy Cunard's Aragon, John Dos Passos's Cendrars, Paul Bowles's Ponge, and the translations by Eugene and Maria Jolas (the editors of *transition*), to mention just a few. Also to be noted are the translations that previously existed only in manuscript. Paul Blackburn's translations of Apollinaire, for example, were discovered among his papers after his death, and are published here for the first time.

Only in cases where translations did not exist or where the available translations seemed inadequate did I commission fresh translations. In each of these instances (Richard Wilbur's version of Apollinaire's "Le Pont Mirabeau," Lydia Davis's Fargue, Robert Kelly's Roubaud, Anselm Hollo's Dadelsen, Michael Palmer's Hocquard, Rosmarie Waldrop's Veinstein, Geoffrey Young's Aragon), I have tried to arrange the marriage with care. My aim was to bring together compatible poets—so that the translator would be able to exploit his particular strengths as a poet in rendering the original into English. The results of this matchmaking have been uniformly satisfying. Richard Wilbur's "Mirabeau Bridge," for instance, strikes me as the first acceptable version of this important poem we have had in English, the only translation that comes close to re-creating the subtle music of the original.

In general, I have followed no consistent policy about translation in making my choices. A few of the translations are hardly more than adaptations, although the vast majority are quite faithful to the originals. Translating poetry is at best an art of approximation, and there are no fixed rules to follow in deciding what works or does not. It is largely a matter of instinct, of ear, of common sense. Whenever I was faced with a choice between literalness and poetry, I did not hesitate to choose poetry. It seemed more important to me to give those readers who have no French a true sense of each poem *as a poem* than to strive for word-by-word exactness. The experience of a poem resides not only in each of its words, but in the interactions among those words— the music, the silences, the shapes—and if a reader is not somehow given the chance to enter the totality of that experience, he will remain cut off from the spirit of the original. It is for this reason, it seems to me, that poems should be translated by poets.

Of all those who helped me in all the ways I needed help during the preparation of this anthology—by talking out problems with me, by suggesting material, by lending me books, by giving up time to ease the burden of drudgery—I would like to single out the following people and send them my

deepest thanks: Siri Hustvedt, Anthony Rudolf, Charles Simic, Jacques Dupin, Samuel Beckett, Madeleine Follain, Anthony Barnett, Mark Rudman, Lydia Davis, Bill Zavatsky, Françoise de Laroque, Eliot Weinberger, Claude Royet-Journoud, Lloyd Hustvedt, Jean-Michel Reynard, George Economou and Raphael Rudnik.

— P.A.
*New York City*
*September 23, 1981*

The Random House Book of
# TWENTIETH-CENTURY
# FRENCH POETRY

ZONE

A la fin tu es las de ce monde ancien

Bergère ô tour Eiffel le troupeau des ponts bêle ce matin

Tu en as assez de vivre dans l'antiquité grecque et romaine

Ici même les automobiles ont l'air d'être anciennes
La religion seule est restée toute neuve la religion
Est restée simple comme les hangars de Port-Aviation

Seul en Europe tu n'es pas antique ô Christianisme
L'Européen le plus moderne c'est vous Pape Pie X
Et toi que les fenêtres observent la honte te retient
D'entrer dans une église et de t'y confesser ce matin
Tu lis les prospectus les catalogues les affiches qui chantent tout haut
Voilà la poésie ce matin et pour la prose il y a les journaux
Il y a les livraisons à 25 centimes pleines d'aventures policières
Portraits des grands hommes et mille titres divers

J'ai vu ce matin une jolie rue dont j'ai oublié le nom
Neuve et propre du soleil elle était le clairon
Les directeurs les ouvriers et les belles sténo-dactylographes
Du lundi matin au samedi soir quatre fois par jour y passent

# Guillaume Apollinaire

## 1880-1918

ZONE

In the end you are weary of this ancient world

This morning the bridges are bleating Eiffel Tower oh herd

Weary of living in Roman antiquity and Greek

Here even the motor-cars look antique
Religion alone has stayed young religion
Has stayed simple like the hangars at Port Aviation

You alone in Europe Christianity are not ancient
The most modern European is you Pope Pius X
And you whom the windows watch shame restrains
From entering a church this morning and confessing your sins
You read the handbills the catalogues the singing posters
So much for poetry this morning and the prose is in the papers
Special editions full of crimes
Celebrities and other attractions for 25 centimes

This morning I saw a pretty street whose name is gone
Clean and shining clarion of the sun
Where from Monday morning to Saturday evening four times a day
Directors workers and beautiful shorthand typists go their way

Le matin par trois fois la sirène y gémit
Une cloche rageuse y aboie vers midi
Les inscriptions des enseignes et des murailles
Les plaques les avis à la façon des perroquets criaillent
J'aime la grâce de cette rue industrielle
Située à Paris entre la rue Aumont-Thiéville et l'avenue des Ternes

Voilà la jeune rue et tu n'es encore qu'un petit enfant
Ta mère ne t'habille que de bleu et de blanc
Tu es très pieux et avec le plus ancien de tes camarades René Dalize
Vous n'aimez rien tant que les pompes de l'Église
Il est neuf heures le gaz est baissé tout bleu vous sortez du dortoir en
    cachette
Vous priez toute la nuit dans la chapelle du collège
Tandis qu'éternelle et adorable profondeur améthyste
Tourne à jamais la flamboyante gloire du Christ
C'est le beau lys que tous nous cultivons
C'est la torche aux cheveux roux que n'éteint pas le vent
C'est le fils pâle et vermeil de la douloureuse mère
C'est l'arbre toujours touffu de toutes les prières
C'est la double potence de l'honneur et de l'éternité
C'est l'étoile à six branches
C'est Dieu qui meurt le vendredi et ressuscite le dimanche
C'est le Christ qui monte au ciel mieux que les aviateurs
Il détient le record du monde pour la hauteur

Pupille Christ de l'œil
Vingtième pupille des siècles il sait y faire
Et changé en oiseau ce siècle comme Jésus monte dans l'air
Les diables dans les abîmes lèvent la tête pour le regarder
Ils disent qu'il imite Simon Mage en Judée
Ils crient s'il sait voler qu'on l'appelle voleur
Les anges voltigent autour du joli voltigeur
Icare Énoch Élie Apollonius de Thyane
Flottent autour du premier aéroplane
Ils s'écartent parfois pour laisser passer ceux que transporte la
    Sainte-Eucharistie
Ces prêtres qui montent éternellement élevant l'hostie
L'avion se pose enfin sans refermer les ailes
Le ciel s'emplit alors de millions d'hirondelles
A tire-d'aile viennent les corbeaux les faucons les hiboux
D'Afrique arrivent les ibis les flamants les marabouts
L'oiseau Roc célébré par les conteurs et les poètes
Plane tenant dans les serres le crâne d'Adam la première tête

And thrice in the morning the siren makes its moan
And a bell bays savagely coming up to noon
The inscriptions on walls and signs
The notices and plates squawk parrot-wise
I love the grace of this industrial street
In Paris between the Avenue des Ternes and the Rue Aumont-Thiéville

There it is the young street and you still but a small child
Your mother always dresses you in blue and white
You are very pious and with René Dalize your oldest crony
Nothing delights you more than church ceremony
It is nine at night the lowered gas burns blue you steal away
From the dormitory and all night in the college chapel pray
Whilst everlastingly the flaming glory of Christ
Wheels in adorable depths of amethyst
It is the fair lily that we all revere
It is the torch burning in the wind its auburn hair
It is the rosepale son of the mother of grief
It is the tree with the world's prayers ever in leaf
It is of honour and eternity the double beam
It is the six-branched star it is God
Who Friday dies and Sunday rises from the dead
It is Christ who better than airmen wings his flight
Holding the record of the world for height

Pupil Christ of the eye
Twentieth pupil of the centuries it is no novice
And changed into a bird this century soars like Jesus
The devils in the deeps look up and say they see a
Nimitation of Simon Magus in Judea
Craft by name by nature craft they cry
About the pretty flyer the angels fly
Enoch Elijah Apollonius of Tyana hover
With Icarus round the first airworthy ever
For those whom the Eucharist transports they now and then make way
Host-elevating priests ascending endlessly
The aeroplane alights at last with outstretched pinions
Then the sky is filled with swallows in their millions
The rooks come flocking the owls the hawks
Flamingoes from Africa and ibises and storks
The roc bird famed in song and story soars
With Adam's skull the first head in its claws
The eagle stoops screaming from heaven's verge
From America comes the little humming-bird

L'aigle fond de l'horizon en poussant un grand cri
Et d'Amérique vient le petit colibri
De Chine sont venus les pihis longs et souples
Qui n'ont qu'une seule aile et qui volent par couples
Puis voici la colombe esprit immaculé
Qu'escortent l'oiseau-lyre et le paon ocellé
Le phénix ce bûcher qui soi-même s'engendre
Un instant voile tout de son ardente cendre
Les sirènes laissant les périlleux détroits
Arrivent en chantant bellement toutes trois
Et tous aigle phénix et pihis de la Chine
Fraternisent avec la volante machine

Maintenant tu marches dans Paris tout seul parmi la foule
Des troupeaux d'autobus mugissants près de toi roulent
L'angoisse de l'amour te serre le gosier
Comme si tu ne devais jamais plus être aimé
Si tu vivais dans l'ancien temps tu entrerais dans un monastère
Vous avez honte quand vous vous surprenez à dire une prière
Tu te moques de toi et comme le feu de l'Enfer ton rire pétille
Les étincelles de ton rire dorent le fond de ta vie
C'est un tableau pendu dans un sombre musée
Et quelquefois tu vas le regarder de près

Aujourd'hui tu marches dans Paris les femmes sont ensanglantées
C'était et je voudrais ne pas m'en souvenir c'était au déclin de la beauté

Entourée de flammes ferventes Notre-Dame m'a regardé à Chartres
Le sang de votre Sacré-Cœur m'a inondé à Montmartre
Je suis malade d'ouïr les paroles bienheureuses
L'amour dont je souffre est une maladie honteuse
Et l'image qui te possède te fait survivre dans l'insomnie et dans l'angoisse
C'est toujours près de toi cette image qui passe

Maintenant tu es au bord de la Méditerranée
Sous les citronniers qui sont en fleur toute l'année
Avec tes amis tu te promènes en barque
L'un est Nissard il y a un Mentonasque et deux Turbiasques
Nous regardons avec effroi les poulpes des profondeurs
Et parmi les algues nagent les poissons images du Sauveur

Tu es dans le jardin d'une auberge aux environs de Prague
Tu te sens tout heureux une rose est sur la table

From China the long and supple
One-winged peehees that fly in couples
Behold the dove spirit without alloy
That ocellate peacock and lyre-bird convoy
The phoenix flame-devoured flame-revived
All with its ardent ash an instant hides
Leaving the perilous straits the sirens three
Divinely singing join the company
And eagle phoenix peehees fraternize
One and all with the machine that flies

Now you walk in Paris alone among the crowd
Herds of bellowing buses hemming you about
Anguish of love parching you within
As though you were never to be loved again
If you lived in olden times you would get you to a cloister
You are ashamed when you catch yourself at a paternoster
You are your own mocker and like hellfire your laughter crackles
Golden on your life's hearth fall the sparks of your laughter
It is a picture in a dark museum hung
And you sometimes go and contemplate it long

To-day you walk in Paris the women are blood-red
It was and would I could forget it was at beauty's ebb

From the midst of fervent flames Our Lady beheld me at Chartres
The blood of your Sacred Heart flooded me in Montmartre
I am sick with hearing the words of bliss
The love I endure is like a syphilis
And the image that possesses you and never leaves your side
In anguish and insomnia keeps you alive

Now you are on the Riviera among
The lemon-trees that flower all year long
With your friends you go for a sail on the sea
One is from Nice one from Menton and two from La Turbie
The polypuses in the depths fill us with horror
And in the seaweed fishes swim emblems of the Saviour

You are in an inn-garden near Prague
You feel perfectly happy a rose is on the table
And you observe instead of writing your story in prose
The chafer asleep in the heart of the rose

Et tu observes au lieu d'écrire ton conte en prose
La cétoine qui dort dans le cœur de la rose

Epouvanté tu te vois dessiné dans les agates de Saint-Vit
Tu étais triste à mourir le jour où tu t'y vis
Tu ressembles au Lazare affolé par le jour
Les aiguilles de l'horloge du quartier juif vont à rebours
Et tu recules aussi dans ta vie lentement
En montant au Hradchin et le soir en écoutant
Dans les tavernes chanter des chansons tchèques

Te voici à Marseille au milieu des pastèques

Te voici à Coblence à l'hôtel du Géant

Te voici à Rome assis sous un néflier du Japon

Te voici à Amsterdam avec une jeune fille que tu trouves belle et qui est
    laide
Elle doit se marier avec un étudiant de Leyde
On y loue des chambres en latin Cubicula locanda
Je m'en souviens j'y ai passé trois jours et autant à Gouda

Tu es à Paris chez le juge d'instruction
Comme un criminel on te met en état d'arrestation

Tu as fait de douloureux et de joyeux voyages
Avant de t'apercevoir du mensonge et de l'âge
Tu as souffert de l'amour à vingt et à trente ans
J'ai vécu comme un fou et j'ai perdu mon temps
Tu n'oses plus regarder tes mains et à tous moments je voudrais sangloter
Sur toi sur celle que j'aime sur tout ce qui t'a épouvanté

Tu regardes les yeux pleins de larmes ces pauvres émigrants
Ils croient en Dieu ils prient les femmes allaitent des enfants
Ils emplissent de leur odeur le hall de la gare Saint-Lazare
Ils ont foi dans leur étoile comme les rois-mages
Ils espèrent gagner de l'argent dans l'Argentine
Et revenir dans leur pays après avoir fait fortune
Une famille transporte un édredon rouge comme vous transportez votre
    cœur
Cet édredon et nos rêves sont aussi irréels
Quelques-uns de ces émigrants restent ici et se logent

Appalled you see your image in the agates of Saint Vitus
That day you were fit to die with sadness
You look like Lazarus frantic in the daylight
The hands of the clock in the Jewish quarter go to left from right
And you too live slowly backwards
Climbing up to the Hradchin or listening as night falls
To Czech songs being sung in taverns

Here you are in Marseilles among the water-melons

Here you are in Coblentz at the Giant's Hostelry

Here you are in Rome under a Japanese medlar-tree

Here you are in Amsterdam with an ill-favoured maiden
You find her beautiful she is engaged to a student in Leyden
There they let their rooms in Latin cubicula locanda
I remember I spent three days there and as many in Gouda

You are in Paris with the examining magistrate
They clap you in gaol like a common reprobate

Grievous and joyous voyages you made
Before you knew what falsehood was and age
At twenty you suffered from love and at thirty again
My life was folly and my days in vain
You dare not look at your hands tears haunt my eyes
For you for her I love and all the old miseries

Weeping you watch the wretched emigrants
They believe in God they pray the women suckle their infants
They fill with their smell the station of Saint-Lazare
Like the wise men from the east they have faith in their star
They hope to prosper in the Argentine
And to come home having made their fortune
A family transports a red eiderdown as you your heart
An eiderdown as unreal as our dreams
Some go no further doss in the stews
Of the Rue des Rosiers or the Rue des Écouffes
Often in the streets I have seen them in the gloaming
Taking the air and like chessmen seldom moving
They are mostly Jews the wives wear wigs and in
The depths of shadowy dens bloodless sit on and on

Rue des Rosiers ou rue des Écouffes dans des bouges
Je les ai vus souvent le soir ils prennent l'air dans la rue
Et se déplacent rarement comme les pièces aux échecs
Il y a surtout des Juifs leurs femmes portent perruque
Elles restent assises exsangues au fond des boutiques

Tu es debout devant le zinc d'un bar crapuleux
Tu prends un café à deux sous parmi les malheureux

Tu es la nuit dans un grand restaurant

Ces femmes ne sont pas méchantes elles ont des soucis cependant
Toutes même la plus laide a fait souffrir son amant

Elle est la fille d'un sergent de ville de Jersey

Ses mains que je n'avais pas vues sont dures et gercées

J'ai une pitié immense pour les coutures de son ventre

J'humilie maintenant à une pauvre fille au rire horrible ma bouche

Tu es seul le matin va venir
Les laitiers font tinter leurs bidons dans les rues

La nuit s'éloigne ainsi qu'une belle Métive
C'est Ferdine la fausse ou Léa l'attentive

Et tu bois cet alcool brûlant comme ta vie
Ta vie que tu bois comme une eau-de-vie

Tu marches vers Auteuil tu veux aller chez toi à pied
Dormir parmi tes fétiches d'Océanie et de Guinée
Ils sont des Christ d'une autre forme et d'une autre croyance
Ce sont les Christ inférieurs des obscures espérances

Adieu Adieu

Soleil cou coupé

You stand at the bar of a crapulous café
Drinking coffee at two sous a time in the midst of the unhappy

It is night you are in a restaurant it is superior

These women are decent enough they have their troubles however
All even the ugliest one have made their lovers suffer

She is a Jersey police-constable's daughter

Her hands I had not seen are chapped and hard

The seams of her belly go to my heart

To a poor harlot horribly laughing I humble my mouth

You are alone morning is at hand
In the streets the milkmen rattle their cans

Like a dark beauty night withdraws
Watchful Leah or Ferdine the false

And you drink this alcohol burning like your life
Your life that you drink like spirit of wine

You walk towards Auteuil you want to walk home and sleep
Among your fetishes from Guinea and the South Seas
Christs of another creed another guise
The lowly Christs of dim expectancies

Adieu Adieu

Sun corseless head

—SAMUEL BECKETT

## LE PONT MIRABEAU

Sous le pont Mirabeau coule la Seine
    Et nos amours
   Faut-il qu'il m'en souvienne
La joie venait toujours après la peine

      Vienne la nuit sonne l'heure
      Les jours s'en vont je demeure

Les mains dans les mains restons face à face
    Tandis que sous
  Le pont de nos bras passe
Des éternels regards l'onde si lasse

      Vienne la nuit sonne l'heure
      Les jours s'en vont je demeure

L'amour s'en va comme cette eau courante
    L'amour s'en va
  Comme la vie est lente
Et comme l'Espérance est violente

      Vienne la nuit sonne l'heure
      Les jours s'en vont je demeure

Passent les jours et passent les semaines
    Ni temps passé
  Ni les amours reviennent
Sous le pont Mirabeau coule la Seine

      Vienne la nuit sonne l'heure
      Les jours s'en vont je demeure

## MIRABEAU BRIDGE

Under the Mirabeau Bridge there flows the Seine
    Must I recall
  Our loves recall how then
After each sorrow joy came back again

    Let night come on bells end the day
    The days go by me still I stay

Hands joined and face to face let's stay just so
    While underneath
  The bridge of our arms shall go
Weary of endless looks the river's flow

    Let night come on bells end the day
    The days go by me still I stay

All love goes by as water to the sea
    All love goes by
  How slow life seems to me
How violent the hope of love can be

    Let night come on bells end the day
    The days go by me still I stay

The days the weeks pass by beyond our ken
    Neither time past
  Nor love comes back again
Under the Mirabeau Bridge there flows the Seine

    Let night come on bells end the day
    The days go by me still I stay

—RICHARD WILBUR

# CRÉPUSCULE

*A Mademoiselle Marie Laurencin.*

Frôlée par les ombres des morts
Sur l'herbe où le jour s'exténue
L'arlequine s'est mise nue
Et dans l'étang mire son corps

Un charlatan crépusculaire
Vante les tours que l'on va faire
Le ciel sans teinte est constellé
D'astres pâles comme du lait

Sur les tréteaux l'arlequin blême
Salue d'abord les spectateurs
Des sorciers venus de Bohême
Quelques fées et les enchanteurs

Ayant décroché une étoile
Il la manie à bras tendu
Tandis que des pieds un pendu
Sonne en mesure les cymbales

L'aveugle berce un bel enfant
La biche passe avec ses faons
Le nain regarde d'un air triste
Grandir l'arlequin trismégiste

# ANNIE

Sur la côte du Texas
Entre Mobile et Galveston il y a
Un grand jardin tout plein de roses
Il contient aussi une villa
Qui est une grande rose

Une femme se promène souvent
Dans les jardin toute seule

# DUSK

*To Mademoiselle Marie Laurencin*

Brushed by the shadows of the dead
On grass where failing daylight falls
The lady harlequin's stripped bare
Admiring herself in a still pool

A twilight juggler a charlatan
Boasts tricks that he knows how to play
Pale as milk the studding stars
Stand in the tall uncolored air

Harlequin pallid on his small stage
Greets the audience first of all
Bohemian sorcerers a train
Of fairies and prestidigitals

Reaching up to unhook a star
He whirls it round with outstretched arm
While cymbals mark a measured beat
Hanging from a hanged man's feet

The sightless one croons to a child
The hind and her troop of fawns pass by
The dwarf sulks at the growing thrust
Of Harlequin the Trismegist

—DUDLEY FITTS

# ANNIE

Between Mobile and Galveston
On the seacoast of Texas
There's a big garden full of rosebushes
And a house like a big rose

Often there is a woman
Walking alone in the garden

Et quand je passe sur la route bordée de tilleuls
Nous nous regardons

Comme cette femme est mennonite
Ses rosiers et ses vêtements n'ont pas de boutons
Il en manque deux à mon veston
La dame et moi suivons presque le même rite

AUTOMNE

Dans le brouillard s'en vont un paysan cagneux
Et son bœuf lentement dans le brouillard d'automne
Qui cache les hameaux pauvres et vergogneux

Et s'en allant là-bas le paysan chantonne
Une chanson d'amour et d'infidélité
Qui parle d'une bague et d'un cœur que l'on brise

Oh! l'automne l'automne a fait mourir l'été
Dans le brouillard s'en vont deux silhouettes grises

1909

La dame avait une robe
En ottoman violine
Et sa tunique brodée d'or
Était composée de deux panneaux
S'attachant sur l'épaule

Les yeux dansants comme des anges
Elle riait elle riait
Elle avait un visage aux couleurs de France

And when I pass along the lime-bordered highway
We look at one another

She is a Mennonite this woman
And her rosebushes and clothes are buttonless
I see that two buttons are missing from my jacket
The lady and I observe almost the same rite

—WILLIAM MEREDITH

## AUTUMN

A bowlegged peasant and his ox receding
Through the mist slowly through the mist of autumn
Which hides the shabby and sordid villages

And out there as he goes the peasant is singing
A song of love and infidelity
About a ring and a heart which someone is breaking

Oh the autumn the autumn has been the death of summer
In the mist there are two gray shapes receding

—W. S. MERWIN

## 1909

The woman had a dress
Of Turkish cloth
And her tunic with a border of gold
Was made of two panels
Attached to each other at the shoulder

Her eyes were dancing like those of angels
She was laughing and laughing
She had a face with the colors of France

Les yeux bleus les dents blanches et les lèvres très rouges
Elle avait un visage aux couleurs de France

Elle était décolletée en rond
Et coiffée à la Récamier
Avec de beaux bras nus

N'entendra-t-on jamais sonner minuit

La dame en robe d'ottoman violine
Et en tunique brodée d'or
Décolletée en rond
Promenait ses boucles
Son bandeau d'or
Et traînait ses petits souliers à boucles

Elle était si belle
Que tu n'aurais pas osé l'aimer

J'aimais les femmes atroces dans les quartiers énormes
Où naissaient chaque jour quelques êtres nouveaux
Le fer était leur sang la flamme leur cerveau
J'aimais j'aimais le peuple habile des machines
Le luxe et la beauté ne sont que son écume
Cette femme était si belle
Qu'elle me faisait peur

AUTOMNE MALADE

Automne malade et adoré
Tu mourras quand l'ouragan soufflera dans les roseraies
Quand il aura neigé
Dans les vergers

Pauvre automne
Meurs en blancheur et en richesse
De neige et de fruits mûrs
Au fond du ciel
Des éperviers planent

Blue eyes white teeth very red lips
She had a face with the colors of France

Her dress was cut low in a circle below her neck
And her hair dressed like Mme. Récamier
With fine naked arms

Shall we never hear midnight sound

The woman in a dress of Turkish cloth
And a tunic with a border of gold
Cut low in a circle
Took her curls for a walk
Her band of gold
Accompanied by her little shoes with buckles

She was so beautiful
That you would never have dared love her

I loved atrocious women in the abysmal quarters of the city
Where some new beings were born every day
Their blood was iron, their brains fire
I loved I loved the people clever with machines
Luxury and beauty are nothing but scum
This woman was so beautiful
That she frightened me

—ROBERT BLY

## AUTOMNE MALADE

   Adored, invalid autumn, you will
die when the hurricane
blows in the rose
parks, when the snow will have come
among orchards

   Poor autumn,
die in the whiteness and richness of ripe
fruit and snow
At the top of the sky hawks

Sur les nixes nicettes aux cheveux verts et naines
Qui n'ont jamais aimé

Aux lisières lointaines
Les cerfs ont bramé

Et que j'aime ô saison que j'aime tes rumeurs
Les fruits tombant sans qu'on les cueille
Le vent et la forêt qui pleurent
Toutes leurs larmes en automne feuille à feuille

Les feuilles
Qu'on foule
Un train
Qui roule
La vie
S'écoule

## CORS DE CHASSE

Notre histoire est noble et tragique
Comme le masque d'un tyran
Nul drame hasardeux ou magique
Aucun détail indifférent
Ne rend notre amour pathétique

Et Thomas de Quincey buvant
L'opium poison doux et chaste
A sa pauvre Anne allait rêvant
Passons passons puisque tout passe
Je me retournerai souvent

Les souvenirs sont cors de chasse
Dont meurt le bruit parmi le vent

glide and hover
over silly young nymphs
with short green hair
who have never loved

   On the far edges of wood the stags
have belled And oh season, season, I
              love your dins
Fruits falling unpicked, the wind
and the woods that weep all of their
tears in the fall, leaf by leaf
            The leaves

                    one tramples
                    underfoot
     A train

                rolls on
     The life that
              runs
                    out

—PAUL BLACKBURN

## HUNTING HORNS

Our story is noble, tragic
as the mask of a tyrant
No dangerous drama or magic
no indifferent detail
can make our love pathetic

And Thomas de Quincey drinking
opium poison mild and chaste
to his poor Anne went dreaming
Let's go, let's go, everything goes
I shall return often

Memories are hunting horns
whose sounds die along the wind

—PAUL BLACKBURN

## LA PETITE AUTO

Le 31 du mois d'août 1914
Je partis de Deauville un peu avant minuit
Dans la petite auto de Rouveyre

Avec son chauffeur nous étions trois

Nous dîmes adieu à toute une époque
Des géants furieux se dressaient sur l'Europe
Les aigles quittaient leur aire attendant le soleil
Les poissons voraces montaient des abîmes
Les peuples accouraient pour se connaître à fond
Les morts tremblaient de peur dans leurs sombres demeures

Les chiens aboyaient vers là-bas où étaient les frontières
Je m'en allais portant en moi toutes ces armées qui se battaient
Je les sentais monter en moi et s'étaler les contrées où elles serpentaient
Avec les forêts les villages heureux de la Belgique
Francorchamps avec l'Eau Rouge et les pouhons
Région par où se font toujours les invasions
Artères ferroviaires où ceux qui s'en allaient mourir
Saluaient encore une fois la vie colorée
Océans profonds où remuaient les monstres
Dans les vieilles carcasses naufragées
Hauteurs inimaginables où l'homme combat
Plus haut que l'aigle ne plane
L'homme y combat contre l'homme
Et descend tout à coup comme une étoile filante
Je sentais en moi des êtres neufs pleins de dextérité
Bâtir et aussi agencer un univers nouveau
Un marchand d'une opulence inouïe et d'une taille prodigieuse
Disposait un étalage extraordinaire
Et des bergers gigantesques menaient
De grands troupeaux muets qui broutaient les paroles
Et contre lesquels aboyaient tous les chiens sur la route

# THE LITTLE CAR

The 31st day of August 1914
I left Deauville a little before midnight
In Rouveyre's little car

With his driver there were three of us

We said goodbye to an entire epoch
Furious giants were rising over Europe
The eagles were leaving their aeries expecting the sun
The voracious fish were rising from the depths
The masses were rushing toward some deeper understanding
The dead were trembling with fear in their dark dwellings

The dogs were barking towards over there where the frontiers are
I went bearing within me all those armies fighting
I felt them rise up in me and spread out over the countries they wound
    through
With the forests the happy villages of Belgium
Francorchamps with l'Eau Rouge and the mineral springs
Region where the invasions always take place
Railway arteries where those who were going to die
Saluted one last time this colorful life
Deep oceans where monsters were moving
In old shipwrecked hulks
Unimaginable heights where man fights
Higher than the eagle soars
There man fights man
And falls like a shooting star
I felt in myself new and totally capable beings
Build and organize a new universe
A merchant of amazing opulence and astounding size
Was laying out an extraordinary display
And gigantic shepherds were leading
Great silent flocks that were browsing on words
With every dog along the road barking at them

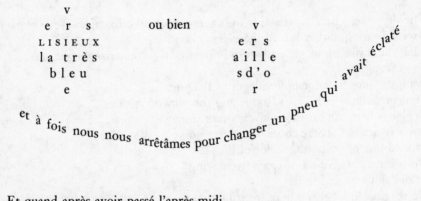

Je n'oublierai jamais de voyage nocturne où nul de nous ne dit un mot

```
O                   o
dé                  nuit
part                tendre            o
sombre              d'avant           vil          s e h â t
où mouraient        la guerre         lages où  t a i l e n
nos 3 phares
```

## MARÉCHAUX-FERRANTS RAPPELÉS

ENTRE MINUIT ET UNE HEURE DU MATIN

```
        v
      e   r   s         ou bien         v
      LISIEUX                         e   r   s
      la très                        a i l l e
      bleu                           s d ' o
        e                                r
```

et à fois nous nous arrêtâmes pour changer un pneu qui avait éclaté


Et quand après avoir passé l'après-midi
Par Fontainebleau
Nous arrivâmes à Paris
Au moment où l'on affichait la mobilisation
Nous comprîmes mon camarade et moi
Que la petite auto nous avait conduits dans une époque Nouvelle
Et bien qu'étant déjà tous deux des hommes mûrs
Nous venions cependant de naître

I'll never for<sub>get</sub> t<sub>h</sub>a<sub>t</sub> <sub>n</sub>i<sub>g</sub>h<sub>t</sub> when <sub>n</sub>o<sub>ne</sub> <sub>of</sub> <sub>us</sub> <sub>s</sub>ai<sub>d</sub> <sub>a</sub> <sub>s</sub>i<sub>ngle</sub> word

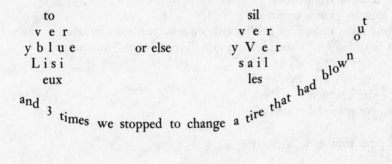

O
dark        O
departure    ten
when our     der
three head    pre-       O
lights were   w a r     vil
d y i n g    night    lages  w<sub>ith</sub>  t<sup>he</sup>r<sub>u</sub> g<sub>n</sub>i<sub>h</sub><sup>s</sup>

B L A C K S M I T H S  C A L L E D  U P

between midnight and one o'clock in the <sub>morning</sub>

to                  sil
v e r             v e r        <sup>t</sup>
y b l u e    or else    y V e r    <sub>o</sub>
L i s i             s a i l
eux                 les

<sup>an</sup>d <sub>3</sub> t<sub>imes</sub> we stopped to change a t<sub>ire</sub> t<sub>hat</sub> <sub>had</sub> <sub>blow</sub><sup>n</sup> <sup>o</sup><sup>u</sup><sup>t</sup>


And when having passed that afternoon
Through Fontainebleau
We arrived in Paris
Just as the mobilization posters were going up
We understood my buddy and I
That the little car had taken us into a New epoch
And although we were both grown men
We had just been born

—RON PADGETT

# TOUJOURS

*A Madame Faure-Favier*

          Toujours
Nous irons plus loin sans avancer jamais
Et de planète en planète

De nébuleuse en nébuleuse
Le don Juan des mille et trois comètes
Même sans bouger de la terre
Cherche les forces neuves
Et prend au sérieux les fantômes

Et tant d'univers s'oublient
Quels sont les grands oublieurs
Qui donc saura nous faire oublier telle ou telle partie du monde
Où est le Christophe Colomb à qui l'on devra l'oubli d'un continent

          Perdre
Mais perdre vraiment
Pour laisser place à la trouvaille
             Perdre
La vie pour trouver la Victoire

# LA JOLIE ROUSSE

Me voici devant tous un homme plein de sens
Connaissant la vie et de la mort ce qu'un vivant peut connaître
Ayant éprouvé les douleurs et les joies de l'amour
Ayant su quelquefois imposer ses idées
Connaissant plusieurs langages
Ayant pas mal voyagé
Ayant vu la guerre dans l'Artillerie et l'Infanterie

# ALWAYS

*To Madame Faure-Favier*

Always

We are going farther without ever advancing
And from planet to planet

From nebula to nebula
The Don Juan of a thousand and three comets
Without even rising from the earth
Look for new forces
And take phantoms seriously

And so many of the universe forget themselves
Who are the great forgetters
Who will know just how to make us forget such and such a part of the
    world
Where is Christopher Columbus to whom is owed the forgetting of a
    continent

To lose

But to lose genuinely
In order to make room for discovery

To lose

Life in order to find Victory

—ROGER SHATTUCK

# THE PRETTY REDHEAD

I stand here in the sight of everyone a man full of sense
Knowing life and knowing of death what a living man can know
Having gone through the griefs and happinesses of love
Having known sometimes how to impose his ideas
Knowing several languages
Having travelled more than a little
Having seen war in the artillery and the infantry

Blessé à la tête trépané sous le chloroforme
Ayant perdu ses meilleurs amis dans l'effroyable lutte
Je sais d'ancien et de nouveau autant qu'un homme seul pourrait des deux
    savoir
Et sans m'inquiéter aujourd'hui de cette guerre
Entre nous et pour nous mes amis
Je juge cette longue querelle de la tradition et de l'invention
        De l'Ordre et de l'Aventure

        Vous dont la bouche est faite à l'image de celle de Dieu
Bouche qui est l'ordre même
Soyez indulgents quand vous nous comparez
A ceux qui furent la perfection de l'ordre
Nous qui quêtons partout l'aventure

Nous ne sommes pas vos ennemis
Nous voulons vous donner de vastes et d'étranges domaines
Où le mystère en fleurs s'offre à qui veut le cueillir
Il y a là des feux nouveaux des couleurs jamais vues
Mille phantasmes impondérables
Auxquels il faut donner de la réalité
Nous voulons explorer la bonté contrée énorme où tout se tait
Il y a aussi le temps qu'on peut chasser ou faire revenir
Pitié pour nous qui combattons toujours aux frontières
De l'illimité et de l'avenir
Pitié pour nos erreurs pitié pour nos péchés

Voici que vient l'été la saison violente
Et ma jeunesse est morte ainsi que le printemps
O Soleil c'est le temps de la Raison ardente
        Et j'attends
Pour la suivre toujours la forme noble et douce
Qu'elle prend afin que je l'aime seulement
Elle vient et m'attire ainsi qu'un fer l'aimant
      Elle a l'aspect charmant
      D'une adorable rousse

Ses cheveux sont d'or on dirait
Un bel éclair qui durerait
Ou ces flammes qui se pavanent
Dans les roses-thé qui se fanent

Wounded in the head trepanned under chloroform
Having lost his best friends in the horror of battle

I know as much as one man alone can know
Of the ancient and the new
And without troubling myself about this war today
Between us and for us my friends
I judge this long quarrel between tradition and imagination
Between order and adventure

You whose mouth is made in the image of God's mouth
Mouth which is order itself
Judge kindly when you compare us
With those who were the very perfection of order
We who are seeking everywhere for adventure

We are not your enemies
Who want to give ourselves vast strange domains
Where mystery flowers into any hands that long for it
Where there are new fires colors never seen
A thousand fantasies difficult to make sense out of
They must be made real
All we want is to explore kindness the enormous country where
    everything is silent
And there is time which somebody can banish or welcome home
Pity for us who fight always on the frontiers
Of the illimitable and the future
Pity our mistakes pity our sins

Here summer is coming the violent season
And so my youth is as dead as spring
Oh Sun it is the time of reason grown passionate
And I am still waiting
To follow the forms she takes noble and gentle
So I may love her alone

She comes and draws me as a magnet draws filaments of iron
She has the lovely appearance
Of an adorable redhead
Her hair turns golden you would say
A beautiful lightning flash that goes on and on
Or the flames that spread out their feathers
In wilting tea roses

Mais riez riez de moi
Hommes de partout surtout gens d'ici
Car il y a tant de choses que je n'ose vous dire
Tant de choses que vous ne me laisseriez pas dire
Ayez pitié de moi

But laugh laugh at me
Men everywhere especially people from here
For there are so many things that I don't dare to tell you
So many things that you would not let me say
Have pity on me

—JAMES WRIGHT

## POÈME DÉCLAMATOIRE

Ce n'est ni l'horreur du crépuscule blanc, ni l'aube blafarde que la lune refuse d'éclairer, c'est la lumière triste des rêves où vous flottez coiffées de paillettes, Républiques, Défaites, Gloires! Quelles sont ces Parques? quelles sont ces Furies? est-ce la France en bonnet phrygien? est-ce toi, Angleterre? est-ce l'Europe? est-ce la Terre sur le Taureau-nuage de Minos? Il y a un grand calme dans l'air et Napoléon écoute la musique du silence sur le plateau de Waterloo. O Lune, que tes cornes le protègent! il y a une larme sur ses joues pâles! si intéressant est le défilé des fantômes. « Salut à toi! salut! nos chevaux ont les crinières mouillées de rosée, nous sommes les cuirassiers! nos casques brillent comme des étoiles et, dans l'ombre, nos bataillons poudreux sont comme la main divine du destin. Napoléon! Napoléon! nous sommes nés et nous sommes morts.—Chargez! chargez! fantômes! j'ordonne qu'on charge!» La lumière ricane: les cuirassiers saluent de l'épée et ricanent; ils n'ont plus ni os, ni chair. Alors, Napoléon écoute la musique du silence et se repent, car où sont les forces que Dieu lui avait données? Mais voici un tambour! C'est un enfant qui joue du tambour: sur son haut bonnet à poils, il y a un drap rouge et cet enfant-là est bien vivant: c'est la France! Ce n'est ici maintenant autour du plateau de Waterloo, dans la lumière triste des rêves où vous flottez, coiffées de paillettes, Républiques, Défaites, Gloires, ni l'horreur du crépuscule blanc, ni l'aube blafarde que la lune refuse d'éclairer.

# Max Jacob
## 1876-1944

### DECLAMATORY POEM

It is neither the horror of the white sunset nor the sickly dawn that the moon refuses to illuminate, but rather it is the sad light of dreams where you float dressed in sequins, O Republics, Defeats, Glories! Who are these Fates? Who are these Furies? Is it France in a Phrygian cap? Is it you, England? Is it Europe? Is it the earth on the Bull-Cloud of Minos? A great stillness fills the air, and Napoleon is listening to the music of silence on the plains of Waterloo. O moon, let your horns protect him! There is a tear on his pale cheeks! So interesting are the ghosts in their procession . . . "Greetings to you! Greetings! The manes of our horses are soaked with dew, we are the cuirassiers! Our helmets shine like the stars, and in the darkness our dusty battalions are like the divine hand of destiny. Napoleon! Napoleon! We are born and we die.—Charge! Charge! Ghosts, I order you to charge!" The light sneers: the cuirassiers salute, their swords drawn, sneering; their flesh and bones are gone. So, Napoleon listens to the music of silence and repents, because where is the power that God had given him? But here is a drum! A child beating a drum: over his tall woven cap there is a red flag, this child really is alive: it is France! Now it is not across the plains of Waterloo where you float, dressed in sequins, in the sad light of dreams, O Republics, Defeats, Glories, nor the horror of the white sunset, nor the sickly dawn that the moon refuses to illuminate.

—MICHAEL BROWNSTEIN

POÈME

La grêle est sur la mer; la nuit tombe: « Allumez le phare à bœufs!»
La vieille courtisane est morte à l'auberge: il n'y a que des rires dans la maison.
Il grêle et le cinématographe fonctionne pour les marins à la maison d'école.
L'instituteur a une belle figure. Me voici dans la campagne; il y a deux hommes qui regardent briller le phare à bœufs.
« Enfin, vous voilà! me dit l'instituteur. Allez-vous prendre des notes pendant le cinématographe? le petit ménage des adjoints vous cédera la table.
—Des notes? quelles notes prendrais-je? les sujets des films?
—Non! vous condenserez le rythme du Cinéma et celui de la grêle et aussi le rire de ceux qui assistent à la mort de la vieille courtisane pour avoir l'idée du Purgatoire.»

LA RUE RAVIGNAN

« On ne se baigne pas deux fois dans le même fleuve» , disait le philosophe Héraclite. Pourtant, ce sont toujours les mêmes qui remontent! Aux mêmes heures, ils passent gais ou tristes. Vous tous, passants de la rue Ravignan, je vous ai donné les noms des défunts de l'Histoire! Voici Agamemnon! voici M^me Hanska! Ulysse est un laitier! Patrocle est au bas de la rue qu'un Pharaon est près de moi. Castor et Pollux sont les dames du cinquième. Mais toi, vieux chiffonnier, toi, qui, au féerique matin, viens enlever les débris encore vivants quand j'éteins ma bonne grosse lampe, toi que je ne connais pas, mystérieux et pauvre chiffonnier, toi, chiffonnier, je t'ai nommé d'un nom célèbre et noble, je t'ai nommé Dostoïevsky.

POEM

Hail falls on the ocean, the night falls: "Have someone turn on the cow-beacons!"

The old courtesan lies dead in the inn: from the house I hear nothing but laughter.

It is hailing and the sailors are watching movies down at the schoolhouse.

The headmaster cuts a fine figure. Here I am out in the fields. Two men are watching the light from the cow-beacons.

"So you're here after all!" the headmaster says to me. "Why don't you take notes during the movie? Our little group of co-workers can give you their table."

"Notes? What kind of notes should I take? On the things in the film?"

"No! You will distill the rhythms of the movie and the rhythms of the hail and you will fuse them with the laughter of those who have witnessed the death of the courtesan: then we will have some inkling of Purgatory."

—JEROME ROTHENBERG

THE RUE RAVIGNAN

"One does not bathe twice in the same stream," said the philosopher Heraclitus. Yet it is always the same ones who mount the street! Always at the same time of day they pass by, happy or sad. All of you, passers-by of the Rue Ravignan, I have named you after the illustrious dead. There is Agamemnon! There is Madame Hanska! Ulysses is a milkman! When Patroclus appears at the end of the street a Pharaoh is beside me! Castor and Pollux are the ladies of the fifth floor. But thou, old ragpicker, who come in the enchanted morning to take away the still living rubbish as I am putting out my good big lamp, thou whom I know not, mysterious and impoverished ragpicker, I have given thee a celebrated and noble name, I have named thee Dostoievsky.

—JOHN ASHBERY

## MŒURS LITTÉRAIRES I

Quand une bande de messieurs rencontre une autre bande, il est rare que les saluts ne s'entremêlent pas de sourires. Quand une bande de messieurs rencontre un monsieur, s'il y a un profond salut, les saluts vont en diminuant et, quelquefois, le dernier de la bande ne salue pas. Il paraît que j'ai écrit que tu avais mordu une femme au bouton du sein et qu'il a coulé du sang. Si tu crois que je l'ai fait, pourquoi me salues-tu? et si je pensais que tu l'eusses fait, te saluerais-je? Nous nous sommes rencontrés chez une grosse dame à lunettes qui a une pèlerine de tricot, tu m'as serré la main, mais nous nous sommes trouvés dans la chambre où est la chaise percée de la dame et tu m'as jeté à la tête les coussins de la chaise percée. Ces coussins étaient très XVIIIᵉ. On dit que je t'ai jeté des coussins aussi au lieu de me disculper. Je ne sais si cela est vrai. Quand ma bande te rencontrera, si je suis le dernier et qui ne salue pas, ne crois pas que ce soit pour l'histoire des coussins; mais, si ma bande rencontre la tienne et qu'il y ait des sourires échangés, ne crois pas qu'il y en ait qui viennent de moi.

## LA CLEF

Quand le sire de Framboisy revint de guerre, sa femme lui fit de grands reproches à l'église, alors il dit: « Madame, voici la clef de tous mes biens, je pars pour jamais. » La dame laissa tomber la clef sur le pavé du temple par délicatesse. Une nonne, dans un coin, priait, parce qu'elle avait égaré la sienne, la clef du couvent et qu'on n'y pouvait pas entrer. « Voyez donc si votre serrure s'accommode de celle-ci. » Mais la clef n'était plus là. Elle était déjà au musée de Cluny: c'était une énorme clef en forme de tronc d'arbre.

## LITERARY MANNERS I

If two groups of writers run into each other the usual thing is to stretch out the greetings with a great many smiles. If one group runs into a stray from another the greetings start at a high level but gradually drop off until the last one on line doesn't even say hello. Or take the time when I was supposed to have said that you had bitten some woman's nipple until you drew blood. If you really believed that I'd said it, why should you greet me? And if I really thought that you'd done it, why should I greet you? But there we were in the house of one of those fabulous ladies with eyeglasses and a knitted cape, and you impulsively reached for my hand. That was how it went until we ended up in the room with the lady's chamberpot and you took the pillows that were piled on her nightstand and threw them at my head. The pillows were very 18th Century, and rumor has it that I threw them back at you instead of explaining what I had done. Or maybe that isn't what happened. But if my group ever runs into you and I'm the last one on line and don't greet you, don't think it's got anything to do with those pillows. Likewise, if my group ever runs into your group and the usual smiles are exchanged, don't think that any are coming from me.

—JEROME ROTHENBERG

## THE KEY

When the sire of Framboisy returned from war his wife reproached him greatly in church, so he said, "My lady, here is the key to all my goods, I am leaving forever." Because of her delicacy the lady let the key fall to the floor of the church. A nun, in a corner, was praying, because she had lost hers too, the key to the convent, and no one could get in. "See then if your lock fits this one." But the key was no longer there. It was already in the Cluny Museum: it was an enormous key in the shape of a tree trunk.

—RON PADGETT

## LES VRAIS MIRACLES

Le bon vieux curé! après qu'il nous eût quitté, nous le vîmes s'envoler au-dessus du lac comme une chauve-souris. Il était assez absorbé dans ses pensées pour ne pas même s'apercevoir du miracle. Le bas de la soutane était mouillé, il s'en étonna.

## MŒURS LITTÉRAIRES II

Un négociant de la Havane m'avait envoyé un cigare enveloppé d'or qui avait été un peu fumé. Les poètes, à table, dirent que c'était pour se moquer de moi, mais le vieux Chinois qui nous avait invités dit qu'ainsi était l'usage à la Havane, quand on voulait faire un grand honneur. Je montrai deux magnifiques poèmes qu'un savant de mes amis avait traduits pour moi sur le papier, parce que je les admirai à sa traduction orale. Les poètes dirent que ces poèmes étaient très connus et qu'ils ne valaient rien. Le vieux Chinois dit qu'ils ne pouvaient pas les connaître, puisqu'ils n'existaient que dans un seul exemplaire manuscrit et en pehlvi, langue qu'ils ignoraient. Les poètes, alors, se mirent à rire bruyamment comme des enfants et le vieux Chinois nous regarda avec tristesse.

## LA MENDIANTE DE NAPLES

Quand j'habitais Naples, il y avait à la porte de mon palais une mendiante à laquelle je jetais des pièces de monnaie avant de monter en voiture. Un jour, surpris de n'avoir jamais de remerciements, je regardai la mendiante. Or, comme je regardais, je vis que ce que j'avais pris pour une mendiante, c'était une caisse de bois peinte en vert qui contenait de la terre rouge et quelques bananes à demi pourries . . .

## MIRACLES REAL MIRACLES

Nice old priest! After he'd left us we saw him fly over the lake, just like a bat, his thoughts absorbing him, not even understanding that this flight was a miracle. His cassock, the hem of his cassock is wet! *That* amazes him.

—ARMAND SCHWERNER

## LITERARY MANNERS II

A Havana businessman sent me a cigar wrapped in goldleaf, only a little chewed at one end. The poets at my table all say that he was playing a joke on me, but the old Chinaman who invited us over reminds them that it's an old Cuban custom and a sign of great esteem. Next I show them two magnificent poems that a friend of mine translated and wrote down for me on a scrap of paper, because I said I liked them when he first read them out loud. The poets tell me that everyone knows those poems and that they really aren't worth much. But the old Chinaman says that the poets couldn't have read them before, since the only copy in the world is a rare manuscript in the Pali language, which none of them understand. Then the poets look at each other and burst out laughing like a bunch of kids, and the old Chinaman stares at us all with such sadness.

—JEROME ROTHENBERG

## THE BEGGAR WOMAN OF NAPLES

When I lived in Naples there was always a beggar woman at the gate of my palace, to whom I would toss some coins before climbing into my carriage. One day, surprised at never being thanked, I looked at the beggar woman. Now, as I looked at her, I saw that what I had taken for a beggar woman was a wooden case painted green which contained some red earth and a few half-rotten bananas . . .

—JOHN ASHBERY

## AU PAYS DES COLLINES

J'arrivai sur une colline couverte de prairies au sommet; des arbres l'entouraient et on apercevait près de soi d'autres collines. Je trouvai à l'hôtel mon père, qui me dit: « Je t'ai fait venir ici pour te marier!—Mais je n'ai pas mon habit noir!—Ça ne fait rien; tu te marieras, c'est l'essentiel! » Je marchai vers l'église et je m'aperçus qu'on m'avait destiné une jeune dame pâle. L'après-midi, j'étais frappé du charme de la fête: la prairie était entourée de bancs; des couples arrivaient, des nobles, quelques savants, des amis de collège, dans des replis de terrains, sous des arbres. Il me prit envie de dessiner. Mais ma femme? Ah! ce n'était qu'une plaisanterie, n'est-ce pas? on ne marie pas les gens sans habit noir, à l'anglaise. Le maire était un directeur d'école communale. Il fit un discours devant la prairie, dit qu'on s'était passé de moi pour me marier, parce qu'on connaissait l'état des fortunes. Alors, j'étouffai des sanglots d'humiliation et j'écrivis cette page-ci, mais avec beaucoup plus de littérature ridicule.

## LE CENTAURE

Oui! j'ai rencontré le Centaure! c'était sur une route de Bretagne: les arbres ronds étaient disséminés sur les talus. Il est couleur café au lait; il a les yeux concupiscents et sa croupe est plutôt la queue d'un serpent que le corps d'un cheval. J'étais trop défaillant pour lui parler et ma famille nous regardait de loin, plus effrayée que moi. Soleil! que de mystères tu éclaires autour de toi.

## LE BIBLIOPHILE

La reliure du livre est un grillage doré qui retient prisonniers des cacatoès aux mille couleurs, des bateaux dont les voiles sont des timbres-poste, des sultanes qui ont des paradis sur la tête pour montrer qu'elles sont très riches.

## IN THE HILL COUNTRY

I arrived on a hill whose top was covered with meadows; trees surrounded it and nearby one could see other hills. At the hotel I found my father, who said: "I summoned you here to marry you off." "But I don't have my black suit!" "No matter, the important thing is for you to get married." I walked toward the church and perceived that they had intended me for a pale young lady. In the afternoon I was struck by the charm of the fête: the meadow was surrounded by benches; couples arrived: nobles, a few scholars, some college friends, in the folds of the ground, under the trees. I had an urge to draw. But my wife? Ah, surely that was just a joke, you don't marry people without a black suit, in the English fashion. The mayor was the director of an elementary school. He made a speech standing in front of the meadow, said that they had gone ahead with the marriage without me, because they knew the condition of the two fortunes. Then I choked with sobs of humiliation and I wrote this page, along with much more ridiculous literature.

—JOHN ASHBERY

## CENTAUR

It's true. I met the Centaur. It was on a Breton road, round trees scattered over the slopes. The Centaur's coloring? very light coffee; concupiscent eyes —and his rump! more a snake's tail than a horse. I couldn't speak to him, felt so weak, and my family kept just staring from a distance, more scared than me. O sun how you do light up what's mysterious around you.

—ARMAND SCHWERNER

## THE BIBLIOPHILE

The binding has some golden grillwork which imprisons cockatoos of a thousand colors, boats with sails made of postage stamps, sultans with bird of paradise feathers on their heads to show how very rich they are. The book

Le livre retient prisonnières des héroïnes qui sont très pauvres, des bateaux à vapeur qui sont très noirs et de pauvres moineaux gris. L'auteur est une tête prisonnière d'un grand mur blanc (je fais allusion au plastron de sa chemise).

## MA VIE

La ville à prendre est dans une chambre. Le butin de l'ennemi n'est pas lourd et l'ennemi ne l'emportera pas car il n'a pas besoin d'argent puisque c'est un conte et seulement un conte. La ville a des remparts en bois peints: nous les découperons pour les coller sur notre livre. Il y a deux chapitres ou parties. Voici un roi rouge à couronne d'or qui monte sur une scie : c'est le chapitre II; quant au chapitre I$^{er}$ je ne m'en souviens plus.

## LE PAPIER DE TENTURE DE M. R. K.

Le plafond de l'enfer est attaché avec de gros clous d'or. Au-dessus, c'est la terre. L'enfer ce sont de grandes fontaines lumineuses tordues. Pour la terre, il y a un peu de pente : un champ de blés coupés ras et un petit ciel en pelure d'oignons, où passe une chevauchée de nains forcenés. De chaque côté un bois de pins et un bois d'aloès. Vous comparaissez, mademoiselle Suzanne, devant le tribunal révolutionnaire pour avoir trouvé un cheveu blanc dans vos cheveux noirs.

imprisons heroines who are very poor, steamboats which are very black, and poor gray sparrows. The author is a head imprisoned by a big white wall (I am alluding to his starched shirt front).

—RON PADGETT

## MY LIFE

The town to take is in a room. The enemy's plunder isn't heavy and the enemy doesn't even take it away because he doesn't need any money since it's a story and only a story. The town has ramparts of painted wood: we'll cut them out and glue them on our book. There are two chapters or parts. Here is a red king with a gold crown riding a saw: that's chapter 2. I don't remember chapter 1 any more.

—RON PADGETT

## THE WALLPAPER OF MR. R.K.

The ceiling of hell was fastened with thick gold nails. Up above was the earth. Hell is all fountains, big, luminous and twisted. For the earth there is a little slope: a field of wheat cut smoothly and a small sky in onion rinds through which passes a cavalcade of mad dwarves. On each side there is a pine forest and an aloe forest. You are now appearing, Miss Suzanne, before a revolutionary court for having found a white hair among your many black ones.

—ANDREI CODRESCU

## LITTÉRATURE ET POÉSIE

C'était aux environs de Lorient, il faisait un soleil brillant et nous nous promenions, regardant par ces jours de septembre la mer monter, monter et couvrir les bois, les paysages, les falaises. Bientôt il ne resta plus à lutter contre la mer bleue que des méandres de sentiers sous les arbres et les familles se rapprochaient. Il y avait parmi nous un enfant habillé en costume de marin. Il était triste; il me prit la main: « Monsieur, me dit-il, j'ai été à Naples; savez-vous qu'à Naples, il y a beaucoup de petites rues; dans les rues on peut rester tout seul sans que personne vous voie : ce n'est pas qu'il y ait beaucoup de monde à Naples mais il y a tant de petites rues qu'il n'y a jamais qu'une rue par personne.—Quel mensonge vous fait encore ce petit, me dit le père, il n'est pas allé à Naples.—Monsieur, votre fils est un poète.—C'est bien, mais si c'est un littérateur je lui tordrai le cou! » Les méandres des sentiers laissés à sec par la mer lui avaient fait songer à des rues de Naples.

## LITERATURE AND POETRY

It was near Lorient, the sun shone brightly and we used to go for walks, watching through those September days the sea rising, rising to cover woods, landscapes, cliffs. Soon there was nothing left to combat the blue sea but the meandering paths under the trees and the families drew closer together. Among us was a child in a sailor suit. He was sad and took me by the hand: "Sir," he said, "I have been in Naples; do you know that in Naples there are lots of little streets; in the streets you can stay all alone without anyone seeing you: it's not that there are many people in Naples but there are so many little streets that there is never more than one street for each person." "What stories is the child telling you now," said the father. "He has never been to Naples." "Sir, your child is a poet." "That's all right, but if he is a man of letters I'll wring his neck." The meandering paths left dry by the sea had made him think of the streets of Naples.

—JOHN ASHBERY

# DANS LES VILLES JAUNES . . .

Dans les villes jaunes sur un ciel d'orage . . .

On parle d'amour derrière une porte. Une vitre où bouge et s'allonge une figure pâle . . . Une lucarne où des fleurs brûlent d'une flamme douce. Une ruelle où l'odeur d'une étable vous lèche . . .

Dans un quartier de cours sombres et de fontaines où je rôdais seul dans l'odeur du soir—j'ai vu les Vieilles. Elles groupaient leurs têtes aux barreaux des fenêtres basses. Leurs yeux brillaient de malice obscène. Ils semblaient tourner dans un bain d'huile. Un rire plein de charbon tirait leur bouche. Une d'elles me désignait d'un gros pouce. Une autre un peu en retrait semblait souffrir.—Je distinguai les Parques, la Belle Heaumière et la sorcière Sycorax. D'autres faisaient marcher la machine à laver, comme dans l'hôpital de Pairis du Lac Noir . . .

Quand elles sabotaient dans le crépuscule, une chauve-souris battait d'une vieille paupière et s'éventait . . . Les bêtes torses des pavés se coulaient dans quelque fissure. Sous les auvents, les nids battaient de pulsations rapides. Un oiseau traversait le ciel où les tours du couchant brûlaient. Tout un bûcher barrait l'impasse . . .

Une pompe comptait dans son auge de pierre. Un gros rat pointa dans la brèche d'une porte, d'une tête tremblante . . . Un chat rampa le long d'un mur comme un flocon de fumée grasse . . .

—Qui est là? dit une voix tremblante derrière une grille . . .

Une plainte arriva du large. Une étoile fixa le soir . . .

Ailleurs, on attend les aimés par la voiture . . . Des bruits de cuisine sonnent.

# Léon-Paul Fargue

## 1876-1947

IN YELLOW TOWNS . . .

In yellow towns against a stormy sky . . .

They talk of love behind a door. A windowpane where a wan face moves and grows long . . . A dormer window where flowers burn with a soft flame. An alley where the fragrance of a stable licks you . . .

In a neighborhood of fountains and dark courtyards where I roamed alone in the fragrance of evening—I saw the Old Women. Their heads were clustered at the bars of the low windows. Their eyes shone with obscene malice. As though revolving in an oil bath. Laughter full of coal strained their mouths. One of them pointed at me with a coarse thumb. Another who stood slightly behind them seemed to be in pain.—I could distinguish the Parcae, the Beautiful Helmet Maker, and the witch Sycorax. Others were running the washing machine, as in the Pairis Hospital in Lac Noir . . .

When at dusk they clattered forth in their wooden shoes, a bat flapped from an old eyelid, fanning itself . . . The twisted creatures of the streets slipped into a crack. Under the eaves, nests beat with quick throbs. A bird crossed the sky, where the towers of the sunset were burning. A whole pile of sticks barred the blind alley . . .

A pump counted into its stone trough. A heavy rat sprang up in the gap of a doorway, its head trembling . . . A cat crept along a wall like a tuft of oily smoke . . .

"Who's there?" said a trembling voice behind a grate . . .

A lamentation came from the sea. A star nailed the evening . . .

Elsewhere, people wait for their loved ones in cars . . . Kitchen noises ring

Le grelot d'un cheval danse dans la rue voisine. Toutes les voix calmes chantent à la ronde, égoïstes et douces . . .

Mais le soir m'emplit d'une ivresse étrange. Et je rôderai dans les cours sombres . . .

## LE BOULEVARD . . .

Le boulevard défile et bâille . . . Un train crie derrière les haies . . .

Des filles en couleurs fortes cousent et attendent aux portes des bouges. Au bruit des pas noirs qui arrivent, leur regard tourne comme un astre . . . Germaine et son amie traînent contre une palissade, au bout d'une rue vide, sous le temps couvert . . .

Souviens-toi des hôtels que ferme à mi-porte une barrière peinte en rouge où tinte un cornet de fer, dans quelque ruelle où les maisons haussent, comme une coupe de jade au bout de mains sales, un pan de ciel crépusculaire . . .

Les murs s'observent avec la lassitude de vieux partenaires, et comme les éternels vis-à-vis d'un bal pauvre . . . Des loques ricanent sur des cordes, aux fenêtres.—Les coins recèlent d'étranges visages. J'entends des fins de scène et des yeux fixes me défient.

Des enfants piaillent dans l'ombre et tombent: Une voix grondeuse les relève.—La ruelle est si mal pavée que tout le monde a l'air d'y boiter. Le dos d'une vieille tourne au bout d'un passage . . . Un chat débuche—et c'est deux pastilles de lune . . .

Le ciel se fonce entre les murs comme une grande fleur, là-haut, dans un vase de fer . . . Un quinquet de travers, couleur d'oignon brûlé. Son maigre bras. Son tintement l'allume . . . De courtes flammes bleues pointent dans les cuisines . . . Des échoppes s'éclairent, baissent et tremblent . . .

Une fille ouvre sa fenêtre. Et je vois sa lampe, coiffée de rose, comme un long flamant debout sur une seule patte . . .

Rappelle-toi nos descentes sourdes dans les escaliers jaunes où flue l'haleine des plombs sans couvercle ouverts sur le soufre des cours, les rais du ciel dans une gouttière, le coin bleu d'un toit où un tuyau bave, et cette femme au casque sombre, aux jambes gantées de bas rouges, et ton cœur qui battait quand tu prenais la fille—et les soldats qui longeaient le chemin de fer—et ce regard d'une femme à sa fenêtre—sage et lourd comme du raisin noir . . .

out. A horse's bell dances in the next street. All the calm voices sing around us, self-absorbed and sweet . . .

But the evening fills me with a strange drunkenness. And I will roam through dark courtyards . . .

—LYDIA DAVIS

## THE BOULEVARD . . .

The boulevard unfurls and yawns . . . A train wails behind the hedge . . .

Girls in bright colors sew and wait in the doorways of brothels. At the noise of black footsteps approaching, their eyes turn like stars . . . Germaine and her friend idle against a billboard at the end of an empty street under stormy skies . . .

Remember the hotels barred by a red-painted half-gate where an iron cornet tinkles, in some lane where houses lift a patch of dusky sky as though it were a jade cup in the tips of dirty hands . . .

The walls gaze upon each other with the weariness of old partners, or of endless confrontations in a miserable dance . . . Tattered clothes cackle on ropes in the windows.—Corners conceal strange faces. I hear the tail ends of quarrels and staring eyes defy me.

Children shriek in the shadow and fall down: A scolding voice lifts them up again.—The lane is so badly paved that everyone seems to limp along it. The back of an old woman rounds the end of a passageway . . . A cat breaks cover—two lozenges of moonlight . . .

The sky darkens between the walls like a large flower, up above, in an iron vase . . . A crooked Argand lamp, the color of burnt onion. Its thin arm. Its tinkling kindles it . . . Short blue flames sprout in kitchens . . . Street stalls light up, lower and tremble . . .

A girl opens her window. And I see her lamp, coiffed in pink like a tall flamingo standing on one leg . . .

Remember our muffled descents down yellow stairways awash with the breath of uncovered drains open to the sulfur of the courtyards, the slanting rays of the sky in a gutter, the blue corner of a roof where a pipe dripped, and that woman with her dark crown of hair, her legs gloved in red stockings, and your heart pounding when you took the girl—and the soldiers who walked along the railway—and that gaze of a woman at her window—wise and heavy as purple grapes . . .

—LYDIA DAVIS

## DANS UN QUARTIER . . .

Dans un quartier qu'endort l'odeur de ses jardins et de ses arbres, la rampe du songe au loin lève et baisse un peu ses accords, par ce temps d'automne . . .

Quels beaux regards se penchent sur leur blanc calvaire? Quels gestes font chanter les rêves couchés et invisibles? Quelles mains ont ouvert les fenêtres sur des paysages où les souvenirs clignent comme au loin des toits, par éclairs?

Une lanterne attend son heure au bout de l'allée sablée qui mène à la villa perdue sous les feuilles où s'égoutte encore une pluie légère.

L'ange est là, sans doute, au clavier, sous l'aile de l'ombre, et son beau visage et ses mains où les bagues sortent leurs griffes à la lumière, brillent d'une flamme qui bouge à peine . . .

Mais l'oiseau qui souffre et se tait sur un secret des Îles se prend à chanter dans son panier d'or!

Un perron d'automne. Une villa blanche posée comme une veilleuse au bout de l'allée à l'odeur amère. Une pensée d'or descend, d'un vol triste . . . On a fermé les persiennes sur des chambres où les idylles sont mortes.

## UNE ODEUR NOCTURNE . . .

Une odeur nocturne, indéfinissable et qui m'apporte un doute obscur, exquis et tendre, entre par la fenêtre ouverte dans la chambre où je travaille.

Mon chat guette la nuit, tout droit, comme une cruche . . . Un trésor au regard subtil me surveille par ses yeux verts . . .

La lampe fait son chant léger, doux comme on l'entend dans les coquillages. Elle étend ses mains qui apaisent. J'entends les litanies, les chœurs et les répons des mouches dans son aréole. Elle éclaire les fleurs au bord de la terrasse. Les plus proches s'avancent timidement pour me voir, comme une troupe de nains qui découvre un ogre . . .

Le petit violon d'un moustique s'obstine. On croirait qu'un soliste joue dans une maison très lointaine . . . Des insectes tombent d'une chute oblique et vibrent doucement, sur la table. Un papillon blond comme un fétu de paille se traine dans la petite vallée de mon livre . . .

Une horloge pleure. Des souvenirs dansent une ronde enfantine . . .

## IN A QUARTER . . .

In a quarter made drowsy by the odor of its gardens and of its trees, the ramp of dreams, in the distance, accelerates and retards its chords, a little, in the autumn weather . . .

What gorgeous aspects cluster over their pale Calvary! What gestures evoke the chants of latent and unrealized dreams! What hands have opened penetrations into landscapes where things remembered come to sight like the perspectives of roofs seen by lightning . . .

A road lamp bides its time at the end of the gravel walk that leads to the villa lost beneath the leaves, in which a light rain still drips.

The angel is there, no doubt, at the keyboard, under the plume of the shade; and his noble visage, and his hands, on which the rings put forth touches toward the light, are bright with a steadfast flame.

The bird troubled by some secret of the Islands, and yet concealing it, picks up its song, in its basketry of gold!

A terrace of autumn. A white villa placed like something on the watch at the terminal of the walk in the bitter odor. A thought as of gold falls down with sad descent. The blinds have been drawn in the rooms in which the idylls are dead.

—WALLACE STEVENS

## A FRAGRANCE OF NIGHT . . .

A fragrance of night, not to be defined, that brings on an obscure doubt, exquisite, tender, comes by the open window into the room where I am at work . . .

My cat watches the darkness, as rigid as a jug. A fortune of subtle seeing looks at me through its green eyes . . .

The lamp sings its slight song quietly, subdued as the song one hears in a shell. The lamp reaches out its placating hands. In its aureole, I hear the litanies, the choruses and the responses of flies. It lights up the flowers at the edge of the terrace. The nearest ones come forward timidly to see me, like a troop of dwarfs that discover an ogre . . .

The minute violin of a mosquito goes on and on. One could believe that a person was playing alone in a house at a remote distance . . . Insects fall with a sidewise fall and writhe gently on the table. A butterfly yellow as a wisp of straw drags itself along the little yellow valley that is my book . . .

Le chat se fend à fond. Son nez dessine en l'air quelque vol invisible . . .
Une mouche a posé ses ciseaux dans la lampe . . .

Des bruits de cuisine s'entassent dans une arrière-cour. Des voix contradic-
toires jouent à pigeon-vole. Une voiture démarre. Un train crie dans la gare
prochaine. Une plainte lointaine et longue s'élève . . .

Et je pense à quelqu'un que j'aime, et qui est si petit d'être si loin, peut-être,
par-delà des pays noirs, par-delà des eaux profondes. Et à son regard qui m'est
invisible . . .

## «ON A TROUVÉ . . .»

« On a trouvé sur le cadavre des lettres, un crayon et quelques cigarettes
espagnoles . . .» On décrit les beaux traits, l'expression de profond chagrin
du visage, et tant de choses, et l'abandon terrible . . .

J'ai peine à suivre . . . Pourquoi faut-il qu'en lisant je revoie fixement la
douce figure d'un des maîtres de notre enfance, avec l'expression qui la tendait
lorsqu'il annotait nos devoirs . . .

Je le vois encore, dans son clair pouvoir, un soir de travail . . . Il causait avec
mon père. On sentait passer dans leur voix contrainte une délicate certitude,
et toute l'estime d'un travailleur pour un autre . . . Notre lampe baissait les
yeux . . . Les oiseaux dormaient dans la cage. Une ombre de barreaux venait
régler ma page blanche . . . On entendait le feu bouger comme un dormeur,
monter dans son rêve et crouler sur ses piliers d'or avec la douceur d'un fruit
mûr . . .

Si c'était lui qu'on a tué . . . Son crayon . . . ses lettres . . .

Est-il vrai? qu'il soit étendu là-bas, par delà cette mince ligne nocturne où
souffrent de pauvres lumières . . .

A big clock outdoors intones drearily. Memories take motion like children dancing in a ring . . .

The cat stretches itself to the uttermost. Its nose traces in the air an imperceptible evolution. A fly fastens its scissors in the lamp . . .

Kitchen clatter mounts in a back-yard. Argumentative voices play at pigeon-vole. A carriage starts up and away. A train chugs at the next station. A long whistle rises far-off . . .

I think of someone whom I love, who is so little to be so separated, perhaps beyond the lands covered by the night, beyond the profundities of water. I am not able to engage her glance . . .

—WALLACE STEVENS

## "ON THE BODY . . ."

"On the body they found some letters, a pencil, and a few Spanish cigarettes . . ." It describes the beautiful features, the expression of profound sadness on the face, and so many other things, and the terrible neglect . . .

I have trouble following . . . Why, as I read, must I keep seeing the gentle face of one of our childhood teachers, with the tense expression it assumed when he was marking our exercises . . .

I can still see him, in his bright power, one working evening . . . He was chatting with my father. We sensed a delicate certainty entering their constrained voices, and all the esteem of one worker for another . . . Our lamp lowered its eyes . . . The birds slept in their cage. A barred shadow lined my white page . . . We heard the fire stir like a sleeper, rise up into its dream and collapse on its golden pillars with the softness of ripe fruit . . .

If it really was he who was killed . . . His pencil . . . his letters . . .

Is it true? that he is lying there, beyond that thin line of night where wretched lights suffer . . .

—LYDIA DAVIS

# COLÈRE

*Pourquoi m'as-tu quitté, moi qui t'aimais tant?*    — Almanach.

Sonnez, flèches de miel, sur les fausses portées fumantes; œil de tigre, frelon fusant, sphinx taupé, navette au chant brumeux, chalumeaux du jour, enclochez-vous dans l'alvéole; fuyez, secrets pointés cachés dans le ciel, petites clefs plumeuses; oreillard, fais ton portemanteau pour la nuit dans les cours chaudronnantes rayées d'animaux inconnus et de linges. Le disque se déclenche au rouge! Voici l'Homme!

Te voilà, zoizonin. Bonjour, monsieur, eh imbécile. Homme, va-t-en, voici les hommes. Quand ils parlent, rien ne pousse. Anatole, tanaos et thanatos, anthropofrime, bœhme, assez de vos mots, assez de vos dieux, assez de vos cloches! Les rais s'épointent, les souffles s'attristent, l'uranie s'endort contre vos plaques, vos chevaux de pierre montent dans le ciel, vos larmiers verdissent, vos cerveaux s'englument, hommes, lâchez-nous! Comment! L'oracle étonné, pas compris, dévêtu pourtant, jonché de patrons et de feuilles d'or par la grande batte, toupies brunisseuses et molettes célestes; l'oracle endormi du soleil dans vos maisons pleines de méduses montées en graine, d'échos et de prismes trompés, de niches prises en alcôve, d'instruments scientifiques en instance, de sacs de fibrine, de lampes capillaires, de tubes de force hantés de résilles sanglantes; vos chambres secouées de haussements d'épaules et de larmes ménagères, fumées qui rabattent, miroirs infestés de tics, grimaces balancées; vos têtes nasardes, hôtels borgnes, sourds à la musique muette des nombres, le tendeur gainé de chair, l'œil à la mèche encrassée, l'écorché dans sa baignoire, le moribond dans son stère, baisers et sommeils qui choquent les pots, traînerie de frotteurs passionnés, prisonnière entre ses lattes, vieux appareils photographiques sautant sur deux pieds sans trouver leur place, vos objectifs tremblants et bègues, meetings de rêves, soufflets digestifs, de potins et d'histoires, et jamais au point; votre cœur vairon, la tendresse impossible avec vous, votre psychologie de vieilles demi-vierges, votre hyperlogorrhée; l'ami qui tousse de traîtrise, l'étudiant en droit qui se croit l'empereur, le grimaud qui mesure la France avec un ver solitaire, le potard qui regarde dans son tube tourner les volants du fromage, l'élève et la femme lui font les poches et l'anévrisme chemine en lui; ce besoin d'échapper au centre de gravité de votre pensée d'hommes, cette envie de sortir avec l'œil d'une mouche, cet archarnement sur les comptes de la terre, espérez-vous faire son prix de revient, c'est bien difficile; vos questions résolues, tout est pire qu'avant; vous oubliez toujours le principal, vous n'avez rien vu comme coulage, vos coutures filent de proche en proche, vos trains les plus rapides s'avancent comme un dessin d'enfant, la fumée mal faite; les constructions de vos têtes les plus fortes roulent sous la table, les cristaux de Descartes mal départis, mal nourris, décroissements, moléculaires, vident la monture, sautent dans les lieux; pas fort, une pichenette, le taon d'un souvenir, le prurit contre la tempe, un revers

# TUMULT

*Why did you leave me I who loved you so.*    — Almanach

Ring, arrows of honey, on the false smoking staffs; tiger eye, fusing hornet, mole-like sphinx, shuttle with the foggy song, reed-pipes for the day, enbell yourselves in the honey cell; flee, pointed secrets hidden in the sky, little feathery keys; lop-eared one make your clothesrack for the night in the caldroned courtyards streaked with unknown animals and linen cloths. The red signal! Here is Man. There you are, lilbirdie. Good-day Sir, hey stupid fool. Man, go away, here are men. When they speak, nothing grows. Anatole, tanaos and thanatos, anthroposham, boehme, enough of your words, enough of your gods, enough of your bells! The spokes break off at the point, breaths become sod, urania goes to sleep against your plaques, your stone horses rise into the sky, your tear-wells turn green, your brains are ensnared, men, let us go! What! The astonished oracle, not understood, but stripped, strewn with patterns and golden leaves by the big lath sword, spinning tops that burnish and celestial grind-stones; the sleeping oracle of the sun in your houses that are full of medusas running to seed, of echoes and deceived prisms, of niches made in alcove form, of expectant scientific instruments, of sacks of fibrine, capillary lamps, force tubes haunted by bloody hair nets, your rooms that are shaken by the raising of shoulders and housewifely tears, fumes that descend, mirrors infested with twitchings, balanced grimaces, your expressive loaf ends, deaf to the mute music of numbers, the layer of snares sheathed in flesh, the eye with the dirty wick, the flayed one in his bath-tub, the dying man in his cubic yard, kisses and slumbers which jar the pottery, dragging along of impassioned polishers, prisoner between her lathes, old cameras jumping on two feet without finding their place, your trembling, stammering lenses, meetings of dreams, digestive bellows, gossip and tales, and never right; the wall-eyed heart, tenderness impossible with you, your psychology of old demi-virgins, your hyperloquacity, the friend who coughs through treachery, the law student who thinks himself emperor, the scribbler who measures France with a tape-worm, the druggist who watches the works of the cheese turn in his tube, the student clerk and the wife go through his pockets and aneurism progresses in him; this need to escape from the center of gravity in your human thought, this desire to go out with the eye of a fly, this rage about the accounts of the earth, do you hope to establish its net price, that is very hard; your questions solved, everything is worse than before; you always forget the principal thing, you have not seen anything in the way of waste, your seams rip first one place then another, your fastest trains go forward like a child's drawing, the smoke badly made; the constructions of your finest brains roll under the table, Descartes' crystals badly distributed, underd, molecular decreasings, empty the stirrups, leap upon the scene; not strong, a fillip, the gad-fly of a memory, itching against the

de la main sur un spectre sucré, (rien, c'est l'Inconnue qui se décroise dans un courant d'air), renversent d'un seul coup vos parties d'échecs les plus longues; vos travaux ne valent pas cher, et votre papier de tirage ne vaut rien! Mais vous m'avez plombé de votre haine, de vos querelles, de vos attentats, de tout cela qui est de l'amour qui se cherche et se tord comme un ver; vous ne pouvez pas trouver la formule, Colin-Maillard béni de gifles, vous le sentez là qui respire, et vous ne pouvez pas l'atteindre, et vous battez la semelle, et vous claquez du bec l'un contre l'autre, et vous soufflez du nez, hein, c'est comme un mot qu'on ne peut pas sortir, pauvres pataurés, petits rageurs noirs; le père chef d'État, le frère chef des chœurs, la fillette horriblement aimée dans son petit lit, la grande sœur jalouse en banlieue, le solitaire brucolaque, les militaires beaux comme des bureaux de tabac, le maréchal doux comme un Bon Dieu de sergents de ville, le pingouin du tribunal, l'ingénieur qui se crotte dans ses calculs, le marin dans ses tripes d'acier, le poète plein de crimes en marcassite, la mère qui pleure dans la cuisine, le piano qui console une dent malade dans une rue pluvieuse; avec ça vos propos n'amusaient pas la route, et vous vous déchiriez, fil à fil, au fond de la turbine. Pourtant, vos pierres creuses étaient posées dans un jardin, vous l'aviez belle, on vous donnait des feuilles neuves chaque matin, des feuilles fraîches comme si elles n'avaient jamais servi. Mais vous alliez trop vite, et vous n'avez rien vu. Si vous m'aviez suivi, si vous aviez parlé moins fort, nous aurions ralenti, moi qui vous aimais tant!

Voix désertes, foulard du soir, tête osseuse contre la vitre. Chaque bête avec son rouet dans son enclos. Votre plainte n'est plus pour moi. Trop tard. A quoi bon, pélican, gonfler éternellement sans pouvoir l'ouvrir ton vieux parapluie nourricier; c'est pour rien, casoar, que tu cours en boxant sous les arbres; vous ne me faites plus plaisir, comme au temps que j'étais enfant, quand un homme de peu de paroles et de grand amour me menait à vous par la main . . . L'organeau qui tintait quand nous passions la porte, on l'a arraché, il n'y a plus de cheval côtier . . . Poète, le resteras-tu, dans cette île tournante musquée de mensonges et de fantômes, qui ne te rendent pas ton amour, qui t'appellent monsieur quand tu les tutoies, mais où tout le monde tire de toi le meilleur, jusqu'au moulage de la mort? Ton rire a fondu dans sa grille, le temps pavoise d'étage en étage, et voici la nuit. La grenade montre son cœur. L'usine de quartz et de pain d'épices s'allume au bord de la Seine. On entend le bruit des marteuses. Va où tu sais. Retourne dans ta galerie de mine, parle à la fille sur sa porte, enfonce-toi comme autrefois dans ce passage sourdement bordé de micas et de chrysalides où s'exile un vieux bec de gaz couronné, noir paponcle; bourre-toi d'images sonores. Musique, maintenant que le moral flanche, tu ne vas pas me lâcher?

temple, a back of the hand on a sugary spectre, nothing, it is the Unknown which uncrosses itself in a draught of air, they overthrow with one blow your longest parts; your labours are not worth much, and your print paper is worth nothing. You have filled me with your hatred, your quarrels, your outrages, with everything about love that seeks and twists itself like a worm, you cannot find the formula, Blindman's Buff, blessed with slaps, you feel him there, he is breathing and you cannot get at him, and you shuffle your feet and you knock each other in the snoot, and you breathe through your nose, eh, it is like a word you can't get out, poor pawgawkies, little black spitfires, the father chief of State, the brother choral director, the little girl fearfully beloved in her little bed, the jealous sister in the suburbs, the solitary vroucolacowamp, the soldiers handsome as tobacco shops, the marshal gentle as a policemen's God, the penguin of the tribunal, the engineer who wallows in his calculations, the sailor in his steel guts, the poet full of marcasite crimes, the mother who weeps in the kitchen, the piano that consoles a bad tooth in a rainy street; at that your remarks did not amuse the road, and you rent yourself, thread for thread, in the bottom of the turbine. Still your hollow stones were placed in a garden, you had it easy, they gave you new leaves each morning, leaves as fresh as if they had never been used. But you went too fast, and you saw nothing. If you had followed me, if you had not spoken so loudly, we would have slowed down, I who loved us so! Deserted voices, evening neckerchief, bony head against the window pane. Each animal with its spinning-wheel in its enclosure. Your complaint is no longer for me. Too late. What is the use, pelican, of eternally inflating your old nurse's umbrella if you are not able to open it; it is no use, cassowary, for you to run under the trees boxing the while, you no longer give me pleasure, as when I was a child, when a man of few words and great love led me by the hand to see you. The anchor-ring that rang as we passed the door, has been torn off, there is no longer a leader horse. Poet, will you remain a poet, in this turning island scented with the musk of lies and phantoms, that do not return your love, that call you sir when you say thou to them, but where everybody takes of your best, even to the molding by death? Your laughter has melted in its grill pan, time is decorating with flags from floor to floor, and night is here. The pomegranate shows its heart. The quartz and gingerbread factory light up on the banks of the Seine. The sound of the hammutes is heard. Go you know where. Return to your minegallery, speak to the girl in the doorway, plunge as before into this passage dully bordered with micas and chrysalids where there lives in exile an old crowned gas lamp, black papuncle; stuff yourself with sonorous images; music, now that my spirit has flopped, you will not leave me in the lurch!

—MARIA JOLAS

## POSTFACE

Un long bras timbré d'or glisse du haut des arbres
Et commence à descendre et tinte dans les branches.
Les fleurs et les feuilles se pressent et s'entendent.
J'ai vu l'orvet glisser dans la douceur du soir.
Diane sur l'étang se penche et met son masque.
Un soulier de satin court dans la clairière
Comme un rappel du ciel qui rejoint l'horizon.
Les barques de la nuit sont prêtes à partir.
D'autres viendront s'asseoir sur la chaise de fer.
D'autres verront cela quand je ne serai plus.
La lumière oubliera ceux qui l'ont tant aimée.
Nul appel ne viendra rallumer nos visages.
Nul sanglot ne fera retentir notre amour.
Nos fenêtres seront éteintes.
Un couple d'étrangers longera la rue grise.
Les voix
D'autres voix chanteront, d'autres yeux pleureront
Dans une maison neuve.
Tout sera consommé, tout sera pardonné,
La peine sera fraîche et la forêt nouvelle,
Et peut-être qu'un jour, pour de nouveaux amis,
Dieu tiendra ce bonheur qu'il nous avait promis.

# NOCTURNE

A long arm embossed with gold slides from the tree tops
And starts to come down and jingle in the branches.
Leaves and flowers crowd together and understand each other.
I have seen the glass snake glide through the evening quiet.
Diana leans over the pond and puts on her mask.
A satin slipper runs in the glade
Like a call from the sky which reaches the horizon.
The boats of night are ready to go.

Other people will come to sit on the iron chair.
Other people will watch it when I am no longer here.
The night will forget the ones who loved it so much.
Never a call will come to light up our faces again,
Never a sob to bring back our love.
Our windows will be put out.
A couple of foreigners will walk along the gray street.
Voices.
Other voices will sing, other eyes weep.

In a new house
Everything will be consummated, everything will be forgiven.
There will be fresh trouble and a new forest,
And maybe someday, for those other friends—
God will hold out the happiness he promised us once.

—KENNETH REXROTH

## L'ÉTRANGÈRE

Tu ne sais rien de ton passé. Tu l'as rêvé,
—Oui, sûrement tu l'as rêvé.
Je vois ton visage dans la lumière grise de la pluie.
Novembre ensevelit le paysage et ma vie.
Je ne sais rien, je ne veux rien savoir de ton passé.

Tes yeux me parlent de brumeuses villes lointaines
Que je ne verrai jamais
Et dont jamais je n'entendrai le nom dans ta voix.
Novembre est sur toute mon âme, novembre est sur toute la plaine.
Je te vois inconnue à travers Autrefois.

Ce sont des choses depuis longtemps mortes,
—Mortes irrémédiablement—
Des musiques étouffées, des luxures flétries.
Je suis sûr que novembre est derrière la porte.
Je vois vivre en ton cœur ce que ton cœur oublie.

Ton âme est loin, bien loin d'ici. Ton âme étrangère
Est une nuit de brume,
De brume et de bruine sale sur des faubourgs
Où la vie a la couleur froide de la terre,
Où des hommes mourront, sans avoir connu l'amour.

# O. V. de L. Milosz

1877-1939

L ' É T R A N G È R E

You know nothing of your past. You have dreamed it,
Yes, most assuredly dreamed it.
I see your face in the rain's gray brillance.
November shrouds the landscape and my life.
And your life I know nothing of, nor do I wish to.

Your eyes murmur of remote cities, hazy—
I shall never see them
Or hear their names in your own voice.
November comes over me, and across the plain.
I watch you, unrecognized, drift this side of formerly.

And things long dead,
Irremediably:
Music and extinguished richnesses.
November stands at the door, I am sure of it.
I can see your heart giving life to what it forgets.

You are distant, alien—you are
The night of fog,
Foul drizzle over the faubourgs
Where life is the earth's cold color,
Where men have died untouched by passion.

Tu m'as déjà rencontré jadis, t'en souvient-il,
Oui, jadis, tristement jadis,
Au pays des vieux livres et des vieilles musiques,
Dans le crépuscule bleu d'une maison tranquille
Aux fenêtres léthargiques.

Le fantôme des paroles dont tu ne te souviens pas
Ou que tu ne prononças pas,
Donne un sens si bizarre à ta lointaine présence.
Je déchiffre dans le livre de ton silence
Ton histoire morte à jamais, même pour toi.

Ma raison pâle est une illusion de clarté,
Un jour de soleil ancien
Sur la route où ta joie rencontra ta douleur.
Tout cela n'a peut-être jamais été
Mais si je te le disais, tu mourrais de peur.

C'est triste comme un jour d'hiver sur les banlieues
Où chemine la mort de la ville,
Comme la maladie et le deuil dans un mauvais lieu,
Comme un bruit de pas dans une maison étrangère
Comme le mot jadis quand l'ombre est sur la mer.

Je ne veux rien savoir de ton passé. Je vois
S'éteindre le jour,
Le dernier jour sur ton visage et sur tes mains.
Laisse-moi la douceur d'ignorer les chemins
Où le hasard a su te guider jusqu'à moi.

Je retrouve en tes yeux des réalités de rêves,
De rêves rêvés dans le vieux temps
Et des visions écloses au soleil de la vie.
Dans le demi-jour empoisonné de la pluie
On dirait que toute une éternité s'achève.

Je reconnais en toi des êtres mystérieux,
Des voyageurs au but secret
Rencontrés autrefois dans la brume des gares
Où tous les bruits ont des inflexions d'adieux.
Parfois aussi tu m'es une atmosphère de foire

Avec ses lumières en pleurs et ses relents
De moisissure et de vice,

We have met already, you will recall,
Yes, long since and unfortunately
In some region of vellum and toccatas
In the blue twilight of a quiet house,
Windows of lassitude.

The ghost of words you will not remember
Or refuse to utter
Gives your remote presence its strange air.
In your voluminous silence I decipher
That story of yours dead as always, even as you are.

My pale rationality is but a figment of clarity,
One day of old sunlight
On that road where your joy meets your sadness.
Perhaps none of this has ever really been—
But, were I to say so, you would die of fear.

This sadness—a winter's day in the banlieues
Where the dying city encroaches
Like disease and bereavement in a fated place,
Like footfalls in a strange house.
Like a stale word when shadow falls on the sea.

I want to know nothing of your past. I watch
The day extinguish itself,
The last day over your face and hands.
Leave me one sweetness—ignorance of those ways
In which chance, knowingly, has brought you close to me.

From your eyes I salvage what is real in dreams,
Dreamed, all of them, in the gone time
And visions blossoming in vivid sun.
One might say the eternal comes full circle
In this twilight poisoned with rain.

In you I recognize those unaccountable
Travellers to the hid destination
Whom I saw once in a haze of terminals
Whose every noise was the inflection of departure.
And then, too, you are the market with its air

Of lights in tears, its odor
Of mould, vice, misery

Avec sa misère et la joie malade de ses musiques.
Des souvenirs de maisons de jeu nostalgiques
Se mêlent au chaos de mon énervement.

Si je sortais, si je fermais la porte, que ferais-tu?
Ce serait peut-être
Comme si tes yeux ne m'avaient jamais connu.
Le bruit de mes pas mourrait sans écho dans la rue
Et je ne verrais que la nuit à tes fenêtres.

C'est comme si tu devais me quitter aujourd'hui
Tout de suite et pour toujours
Sans songer à me dire d'où tu viens, où tu vas.
Il pleut sur les grands jardins nus, ton âme a froid,
Novembre ensevelit le paysage et ma vie.

## LE ROIS DON LUIS . . .

Le roi don Luis voulut revoir
Le château des Douces Années.

Manteau de deuil et cheval noir.

Jamais heure au vide du soir
N'a si lugubrement sonné.

C'est pire que le bruit du vent
Dans les maisons abandonnées.

Ah c'est un son, un son vraiment
Qui vient de plus loin que le temps.

C'est pire que le bruit des portes
Alors qu'on songe aux morts, aux mortes.

Ce son félon me vient, m'arrive
De quels rêves, de quelles rives.

And the stale gaiety of its music.
Familiar old cards, what rooms of roulette,
Shuffle themselves through my formless enervation.

Were I to leave, close the door, what would you do?
Perhaps it would be as if
You had never laid eyes on me.
My steps in the street sponging echoless
And only the night in your windows.

That is how you will leave me presently,
At once and forever,
Without a word of how you got here, where you are going.
It rains in the great naked gardens, you gather to coldness,
November shrouding the landscape and my life.

—JOHN PECK

## KING DON LUIS

King don Luis wanted to see again
The palace called Sweet Years.

Cloak of grief and a black horse.

Bell in the blank of evening:
Never so ominous as this—

Harsh as the wind's hurry
Through abandoned houses.

Indeed, it is a sound
Travelling farther than time.

Doors swinging into reveries
Over men dead, and women.

Treacherous advent, entering
From what dreams, what shores.

Il se couche sur ma raison
En lueurs fausses de poison.

Le long mendiant de la route
Est la chair de ce son sans doute.

Rencontre de chemin d'exil.
O le sinistre qui s'arrête!

Je vois deux yeux presque sans tête,
Deux yeux sur deux jambes de fil.

De plus loin que les oubliés
De plus profond que les noyés.

Le cheval noir dresse l'oreille.

Le sang du roi voudrait crier
L'odeur du silence est si vieille.


## QUAND ELLE VIENDRA . . .

Quand elle viendra—fera-t-il gris ou vert dans ses yeux,
Vert ou gris dans le fleuve?
L'heure sera nouvelle dans cet avenir si vieux,
Nouvelle, mais si peu neuve . . .
Vieilles heures où l'on a tout dit, tout vu, tout rêvé!
Je vous plains si vous le savez . . .

Il y aura de l'aujourd'hui et des bruits de la ville
Tout comme aujourd'hui et toujours—dures épreuves!—
Et des odeurs,—selon la saison—de septembre ou d'avril
Et du ciel faux et des nuages dans le fleuve;

Et des mots—selon le moment—gais ou sanglotants
Sous des cieux qui se réjouissent ou qui pleuvent,
Car nous aurons vécu et simulé, ah! tant et tant,
Quand elle viendra avec ses yeux de pluie sur le fleuve.

Over my mind it sleeps
In false glimmers of poison.

And the tall beggar, most certainly,
Is that sound's body.

On the road into exile.
Sinister, self-encountering!

I see two eyes nearly headless,
Two eyes on two legs of thread.

Farther than the forgotten,
Deeper than the drowned.

The black horse pricks its ears.

The king's blood would cry out
The smell of silence is so old.

—JOHN PECK

## WHEN SHE COMES

When she comes—will her eyes go green, gray,
Gray or green in the river?
The hours will be new in that archaic future,
New, but hardly novel—
Old hours: one has seen, dreamed, spoken them all!
I pity you the knowledge . . .

There will be something of the present and its street-sounds
Just as today and always—stern ordeals—
And odors, depending on the season, September's, April's,
And the false sky, and clouds in the river;

And words, depending on the moment, spirited, broken,
Under skies arranged correspondingly,
For we shall have lived a great deal, shall have pretended to live such a
     great deal
When she comes with her eyes of rain over that river.

Il y aura (voix de l'ennui, rire de l'impuissance)
Le vieux, le stérile, le sec moment présent,
Pulsation d'une éternité sœur du silence;
Le moment présent, tout comme à présent.

Hier, il y a dix ans, aujourd'hui, dans un mois,
Horribles mots, pensées mortes, mais qu'importe.
Bois, dors, meurs,—il faut bien qu'on se sauve de soi
De telle ou d'autre sorte . . .

## SYMPHONIE DE NOVEMBRE

Ce sera tout à fait comme dans cette vie. La même chambre.
—Oui, mon enfant, la même. Au petit jour, l'oiseau des temps dans la
      feuillée
Pâle comme une morte: alors les servantes se lèvent
Et l'on entend le bruit glacé et creux des seaux

A la fontaine. O terrible, terrible jeunesse! Cœur vide!
Ce sera tout à fait comme dans cette vie. Il y aura
Les voix pauvres, les voix d'hiver des vieux faubourgs,
Le vitrier avec sa chanson alternée,

La grand-mère cassée qui sous le bonnet sale
Crie des noms de poissons, l'homme au tablier bleu
Qui crache dans sa main usée par le brancard
Et hurle on ne sait quoi, comme l'Ange du jugement.

Ce sera tout à fait comme dans cette vie. La même table,
La Bible, Gœthe, l'encre et son odeur de temps,
Le papier, femme blanche qui lit dans la pensée,
La plume, le portrait. Mon enfant, mon enfant!

Ce sera tout à fait comme dans cette vie!—Le même jardin,
Profond, profond, touffu, obscur. Et vers midi
Des gens se réjouiront d'être réunis là
Qui ne se sont jamais connus et qui ne savent

There will be (weary voice, impotent smile)
The moment we now have, senile, sterile, dry,
The pulsing of eternity, sister of silence;
The moment we now have, just as we have it now.

Yesterday, ten years ago, today, in a month—
Frightful words, clichés, but what does it matter.
Drink, sleep, die—one must escape from himself
In some way or another . . .

—JOHN PECK

## STROPHES

It will be as it is in this life, the same room,
Yes, the same! and at daybreak, the bird of time in the leafage,
Pale as a dead woman's face; and the servants
Moving; and the icy, hollow noise of the fountain-taps,

Terrible, terrible youth; and the heart empty.
Oh! it will be as it is in this life; the poor voices,
The winter voices in the worn-out suburbs;
And the window-mender's cracked street-cry;

The dirty bonnet, with an old woman under it
Howling a catalogue of stale fish, and the blue-apron'd fellow
Spitting on his chapped hands
And bellowing like an angel of judgement,

It will be exactly as here and in this life, and the table,
The bible, Goethe, the ink with the same temporal odor,
Paper, pale; woman, white thought-reader!
Pen, the portrait,
                    It will be the same,
My child, as in this life, the same garden,
Long, long, tufted, darkish, and, at lunch-time,
Pleasure of being together; that is—
People unacquainted, having only in common
A knowledge of their unacquaintance—

Les uns des autres que ceci: qu'il faudra s'habiller
Comme pour une fête et aller dans la nuit
Des disparus, tout seul, sans amour et sans lampe.
Ce sera tout à fait comme dans cette vie. La même allée:

Et (dans l'après-midi d'automne), au détour de l'allée,
Là où le beau chemin descend peureusement, comme la femme
Qui va cueillir les fleurs de la convalescence—écoute, mon enfant,—
Nous nous rencontrerons, comme jadis ici;

Et tu as oublié, toi, la couleur d'alors de ta robe;
Mais moi, je n'ai connu que peu d'instants heureux.
Tu seras vêtu de violet pâle, beau chagrin!
Et les fleurs de ton chapeau seront tristes et petites

Et je ne saurai pas leur nom: car je n'ai connu dans la vie
Que le nom d'une seule fleur petite et triste, le myosotis,
Vieux dormeur des ravins au pays Cache-Cache, fleur
Orpheline. Oui, oui, cœur profond! comme dans cette vie.

Et le sentier obscur sera là, tout humide
D'un écho de cascades. Et je te parlerai
De la cité sur l'eau et du Rabbi de Bacharach
Et des Nuits de Florence. Il y aura aussi

Le mur croulant et bas où somnolait l'odeur
Des vieilles, vieilles pluies, et une herbe lépreuse
Froide et grasse secouera là ses fleurs creuses
Dans le ruisseau muet.

And that one must put on one's best clothes
To go into the night—at the end of things,
Loveless and lampless;
It will be the same as in this life,
The same lane in the forest; and at mid-day, in mid-autumn
When the clean road turns like a weeping woman
To gather the valley flowers,
We will cross in our walks,
  As in the yesterday you have forgotten,
  In the gown whose color you have forgotten.

—EZRA POUND

H

Le jardin descend vers la mer. Jardin pauvre, jardin sans fleurs, jardin
Aveugle. De son banc, une vieille vêtue
De deuil lustré, jauni avec le souvenir et le portrait,
Regarde s'effacer les navires du temps. L'ortie, dans le grand vide

De deux heures, velue et noire de soif, veille.
Comme du fond du cœur du plus perdu des jours, l'oiseau
De la contrée sourde pépie dans le buisson de cendre.
C'est la terrible paix des hommes sans amour. Et moi,

Moi je suis là aussi, car ceci est mon ombre; et dans la triste et basse
Chaleur elle a laissé retomber sa tête vide sur
Le sein de la lumière; mais
Moi, corps et esprit, je suis comme l'amarre

Prête à rompre. Qu'est-ce donc qui vibre ainsi en moi,
Mais qu'est-ce donc qui vibre ainsi et geint je ne sais où
En moi, comme la corde autour du cabestan
Des voiliers en partance? Mère

Trop sage, éternité, ah laissez-moi vivre mon jour!
Et ne m'appelez plus Lémuel; car là-bas
Dans une nuit de soleil, les paresseuses
Hèlent, les îles de jeunesse chantantes et voilées! Le doux

Lourd murmure de deuil des guêpes de midi
Vole bas sur le vin et il y a de la folie
Dans le regard de la rosée sur les collines mes chères
Ombreuses. Dans l'obscurité religieuse les ronces

Ont saisi le sommeil par ses cheveux de fille. Jaune dans l'ombre
L'eau respire mal sous le ciel lourd et bas des myosotis.
Cet autre souffre aussi, blessé comme le roi
Du monde, au côté; et de sa blessure d'arbre

S'écoule le plus pur désaltérant du cœur.
Et il y a l'oiseau de cristal qui dit mlî d'une gorge douce
Dans le vieux jasmin somnambule de l'enfance.
J'entrerai là en soulevant doucement l'arc-en-ciel

H

The garden descends towards the sea. Poor garden, garden without
    flowers, blind
Garden. On her bench, an old woman clad
In glossy mourning, yellowed like the memento and the portrait,
Watches the vessels of time departing. The nettle, in the great emptiness

Of two o'clock, hairy and black with thirst, keeps watch.
As though from the depths of the heart of the most lost of days, the bird
Of the dull district chirps in the bush of slag.
The peace is the same as the terrible stillness of men devoid of love.
    And I,

    I too am there, for this is my shadow; and in the sad and vile
Heat she has let her empty head fall back upon
The bosom of the light; but I,
Body and soul, myself am like the rope
About to break. What is it then in me that so vibrates and frets I know
    not where
In me, like the cord bound round about the capstan
Of sailing-ships preparing to depart? O overwise

Mother, eternity, ah! let me live my day!
And no longer call me Lemuel; because down there
In a sunlit night, the lazy girls
Hail the islands of their singing and veiled youth! The sweet

And heavy mourning murmur of the wasps of noon
Floats low above the wine and there is a kind of craziness
About the look of the dew upon the hills of my beloved
Shady ones. In the religious gloom the brambles

Have seized hold of the girl's hair of sleep. Yellow in the shade
The water difficultly breathes beneath the heavy, low forget-me-not blue
    sky.
That other suffers too, bearing like the king
Of the world, a wounded side; and from his scarred-tree wound

There flows the purest stream ever to quench the thirsty heart.
And there is the crystal bird that sweetly trills
In the old somnabulistic jasmine-tree of childhood.
I will enter in there gently raising the rainbow's arch

Et j'irai droit à l'arbre où l'épouse éternelle
Attend dans les vapeurs de la patrie. Et dans les feux du temps
    apparaîtront
Les archipels soudains, les galères sonnantes—
Paix, paix. Tout cela n'est plus. Tout cela n'est plus ici, mon fils Lémuel.

Les voix que tu entends ne viennent plus des choses.
Celle qui a longtemps vécu en toi obscure
T'appelle du jardin sur la montagne! Du royaume
De l'autre soleil! Et ici, c'est la sage quarantième

Année, Lémuel.
Le temps pauvre et long.
Une eau chaude et grise.
Un jardin brûlé.

And I will go straight to the tree where the eternal bride
Awaits amongst the mists of the native land. And in the fires of time
    there will appear
The sudden archipelagos, the sonorous hulks—
Peace, peace. All that is no more. All that is no longer here, my son
    Lemuel.

The voices you hear no longer come from things.
That which has long lived in the dark in you
Calls you from the garden on the mountains! From the kingdom
Of the other sun! And here, it is the disillusioned fortieth

Year, Lemuel.
The poor long time.
A water warm and grey.
A garden burnt.

—DAVID GASCOYNE

## AUX DIX MILLE ANNÉES

Ces barbares, écartant le bois, et la brique et la terre, bâtissent dans le roc afin de bâtir éternel!

Ils vénèrent des tombeaux dont la gloire est d'exister encore; des ponts renommés d'être vieux et des temples de pierre trop dure dont pas une assise ne joue.

Ils vantent que leur ciment durcit avec les soleils; les lunes meurent en polissant leurs dalles; rien ne disjoint la durée dont ils s'affublent ces ignorants, ces barbares!

Vous! fils de Han, dont la sagesse atteint dix mille années et dix mille dix milliers d'années, gardez-vous de cette méprise.

Rien d'immobile n'échappe aux dents affamées des âges. La durée n'est point le sort du solide. L'immuable n'habite pas vos murs, mais en vous, hommes lents, hommes continuels.

Si le temps ne s'attaque à l'œuvre, c'est l'ouvrier qu'il mord. Qu'on le rassasie: ces troncs pleins de sève, ces couleurs vivantes, ces ors que la pluie lave et que le soleil éteint.

Fondez sur le sable. Mouillez copieusement votre argile. Montez les bois

# Victor Segalen

## 1878-1919

TO THE TEN THOUSAND YEARS

萬歲
萬萬歲

These barbarians, laying wood aside, and brick, and clay, build in rock so as to build forever!

They venerate tombs whose glory is to exist even now; bridges famed for their age and temples of too hard a stone, not one of whose foundations gives an inch.

They boast that their cement hardens with the suns; moons die while polishing their flagstones; nothing can unseam the duration they dress up in, these ignorant barbarians!

You! sons of Han, whose wisdom reaches to ten thousand years and ten thousand times ten thousand years, protect yourselves from this misapprehension.

Nothing that's motionless escapes the ravenous teeth of time. Not one thing solid is fated to last. The unchangeable does not dwell in your walls—but in yourselves, slow men, uninterruptible men.

Should time fail to invest the work, the worker's bitten. Let time be fed: these tree-trunks full of sap, these living colors, these golds refined by rain, extinguished by the sun.

Build upon sand. Saturate your clay. Scaffold this wood for sacrifice; soon

pour le sacrifice; bientôt le sable cédera, l'argile gonflera, le double toit criblera le sol de ses écailles:

Toute l'offrande est agréée!

Or, si vous devez subir la pierre insolente et le bronze orgueilleux, que la pierre et que le bronze subissent les contours du bois périssable et simulent son effort caduc:

Point de révolte: honorons les âges dans leurs chutes successives et le temps dans sa voracité.

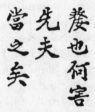

## A CELUI-LÀ

A celui-là qui parvient jusqu'ici malgré les détours et les faux pas; au compagnon qui me livre ses yeux,—que livrer en échange de ce compagnon-nage?

Non pas mon dévouement: le Prince est là: je suis tout entier pour le Prince. La servitude glorieuse pèse sur chacun de mes gestes comme le sceau sur l'acte impérial et le tribut.

Non pas ma tendresse et de faibles émois: sachez qu'elle les garde et boit jalousement toutes les fraîches gouttes écloses de mon âme.

Non pas enfin l'ardeur d'une mort filiale: cela ne m'appartient pas car le père de mes jours est vivant.

A celui qui me dévisage et m'observe amicalement; à celui comme une caverne en qui retentit mon aboi,

Je propose ma vie singulière: seule ma vie est à moi.—Qu'il vienne plus avant. Qu'il écoute plus profondément:

Là même où ni père ni amante ni le Prince lui-même ne pourront accéder jamais.

## ON ME DIT

On me dit: Vous ne devez pas l'épouser. Tous les présages sont d'accord, et néfastes: remarquez bien, dans son nom, l'EAU, jetée au sort, se remplace par le VENT.

sand will give, the clay will swell and rise, the double roof will riddle the ground with its scales:

The whole offering is accepted!

And if you must submit to insolence of stone and bronze's pride, let stone and bronze follow the contours of perishable wood and counterfeit its thwarted effort:

Let there be no revolt: honor the ages in their cataracts, the gluttony of time.

—NATHANIEL TARN

## TO THAT PERSON

To that person who arrives here despite detours and wrong turnings: to the companion who grants me his eyes—what shall I give in exchange for this companionship?

Not my devotion: I have a Prince and I am all the Prince's. A glorious servitude weighs on my every gesture like the seal on an imperial edict and on tribute.

Not my tenderness nor my weak-hearted emotions: know that she guards those and jealously drinks every fresh drop my soul distills.

Nor, in short, a filial death's ardor: this is not mine to give for the father of my days is alive.

To him who scrutinizes me and observes me like a friend; who is like a cavern which echoes my halloo,

I propose my particular life: only my life is mine. Let him come further forward and listen with more attention:

There where neither father nor mistress nor Prince himself can ever reach.

—NATHANIEL TARN

菱先當
也夫之
何矣
害

## I AM TOLD

I am told: you must not marry her. All the omens agree and they are inauspicious. Mark it well: in her name, *water,* cast by lot, is replaced by *wind.*

Or, le vent renverse, c'est péremptoire. Ne prenez donc pas cette femme. Et puis il y a le commentaire: écoutez: « Il se heurte aux rochers. Il entre dans les ronces. Il se vêt de poil épineux . . . » et autres gloses qu'il vaut mieux ne pas tirer.

Je réponds: Certes, ce sont là présages douteux. Mais ne donnons pas trop d'importance. Et puis, elle est veuve et tout cela regarde le premier mari.
Préparez la chaise pour les noces.

## LIBATION MONGOLE

C'est ici que nous l'avons pris vivant. Comme il se battait bien nous lui offrîmes du service: il préféra servir son Prince dans la mort.
Nous avons coupé ses jarrets: il agitait les bras pour témoigner son zèle.
Nous avons coupé ses bras: il hurlait de dévouement pour Lui.
Nous avons fendu sa bouche d'une oreille à l'autre: il a fait signe, des yeux, qu'il restait toujours fidèle.

Ne crevons pas ses yeux comme au lâche; mais tranchant sa tête avec respect, versons le koumys des braves, et cette libation:
Quand tu renaîtras, Tch'en Houo-chang, fais-nous l'honneur de renaître chez nous.

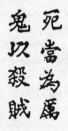

## ÉCRIT AVEC DU SANG

Nous sommes à bout. Nous avons mangé nos chevaux, nos oiseaux, des rats et des femmes. Et nous avons faim encore.
Les assaillants bouchent les créneaux. Ils sont plus de quatre myriades; nous, moins de quatre cents.
Nous ne pouvons plus bander l'arc ni crier des injures sur eux; seulement grincer des mâchoires par envie de les mordre.

Now wind knocks over, that brooks no argument. So, do not take this woman. And then the gloss: Listen: "Wind dashes against rock, darts into brambles, covers itself with a spiny fur . . . " and other footnotes better left in the pack.

I answer: Yes, these are dubious omens. Let's not exaggerate, however. And then, she is a widow: all that is her first husband's business.
Prepare the marriage chair.

—NATHANIEL TARN

他日再生
當令我
得之

## MONGOL LIBATION

It's here we took him alive. As he fought well we offered him some office: he preferred to serve his Prince in death.
We cut his hamstrings: he waved his arms about to witness to his zeal. We cut his arms: he bellowed his devotion to Him.
We sliced his mouth from ear to ear: he signalled with his eyes that he remained faithful.

Let's not pierce his eyes as one does to cowards. Let's cut his head off respectfully, and pour the *koumys* of the brave, with this libation:
When you are reborn, Cheng-ho-chang, do us the honor of being reborn among us.

—NATHANIEL TARN

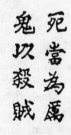

死當為屬
鬼以殺賊

## WRITTEN IN BLOOD

We are at the end of our tethers. We have eaten our horses, our birds, rats and women. And we are still hungry.
The attackers block the battlements. They number more than four myriad; we have only four hundred.
We can no longer draw our bows nor heap insults upon them: we can only gnash our teeth out of a longing to bite them.

Nous sommes vraiment à bout. Que l'Empereur, s'il daigne lire ceci de notre sang, n'ait point de reproches pour nos cadavres.

Mais qu'Il n'évoque point nos esprits: nous voulons devenir démons, et de la pire espèce:
Par envie de toujours mordre et de dévorer ces gens-là!

雖則七襄
不成報章

## LES MAUVAIS ARTISANS

Ce sont, dans les vingt-huit maisons du Ciel; la Navette étoilée qui jamais n'a tissé de soie;
Le Taureau constellé, corde au cou, et qui ne peut traîner sa voiture;
Le Filet myriadaire si bien fait pour coiffer les lièvres et qui n'en prend jamais;
Le Van qui ne vanne pas; la Cuiller sans usage même pour mesurer l'huile!
Et le peuple des artisans terrestres accuse les célestes d'imposture et de nullité.
Le poète dit: Ils rayonnent.

諱名

## NOM CACHÉ

Le véritable Nom n'est pas celui qui dore les portiques, illustre les actes; ni que le peuple mâche de dépit;
Le véritable Nom n'est point lu dans le Palais même, ni aux jardins ni aux grottes, mais demeure caché par les eaux sous la voûte de l'aqueduc où je m'abreuve.
Seulement dans la très grande sécheresse, quand l'hiver crépite sans flux, quand les sources, basses à l'extrême, s'encoquillent dans leurs glaces,
Quand le vide est au cœur du souterrain et dans le souterrain du cœur,—où le sang même ne roule plus,—sous la voûte alors accessible se peut recueillir le Nom.
Mais fondent les eaux dures, déborde la vie, vienne le torrent dévastateur plutôt que la Connaissance!

We are really at the end of our tethers. We hope the Emperor will not reproach our corpses, if he should deign to read our blood.

But let Him not evoke our spirits: we wish to become demons, and of the bloodiest kind:

Out of a longing forever to bite and devour that lot!

—NATHANIEL TARN

雖則七襄
不成報章

## BAD CRAFTSMEN

In the twenty-eight houses of the Sky: the starry Shuttle which has never woven silk;

The Bull constellation, roped at the neck, which cannot draw its cart;

The myriad-knotted Net so well laid to take hares by the ears and which never catches any;

The Fan which fails to winnow; the Spoon which doesn't even measure oil!

And a congregation of politic craftsmen accuse the celestials of imposture and rate them nil.

The poet says: They are radiant.

—NATHANIEL TARN

譚名

## HIDDEN NAME

The true Name is not the one that gilds portals, illustrates proceedings; nor the one the populace chews with vexation;

The true Name is not to be read in the Palace itself, nor in gardens or grottos, but remains hidden in the waters under an aqueduct I drink from.

Only when there is great drought, when frostbound winter crackles, when springs, at their lowest ebb, spiral in shells of ice,

When the void gapes underground in the heart's cavern—where blood itself has ceased to flow—under the vault, now accessible, the Name can be received.

But let the hard waters melt, let life overflow, let the devastating torrent surge rather than Knowledge!

—NATHANIEL TARN

# ODE

Prête-moi ton grand bruit, ta grande allure si douce,
Ton glissement nocturne à travers l'Europe illuminée,
O train de luxe! et l'angoissante musique
Qui bruit le long de tes couloirs de cuir doré,
Tandis que derrière les portes laquées, aux loquets de cuivre lourd,
Dorment les millionnaires.
Je parcours en chantonnant tes couloirs
Et je suis ta course vers Vienne et Budapesth,
Mêlant ma voix à tes cent mille voix,
O Harmonika-Zug!

J'ai senti pour la première fois toute la douceur de vivre,
Dans une cabine du Nord-Express, entre Wirballen et Pskow.
On glissait à travers des prairies où des bergers,
Au pied de groupes de grands arbres pareils à des collines,
Étaient vêtus de peaux de moutons crues et sales . . .
(Huit heures du matin en automne, et la belle cantatrice
Aux yeux violets chantait dans la cabine à côté.)
Et vous, grandes places à travers lesquelles j'ai vu passer la Sibérie et les
        monts du Samnium,
La Castille âpre et sans fleurs, et la mer de Marmara sous une pluie tiède!

Prêtez-moi, ô Orient-Express, Sud-Brenner-Bahn, prêtez-moi
Vos miraculeux bruits sourds et

# Valery Larbaud

1881-1957

## ODE

Lend me thy great noise, thy powerful, gentle gait,
Thy delicate nocturnal glide across illuminated Europe,
O luxurious train! And the agonizing music
Running the length of thy gilt, embossed corridors,
While behind the brass knobs of lacquered doors,
Millionaires slumber.
Humming I pace thy corridors
And follow thy course toward Vienna and Budapest,
Mingling my voice with thy hundred thousand voices,
O Harmonika-Zug!

I experienced for the first time all the joy of living
In a compartment of the Nord-Express, between Wirballen and Pskov.
We were gliding over fields where shepherds,
Under clumps of huge trees like hills,
Were clad in filthy, raw sheepskins . . .
(Eight o'clock one autumn morning, and the beautiful blue-eyed
Singer was singing in the neighboring compartment.)
Wide windows beyond which I have seen Siberia and the Mountains of
    Samnium,
Bleak, blossomless Castile, and the Sea of Marmara under a warm rain!

Lend me, O Orient Express, Sud-Brenner-Bahn, lend me
Your miraculous deep tones and

Vos vibrantes voix de chanterelle;
Prêtez-moi la respiration légère et facile
Des locomotives hautes et minces, aux mouvements
Si aisés, les locomotives des rapides,
Précédant sans effort quatre wagons jaunes à lettres d'or
Dans les solitudes montagnardes de la Serbie,
Et, plus loin, à travers la Bulgarie pleine de roses . . .

Ah! il faut que ces bruits et que ce mouvement
Entrent dans mes poèmes et disent
Pour moi ma vie indicible, ma vie
D'enfant qui ne veut rien savoir, sinon
Espérer éternellement des choses vagues.


## LE MASQUE

J'écris toujours avec un masque sur le visage;
Oui, un masque à l'ancienne mode de Venise,
Long, au front déprimé,
Pareil à un grand mufle de satin blanc.
Assis à ma table et relevant la tête,
Je me contemple dans le miroir, en face
Et tourné de trois quarts, je m'y vois
Ce profil enfantin et bestial que j'aime.
Oh, qu'un lecteur, mon frère, à qui je parle
A travers ce masque pâle et brillant,
Y vienne déposer un baiser lourd et lent
Sur ce front déprimé et cette joue si pâle.
Afin d'appuyer plus fortement sur ma figure
Cette autre figure creuse et parfumée.

Your vibrant string-voices;
Lend me the light, easy respiration
Of your high, thin locomotives with their graceful
Movement, the express engines
Drawing effortlessly four yellow gold-lettered carriages
Through the mountain solitudes of Serbia,
And farther on, through rose-heaped Bulgaria . . .

Ah, these sounds and this movement
Must enter into my poems and express
For me my inexpressible life,
The life of a child whose only desire
Is to hope eternally for airy, distant things.

—WILLIAM JAY SMITH

## THE MASK

I always write with a mask upon my face;
Yes, a mask in the old Venetian style,
Long, with a low forehead,
Like a big muzzle of white satin.
Seated at my desk and raising my head
I look at myself in the mirror, opposite
Me and three-quarters turned, I see me there,
That childish bestial profile that I love.
Oh, that some reader, my brother, to whom I speak
Through this pale and shining mask,
Might come and place a slow and heavy kiss
On this low forehead and cheek so pale,
All the more to press upon my face
That other face, hollow and perfumed.

—RON PADGETT & BILL ZAVATSKY

## MATIN DE NOVEMBRE PRÈS D'ABINGDON

Les collines dans le brouillard, sous le ciel de cendre bleue
Comme elles sont hautes et belles!
O jour simple, mêlé de brume et de soleil!
Marcher dans l'air froid, à travers ces jardins,
Le long de cette Tamise qui me fait songer aux vers de Samain,
Marcher sur la terre de nouveau inconnue, toute changée,
Et pareille au pays des fées, ce matin d'arrière-automne . . .
O nature voilée, mystérieux paysages, vous ressemblez
Aux blocs des maisons géantes et aux avenues brumeuses de la ville,
Vous avez l'imprécis grandiose des horizons urbains.

## ALMA PERDIDA

A vous, aspirations vagues; enthousiasmes;
Pensers d'après déjeuner; élans du cœur;
Attendrissement qui suit la satisfaction
Des besoins naturels; éclairs du génie; agitation
De la digestion qui se fait; apaisement
De la digestion bien faite; joies sans causes;
Troubles de la circulation du sang; souvenirs d'amour;
Parfum de benjoin du tub matinal; rêves d'amour;
Mon énorme plaisanterie castillane, mon immense
Tristesse puritaine, mes goûts spéciaux:
Chocolat, bonbons sucrés jusqu'à brûler, boissons glacées;
Cigares engourdisseurs; vous, endormeuses cigarettes;
Joies de la vitesse; douceur d'être assis; bonté
Du sommeil dans l'obscurité complète;
Grande poésie des choses banales: faits divers; voyages;
Tziganes; promenades en traineau; pluie sur la mer;
Folie de la nuit fiévreuse, seul avec quelques livres;
Hauts et bas du temps et du tempérament;
Instants reparus d'une autre vie; souvenirs, prophéties
O splendeurs de la vie commune et du train-train ordinaire,
A vous cette âme perdue.

# NOVEMBER MORNING NEAR ABINGDON

The hills in the fog, under an ash blue sky
How high and beautiful they are!
O simple day, mingled with mist and sun!
Walking in cold air through these gardens,
Along this Thames which makes me think of the poems of Samain,
Walking the earth made strange again, all changed,
And like fairylands this late autumn morning . . .
O veiled nature, mysterious landscapes, you resemble
The blocks of giant houses and the misty avenues of the city,
You have the grandiose vagueness of urban horizons.

—RON PADGETT & BILL ZAVATSKY

# ALMA PERDIDA

To you, vague aspirations; enthusiasms;
Thoughts after lunch; emotional impulses;
Feelings that follow the gratification
Of natural needs; flashes of genius; agitation
Of the digestive process; appeasement
Of good digestion; inexplicable joys;
Circulatory problems; memories of love;
Scent of benzoin in the morning tub; dreams of love;
My tremendous Castilian joking, my vast
Puritan sadness, my special tastes:
Chocolate, candies so sweet they almost burn, iced drinks;
Drowsy cigars; you, sleepy cigarettes;
Joys of speed; sweetness of being seated; excellence
Of sleeping in total darkness;
Great poetry of banal things: news items; trips;
Gypsies; sleigh rides; rain on the sea;
Delirium of feverish night, alone with a few books;
Ups and downs of temperature and temperament;
Recurring moments from another life; memories, prophecies;
O splendors of the common life and the usual this and that,
To you this lost soul.

—RON PADGETT & BILL ZAVATSKY

# MUSIQUE APRÈS UNE LECTURE

Assez de mots, assez de phrases! ô vie réelle,
Sans art et sans métaphores, sois à moi.
Viens dans mes bras, sur mes genoux,
Viens dans mon cœur, viens dans mes vers, ma vie.
Je te vois devant moi, ouverte, interminable,
Comme une rue du Sud béni, étroite et chaude,
Et tortueuse entre des maisons très hautes, dont les faîtes
Trempent dans le ciel du soir, heurtés
Par des chauves-souris mou-volantes;
Rue, comme un grand corridor parfumé
D'un Barrio del Mar dont la mer est en effet voisine,
Et où, dans la nuit calme, tout à l'heure,
Les serenos psalmodieront les heures . . .

Mais, ma vie, c'est toujours cette rue à la veille
Du jour de Saint-Joseph, quand des musiciens,
Des guitares sous leurs capes, donnent des sérénades:
On entendra, jusqu'au sommeil très doux, le bruit
Plus doux encore que le sommeil, des cordes et du bois,
Si tremblant, si joyeux, si attendrissant et si timide,
Que si seulement je chante
Toutes les Pepitas vont danser dans leurs lits.

Mais non!
Mon chant entrecoupé de cris! mon chant à moi!
(Ce n'est pas toi, Amérique, tes cataractes, tes forêts
Où frémit la venue du printemps, ce n'est pas toi,
Grand silence des Andes prodigieux et solitaires,
Ce n'est pas vous, non, qui remplissez ce cœur
D'une harmonie indescriptible, où se mêlent
Une joie féroce et des sanglots d'orgueil! . . . )
Oh! que j'aille dans les lieux inhabités, loin des livres,
Et que j'y laisse rire et hurler
La bête lyrique qui bondit dans mon sein!

# MUSIC AFTER READING

Enough words, enough sentences! O real life,
Artless and unmetaphored, be mine.
Come into my arms, sit on my lap.
Come into my heart, come into my lines, my life.
I see you in front of me, open, interminable,
Like a street in the blessed South, narrow and warm,
Winding between such high houses, whose tops
Dip into the evening sky, with
Soft-flying bats brushing past them;
Street like a large fragrant passageway
Of a Barrio del Mar whose neighbor is indeed the sea,
And where, in the peaceful darkness, in a little while,
The serenos will sing the hours like psalms . . .

But my life—it's always this street on the eve
Of Saint Joseph's Day, when the musicians,
Guitars under their capes, go serenading:
Very gently on the brink of sleep you'll hear
The sound of strings and wood, even gentler than sleep,
So trembling, so joyful, so touching and so tentative,
That if only I were to sing
All the Pepitas would dance in their beds.

But no!
Cries shatter my song! My own song!
(You're not the one, America, your cataracts, your forests
Where the coming spring trembles, you're not the one,
Great silence of the stupendous, lonely Andes,
No, you're not the ones who fill this heart
With an indescribable harmony, mingling
Fierce joy and sobs of pride! . . .)
Oh! If I could only go where no one lives, far from books,
And let the lyrical beast leaping in my breast laugh and howl!

—RON PADGETT & BILL ZAVATSKY

MA MUSE

Je chante l'Europe, ses chemins de fer et ses théâtres
Et ses constellations de cités, et cependant
J'apporte dans mes vers les dépouilles d'un nouveau monde:
Des boucliers de peaux peints de couleurs violentes,
Des filles rouges, des canots de bois parfumés, des perroquets,
Des flèches empennées de vert, de bleu, de jaune,
Des colliers d'or vierge, des fruits étranges, des arcs sculptés,
Et tout ce qui suivait Colomb dans Barcelone.
Mes vers, vous possédez la force, ô mes vers d'or,
Et l'élan de la flore et de la faune tropicales,
Toute la majesté des montagnes natales,
Les cornes du bison, les ailes du condor!
La muse qui m'inspire est une dame créole,
Ou encore la captive ardente que le cavalier emporte
Attachée à sa selle, jetée en travers de la croupe,
Pêle-mêle avec des étoffes précieuses, des vases d'or et des tapis,
Et tu es vaincu par ta proie, ô llanero!
Mes amis reconnaissent ma voix, ses intonations
Familières d'après dîner, dans mes poèmes.
(Il suffit de savoir mettre l'accent où il faut.)
Je suis agi par les lois invincibles du rythme,
Je ne les comprends pas moi-même: elles sont là.
O Diane, Apollon, grands dieux neurasthéniques
Et farouches, est-ce vous qui me dictez ces accents,
Ou n'est-ce qu'une illusion, quelque chose
De moi-même purement—un borborygme?

LE DON DE SOI-MÊME

Je m'offre à chacun comme sa récompense;
Je vous la donne même avant que vous l'ayez méritée.

Il y a quelque chose en moi,
Au fond de moi, au centre de moi,
Quelque chose d'infiniment aride

## MY MUSE

I sing Europe, its railways and its theaters
And its constellations of cities, and yet
In my lines I bring the spoils from a new world:
Shields of hide painted violent colors,
Red girls, canoes of scented wood, parrots,
Arrows feathered with green, blue, yellow,
Necklaces of pure gold, strange fruit, carved bows,
And everything that followed Columbus into Barcelona.
My lines, you have the power, O my golden lines,
And the zest of tropical fauna and flora,
All the majesty of my native mountains,
Buffalo horns, the condor's wings!
The muse that inspires me is a Creole lady,
Or the fiery captive the cavalier sweeps away
Lashed to his saddle, thrown across the rump,
Helter-skelter with precious stuffs, gold urns and rugs,
And you have been conquered by your prey, O llanero!
My friends recognize my voice, its familiar
After-dinner intonations, in my poems.
(Just put the emphasis in the right place.)
I am set in motion by the invincible laws of rhythm,
I don't understand them myself: they're just there.
O Diana, Apollo, great neurasthenic
Savage gods, is it you who dictate these strains to me,
Or is this only an illusion, something
Purely mine—a borborygmus?

—RON PADGETT & BILL ZAVATSKY

## THE GIFT OF ONESELF

I offer myself to each as his reward;
Here it is, even before you deserved it.

There is something in me,
In the deepest part of me, at the center of me,
Something infinitely barren

Comme le sommet des plus hautes montagnes;
Quelque chose de comparable au point mort de la rétine,
Et sans écho,
Et qui pourtant voit et entend;
Un être ayant une vie propre, et qui, cependant,
Vit toute ma vie, et écoute, impassible,
Tous les bavardages de ma conscience.

Un être fait de néant, si c'est possible,
Insensible à mes souffrances physiques,
Qui ne pleure pas quand je pleure,
Qui ne rit pas quand je ris,
Qui ne rougit pas quand je commets une action honteuse,
Et qui ne gémit pas quand mon cœur est blessé;
Qui se tient immobile et ne donne pas de conseils,
Mais semble dire éternellement:
« Je suis là, indifférent à tout. »

C'est peut-être du vide comme est le vide.
Mais si grand que le Bien et le Mal ensemble
Ne le remplissent pas.
La haine y meurt d'asphyxie,
Et le plus grand amour n'y pénètre jamais.

Prenez donc tout de moi: le sens de ces poèmes,
Non ce qu'on lit, mais ce qui paraît au travers malgré moi:
Prenez, prenez, vous n'avez rien.
Et où que j'aille, dans l'univers entier,
Je rencontre toujours,
Hors de moi comme en moi,
L'irremplissable Vide,
L'inconquérable Rien.

Like the tops of the highest mountains;
Something comparable to the blind spot in the retina,
And with no echo,
And yet which sees and hears;
A being with a life of its own, which nonetheless
Lives my whole life, and listens, impassive,
To all the chitchat of my consciousness.

A being made of nothing, if that's possible,
Insensitive to my physical suffering,
That doesn't weep when I weep,
That doesn't laugh when I laugh,
That doesn't blush when I do something shameful,
And that doesn't moan when my heart is aching;
That doesn't make a move and gives no advice,
But seems to say eternally:
"I'm here, indifferent to everything."

Maybe it is as empty as emptiness is,
But so big that Good and Evil together
Do not fill it.
Where hatred dies of suffocation
And the greatest love never penetrates.

So take all of me: the meaning of these poems,
Not what can be read, but what comes across in spite of me:
Take, take, you have nothing.
Wherever I go, in the whole world,
I always meet,
Around me as in me,
The unfillable Void,
The unconquerable Nothing.

—RON PADGETT & BILL ZAVATSKY

CRÉPITEMENTS

Les arcencielesques dissonances de la Tour dans sa télégraphie sans fil
Midi
Minuit
On se dit merde de tous les coins de l'univers

Étincelles
Jaune de chrome
On est en contact
De tous les côtés les transatlantiques s'approchent
S'éloignent
Toutes les montres sont mises à l'heure
Et les cloches sonnent
*Paris-Midi* annonce qu'un professeur allemand a été mangé par les
    cannibales au Congo
C'est bien fait
*L'Intransigeant* ce soir publie des vers pour cartes postales
C'est idiot quand tous les astrologues cambriolent les étoiles
On n'y voit plus
J'interroge le ciel
L'Institut Météorologique annonce du mauvais temps

Il n'y a pas de futurisme
Il n'y a pas de simultanéité

# Blaise Cendrars
## 1887-1961

SPUTTERINGS

The rainbowesque dissonances of the Tower in its wireless
Noon
Midnight
Shit is said in all corners of the universe

Sparks
Chrome yellow
We're in contact
The transatlantics approach from all shores
Go away
Every watch is set
And bells ring
*Paris-Midi* announces that a German professor was eaten by
    cannibals in the Congo
Well done
This evening *L'Intransigeant* published poems for post cards
It's stupid when all the astrologers burglarize the stars
You don't see any more there
I question the sky
The Meteorological Institute announces bad weather

There is no futurism
There is no simultaneity

Bodin a brûlé toutes les sorcières
Il n'y a rien
Il n'y a plus d'horoscopes et il faut travailler
Je suis inquiet
L'Esprit
Je vais partir en voyage
Et j'envoie ce poème dépouillé à mon ami R . . .


## DERNIÈRE HEURE

OKLAHOMA, *20 janvier 1914*
Trois forçats se procurent des revolvers
Ils tuent leur geôlier et s'emparent des clefs de la prison
Ils se précipitent hors de leurs cellules et tuent quatre gardiens dans la
　　cour
Puis ils s'emparent de la jeune sténo-dactylographe de la prison
Et montent dans une voiture qui les attendait à la porte
Ils partent à toute vitesse
Pendant que les gardiens déchargent leurs revolvers dans la direction des
　　fugitifs

Quelques gardiens sautent à cheval et se lancent à la poursuite des forçats
Des deux côtés des coups de feu sont échangés
La jeune fille est blessée d'un coup de feu tiré par un des gardiens

Une balle frappe à mort le cheval qui emportait la voiture
Les gardiens peuvent approcher
Ils trouvent les forçats morts le corps criblé de balles
Mr. Thomas, ancien membre du Congrès qui visitait la prison
Félicite la jeune fille

Télégramme-poème copié dans *Paris-Midi*

Bodin burned every witch
There is nothing
There are no more horoscopes and you have to work
I'm upset
The Spirit
I'm going to take a trip
And I send this poem to my friend R . . .

—RON PADGETT


## STOP PRESS

OKLAHOMA, *January 20, 1914:*
Three convicts procure handguns
Kill their warder, seize the keys
Then rush out of their cells and kill four guards in the yard
Grab the young shorthand typist employed at the prison
And get into a wagon waiting by the gate
Leave at top speed
While guards discharge their guns in their direction

Some jump on horses and give chase
Shots are fired from both sides
The girl is wounded by a shot fired by one of the guards

A bullet strikes and kills the horse pulling the wagon
The guards catch up with it and find
The convicts dead, their bodies riddled with bullets
Mr. Thomas, former Congressman, visiting the prison
Congratulates the young woman

Cable-poem from *Paris-Midi.*

—ANSELM HOLLO

## AUX 5 COINS

Oser et faire du bruit
Tout est couleur mouvement explosion lumière
La vie fleurit aux fenêtres du soleil
Qui se fond dans ma bouche
Je suis mûr
Et je tombe translucide dans la rue

Tu parles, mon vieux

Je ne sais pas ouvrir les yeux?
Bouche d'or
La poésie est en jeu

## MEE TOO BUGGI

Comme chez les Grecs on croit que tout homme bien élevé doit savoir
    pincer la lyre
Donne-moi le fango-fango
Que je l'applique à mon nez
Un son doux et grave
De la narine droite
Il y a la description des paysages
Le récit des événements passés
Une relation des contrées lointaines
Bolotoo
Papalangi
Le poète entre autres choses fait la description des animaux
Les maisons sont renversées par d'énormes oiseaux
Les femmes sont trop habillées
Rimes et mesures dépourvues
Si l'on fait grâce à un peu d'exagération
L'homme qui se coupa lui-même la jambe réussissait dans le genre simple
    et gai
Mee low folla
Mariwagi bat le tambour à l'entrée de sa maison

## AT THE FIVE CORNERS

To be brave enough to make noise, and to make it:
Everything's color, motion, explosion, light
Life's flowering in the windows of the sun
Which melts in my mouth—
I'm ripe—
Translucent, I fall down in the street

No kidding!

I don't know how to open my eyes?
Mouth of gold—
In this game, the stakes are poetry

—ANSELM HOLLO


## ME TOO BOOGIE

Like the Greeks, we believe that every well-educated person should know
    how to pluck the lyre
Now give me that fango-fango
So I can put it to my nose
And make a sweet and resonant sound
With the right nostril
There is the description of landscapes
The narration of past events
A relation of distant lands
Bolotoo
Papalangi
Among other things, the poet describes animal life
Houses are knocked over by huge birds
The women wear too many clothes
No rhymes or meters provided
If you don't mind a little hyperbole
The man who cut off his own leg was a success in the simple
    light-hearted genre
Mee low fellah
Mariwagi sits beating the drum in the doorway of his house

—ANSELM HOLLO

## LA TÊTE

La guillotine est le chef-d'œuvre de l'art plastique
Son déclic
Crée le mouvement perpétuel
Tout le monde connaît l'œuf de Christophe Colomb
Qui était un œuf plat, un œuf fixe, l'œuf d'un inventeur
La sculpture d'Archipenko est le premier œuf ovoïdal
Maintenu en équilibre intense
Comme une toupie immobile
Sur sa pointe animée
Vitesse
Il se dépouille
Des ondes multicolores
Des zones de couleur
Et tourne dans la profondeur
Nu.
Neuf.
Total.


## EN ROUTE POUR DAKAR

L'air est froid
La mer est d'acier
Le ciel est froid
Mon corps est d'acier
Adieu Europe que je quitte pour la première fois depuis 1914
Rien ne m'intéresse plus à ton bord pas plus que les émigrants de l'entrepont
    juifs russes basques espagnols portugais et saltimbanques allemands qui
    regrettent Paris
Je veux tout oublier ne plus parler tes langues et coucher avec des nègres et
    des négresses des indiens et des indiennes des animaux des plantes
Et prendre un bain et vivre dans l'eau
Et prendre un bain et vivre dans le soleil en compagnie d'un gros bananier
Et aimer le gros bourgeon de cette plante

THE HEAD

The guillotine is the masterpiece of plastic art
Its click
Creates perpetual motion
Everyone knows about Christopher Columbus' egg
Which was a flat egg, a fixed egg, the egg of an inventor
Archipenko's sculpture is the first ovoidal egg
Held in intense equilibrium
Like an immobile top
On its animated point
Speed
It throws off
Multicolored waves
Color zones
And turns in depth
Nude.
New.
Total.

—RON PADGETT

ON THE WAY TO DAKAR

The air is cold
The sea is steel
The sky is cold
My flesh is steel
Goodby Europe that I'm leaving for the first time since 1914
Nothing about you means anything to me anymore than to emigrants in the
    steerage Jews Russians Basques Spaniards Portuguese and the German
    acrobats who are homesick for Paris
I want to forget everything not to speak your languages anymore to go to bed
    with negroes and negresses and Indians and Indianwomen and animals and
    plants
And take a bath and live in the water
And take a bath and live in the sun in the company of a big bananatree

Me segmenter moi-même
Et devenir dur comme un caillou
Tomber à pic
Couler à fond


ORION

C'est mon étoile
Elle a la forme d'une main
C'est ma main montée au ciel
Durant toute la guerre je voyais Orion par un créneau
Quand les Zeppelins venaient bombarder Paris ils venaient toujours d'Orion
Aujourd'hui je l'ai au-dessus de ma tête
Le grand mât perce la paume de cette main qui doit souffrir
Comme ma main coupée me fait souffrir percée qu'elle est par un dard
    continuel


TROUÉES

Échappées sur la mer
Chutes d'eau
Arbres chevelus moussus
Lourdes feuilles caoutchoutées luisantes
Un vernis de soleil
Une chaleur bien astiquée
Reluisance
Je n'écoute plus la conversation animée de mes amis qui se partagent les
    nouvelles que j'ai apportées de Paris

And fall in love with the great bud of that palm
Come out in segmentations
Get hard as a pebble
Fall headlong
Sink to the bottom

—JOHN DOS PASSOS

## ORION

That's my star
In the form of a hand
My hand gone up to heaven
All through the war I used to look at Orion through the crenellations of the
    trenches
When the zeppelins bombarded Paris they always came from Orion
Now it's directly overhead
The mainmast is piercing the palm of that hand it must hurt
The way my hand they cut off hurts pierced as it is by a continual ache

—JOHN DOS PASSOS

## CLEARINGS

Halfglimpses of the sea
Waterfalls
Shockheaded trees dripping moss
Heavy leaves rubbery shiny
Varnished with sun
A finely polished heat
Glitter
I'm not listening anymore to the animated conversation of my friends who
    are mulling over among themselves all the gossip I brought from Paris

Des deux côtés du train toute proche ou alors de l'autre côté de la vallée
    lointaine
La forêt est là et me regarde et m'inquiète et m'attire comme le masque d'une
    momie
Je regarde
Pas l'ombre d'un œil

# HOMMAGE À GUILLAUME APOLLINAIRE

Le pain lève
La France
Paris
Toute une génération
Je m'adresse aux poètes qui étaient présents
Amis
Apollinaire n'est pas mort
Vous avez suivi un corbillard vide
Apollinaire est un mage
C'est lui qui souriait dans la soie des drapeaux aux fenêtres
Il s'amusait à vous jeter des fleurs et des couronnes
Tandis que vous passiez derrière son corbillard
Puis il a acheté une petite cocarde tricolore
Je l'ai vu le soir même manifester sur les boulevards
Il était à cheval sur le moteur d'un camion américain et brandissait un
    énorme drapeau international déployé comme un avion
VIVE LA FRANCE
Les temps passent
Les années s'écoulent comme des nuages
Les soldats sont rentrés chez eux
A la maison
Dans leur pays
Et voilà que se lève une nouvelle génération
Le rêve des MAMELLES se réalise!
Des petits Français, moitié anglais, moitié nègre, moitié russe, un peu
    belge, italien, annamite, tchèque
L'un à l'accent canadien, l'autre les yeux hindous
Dents face os jointures galbe démarche sourire

On both sides of the train over our heads or else on the slope of a distant valley
    opposite
The forest is there staring me down disturbing me attracts my eye like the
    blank maskstare of a mummy
I stare back
Not a trace of an eye

—JOHN DOS PASSOS


## HOMAGE TO GUILLAUME APOLLINAIRE

The bread rises
France
Paris
An entire generation
I address myself to the poets who were there:
Friends
Apollinaire is not dead
You followed an empty hearse
Apollinaire is a magus
It was him, smiling in the silk of flags at the windows
Having fun, tossing flowers and wreaths at you
As you went by, behind his hearse
Then he went and bought himself a little tricolor cockade
I saw him appear on the boulevards that same evening
Riding the hood of an American truck and waving an enormous
    international flag, spread out like an airplane
VIVE LA FRANCE
Times change
Years glide by like clouds
The soldiers have come home
Their home
in their country
And before you know it, there's a new generation:
The dream of THE BREASTS OF TIRESIAS come true!
Little Frenchmen, half English, half Negro, half Russian, with a touch of
    Belgian, Italian, Annamite, Czech
One speaks like a Canadian, another has Hindu eyes
Teeth face bones joints figure gait smile

Ils ont tous quelque chose d'étranger et sont pourtant bien de chez nous
Au milieu d'eux, Apollinaire, comme cette statue du Nil, le père des eaux,
    étendu avec des gosses qui lui coulent de partout
Entre les pieds, sous les aisselles, dans la barbe
Ils ressemblent à leur père et se départent de lui
Et ils parlent tous la langue d'Apollinaire

## AU COEUR DU MONDE

*Fragment retrouvé*

Ce ciel de Paris est plus pur qu'un ciel d'hiver lucide de froid
Jamais je ne vis de nuits plus sidérales et plus touffues que ce printemps
Où les arbres des boulevards sont comme les ombres du ciel,
Frondaisons dans les rivières mêlées aux oreilles d'éléphant,
Feuilles de platanes, lourds marronniers.

Un nénuphar sur la Seine, c'est la lune au fil de l'eau
La Voie Lactée dans le ciel se pâme sur Paris et l'étreint
Folle et nue et renversée, sa bouche suce Notre-Dame.
La Grande Ourse et la Petite Ourse grognent autour de Saint-Merry.
Ma main coupée brille au ciel dans la constellation d'Orion.

Dans cette lumière froide et crue, tremblotante, plus qu'irréelle,
Paris est comme l'image refroidie d'une plante
Qui réapparaît dans sa cendre. Triste simulacre.
Tirées au cordeau et sans âge, les maisons et les rues ne sont
Que pierre et fer en tas dans un désert invraisemblable.
Babylone et la Thébaïde ne sont pas plus mortes, cette nuit, que la ville
    morte de Paris
Bleue et verte, encre et goudron, ses arêtes blanchies aux étoiles.
Pas un bruit. Pas un passant. C'est le lourd silence de guerre.
Mon œil va des pissotières à l'œil violet des réverbères.
C'est le seul espace éclairé où traîner mon inquiétude.
C'est ainsi que tous les soirs je traverse tout Paris à pied
Des Batignolles au Quartier Latin comme je traverserais les Andes
Sous les feux de nouvelles étoiles, plus grandes et plus consternantes,

All a little alien, yet right at home
Among them Apollinaire, like that statue of the Nile, Father of the
    Waters, stretched out, with children flowing out of him everywhere:
From between his feet, from under his armpits, from his beard
They resemble their father and are different, too
And all of them speak the language of Apollinaire

—ANSELM HOLLO


## IN THE WORLD'S HEART

*Found fragment*

This Paris sky, cleaner than winter sky lucid with cold—
I've never seen nights more starry, more bushy, than this spring
With boulevard trees like shadows of heaven,
Great fronds in rivers choked with elephant ears,
Heavy chestnuts, leaves of plane trees—

White water lily on the Seine, moon held by water's thread,
Milky Way in the sky flops down on Paris, embraces
The city, crazy, naked, upside down, mouth sucking Notre Dame.
Great Bear and Little Bear prowl around Saint-Merry, growling.
My cut-off hand shines in the skies—in Orion.

In this hard cold light, trembling, more than unreal,
Paris is like the frozen image of a plant
That reappears in its ashes. A sad simulacrum.
Linear, ageless, the buildings and streets are only
Stone and steel, heaped up, an unlikely desert.

Babylon, Thebes, no more dead tonight than the dead city of Paris
Blue, green, inky, pitchy, its bones bleached in starlight.
Not a sound. Not a footfall. The heavy silence of war.
Eye pans from pissoirs to violet eye of streetlights:
The only lit space into which I can drag my restlessness.

And that's the way I walk Paris each night,
From Batignolles to the Quartier Latin, crossing the Andes

La Croix du Sud plus prodigieuse à chaque pas que l'on fait vers elle
    émergeant de l'ancien monde
Sur son nouveau continent.

Je suis l'homme qui n'a plus de passé.—Seul mon moignon me fait mal.—
J'ai loué une chambre d'hôtel pour être bien seul avec moi-même.
J'ai un panier d'osier tout neuf qui s'emplit de mes manuscrits.
Je n'ai ni livres ni tableau, aucun bibelot esthétique.

Un journal traîne sur ma table.
Je travaille dans ma chambre nue, derrière une glace dépolie,
Pieds nus sur du carrelage rouge, et jouant avec des ballons et une petite
    trompette d'enfant:
Je travaille à la FIN DU MONDE.

Under the lights of new stars, greater, more puzzling:
Southern Cross more prodigious, each step one takes toward it as it
     emerges from the old world
Above the new continent.

I'm the one who has run out of past. Only my stump still hurts me.
I've rented a hotel room to be alone with myself.
A brand-new wicker basket to fill up with manuscripts.
No books, no pictures, no knick-knacks to please me.

Desk cluttered with newsprint,
I work in this empty room, behind a blind window,
Bare feet on red congoleum, play with balloons, a child's trumpet.
I work on THE END OF THE WORLD.

—ANSELM HOLLO

## POÈME POUR VALERY LARBAUD

Servante, l'homme bâille. J'appelle!
Voici des pence pour Hændel, voici nos livres pour le Fleuve.
Et il y eut un jour qu'on appela Dimanche—ennui solaire des Empires dans
    toutes glaces de nos chambres.
On dit que les coucous fréquentent aux jardins d'hôtels, on dit que les oiseaux
    de mer, par-dessus les Comtés, jusqu'aux jardins des villes . . .
Et l'étranger lit les gazettes sous un vieil arbre de Judée:
On lui remet deux lettres
Qu'il ne lit.

« . . . Roses, rosemaries, marigold leaves and daisies . . . » Vous arrosez les
roses avec du thé.
Car il y eut un jour qu'on appela Dimanche et, par-dessus les villes à cantiques
    et les lawns,
De ces grands ciels à houppes comme on en vit à Santa-Fé.
Allez et nous servez, qui sommes vieux comme l'insecte sur ce monde, allez
    et nous laissez à nos façons de vivre qui sont telles, sur toutes rives de ce
    monde . . .
Et l'étranger inscrit un nom, et ce n'est point le sien; inscrit la ville qu'il habite,
    et il n'est point de ville qu'il habite.
« . . . Roses, rosemaries, marigold leaves and daisies . . . »

Un peu avant le gong du soir et la saison d'un souffle dans les tentes,
Mon cœur est plein d'une science,

# Saint-John Perse

## 1887-1975

POEM FOR VALERY LARBAUD

Maidservant, the man yawns. I call!
Herewith pence for Handel, here our books for the River.
And there was a day called Sunday—solar tedium of Empires in all our
  bedroom mirrors.
It is said the cuckoos come often to the hotel gardens, it is said the seabirds
  pass over the Counties for the city gardens . . .
And the foreigner is reading the newspapers under an old Judas-tree:
They hand him two letters
Which he does not read.

". . . *Roses, rosemaries, marigold leaves and daisies* . . ."
  You sprinkle the roses with tea.
For there was a day called Sunday and, passing over the cities with their
  hymns and lawns,
Those great cottony skies like the ones seen in Santa Fe.
Come and serve us, who are old as insects upon this earth, come and leave
  us to our ways of living which are even so, upon every shore of this
  earth . . .
And the foreigner writes down a name, and it is not his name; writes down
the city he inhabits, and there is no city he inhabits.
". . . *Roses, rosemaries, marigold leaves and daisies* . . ."

A little before the evening gong and the season of a breeze in the awnings,
My heart is full of a knowledge,

Mon cœur est plein d'extravagance, et danse, comme la fille de Lady J . . .
en souliers de soie d'or, et nue, entre ses glaces, au son des clefs de malles
par le monde et des orchestres mis en serre sur toutes rives de l'Empire.
Bonheur à naître sous l'écaille et toutes roses de l'Empire! De quelles pures
Zambézies nous souvient-il au soir? . . .
Un peu avant le gong du soir et la saison d'un souffle dans les toiles, quand
le soleil fait son miel du corps des femmes dans les chambres, et c'est
bonheur a naître aux percées d'Isthmes, sur toutes routes de l'Empire, et
les vaisseaux pleins de voyelles et d'incestes, aux fifres des cristaux d'Eu-
rope, vont sur la mer déserte . . .

Servante! l'homme bâille. J'appelle!
Ouvrez les portes sur le fleuve! toutes choses dites à la mer!
Et pour ce soir encore, c'est fort bien—mais demain, ô ma fille, nous verrons
à changer
Ce grand parfum irrespirable de l'année.

## ANABASE

### VII

Nous n'habiterons pas toujours ces terres jaunes, notre délice . . .

L'Été plus vaste que l'Empire suspend aux tables de l'espace plusieurs étages
de climats. La terre vaste sur son aire roule à pleins bords sa braise pâle sous
les cendres.—Couleur de soufre, de miel, couleur de choses immortelles, toute
la terre aux herbes s'allumant aux pailles de l'autre hiver—et de l'éponge verte
d'un seul arbre le ciel tire son suc violet.

Un lieu de pierres à mica! Pas une graine pure dans les barbes du vent. Et
la lumière comme une huile.—De la fissure des paupières au fil des cimes
m'unissant, je sais la pierre tachée d'ouïes, les essaims du silence aux ruches
de lumière; et mon cœur prend souci d'une famille d'acridiens . . .

Chamelles douces sous la tonte, cousues de mauves cicatrices, que les col-
lines s'acheminent sous les données du ciel agraire—qu'elles cheminent en
silence sur les incandescences pâles de la plaine; et s'agenouillent à la fin, dans
la fumée des songes, là où les peuples s'abolissent aux poudres mortes de la
terre.

My heart is full of extravagance, and dances, like Lady J . . .'s daughter in gold
  silk slippers, and naked, among the mirrors, to the sound of steamer-trunk
  keys the world over and of orchestras set under glass on every shore of the
  Empire . . .
Happiness to come beneath the tortoise-shell and all the roses of the Empire!
  What pure Zambesis do we recall in the evening?
A little before the evening gong and the season of a breeze in the canvas, when
  the sun makes its honey from the women's bodies in the bedrooms, and it is
  happiness to come at the opening of each Isthmus, upon every route of the
  Empire, and the vessels full of vowels and incest, to the fifes of crystal from
  Europe, go upon the empty sea . . .

Maidservant! the man yawns. I call!
Open the doors upon the river! all things spoken to the sea!
And for this one more evening, it is well—but tomorrow, my girl, we must
  see to changing
This great unbreathable perfume of the year.

—RICHARD HOWARD

# ANABASIS

### VII
We shall not dwell forever in these yellow lands, our pleasance. . . .

The Summer vaster than the Empire hangs over the tables of space several
terraces of climate. The huge earth rolls on its surface over-flowing its pale
embers under the ashes.—Sulphur colour, honey colour, colour of immortal
things, the whole grassy earth taking light from the straw of last winter—and
from the green sponge of a lonely tree the sky draws its violet juices.

A place of stone of quartz! Not a pure grain in the wind's barbs. And light
like oil.—From the crack of my eye to the level of the hills I join myself, I
know the stones gillstained, the swarms of silence in the hives of light; and
my heart gives heed to a family of crickets. . . .

Milch-camels, gentle beneath the shears, sewn with mauve scars, let the hills
march forth under the facts of the harvest sky—let them march in silence over
the pale incandescence of the plain; and kneeling at last, in the fantasy of
dreams, there where the peoples annihilate themselves in the dead powder of
earth.

Ce sont de grandes lignes calmes qui s'en vont à des bleuissements de vignes improbables. La terre en plus d'un point mûrit les violettes de l'orage; et ces fumées de sable qui s'élèvent au lieu des fleuves morts, comme des pans de siècles en voyage . . .

A voix plus basse pour les morts, à voix plus basse dans le jour. Tant de douceur au cœur de l'homme, se peut-il qu'elle faille à trouver sa mesure? . . . "Je vous parle, mon âme!—mon âme tout enténébrée d'un parfum de cheval!" Et quelques grands oiseaux de terre, naviguant en Ouest, sont de bons mimes de nos oiseaux de mer.

À l'orient du ciel si pâle, comme un lieu saint scellé des linges de l'aveugle, des nuées calmes se disposent, où tournent les cancers du camphre et de la corne . . . Fumées qu'un souffle nous dispute! la terre tout attente en ses barbes d'insectes, la terre enfante des merveilles! . . .

Et à midi, quand l'arbre jujubier fait éclater l'assise des tombeaux, l'homme clôt ses paupières et rafraîchit sa nuque dans les âges . . . Cavaleries du songe au lieu des poudres mortes, ô routes vaines qu'échevèle un souffle jusqu'à nous! où trouver, où trouver les guerriers qui garderont les fleuves dans leurs noces?

Au bruit des grandes eaux en marche sur la terre, tout le sel de la terre tressaille dans les songes. Et soudain, ah! soudain que nous veulent ces voix? Levez un peuple de miroirs sur l'ossuaire des fleuves, qu'ils interjettent appel dans la suite des siècles! Levez des pierres à ma gloire, levez des pierres au silence, et à la garde de ces lieux les cavaleries de bronze vert sur de vastes chaussées! . . .

(L'ombre d'un grand oiseau me passe sur la face.)

EXIL

7

« . . . Syntaxe de l'éclair! ô pur langage de l'exil! Lointaine est l'autre rive où le message s'illumine:

Deux fronts de femmes sous la cendre, du même pouce visités; deux ailes de femmes aux persiennes, du même souffle suscitées . . .

Dormiez-vous cette nuit, sous le grand arbre de phosphore, ô cœur d'orante par le monde, ô mère du Proscrit, quand dans les glaces de la chambre fut imprimée sa face?

Et toi plus prompte sous l'éclair, ô toi plus prompte à tressaillir sur l'autre rive de son âme, compagne de sa force et faiblesse de sa force, toi dont le souffle au sien fut à jamais mêlé,

These are the great quiet lines that disperse in the fading blue of doubtful vines. The earth here and there ripens the violets of storm; and these sand-smokes that rise over dead river courses, like the skirts of centuries on their route . . .

Lower voice for the dead, lower voice by day. Such mildness in the heart of man, can it fail to find its measure? . . . "I speak to you, my soul!—my soul darkened by the horse smell!" and several great land birds, voyaging west-wards, make good likeness of our sea birds.

In the east of so pale a sky, like a holy place sealed by the blind man's linen, calm clouds arrange themselves, where the cancers of camphor and horn revolve. . . . Smoke which a breath of wind claims from us! the earth poised tense in its insect barbs, the earth is brought to bed of wonders! . . .

And at noon, when the jujuba tree breaks the tombstone, man closes his lids and cools his neck in the ages. . . . Horse-tramplings of dreams in the place of dead powders, O vain ways swept away by a breath, to our feet! where find, where find, the warriors who shall watch the streams in their nuptials?

At the sound of great waters on march over the earth, all the salt of the earth shudders in dream. And sudden, ah sudden, what would these voices with us? Levy a wilderness of mirrors on the boneyard of streams, let them appeal in the course of ages! Erect stones to my fame, erect stones to silence; and to guard these places, cavalcades of green bronze on the great causeways! . . .

(The shadow of a great bird falls on my face.)

—T. S. ELIOT

# EXILE

7

". . . Syntax of lightning! O pure speech of exile! Far is that other shore where the message lights up:

Two women, their foreheads signed with ashes by the same thumb; two women, at the slatted blinds, their wings upraised on the same breath . . .

Were you asleep that night, under the great phosphorus tree, O heart of prayers about the world, O mother of the Proscript, when his likeness was stamped on the mirrors in your room?

And you more swift beneath the lightning, O you more swift to spring up in answer on the other shore of his soul, companion of his strength and weakness of his strength, you whose breathing was with his forever mingled,

T'assiéras-tu encore sur sa couche déserte, dans le hérissement de ton âme de femme?

L'exil n'est point d'hier! l'exil n'est point d'hier! . . . Exècre, ô femme, sous ton toit un chant d'oiseau de Barbarie . . .

Tu n'écouteras point l'orage au loin multiplier la course de nos pas sans que ton cri de femme, dans la nuit, n'assaille encore sur son aire l'aigle équivoque du bonheur!»

. . . Tais-toi, faiblesse, et toi, parfum d'épouse dans la nuit comme l'amande même de la nuit.

Partout errante sur les grèves, partout errante sur les mers, tais-toi, douceur, et toi présence, gréée d'ailes à hauteur de ma selle.

Je reprendrai ma course de Numide, longeant la mer inaliénable . . . Nulle verveine aux lèvres, mais sur la langue encore, comme un sel, ce ferment du vieux monde.

Le nitre et le natron sont thèmes de l'exil. Nos pensers courent à l'action sur des pistes osseuses. L'éclair m'ouvre le lit de plus vastes desseins. L'orage en vain déplace les bornes de l'absence.

Ceux-là qui furent se croiser aux grandes Indes atlantiques, ceux-là qui flairent l'idée neuve aux fraîcheurs de l'abîme, ceux-là qui soufflent dans les cornes aux portes du futur

Savent qu'aux sables de l'exil sifflent les hautes passions lovées sous le fouet de l'éclair . . . O Prodigue sous le sel et l'écume de juin! garde vivante parmi nous la force occulte de ton chant!

Comme celui qui dit à l'émissaire, et c'est là son message: « Voilez la face de nos femmes; levez la face de nos fils; et la consigne est de laver la pierre de vos seuils . . . Je vous dirai tout bas le nom des sources où, demain, nous baignerons un pur courroux.»

Et c'est l'heure, ô Poète, de décliner ton nom, ta naissance, et ta race . . .


NEIGES

4

Seul à faire le compte, du haut de cette chambre d'angle qu'environne un Océan de neiges.—Hôte précaire de l'instant, homme sans preuve ni témoin, détacherai-je mon lit bas comme une pirogue de sa crique? . . . Ceux qui

Will you then sit on his deserted bed, amid the shuddering of your woman's soul?

Exile is not of yesterday! exile is not of yesterday! . . . O woman! Loathe that song a Barbary bird sings beneath your roof. . . .

You shall not hear the storm far off multiplying the flight of our feet but that your woman's cry in the night assault once more in his eyrie the ambiguous eagle of happiness!"

. . . Be silent, weakness, and you, beloved fragrance in the night like the very almond of night.

Wandering all over the shores, wandering all over the seas, be silent, gentleness, and you, presence, arrayed with wings at my saddle's height.

I shall resume my Numidian flight, skirting the inalienable sea . . . No vervain on the lips, but still on the tongue, like a salty substance, this ferment of the old world.

Nitre and natron are themes of exile. Our thoughts run to action on bony tracks. Lightning lays bare to me the bed of immense designs. In vain the storm removes the bourns of absence.

Those who went on their quest to the great Atlantic Indies, those who scent the new idea in the freshness risen from the abyss, those who blow with horns at the gates of the future

Know that on the sands of exile there hiss the high passions coiled beneath the lightning's whip . . . O Prodigal in the salt and foam of June! keep alive in our midst the occult power of your song!

Like him who says to the emissary, and this is his message: "Veiled be the faces of our women; raised be the faces of our sons; and the order is: wash the stone of your sills. . . . I shall whisper low the name of the springs in which tomorrow we shall plunge a pure wrath."

And the time is come, O Poet, to declare your name, your birth, and your race. . . .

—DENIS DEVLIN

# SNOWS

4

I, only accountant, from the height of this corner room surrounded by an Ocean of snows.—Precarious guest of the moment, man without proof or witness, shall I unmoor my low bed like a canoe from its cove? . . . Those

campent chaque jour plus loin du lieu de leur naissance, ceux qui tirent chaque jour leur barque sur d'autres rives, savent mieux chaque jour le cours des choses illisibles; et remontant les fleuves vers leur source, entre les vertes apparences, ils sont gagnés soudain de cet éclat sévère où toute langue perd ses armes.

Ainsi l'homme mi-nu sur l'Océan des neiges, rompant soudain l'immense libration, poursuit un singulier dessein où les mots n'ont plus prise. Épouse du monde ma présence, épouse du monde ma prudence! . . . Et du côté des eaux premières me retournant avec le jour, comme le voyageur, à la néoménie, dont la conduite est incertaine et la démarche est aberrante, voici que j'ai dessein d'errer parmi les plus vieilles couches du langage, parmi les plus hautes tranches phonétiques: jusqu'à des langues très lointaines, jusqu'à des langues très entières et très parcimonieuses,

comme ces langues dravidiennes qui n'eurent pas de mots distincts pour « hier» et pour « demain» . . . Venez et nous suivez, qui n'avons mots à dire: nous remontons ce pur délice sans graphie où court l'antique phrase humaine; nous nous mouvons parmi de claires élisions, des résidus d'anciens préfixes ayant perdu leur initiale, et devançant les beaux travaux de linguistique, nous nous frayons nos voies nouvelles jusqu'à ces locutions inouïes, où l'aspiration recule au delà des voyelles et la modulation du souffle se propage, au gré de telles labiales mi-sonores, en quête de pures finales vocaliques.

. . . Et ce fut au matin, sous le plus pur vocable, un beau pays sans haine ni lésine, un lieu de grâce et de merci pour la montée des sûrs présages de l'esprit; et comme un grand *Ave* de grâce sur nos pas, la grande roseraie blanche de toutes neiges à la ronde . . . Fraîcheur d'ombelles, de corymbes, fraîcheur d'arille sous la fève, ha! tant d'azyme encore aux lèvres de l'errant! . . . Quelle flore nouvelle, en lieu plus libre, nous absout de la fleur et du fruit? Quelle navette d'os aux mains des femmes de grand âge, quelle amande d'ivoire aux mains des femmes de jeune âge

nous tissera linge plus frais pour la brûlure des vivants? . . . Épouse du monde notre patience, épouse du monde notre attente! . . . Ah! tout l'hièble du songe à même notre visage! Et nous ravisse encore, ô monde! ta fraîche haleine de mensonge! . . . Là où les fleuves encore sont guéables, là où les neiges encore sont guéables, nous passerons ce soir une âme non guéable . . . Et au delà sont les grands lés du songe, et tout ce bien fongible où l'être engage sa fortune . . .

Désormais cette page où plus rien ne s'inscrit.

who, each day, pitch camp farther from their birthplace, those who, each day, haul in their boat on other banks, know better, day by day, the course of illegible things; and tracing the rivers towards their source, through the green world of appearances they are caught up suddenly into that harsh glare where all language loses its power.

Thus man, half naked on the Ocean of the snows, suddenly breaking asunder the vast libration, follows a singular design in which words cease to take hold. Spouse of the world, my presence, spouse of the world, my prudence! . . . And turning with the day towards the primal waters, like the traveller, at new moon, whose direction is uncertain and whose gait is aberrant, it is my design, now to wander among the oldest layers of speech, among the farthest phonetic strata: as far as the most far-off languages, as far as the most whole and most parsimonious languages,

like those Dravidian languages which had no distinct words for "yesterday" and "tomorrow." . . . Come and follow us, who have no words to say: ascending that pure unwritten delight where runs the ancient human phrase, we move about among clear elisions, the residues of old prefixes that have lost their initial, and, preceding the master works in linguistics, we clear our new ways to those unheard-of locutions where the aspiration withdraws behind its vowels and the modulation of the breath spreads out, under the sway of certain half-voiced labials, in search of pure vocalic finals.

. . . And it was at morning, beneath the purest of word-forms, a beautiful country without hatred or meanness, a place of grace and of mercy for the ascension of the unfailing presages of the mind; and like a great *Ave* of grace on our path, the great white rose-garden of all the snows all around. . . . Freshness of umbels, of corymbs, freshness of aril under the bean, ah! such a wafer-thin taste on the lips of the wanderer! . . . What new flora, in a freer place, absolves us from the flower and from the fruit? What bone shuttle in the hands of very old women, what ivory almond in the hands of very young women

will weave us fresher linen for the burns of the living? . . . Spouse of the world, our patience, spouse of the world, our vigil! . . . Ah! all the dwarf-elder of dream against our faces! And once again, O world! may your fresh breath of falsehood ravish us! . . . There where the rivers are still fordable, there where the snows are still fordable, we shall pass on, this night, an unfordable soul. . . . And beyond are the great linens of dream and all that fungible wealth in which man involves his fate. . . .

Henceforth this page on which no more is written.

—DENIS DEVLIN

# OISEAUX

8

Oiseaux, et qu'une longue affinité tient aux confins de l'homme . . . Les voici, pour l'action, armés comme filles de l'esprit. Les voici, pour la transe et l'avant-création, plus nocturnes qu'à l'homme la grande nuit du songe clair où s'exerce la logique du songe.

Dans la maturité d'un texte immense en voie toujours de formation, ils ont mûri comme des fruits, ou mieux comme des mots: à même la sève et la substance originelle. Et bien sont-ils comme des mots sous leur charge magique: noyaux de force et d'action, foyers d'éclairs et d'émissions, portant au loin l'initiative et la prémonition.

Sur la page blanche aux marges infinies, l'espace qu'ils mesurent n'est plus qu'incantation. Ils sont, comme dans le mètre, quantités syllabiques. Et procédant, comme les mots, de lointaine ascendance, ils perdent, comme les mots, leur sens à la limite de la félicité.

A l'aventure poétique ils eurent part jadis, avec l'augure et l'aruspice. Et les voici, vocables assujettis au même enchaînement, pour l'exercice au loin d'une divination nouvelle . . . Au soir d'antiques civilisations, c'est un oiseau de bois, les bras en croix saisis par l'officiant, qui tient le rôle du scribe dans l'écriture médiumnique, comme aux mains du sourcier ou du géomancien.

Oiseaux, nés d'une inflexion première pour la plus longue intonation . . . Ils sont, comme les mots, portés du rythme universel; ils s'inscrivent d'eux-mêmes, et comme d'affinité, dans la plus large strophe errante que l'on ait vue jamais se dérouler au monde.

Heureux, ah! qu'ils tendent jusqu'à nous, d'un bord à l'autre de l'océan céleste, cet arc immense d'ailes peintes qui nous assiste et qui nous cerne, ah! qu'ils en portent tout l'honneur à force d'âme, parmi nous! . . .

L'homme porte le poids de sa gravitation comme une meule au cou, l'oiseau comme une plume peinte au front. Mais au bout de son fil invisible, l'oiseau de Braque n'échappe pas plus à la fatalité terrestre qu'une particule rocheuse dans la géologie de Cézanne.

# BIRDS

8

Birds, birds held by long affinity close to man's frontiers . . . Behold them armed for action, like daughters of the spirit. Behold them here for the trance and prelude to creation, more nocturnal than the great night of clear dream where the logic of dream holds sway over men.

In the maturity of an immense text always in formation, they have ripened like fruits or even more like words: at one with an original sap and substance. They are indeed like words in being magically changed: nuclei of force and action, sources of lightning and radiation, bearing afar initiative and premonition.

On the white page with infinite margins, the space they measure is all incantation. They are like syllabic quantities in metre. And proceeding as words do from a distant ancestry, they lose their meaning, as words do, on the last verge of happiness.

In ancient days they took part in the adventure of poetry with the haruspex and the augur. And behold them now, vocables engaged in the same venture for the distant exercise of a new divination. . . . At the twilight hour of ancient civilizations, it is a wooden bird who plays the role of scribe in mediumistic writing, his pinions held by the officiating priest as a rod is held in the hands of a water-diviner or geomancer.

Birds, once born from a first inflection of life, and destined for the longest intonation . . . They are carried, like words, on the rhythm of the universe, and inscribe themselves, by natural affinity, in the widest wandering strophe that has ever been seen unfolding in the world.

Happy birds, ah, may they extend towards us, from one shore to the other of heaven's ocean, that huge arc of painted wings that will assist and encircle us! May they bear the full honour of it among us by strength of soul! . . .

Man carries the weight of gravity like a millstone around his neck, the bird like a feather painted on his brow. But at the end of his invisible thread, Braque's bird does not escape the doom of earth any more than does a particle of rock in Cézanne's geology.

—ROBERT FITZGERALD

## POUR LE MOMENT

La vie est simple et gaie
Le soleil clair tinte avec un bruit doux
Le son des cloches s'est calmé
Ce matin la lumière traverse tout
Ma tête est une rampe rallumée
Et la chambre où j'habite est enfin éclairée

Un seul rayon suffit
Un seul éclat de rire
Ma joie qui secoue la maison
Retient ceux qui voudraient mourir
Par les notes de sa chanson

Je chante faux
Ah que c'est drôle
Ma bouche ouverte à tous les vents
Lance partout des notes folles
Qui sortent je ne sais comment
Pour voler vers d'autres oreilles

Entendez je ne suis pas fou
Je ris au bas de l'escalier
Devant la porte grande ouverte

# Pierre Reverdy

1889-1960

FOR THE MOMENT

Life is simple and gay
The bright sun rings with a quiet sound
The sound of the bells has quieted down
This morning the light hits it all
The footlights of my head are lit again
And the room I live in is finally bright

Just one beam is enough
Just one burst of laughter
My joy that shakes the house
Restrains those wanting to die
By the notes of its song

I sing off-key
Ah it's funny
My mouth open to every breeze
Spews mad notes everywhere
That emerge I don't know how
To fly toward other ears

Listen I'm not crazy
I laugh at the bottom of the stairs
Before the wide-open door

Dans le soleil éparpillé
Au mur parmi la vigne verte
Et mes bras sont tendus vers vous

C'est aujourd'hui que je vous aime


AUBERGE

Un œil se ferme

    Au fond plaquée contre le mur
    la pensée qui ne sort pas

    Des idées s'en vont pas à pas

  On pourrait mourir
Ce que je tiens entre mes bras pourrait partir

  Un rêve

L'aube à peine née qui s'achève
   Un cliquetis
Les volets en s'ouvrant l'ont abolie

    Si rien n'allait venir

Il y a un champ où l'on pourrait encore courir
        Des étoiles à n'en plus finir
    Et ton ombre au bout de l'avenue
      Elle s'efface
On n'a rien vu
De tout ce qui passait on n'a rien retenu
Autant de paroles qui montent
Des contes qu'on n'a jamais lus
        Rien
Les jours qui se pressent à la sortie
    Enfin la cavalcade s'est évanouie

En bas entre les tables où l'on jouait aux cartes

In the sunlight scattered
On the wall among green vines
And my arms are held out toward you

It's today I love you

—RON PADGETT

INN

An eye closes
In the dark fast against the wall the thought that does not emerge
Ideas leave step by step
We could die
That which I hold in my arms could depart
A dream
Dawn hardly born is ended
A jingling
The opening shutters have destroyed it
If nothing should come
There is a field where we could still run
           Stars without number
And your shadow down the avenue
It is fading and we have seen nothing
Of all that passed we have retained nothing
So many words that rise
Stories one has never read
              Nothing
The days swarming at the exit
The cavalcade has vanished at last
Down there between the card-players' tables.

—EUGENE JOLAS

## MÉMOIRE

Une minute à peine
            Et je suis revenu
De tout ce qui passait je n'ai rien retenu
Un point
      Le ciel grandi
            Et au dernier moment
La lanterne qui passe
          Le pas que l'on entend
  Quelqu'un s'arrête entre tout ce qui marche
On laisse aller le monde
          Et ce qu'il y a dedans
Les lumières qui dansent
          Et l'ombre qui s'étend
Il y a plus d'espace
         En regardant devant
Une cage où bondit un animal vivant
La poitrine et les bras faisaient le même geste
Une femme riait
        En renversant la tête
Et celui qui venait nous avait confondus
Nous étions tous les trois sans nous connaître
Et nous formions déjà
        Un monde plein d'espoir

## CLAIR HIVER

L'espace d'or ridé où j'ai passé le temps
Dans le lit de décembre aux flammes descendantes
Les haies du ciel jetées sur les enceintes
Et les astres gelés dans l'air qui les éteint
   Ma tête passe au vent du Nord
        Et les couleurs déteintes
       L'eau suivant le signal
Tous les corps retrouvés dans le champ des averses
Et les visages revenus

MEMORY

Just a minute
        And I am back
Of everything that's gone I have kept nothing
A point
      The wide sky
             And at the last moment
The lantern goes by
        The step you hear
   Somebody stops and everything else goes on
You let the world go
          And what is inside
Dancing lights
          Outstretched shadows
There is still space
         Looking ahead
A cage where a live animal leaps
Breast and arms make the same motion
A woman was laughing
        With her head thrown back
And the man who came mistook us
We didn't know each other all three of us
And yet we formed
         A world full of hope

—KENNETH REXROTH

CLEAR WINTER

The space of wrinkled gold where I passed the time
In the bed of December with descending flames
The hedges of the sky erect on the boundaries
And the frozen stars in the air which extinguishes them
   My head goes on to the north wind
        And the faded colors
        The water following the signal
All the bodies recovered in the field of showers
And the faces come back

Devant les flammes bleues de l'âtre matinal
Autour de cette chaîne où les mains sonnent
Où les yeux brillent du feu des pleurs
Et que les ronds de cœurs couvrent d'une auréole
Les rayons durs brisés dans le soir qui descend


QUAI AUX FLEURS

Petite poitrine
   O
nuages
      Dans l'étang où elle se noya
      L'hiver ne souffle plus
Et
loin de son bord
Il passe ayant remis son pardessus
Dans la vitrine tout le monde la regarde
Elle est morte et sourit à ces gens
          qui ne savent que douter
Sa petite poitrine a l'air de remuer
Avec vos lèvres vous soufflez dessus
Et ses yeux se ferment en vous regardant
Ces messieurs habillés de noir
Ont les yeux brillants de malice
Une petite femme que j'ai beaucoup connue
La misère passe avec le vent
et balaie le boulevard
         Elle avait de bien jolies jambes
         Elle dansait elle riait
Et maintenant que va-t-elle devenir
Tournant la tête
elle demandait qu'on la laissât dormir

Before the blue flames of the morning hearth
Around that chain where hands sound
Where eyes shine with the fire of tears
And which circles of hearts cover with a halo
The hard rays broken in the falling evening

—JOHN ASHBERY

## FLOWER MARKET

Little breast
   O
clouds
     In the pond where she drowned herself
     Winter blows no more
And
far from its shore
He puts on his overcoat and goes away
Everybody stares at her in the showcase
She is dead and smiles at the people
        who don't know what to think
Her little breast seems to stir
When you blow on it with your lips
And her eyes close as they watch you
These gentlemen dressed in black
Have eyes brilliant with malice
A little woman I once knew well
Misery goes with the wind
sweeping the boulevard
      She had very pretty legs
      She danced and laughed
And now what will become of her
She turns her head
and asks to be left asleep

—KENNETH REXROTH

## VOYAGES SANS FIN

Tous ceux qui vus de dos s'éloignaient en chantant
Qu'on avait vus passer le long de la rivière
Où même les roseaux redisaient leurs prières
Que reprenaient plus fort et plus loin les oiseaux
Ils viennent les premiers et ne s'en iront pas
Le chemin qu'ils ont fait se comptait pas à pas
Et disparaissait à mesure
             Ils marchaient sur la pierre dure
Au bord des champs ils se sont arrêtés
Au bord de l'eau ils se désaltéraient
    Leurs pieds soulevaient la poussière
Et c'était un manteau brodé par la lumière
Tous ceux qui s'en allaient
marchant dans ce désert
Et pour qui maintenant le ciel s'était ouvert
Cherchaient encore le bout où finirait le monde
Le vent qui les poussait continuait sa ronde
       Et la porte se refermait
   Une porte noire
         La nuit

## PERSPECTIVE

La même voiture
M'a-t-elle emporté
         Je vois d'où tu viens
         Tu tournes la tête
Minuit
Sur la lune
Finit de sonner
         Au coin de la rue
         Tout est retourné
J'ai vu sa figure
Et même ses mains
         La dernière étoile
         Est dans le jardin

# ENDLESS JOURNEYS

All those seen from behind who were moving away singing
Who had been seen passing along the river
Where even the reeds repeated their prayers
Which the birds took up louder and farther on
They are the first to arrive and will not go away
They counted each step of the road
Which vanished as they went along
          They walked on the hard rock
At the edge of the fields they stopped
At the edge of the water they slaked their thirst
    Their feet raised a cloud of dust
And it was a coat embroidered by the sunlight
All who were going away
walking in that desert
And for whom the sky had now opened
Were still looking for the tip of land at the world's end
The wind that pushed them continued on its rounds
    And the door closed again
A black door
      Night

—JOHN ASHBERY

# PERSPECTIVE

Has the same carriage
  Carried me off
        I see where you come from
        You turn your head
Midnight
On the moon
Has ceased striking
        At the street corner
        All has been turned about
I've seen his face
And even his hands
        The last star
        Is in the garden

Comme la première
On pense à demain
    Mais où seront-ils
    Morts sans y penser
Quand le mur s'efface
    Le ciel va tomber


## ENCORE L'AMOUR

Je ne veux plus partir vers ces grands bols du soir
Serrer les mains glacées des ombres les plus proches
Je ne peux plus quitter ces airs de désespoir
Ni gagner les grands ronds qui m'attendent au large
C'est pourtant vers ces visages sans forme que je vais
Vers ces lignes mouvantes qui toujours m'emprisonnent
Ces lignes que mes yeux tracent dans l'incertain
Ces paysages confus ces jours mystérieux
Sous le couvert du temps grisé quand l'amour passe
Un amour sans objet qui brûle nuit et jour
Et qui use sa lampe ma poitrine si lasse
D'attacher les soupirs qui meurent dans leur tour
Les lointains bleus les pays chauds les sables blancs
La grève où roule l'or où germe la paresse
Le môle tiède où le marin s'endort
L'eau perfide qui vient flatter la pierre dure
Sous le soleil gourmand qui broute la verdure
La pensée assoupie lourde clignant des yeux
Les souvenirs légers en boucles sur le front
Les repos sans reveil dans un lit trop profond
La pente des efforts remis au lendemain
Le sourire du ciel qui glisse dans la main
Mais surtout les regrets de cette solitude
O cœur fermé ô cœur pesant ô cœur profond
Jamais de la douleur prendras-tu l'habitude

Like the first one
Tomorrow's coming
               But where will they be
               Dead unawares
When the wall vanishes
               The sky will come down

—DAVID GASCOYNE


## LOVE AGAIN

I no longer want to go away toward those vast bowls of evening
To grip the icy hands of the nearest shadows
I can no longer put off this look of despair
Nor reach the great circles waiting for me out there
Yet it is toward those formless faces that I go
Toward those moving lines which still imprison me
Those lines my eyes trace in the vagueness
Those dim landscapes those mysterious days
Under cover of gray weather when love passes by
A love without an object burning night and day
Which wears out its lamp my chest so tired
Of fixing sighs which in turn die
Blue distances hot countries white sands
Shore where gold tosses where laziness takes root
Tepid wharf where the sailor falls asleep
Treacherous water which comes to flatter the hard rock
Under the greedy sun which is browsing on the foliage
Thought heavy with sleep blinking
Light memories with curls at the forehead
Nights of sleep without waking in a bed that is too deep
Efforts continually put off until tomorrow
Smile of the sky sliding in the hand
But above all homesickness for that solitude
O closed heart O heavy heart O deep heart
You will never get used to sorrow

—JOHN ASHBERY

# L'INVASION

Cette tête
L'œil net
La calme rue du port
      Et les bateaux du large
Je prends la direction du vent sur l'avenue
Aux armes des allées
      De la ville
En été
Pendant que d'autres ouvrent leurs livres
Traité de médecine
Arithmétique
Géométrie
Les lunettes fermées entre l'œil et la vie
Le jeune étudiant remonte à sa famille
Et l'autre dans la vie
Ayant sauté les grilles
Sans savoir où il va
Et le bateau arrive apportant les moutons
La ville s'est ouverte au flanc
La foule entre
Voilà le premier son de cloche au nouveau la
Des enfants multiformes
Et la tête en feu du compagnon malade
      Tout ce qu'il y a

# CASCADE

A la rencontre des froids silences
A la rencontre des regards détournés
Brusquement
Quand une porte s'ouvre sur l'abîme étoilé
Brusquement
Devant la perspective semée d'obstacles
Parcourue de rivières abandonnées dans le métal
Sous les arbres froissés qui tombent de tes mains

# THE INVASION

This head
The eye distinct
The calm street of the port
   And the boats in from the sea
I take the direction of the wind on the avenue
That bears the coat-of-arms of the lanes
         Of the city
In summer
While others open their books
A treatise on medicine
Arithmetic
Geometry
Their glasses closed between eyes and life
The young student goes back up to his family
And the other in life
Having climbed over the iron gates
Without knowing where he is going
And the boat arrives bringing the sheep
The city has opened its side
The crowd enters
And now the bell's first note in a new key
Different kinds of children
And the fiery head of the sick companion
   All there is

—JOHN ASHBERY

# WATERFALL

At the meeting of the icy silences
At the meeting of the furtive glances
Abruptly
When a door opens on the starry deep
Abruptly
Traveled by rivers abandoned in metal
Under the crumpled trees which fall from your hands
Under the odor of mutilated plants which line the road

Sous l'odeur des plantes mutilées qui bordent le chemin
Tout est tiède dans l'air
Tout est froid dans le cœur
La tête embusquée dans les sillons troubles de la discorde
Le meurtre aux dents vernies
Remonte de la source
Quand le sang a fini la boucle de sa course

Ne rien vouloir prendre à sa faim
Ne rien vouloir laisser mourir dans la misère
Garder le plein de vie qui crève la barrière
S'il faut bondir à la lumière du hasard
Briser l'amour qui tamisait la réalité trop grossière
Contre le coude de la nuit
Contre le fil perçant la parole assourdie
D'un feu à l'autre du torrent
D'un cri à l'autre de la pente
Quand l'écho roule sous le pont et se lamente

J'ouvre mon corps au soleil pétillant
J'ouvre mes yeux à la lumière de ta bouche
Et mon sang pour le tien dans l'ornière du temps
A grands traits notre vie coule de roche en roche

## CHAIR VIVE

Lève-toi carcasse et marche
Rien de neuf sous le soleil jaune
Le der des der des louis d'or
La lumière qui se détache
sous les pellicules du temps
La serrure au cœur qui éclate
Un fil de soie
Un fil de plomb
Un fil de sang
Après ces vagues de silence
Ces signes d'amour au crin noir
Le ciel plus lisse que ton œil
Le cou tordu d'orgueil

Everything in the air is tepid
Everything is chilled in the heart
The head trapped in the wake of discord
Murder with gleaming teeth
When the blood has finished the winding of its loop

Not wanting to be glutted
Not wanting anything to die of hunger
Keep the fullness of life which cracks the barrier
We must risk a leap into the light
Smash the love which sifts coarseness from reality
Against the elbow of night
Against the shrillness of the deafened word
From one fire of the rapids to another
From one scream of the slopes to another
When the echo rolls under the bridge and laments

I open my body to the sparkling sun
I open my eyes to the light of your mouth
And exchange my blood for yours in the groove of time
In sweeping strokes our life flows from stone to stone

—MARK RUDMAN

LIVE FLESH

Rise up carcass and walk
Nothing new under the yellow sun
The very last of the very last gold pieces
The light which detaches itself
under the films of time
The lock of the bursting heart
A silk thread
A lead wire
A trickle of blood
After waves of silence
These signs of love's black pelt
Heaven slippery as your eye
The neck wrenched with pride

Ma vie dans la coulisse
D'où je vois onduler les moissons de la mort
Toutes ces mains avides qui pétrissent des boules de fumée
Plus lourdes que les piliers de l'univers
Têtes vides
Cœurs nus
Mains parfumées
Tentacules des singes qui visent les nuées
Dans les rides de ces grimaces
Une ligne droite se tend
Un nerf se tord
La mer repue
L'amour
L'amer sourire de la mort

My life in the wings
Where I can watch the harvests of death undulate
All these avid hands kneading balls of smoke
Heavier than the pillars of the universe
Empty heads
Naked hearts
Perfumed hands
Monkey tentacles aiming at the clouds
In the wrinkles of those grimaces
A straight line bends
A nerve twists
The sated sea
Love
Death's bitter smile

—KENNETH REXROTH

## APRÈS LE DÉLUGE

La lune diminue, divin septembre.
Les montagnes sont apaisées dans leur lumière,
L'ombre plus tôt fait ombre et l'or se repose
Subtilement dans le vert. Toute chaleur
Est morte hier comme une muraille était noire
Que dissipa la nuit avec étoiles claires,
Avec vent et silence déjà, pensée de la mort.

## CAR LA PEAU BLANCHE . . .

Car la peau blanche est une expression nocturne
Et quels déserts n'ont-ils pas foulés ses pieds diurnes?
Une ombre—ce qu'elle est—n'est pas plus effrayée
Ni plus obscène, ni plus horriblement méchante.

# Pierre Jean Jouve

1887-1976

## AFTER THE FLOOD

Divine September, the moon wanes.
The mountains are lulled in their light,
Shadows no longer lengthen and green
Lies down subtly with gold. All that heat
Fell yesterday like a black battlement
Night undermined. Clear wind and stars
And silence spreading, a foretaste of death.

—JOHN MONTAGUE

## FOR WHITE SKIN . . .

For white skin is an idiom of night
And what wastes have its feet not trod by day?
A shadow—which it is—is not more frightened
Nor more obscene, nor more horribly wicked.

L'homme sans péché
Est celui qui ne devrait pas mourir, est donc celui
Qui ne connaîtrait nulle interdiction, est donc celui
Qui n'aurait point de semblable, et qui ne devrait pas vivre.

## GRAVIDA

Le chemin de rocs est semé de cris sombres
Archanges gardant le poids des défilés
Les pierres nues sont sous les flots au crépuscule
Vert émeraude avec des mousses et du sang.

C'est beau! la paroi triste illustration
Chante la mort mais non le sexe chaud du soir
Cela tressaille en s'éloignant infiniment
Jusqu'au lieu grave où j'ai toujours désiré vivre.

Là, muraille et frontière amère, odeur de bois
De larmes et fumier
Et le fils émouvant tremble encore une fois
De revoir dur ce qu'il a vu doux dans le ventre.

## UNE SEULE FEMME ENDORMIE

Par un temps humide et profond tu étais plus belle
Par une pluie désespérée tu étais plus chaude
Par un jour de désert tu me semblais plus humide
Quand les arbres sont dans l'aquarium du temps
Quand la mauvaise colère du monde est dans les cœurs
Quand le malheur est las de tonner sur les feuilles

The sinless man
Is he who should not die, is therefore he
Who would not know what no means, is therefore he
Who would be like no one else, and should not live.

—KEITH BOSLEY


GRAVIDA

The rocky path is sown with sombre cries
Archangels keeping guard over the gorges' weight
The naked stones beneath the twilight waves
Are emerald green with foam and blood.

How beautiful! in illustration the sad mountainside
Sings of the death but not of the warm sex of night
Which trembles as it passes endlessly away
Towards that awesome place where I have always longed to live.

There, wall and bitter frontier, smell of wood,
Of tears and manure
And the touching son trembles once more to see
How hard is what was tender when he saw it in the womb.

—DAVID GASCOYNE


A LONE WOMAN ASLEEP

When there came days sunk deep in damp your beauty seemed increased
And ever warmer grew your glow when rain fell in despair
And when days came that were like deserts you
Grew moister than the trees in the aquarium of time
And when the ugly anger of the world raged in our hearts
And sadness lisped exhausted through the leaves

Tu étais douce
Douce comme les dents de l'ivoire des morts
Et pure comme le caillot de sang
Qui sortait en riant des lèvres de ton âme.

Par un temps humide et profond le monde est plus noir
Par un jour de désert le cœur est plus humide.

## BLANCHES HANCHES

Une joie souterraine est partie loin de moi
Blanches hanches! je cours et recours et brandis vers!
Je soulève le beau vêtement
Reculé dans les parfums les plus chauds et les plus noirs
J'épuise dans des bras
La chaleur de Saturne et la désolation de l'ardeur
Je tremble encore une fois jusqu'à perdre la raison
A cause des rutilants soleils de la privation future

Les azurs sonnent clair
Les dents blanches sont ivres
Les silences des hanches quand les oiseaux du temps
Ont presque fini de vivre.

## NOUS AVONS ÉTONNÉ . . .

Nous avons étonné par nos grandes souffrances
L'inclinaison des astres indifférents
Nous avons regardé le sang de la blessure
D'un œil externe et dur, nous avons clandestins
Baisé par la porte fausse de derrière,

You became as sweet as death
Sweet as teeth in the ivory skull-box of the dead
And pure as the skein of blood
Your laughter made to trickle down from your soul's parted lips

When there come days deep-sunk and damp the world grows still more
    dark
When days like deserts come, the heart is drenched with tears.

—DAVID GASCOYNE

## WHITE HAUNCHES

An underground joy goes out from me.
I run around and around waving my arms.
I lift up your beautiful dress
And recoil in the hottest and blackest of perfumes.
Strength drains out of my arms.
The heat of Saturn. The desolation of ardor.
I still tremble as though I had lost my reason,
Because of the bright red suns of future privation.

The azure sings clearly.
The white teeth are drunk.
The silences of your haunches when the birds of time
Have almost stopped living.

—KENNETH REXROTH

## WE HAVE AMAZED . . .

We have amazed by our great sufferings
The inclination of the indifferent stars
We have stared at the blood of the wound
With an outsider's eye, in secret we
Have coupled through the false back door,

Nous sommes devenus ces systèmes de fer
Qui errent sans lointain cavaliers à chenilles
Du dernier jugement, un vaste ennui funèbre
Nous porte à vos sabots de consommation
Cheval roux Cheval noir Cheval jaune Cheval blanc.

## LORSQUE

Lorsque l'agneau comme sacrifié
Aux sept yeux aveuglés d'amour et reconnu digne
Aura posé la main sur les sceaux
Du livre avec la profondeur de la mer éternelle
Du livre empli par la mort la faute et l'été
Et la vie et le futur et la servitude
Et le passé et la bestialité et la sainte liberté
Du livre empli par la mort avec la transparence de la mer
Recouvert par le péché de vie et fermé
Gonflé par le vent de feu de la grâce désirée
Du livre assis à la droite
De Celui qui voulut tout et l'agneau sacrifié . . .

## A SOI-MÊME

Écris maintenant pour le ciel
Écris pour la courbe du ciel
Et que nul plomb de lettre noire
N'enveloppe ton écriture

Écris pour l'odeur et le vent
Écris pour la feuille d'argent

We have become these iron systems
Which wander distanceless, caterpillar horsemen
Of the last judgement, a vast, dismal boredom
Bears us to your hoofs of consummation
Red Horse black Horse yellow Horse white Horse.

—KEITH BOSLEY

WHEN

When as if sacrificed the lamb
With seven love-blinded eyes and seen to be worthy
Has placed his hand upon the seals
Of the book deep as the eternal sea
The book filled with death and guilt and summer
And life and things to come and servitude
And things past and the beast and holy liberty
The book filled with death transparent as the sea
Covered anew by the sin of life and closed
Swollen by the fiery wind of wished for grace
The book at the right hand
Of Him who willed all things and the slain lamb . . .

—KEITH BOSLEY

TO HIMSELF

Write now for the sky
Write for heaven's curve
Let no leaded saxon black
Obfuscate your verse

Write for smell and wind
For the silver leaf

Que nulle laide face humaine
N'ait regard connaissance haleine

Écris pour le dieu et le feu
Écris pour un amour de lieu
Et que rien de l'homme n'ait place
Au vide qu'une flamme glace.

## LE TRAVAIL . . .

Le travail est abîme. Oh cache-moi de moi
Qui n'ai cessé d'aimer de dévorer d'écrire:
Une cruelle goule ensorcela ma vie en des milliers de mots
Qui n'ont eu que l'écho de plomb pour espérance;
Et sans jamais changer le pleur originel,
Et sans guérir jamais le ricanement faible
Du jeune homme douteur de ses labeurs formels.

## PROMENADE

Je suis dans ces chemins de douceur rude
Où l'on va lentement
A cause de la hauteur où le coeur respire,
Les grands arbres plaintifs
Hier encore sous la neige
M'escortent dans l'odeur parfumante du vent;

Je sens les pas dans les pas
Devenir plus sûrs de lumière belle
A la fois comme monte énorme entre les troncs
La muraille affirmant que la fin est mortelle.

Let no ugly human face
Look or know or breathe

Write for god and fire
For a love of place
Let the void be rid of man
Frozen by a flame.

—KEITH BOSLEY

## WORK . . .

Work is a gulf. Oh protect me from that self
Who has never lost the devouring love to write;
A cruel spectre weaves my life in millions of words
To which only the plumb line's echo gives hope.
Without ever changing the original complaint
Without ever healing the weak derisive laughter
Of the young man who scorned such classic labors.

—JOHN MONTAGUE

## A WALK

I am among those ways of harsh sweetness
Where the going is slow
Because of the height where the heart takes breath.
The great grieving trees
Yesterday still under snow
Escort me in the fragrance of the wind;

I feel steps in my steps
Growing more confident of lovely light,
Meanwhile immense between the treetrunks looms
The wall asserting that the end is death.

—KEITH BOSLEY

## QUE M'IMPORTE . . .

Que m'importe le cirque odorant des montagnes,
    La plaine au soleil aiguisé
    Et la chèvre, sœur du rocher,
Et le chêne têtu qui dompte la campagne.

Je ne sais plus, nature, entendre ta prière,
    Ni l'angoisse de l'horizon,
Et me voici parmi les arbres et les joncs
Sans mémoire et sans yeux comme l'eau des rivières.

## POINTE DE FLAMME

Tout le long de sa vie
Il avait aimé à lire
Avec une bougie
Et souvent il passait
La main dessus la flamme

# Jules Supervielle
## 1884-1960

---

## WHAT DO I CARE . . .

What do I care for the fragrant ring of mountains,
   The stabbing sun on the plains,
   The rock's sister the goat,
And, lord of the landscape, the stubborn oak.

No more do I know you, Nature, nor hear your cries,
   Nor heed the martyred horizon,
I am here amid tree and reed
Like the river—without reason, without eyes.

—WILLIAM ALWYN

## FLAME POINT

All his life
He loved to read
By candlelight
And often passed
His hand across

Pour se persuader
Qu'il vivait,
Qu'il vivait.
Depuis le jour de sa mort
Il tient à côté de lui
Une bougie allumée
Mais garde les mains cachées.

## HAUTE MER

*A Maurice Guillaume*

Parmi les oiseaux et les lunes
Qui hantent le dessous des mers
Et qu'on devine à la surface
Aux folles phases de l'écume,

Parmi l'aveugle témoignage
Et les sillages sous-marins
Des mille poissons sans visage
Qui cachent en eux leur chemin,
Le noyé cherche la chanson
Où s'était formé son jeune âge,
Écoute en vain les coquillages
Et les fait choir au sombre fond.

The flame
In order to
Persuade
Himself that he
Was alive,
Was alive.

And since the day
He died,
He keeps
A burning candle
At his side,
And yet
His hands—
He hides.

—ALLEN MANDELBAUM

## DEEP SEA

Among the birds and moons that haunt
the sea depths

      presences
      evinced at the surface by
      strange gestures of foam,

      blindly witnessed among their
underwater wakes by a thousand
faceless fishes, their
ongoing roads concealed in water,

the drowned man seeks for that song
his youth took form in,
listens in vain to shells
and lets them
drop to the
dark sea-floor.

—DENISE LEVERTOV

## PONT SUPÉRIEUR

Plante verte sur le pont,
Plante qui changes d'étoiles
Et vas d'escale en escale.
Goûtant à chaque horizon,

Plante, branches et ramilles,
L'hélice te fait trembler
Et ma main qui te dessine
Tremble d'être sur la mer.

Mais je découvre la terre
Prise dans ton pot carré
Celle-là que je cherchais
Dans le fond de ma jumelle.


## EMMÊLÉ . . .

Emmêlé à tant d'étoiles,
Me dégageant peu à peu,
Je sens que poussent mes lois
Dans le désordre des cieux.
La solitude du monde
Et la mienne se confondent,
Ah! nul n'est plus seul que Dieu
Dans sa poitrine profonde.

Il faut que quelque part
Quelqu'un vive et respire
Et sans bien le savoir
Soit dans ma compagnie,
Qu'il sache dans son sein

A POT OF EARTH

Green plant on shipboard, changing
with changing stars, plying
from port to port
                    you taste
every horizon

the propeller makes you
tremble from root to branch to
uttermost tendril
and my hand drawing you trembles at being
out at sea

but I discover
the earth set in your square pot
is the same earth I looked for
at the far end of my telescope.

—DENISE LEVERTOV


ENTANGLED . . .

Entangled in so many stars,
From which I gradually free myself,
I feel my laws take shape
In the disorder of the skies.
The earth's solitude
And my own are mingled.
Ah! none is more alone than God
In his heart's great pit.

Someone somewhere
Must live and breathe
And without quite realizing it
Be my companion:
Let him know in his heart

Évasif que j'existe,
Qu'il me situe au loin
Et que je lui résiste,

Moi qui serai en lui.


## LA PLUIE ET LES TYRANS

Je vois tomber la pluie
Dont les flaques font luire
Notre grave planète,
La pluie qui tombe nette
Comme du temps d'Homère
Et du temps de Villon
Sur l'enfant et sa mère
Et le dos des moutons,
La pluie qui se répète
Mais ne peut attendrir
La dureté de tête
Ni le coeur des tyrans
Ni les favoriser
D'un juste étonnement,
Une petite pluie
Qui tombe sur l'Europe
Mettant tous les vivants
Dans la même enveloppe
Malgré l'infanterie
Qui charge ses fusils
Et malgré les journaux
Qui nous font des signaux,
Une petite pluie
Qui mouille les drapeaux.

In spite of its evasions that I exist;
Let him set me up on high,
And let me not yield to him,

I who shall be in him forever.

—JAMES KIRKUP


## RAIN AND THE TYRANTS

I stand and watch the rain
Falling in pools which make
Our grave old planet shine;
The clear rain falling, just the same
As that which fell in Homer's time
And that which dropped in Villon's day
Falling on mother and on child
As on the passive backs of sheep;
Rain saying all it has to say
Again and yet again, and yet
Without the power to make less hard
The wooden heads of tyrants or
To soften their stone hearts,
And powerless to make them feel
Amazement as they ought;
A drizzling rain which falls
Across all Europe's map,
Wrapping all men alive
In the same moist envelope;
Despite the soldiers loading arms,
Despite the newspapers' alarms,
Despite all this, all that,
A shower of drizzling rain
Making the flags hang wet.

—DAVID GASCOYNE

# HOMMAGE À LA VIE

C'est beau d'avoir élu
Domicile vivant
Et de loger le temps
Dans un cœur continu,
Et d'avoir vu ses mains
Se poser sur le monde
Comme sur une pomme
Dans un petit jardin,
D'avoir aimé la terre,
La lune et le soleil,
Comme des familiers
Qui n'ont que leurs pareils,
Et d'avoir confié
Le monde à sa mémoire
Comme un clair cavalier
A sa monture noire,
D'avoir donné visage
A ces mots: femme, enfants,
Et servi de rivage
A d'errants continents,
Et d'avoir atteint l'âme
A petits coups de rame
Pour ne l'effaroucher
D'une brusque approchée.
C'est beau d'avoir connu
L'ombre sous le feuillage
Et d'avoir senti l'âge
Ramper sur le corps nu,
Accompagné la peine
Du sang noir dans nos veines
Et doré son silence
De l'étoile Patience,
Et d'avoir tous ces mots
Qui bougent dans le tête,
De choisir les moins beaux
Pour leur faire un peu fête,
D'avoir senti la vie
Hâtive et mal aimée,
De l'avoir enfermée
Dans cette poésie.

# HOMAGE TO LIFE

It is beautiful to have chosen
A living home
And stayed awhile,
And had its hands
Alight on the world,
As on an apple
In a little garden,
To have loved the earth,
The moon and the sun
Like old friends
Who have no equals,
And to have committed
The world to memory
Like a bright horseman
To his black steed,
To have given a face
To these words—woman, children,
And to have been a shore
On the wandering continents,
And to have come upon the soul
With tiny strokes of the oars,
For it is scared away
By a brusque approach.
It is beautiful to have known
The shade under the leaves,
And to have felt age
Creep over the naked body,
Accompanying the pain
Of black blood in ourselves,
And gilding its silence
With the star, Patience,
And to have all these words
Moving around in the head
To choose the least beautiful of them
And make a little feast,
To have felt life,
Hurried and ill loved,
To have ended it
In this poetry.

—KENNETH REXROTH

## LE CLOS

Avec un mouvement
Qui vient de ses paupières,
Il fait un clos de pierres
Où il n'y avait rien,
Et puis, sans y songer,
Un second clos, de lierre,
Pour cacher le premier
Aux regards de la terre,
Et par-dessus le tout
Une petite brume
Où vous êtes aussi
O jamais importune,
Du poids de vos glycines
Devenues des fumées.
Et cela, il le fait
Avec rien qu'un petit
Battement de ses cils
Mais ne le dites pas
Il convient d'avancer
Avec indifférence
Et que rien ne se passe
Pour ceux qui ne sont pas
Dans le double secret
De tout ce faux silence.

## JE VOUS RÊVE . . .

Je vous rêve de loin, et, de près, c'est pareil,
Mais toujours vous restez précise, sans réplique,
Sous mes tranquilles yeux vous devenez musique,
Comme par le regard, je vous vois par l'oreille.

Vous savez être en moi comme devant mes yeux,
Tant vous avez le cœur offert, mélodieux,
Et je vous entends battre à mes tempes secrètes
Lorsque vous vous coulez en moi pour disparaître.

# THE ENCLOSURE

With a movement
That comes from his eyelids,
He makes a stone enclosure
Where once there was nothing.
And then, without thinking,
He makes another, of ivy
To conceal the first
From the eyes of earth.
And above it all
A little smoke
Where, O ever
Importunate, also abide,
Your heavy wistaria
Turned to smoke.
And this he does
With only a little
Beat of his eyelids.
But never repeat it:
It's best to proceed
With an indifferent air.
And for those who are not
In the double secret
Of all this contrived silence,
Let nothing take place.

—JAMES KIRKUP

# I DREAM YOU . . .

I dream you into being, whether far away or near,
But always you remain distinct, and dumb,
Under my tranquil gazing you become
Music: as if it were an eye, I see you with my ear.

You can inhabit me as if you were before my eyes,
So wide-open and melodious is your heart,
And I hear you beating in my secret thought
When into my dream your disappearing presence flows.

—JAMES KIRKUP

# SOIR

les pêcheurs reviennent avec les étoiles des eaux
ils partagent du pain aux pauvres
enfilent des colliers aux aveugles
les empereurs sortent dans les parcs à cette heure qui ressemble à
    l'amertume des gravures

les domestiques baignent les chiens de chasse
la lumière met des gants
ferme-toi fenêtre par conséquent
sors lumière de la chambre comme le noyau de l'abricot
comme le prêtre de l'église

bon dieu: fais la laine tendre aux amoureux dolents
peins les petits oiseaux à l'encre et renouvelle l'image sur la lune

—allons attraper des scarabées
pour les enfermer dans la boîte
—allons au ruisseau
faire des cruches en terre cuite

—allons nous embrasser
à la fontaine

# Tristan Tzara

1896-1963

EVENING

fishermen return with the stars of the waters
they pass out bread to the poor
thread beads for the blind
emperors stroll out into parks at this hour which is as bitter and precise as
    some old engraving

servants bathe hunting hounds
the light is putting on gloves
therefore shut the window
put out the light in your window as you would spit out the pit of an
    apricot
a priest from his church

good lord: weave soft wool for melancholy lovers
dip little chickadees in ink and clean the face of the moon

—let's catch beetles
and put them in a box
—let's go down by the riverside
to make earthen jugs
—let's hug
beside the fountain

—allons au parc communal
jusqu'à ce que le coq chante
et la ville se scandalise

ou au grenier
le foin picote on entend les vaches mugir
puis elles se souviennent des petits
allons

## LA MORT DE GUILLAUME APOLLINAIRE

nous ne savons rien
nous ne savions rien de la douleur
la saison amère du froid
creuse de longues traces dans nos muscles
il aurait plutôt aimé la joie de la victoire
sages sous les tristesses calmes     en cage
ne pouvoir rien faire
si la neige tombait en haut
si le soleil montait chez nous pendant la nuit
pour nous chauffer
et les arbres pendaient avec leur couronne
—unique pleur—
si les oiseaux étaient parmi nous pour se mirer
dans le lac tranquille au-dessus de nos têtes
ON POURRAIT COMPRENDRE
la mort serait un beau long voyage
et les vacances illimitées de la chair des structures et des os

—let's loiter in the public park
until cockcrow
and the town's up in arms

or in the granary
the hay prickles there we hear the cows moo
as they think about their little ones
let's make it

—CHARLES SIMIC & MICHAEL BENEDIKT

# THE DEATH OF GUILLAUME APOLLINAIRE

we know nothing
we knew nothing of grief
the bitter season of cold
carves long scars in our muscles
he would have sooner loved the joy of victory
wise with quiet sadnesses      caged
can do nothing
if snow fell upwards
if the sun rose here during the night
to warm us
and the trees hung with their wreath
—the only tear—
if the birds were among us to be reflected
in the quiet lake above our heads
ONE WOULD UNDERSTAND
death would be a fine long journey
and limitless holidays for flesh structures and bones

—LEE HARWOOD

VOIE

quel est ce chemin qui nous sépare
à travers lequel je tends la main de ma pensée
une fleur est écrite au bout de chaque doigt
et le bout du chemin est une fleur qui marche avec toi

ACCÈS

magique démarche des nuits incomplètes
des nuits avalées en hâte de boissons amères avalées en hâte
nuits enfouies sous le terreux paillasson de nos lentes passions
rêves arides par de longs regards de corbeaux becquetés

salis mouillés lambeaux de nuit nous avons élevé
en nous chacun de nous une tour de couleur si hautaine
que la vue ne s'accroche plus au-delà des montagnes et des eaux
que le ciel ne se détourne plus de nos filets de pêche aux étoiles
que les nuages se couchent à nos pieds comme chiens de chasse
et que nous pouvons regarder le soleil en face jusqu'à l'oubli

et pourtant mon repos ne trouve sa raison
que dans le nid de tes bras la marée de la nuit
après l'éclat des orages criards ruisselle la mort
c'est le corps décousu d'une panoplie de la terre
qui s'égrène au collier de nos rêves d'oubli

VOLT

les tours penchées les cieux obliques
les autos tombant dans le vide des routes
les animaux bordant les routes rurales

WAY

what is this road that separates us
across which I hold out the hand of my thoughts
a flower is written at the end of each finger
and the end of the road is a flower which walks with you

—LEE HARWOOD

APPROACH

magic step of unfinished nights
nights gulped down in haste bitter drinks gulped down in haste
nights buried under the muddy mat of our slow passions
barren dreams in far looks of pecking crows

soiled sodden night rags we have built
within us each one of us a coloured tower so lofty
that the view is no longer blocked beyond mountains and waters
that the sky no longer turns away from our star nets
that the clouds lie down at our feet like hunting dogs
and we can stare into the sun until oblivion

and yet my peace only finds its reason
in the nest of your arms the night tide
after the burst of squalling storms streams down death
it's the loose body of an earthly suit of armour
that drops away from the necklace of our dreams of oblivion

—LEE HARWOOD

VOLT

the leaning towers the slanted skies
cars falling into the void of roads
animals lining the country roads

avec des branches couvertes d'hospitalières qualités
et d'oiseaux en forme de feuilles sur leurs têtes
tu marches mais c'est une autre qui marche sur tes pas
distillant son dépit à travers les fragments de mémoire et d'arithmétique
entourée d'une robe presque sourde le bruit caillé des capitales

la ville bouillonnante et épaisse de fiers appels et de lumières
déborde de la casserole de ses paupières
ses larmes s'écoulent en ruisseaux de basses populations
sur la plaine stérile vers la chair et la lave lisses
des montagnes ombrageuses les apocalyptiques tentations

perdu dans la géographie d'un souvenir et d'une obscure rose
je rôde dans les rues étroites autour de toi
tandis que toi aussi tu rôdes dans d'autres rues plus grandes
autour de quelque chose

## L'HOMME APPROXIMATIF

I

dimanche lourd couvercle sur le bouillonnement du sang
hebdomadaire poids accroupi sur ses muscles
tombé à l'intérieur de soi-même retrouvé
les cloches sonnent sans raison et nous aussi
sonnez cloches sans raison et nous aussi
nous nous réjouirons au bruit des chaînes
que nous ferons sonner en nous avec les cloches

quel est ce langage qui nous fouette nous sursautons dans la lumière
nos nerfs sont des fouets entre les mains du temps
et le doute vient avec une seule aile incolore
se vissant se comprimant s'écrasant en nous
comme le papier froissé de l'emballage défait
cadeau d'un autre âge aux glissements des poissons d'amertume

les cloches sonnent sans raison et nous aussi
les yeux des fruits nous regardent attentivement

with branches covered in liberal properties
and leaf-like birds on their heads
you walk but it's another who follows in your footsteps
distilling her spite through scraps of memory and arithmetic
wrapped in a gown the curdled sound of capitals nearly muffled

the seething town thick with proud calls and lights
boils over with the stewpan of its eyelids
its tears flow in streams of low populations
on the sterile plain towards the flesh and lava smoothes
shadowy mountains the apocalyptic temptations

lost in the geography of a memory and a dark rose
I prowl the narrow streets around you
while you too you prowl other greater streets
around something

—LEE HARWOOD

## APPROXIMATE MAN

I

sunday heavy lid on the boiling of blood
weekly weight squatting on its muscles
fallen within itself and found again
the bells chime for no reason and we too
chime bells for no reason and we too
will rejoice in the noise of chains
that will chime within us with the bells

what is this language that whips us as we tumble into the light
our nerves are whips in the hands of time
and doubt comes with a single colorless wing
twisting tightening shriveling inside us
like the crumpled paper of an unpacked box
gift from another age to the slithering fish of bitterness

the bells chime for no reason and we too
the eyes of fruits closely watching us

et toutes nos actions sont contrôlées il n'y a rien de caché
l'eau de la rivière a tant lavé son lit
elle emporte les doux fils des regards qui ont traîné
aux pieds des murs dans les bars léché des vies
alléché les faibles lié des tentations tari des extases
creusé au fond des vieilles variantes
et délié les sources des larmes prisonnières
les sources asservies aux quotidiens étouffements
les regards qui prennent avec des mains desséchées
le clair produit du jour ou l'ombrageuse apparition
qui donnent la soucieuse richesse du sourire
vissée comme une fleur à la boutonnière du matin
ceux qui demandent le repos ou la volupté
les touchers d'électriques vibrations les sursauts
les aventures le feu la certitude ou l'esclavage
les regards qui ont rampé le long des discrètes tourmentes
usé les pavés des villes et expié maintes bassesses dans les aumônes
se suivent serrés autour des rubans d'eau
et coulent vers les mers en emportant sur leur passage
les humaines ordures et leurs mirages

l'eau de la rivière a tant lavé son lit
que même la lumière glisse sur l'onde lisse
et tombe au fond avec le lourd éclat des pierres

les cloches sonnent sans raison et nous aussi
les soucis que nous portons avec nous
qui sont nos vêtements intérieurs
que nous mettons tous les matins
que la nuit défait avec des mains de rêve
ornés d'inutiles rébus métalliques
purifiés dans le bain des paysages circulaires
dans les villes préparées au carnage au sacrifice
près des mers aux balayements de perspectives
sur les montagnes aux inquiètes sévérités
dans les villages aux douloureuses nonchalances
la main pesante sur la tête
les cloches sonnent sans raison et nous aussi
nous partons avec les départs arrivons avec les arrivées
partons avec les arrivées arrivons quand les autres partent
sans raison un peu secs un peu durs sévères
pain nourriture plus de pain qui accompagne
la chanson savoureuse sur la gamme de la langue

all our actions are controlled nothing is hidden
the river water has washed its bed so bare
it bears away the sweet threads of glances that have dragged
at the foot of walls licking up lives in bars
tempting the weak increasing temptation drying up ecstasies
digging to the depths of old possibilities
and unblocking the ducts of imprisoned tears
ducts enslaved by daily suffocations
glances that clutch with withered hands
the bright yield of day or the shadowy apparition
offering the anxious riches of a smile
screwed on like a flower in the buttonhole of morning
those asking for calm or lust
electric shocks vibrations jolts
adventures fires certainty or slavery
glances that have edged along discreet torments
worn the city paths paid back so many degradations with charity
following in bunches round the ribbons of water
flowing toward the seas bearing
human filth and all its mirages

the river water has washed its bed so bare
that even the light slides on the smooth wave
and falls to the bottom with the heavy shattering of stones

the bells chime for no reason and we too
cares carried with us
the inner clothes
we put on each morning
unbuttoned by night's dreaming hands
adorned with useless metal puzzles
purified in the bath of circular landscapes
in cities prepared for carnage and sacrifice
near vast expansive seas
on mountains of troubled severities
in villages of painful swagger
the hand weighing on the head
the bells chime for no reason and we too
we leave with those leaving arrive with those arriving
leave with those arriving arrive when the others leave
for no reason a bit dry a bit hard severe
bread food no more bread to accompany
the tasty song on the scale of the tongue

les couleurs déposent leur poids et pensent
et pensent ou crient et restent et se nourrissent
de fruits légers comme la fumée planent
qui pense à la chaleur que tisse la parole
autour de son noyau le rêve qu'on appelle nous

les cloches sonnent sans raison et nous aussi
nous marchons pour échapper au fourmillement des routes
avec un flacon de paysage une maladie une seule
une seule maladie que nous cultivons la mort
je sais que je porte la mélodie en moi et n'en ai pas peur
je porte la mort et si je meurs c'est la mort
qui me portera dans ses bras imperceptibles
fins et légers comme l'odeur de l'herbe maigre
fins et légers comme le départ sans cause
sans amertume sans dettes sans regret sans
les cloches sonnent sans raison et nous aussi
pourquoi chercher le bout de la chaîne qui nous relie à la chaîne
sonnez cloches sans raison et nous aussi
nous ferons sonner en nous les verres cassés
les monnaies d'argent mêlées aux fausses monnaies
les débris des fêtes éclatées en rire et en tempête
aux portes desquelles pourraient s'ouvrir les gouffres
les tombes d'air les moulins broyant les os arctiques
ces fêtes qui nous portent les têtes au ciel
et crachent sur nos muscles la nuit du plomb fondu

je parle de qui parle qui parle je suis seul
je ne suis qu'un petit bruit j'ai plusieurs bruits en moi
un bruit glacé froissé au carrefour jeté sur le trottoir humide
aux pieds des hommes pressés courant avec leurs morts
autour de la mort qui étend ses bras
sur le cadran de l'heure seule vivante au soleil

le souffle obscur de la nuit s'épaissit
et le long des veines chantent les flûtes marines
transposées sur les octaves des couches de diverses existences
les vies se répètent à l'infini jusqu'à la maigreur atomique
et en haut si haut que nous ne pouvons pas voir
et avec ces vies à côté que nous ne voyons pas
l'ultra-violet de tant de voies parallèles
celles que nous aurions pu prendre
celles par lesquelles nous aurions pu ne pas venir au monde

colors put down their weights thinking
thinking or crying or staying or eating
fruits as light as hovering smoke
thinking of the heat that weaves the word
around its kernel the dream called us

the bells chime for no reason and we too
we walk to escape the swarming roads
with a flask of landscape a single disease
a single disease sowing our death
I know I carry the song in me and I am not afraid
I carry death and if I die it is death
who will carry me in his unseen arms
fine and light like the smell of thin grass
fine and light like departure without cause
without bitterness without debts without regret without
the bells chime for no reason and we too
why seek the end of the chain that links us to the chain
chime bells for no reason and we too
we will make the broken glasses chime within us
silver coins mingling with the counterfeit
the debris of festivals breaking into laughter and storm
at whose doors the void might open
the tombs of air the mills hackling arctic bones
these festivals bearing our heads to the sky
spitting molten night upon our muscles

I speak of who speaks who is speaking I'm alone
I'm nothing but a faint noise I have several noises inside me
a crumpled noise frozen on the street tossed onto the wet sidewalk
at the feet of rushing men running with their deaths
round death stretching his arms
on the dial of the sun's only living hour

the night's dark breath thickens
and along my veins sailors' flutes are singing
transposed into octaves from the layers of many existences
lives are infinitely repeated down to atomic thinness
and high so high we cannot see
with these lives beside us we cannot see
the ultraviolet of so many parallel paths
those we might have taken
those that might not have led us to the world

ou en être déjà partis depuis longtemps si longtemps
qu'on aurait oublié et l'époque et la terre qui nous aurait sucé la chair
sels et métaux liquides limpides au fond des puits

je pense à la chaleur que tisse la parole
autour de son noyau le rêve qu'on appelle nous


# MONSIEUR AA L'ANTIPHILOSOPHE

I

Capitaine!
les bolides, les forces ouvertes de la cascade nous
menacent, le nœud des serpents, le fouet de chaînes,
avancent triomphalement dans les pays
contaminés de fureur perpétuelle;
Capitaine!
toutes les accusations des animaux maltraités, en
morsures au-dessus du lit, bâillent en rosaces de
sang, la pluie des dents de pierre et les taches
d'excrément dans les cages nous ensevelissent
dans des manteaux interminables comme la
neige;
Capitaine!
les clartés du charbon devenant phoque, foudre,
insecte sous tes yeux, les escadrons d'hallucinés,
les monstres à roue, les cris des somnambules
mécaniques, les estomacs liquides sur des tablettes
d'argent, les cruautés des fleurs carnivores
envahiront la journée simple et rurale et le cinéma
de ton sommeil;
Capitaine!
prends garde aux yeux bleus.

or have led us out of it already long ago so long ago
we would have forgotten the age and the earth that would have sucked
    our flesh
salts and liquid metals limpid at the bottom of wells

I think of the heat weaving the word
around its kernel the dream called us

—PAUL AUSTER


# MONSIEUR AA, ANTIPHILOSOPHER

I

Captain!
the rockets, the open forces of the waterfall threaten us; the
serpents' knot, the whip of chains advances triumphantly in
the countries contaminated with perpetual fury;
Captain!
all the accusations of the mistreated animals, engraved over
the bed, yawn in rosettes of blood, the rain of stone teeth
and the patches of excrement in the cages bury us in cloaks as
endless as the snow;
Captain!
the brilliance of the coal becoming seal, lightning, bug before
your eyes, the squadrons of madmen, the wheel monsters, the cries
of the mechanical somnambulists, the liquid stomachs on silver
tablets, the cruelties of the carnivorous flowers will invade the
simple rural day, and the cinema of your sleep;
Captain!
watch out for blue eyes.

—RICHARD HOWARD

## POÈME POUR UNE ROBE
## DE MME SONIA DELAUNAY

L'Ange a glissé sa main
dans la corbeille l'œil des fruits
Il arrête les roues des autos
et le gyroscope vertigineux du cœur humain.

## A POEM IN YELLOW
## AFTER TRISTAN TZARA

angel slide your hand
into my basket eat my yellow fruit
my eye is craving it
my yellow tires screech
o dizzy human heart
my yellow dingdong

—JEROME ROTHENBERG

## TOURNESOL

La voyageuse qui traversa les Halles à la tombée de l'été
Marchait sur la pointe des pieds
Le désespoir roulait au ciel ses grands arums si beaux
Et dans le sac à main il y avait mon rêve ce flacon de sels
Que seule a respirés la marraine de Dieu
Les torpeurs se déployaient comme la buée
Au Chien qui fume
Où venaient d'entrer le pour et le contre
La jeune femme ne pouvait être vue d'eux que mal et de biais
Avais-je affaire à l'ambassadrice du salpêtre
Ou de la courbe blanche sur fond noir que nous appelons pensée
Le bal des innocents battait son plein
Les lampions prenaient feu lentement dans les marronniers
La dame sans ombre s'agenouilla sur le Pont-au-Change
Rue Gît-le-Coeur les timbres n'étaient plus les mêmes
Les promesses des nuits étaient enfin tenues
Les pigeons-voyageurs les baisers de secours
Se joignaient aux seins de la belle inconnue
Dardés sous le crêpe des significations parfaites
Une ferme prospérait en plein Paris
Et ses fenêtres donnaient sur la voie lactée
Mais personne ne l'habitait encore à cause des survenants
Des survenants qu'on sait plus dévoués que les revenants

# André Breton

1896-1966

## SUNFLOWER

The traveller who crossed Les Halles at summer's end
Tiptoed as she walked
Despair stirred in the sky its great lilies so lovely
And in her purse she had my dream that bottle of salts
That only God's godmother had breathed
Torpors were spreading like mists
At the Smoking Dog
The Pro and Con had just dropped in
And the young woman could be seen by them but badly and in profile
Was I dealing with the Ambassadress of saltpeter
Or of the white curve on a black background that we call thought
The Ball of the Innocents was in full swing
The lanterns were slowly catching fire in the chestnut trees
The shadowless girl knelt down on the Pont au Change
Rue Gît-le-Coeur things no longer rang with the same note
The promises of the nights had at last been kept
The homing pigeons and the emergency kisses
Were clustering round the breasts of the lovely unknown girl
That stood out beneath the veil of perfect meaning
A farm was prospering in the heart of Paris
And its windows looked out on the Milky Way
But nobody lived in it because of the guests
The guests that are more faithful one knows than ghosts

Les uns comme cette femme ont l'air de nager
Et dans l'amour il entre un peu de leur substance
Elle les intériorise
Je ne suis le jouet d'aucune puissance sensorielle
Et pourtant le grillon qui chantait dans les cheveux de cendres
Un soir près de la statue d'Étienne-Marcel
M'a jeté un coup d'oeil d'intelligence
André Breton a-t-il dit passe

## L'UNION LIBRE

Ma femme à la chevelure de feu de bois
Aux pensées d'éclairs de chaleur
A la taille de sablier
Ma femme à la taille de loutre entre les dents du tigre
Ma femme à la bouche de cocarde et de bouquet d'étoiles de dernière
    grandeur
Aux dents d'empreintes de souris blanche sur la terre blanche
A la langue d'ambre et de verre frottés
Ma femme à la langue d'hostie poignardée
A la langue de poupée qui ouvre et ferme les yeux
A la langue de pierre incroyable
Ma femme aux cils de bâtons d'écriture d'enfant
Aux sourcils de bord de nid d'hirondelle
Ma femme aux tempes d'ardoise de toit de serre
Et de buée aux vitres
Ma femme aux épaules de champagne
Et de fontaine à têtes de dauphins sous la glace
Ma femme aux poignets d'allumettes
Ma femme aux doigts de hasard et d'as de cœur
Aux doigts de foin coupé
Ma femme aux aisselles de martre et de fênes
De nuit de la Saint-Jean
De troène et de nid de scalares
Aux bras d'écume de mer et d'écluse
Et de mélange du blé et du moulin
Ma femme aux jambes de fusée

Those like that woman seem to be swimming
And there is in love some of their substance
She makes them part of herself
I am the plaything of no sensory power
Yet the cricket that chirped in the locks of cinders
Close to the statue of Étienne Marcel
Gave me a look of intelligence
André Breton he said may pass here.

—EDOUARD RODITI

## FREE UNION

My wife whose hair is a brush fire
Whose thoughts are summer lightning
Whose waist is an hourglass
Whose waist is the waist of an otter caught in the teeth of a tiger
Whose mouth is a bright cockade with the fragrance of a star of the first
     magnitude
Whose teeth leave prints like the tracks of white mice over snow
Whose tongue is made out of amber and polished glass
Whose tongue is a stabbed wafer
The tongue of a doll with eyes that open and shut
Whose tongue is incredible stone
My wife whose eyelashes are strokes in the handwriting of a child
Whose eyebrows are nests of swallows
My wife whose temples are the slate of greenhouse roofs
With steam on the windows
My wife whose shoulders are champagne
Are fountains that curl from the heads of dolphins under the ice
My wife whose wrists are matches
Whose fingers are raffles holding the ace of hearts
Whose fingers are fresh cut hay
My wife with the armpits of martens and beech fruit
And Midsummer Night
That are hedges of privet and nesting places for sea snails
Whose arms are of sea foam and a landlocked sea
And a fusion of wheat and a mill
Whose legs are spindles

Aux mouvements d'horlogerie et de désespoir
Ma femme aux mollets de moelle de sureau
Ma femme aux pieds d'initiales
Aux pieds de trousseaux de clés aux pieds de calfats qui boivent
Ma femme au cou d'orge imperlé
Ma femme à la gorge de Val d'or
De rendez-vous dans le lit même du torrent
Aux seins de nuit
Ma femme aux seins de taupinière marine
Ma femme aux seins de creuset du rubis
Aux seins de spectre de la rose sous la rosée
Ma femme au ventre de dépliement d'éventail des jours
Au ventre de griffe géante
Ma femme au dos d'oiseau qui fuit vertical
Au dos de vif-argent
Au dos de lumière
A la nuque de pierre roulée et de craie mouillée
Et de chute d'un verre dans lequel on vient de boire
Ma femme aux hanches de nacelle
Aux hanches de lustre et de pennes de flèche
Et de tiges de plumes de paon blanc
De balance insensible
Ma femme aux fesses de grès et d'amiante
Ma femme aux fesses de dos de cygne
Ma femme aux fesses de printemps
Au sexe de glaïeul
Ma femme au sexe de placer et d'ornithorynque
Ma femme au sexe d'algue et de bonbons anciens
Ma femme au sexe de miroir
Ma femme aux yeux pleins de larmes
Aux yeux de panoplie violette et d'aiguille aimantée
Ma femme aux yeux de savane
Ma femme aux yeux d'eau pour boire en prison
Ma femme aux yeux de bois toujours sous la hache
Aux yeux de niveau d'eau de niveau d'air de terre et de feu

In the delicate movements of watches and despair
My wife whose calves are sweet with the sap of elders
Whose feet are carved initials
Keyrings and the feet of steeplejacks who drink
My wife whose neck is fine milled barley
Whose throat contains the Valley of Gold
And encounters in the bed of the maelstrom
My wife whose breasts are of the night
And are undersea molehills
And crucibles of rubies
My wife whose breasts are haunted by the ghosts of dew-moistened roses
Whose belly is a fan unfolded in the sunlight
Is a giant talon
My wife with the back of a bird in vertical flight
With a back of quicksilver
And bright lights
My wife whose nape is of smooth worn stone and wet chalk
And of a glass slipped through the fingers of someone who has just drunk
My wife with the thighs of a skiff
That are lustrous and feathered like arrows
Stemmed with the light tailbones of a white peacock
And imperceptible balance
My wife whose rump is sandstone and flax
Whose rump is the back of a swan and the spring
My wife with the sex of an iris
A mine and a platypus
With the sex of an alga and old-fashioned candies
My wife with the sex of a mirror
My wife with eyes full of tears
With eyes that are purple armor and a magnetized needle
With eyes of savannahs
With eyes full of water to drink in prisons
My wife with eyes that are forests forever under the ax
My wife with eyes that are the equal of water and air and earth and fire

—DAVID ANTIN

## NON-LIEU

Art des jours art des nuits
La balance des blessures qui s'appelle Pardonne
Balance rouge et sensible au poids d'un vol d'oiseau
Quand les écuyères au col de neige les mains vides
Poussent leurs chars de vapeur sur les prés
Cette balance sans cesse affolée je la vois
Je vois l'ibis aux belles manières
Qui revient de l'étang lacé dans mon cœur
Les roues du rêve charment les splendides ornières
Qui se lèvent très haut sur les coquilles de leurs robes
Et l'étonnement bondit de-ci de-là sur la mer
Partez ma chère aurore n'oubliez rien de ma vie
Prenez ces roses qui grimpent au puits des miroirs
Prenez les battements de tous les cils
Prenez jusqu'aux fils qui soutiennent les pas des danseurs de corde et des
    gouttes d'eau
Art des jours art des nuits
Je suis à la fenêtre très loin dans une cité pleine d'épouvante
Dehors des hommes à chapeau claque se suivent à intervalle régulier
Pareils aux pluies que j'aimais
Alors qu'il faisait si beau
« A la rage de Dieu» est le nom d'un cabaret où je suis entré hier
Il est écrit sur la devanture blanche en lettres plus pâles
Mais les femmes-marins qui glissent derrière les vitres
Sont trop heureuses pour être peureuses
Ici jamais de corps toujours l'assassinat sans preuves
Jamais le ciel toujours le silence
Jamais la liberté que pour la liberté

## FACTEUR CHEVAL

Nous les oiseaux que tu charmes toujours du haut de ces belvédères
Et qui chaque nuit ne faisons qu'une branche fleurie de tes épaules aux
    bras de ta brouette bien-aimée
Qui nous arrachons plus vifs que des étincelles à ton poignet
Nous sommes les soupirs de la statue de verre qui se soulève sur le coude
    quand l'homme dort

# NO GROUNDS FOR PROSECUTION

Art of days art of nights
The scale of wounds called Pardon
Red scale that quivers under the weight of a wing
When the snow-collared horsewomen with empty hands
Push their vaporous chariots across the meadows
I see this scale jumping madly up and down
I see the graceful ibis
Returning from the pool laced within my heart
The wheels of the charming dream and its splendid ruts
Mounting high upon the shells of their dresses
And surprise bounding wildly over the sea
Depart my darling dawn forget nothing of my life
Take these roses creeping in the mirror-well
Take every beating of every lid
Take everything down to the threads that hold the steps of rope and
    waterdrop dancers
Art of days art of nights
I stand before a distant window in a city filled with horror
Outside men with stovepipe hats follow one another at regular intervals
Like the rains I loved
When the weather was fine
"The Wrath of God" was the name of the cabaret I entered last night
It was written on the white facade in even whiter letters
But the lady sailors gliding behind the windows
Are too happy to be afraid
Never a body here always the murder without proof
Never the sky always the silence
Never freedom but for freedom

—PAUL AUSTER

# POSTMAN CHEVAL

We are the birds always charmed by you from the top of these belvederes
And that each night form a blossoming branch between your shoulders
    and the arms of your well beloved wheelbarrow
Which we tear out swifter than sparks at your wrist
We are the sighs of the glass statue that raises itself on its elbow when
    man sleeps

Et que des brèches brillantes s'ouvrent dans son lit
Brèches par lesquelles on peut apercevoir des cerfs aux bois de corail dans
    une clairière
Et des femmes nues tout au fond d'une mine
Tu t'en souviens tu te levais alors tu descendais du train
Sans un regard pour la locomotive en proie aux immenses racines
    barométriques
Qui se plaint dans la forêt vierge de toutes ses chaudières meurtries
Ses cheminées fumant de jacinthes et mue par des serpents bleus
Nous te précédions alors nous les plantes sujettes à métamorphoses
Qui chaque nuit nous faisons des signes que l'homme peut surprendre
Tandis que sa maison s'écroule et qu'il s'étonne devant les emboîtements
    singuliers
Que recherche son lit avec le corridor et l'escalier
L'escalier se ramifie indéfiniment
Il mène à une porte de meule il s'élargit tout à coup sur une place
    publique
Il est fait de dos de cygnes une aile ouverte pour la rampe
Il tourne sur lui-même comme s'il allait se mordre
Mais non il se contente sur nos pas d'ouvrir toutes ses marches comme
    des tiroirs
Tiroirs de pain tiroirs de vin tiroirs de savon tiroirs de glaces tiroirs
    d'escaliers
Tiroirs de chair à la poignée de cheveux
A cette heure où des milliers de canards de Vaucanson se lissent les
    plumes
Sans te retourner tu saisissais la truelle dont on fait les seins
Nous te souriions to nous tenais par la taille
Et nous prenions les attitudes de ton plaisir
Immobiles sous nos paupières pour toujours comme la femme aime voir
    l'homme
Après avoir fait l'amour

## UNE BRANCHE D'ORTIE
## ENTRE PAR LA FENÊTRE

La femme au corps de papier peint
La tanche rouge des cheminées
Dont la mémoire est faite d'une multitude de petits abreuvoirs
Pour les navires au loin
Et qui rit comme un peu de braise qu'on aurait enchâssée dans la neige

And shining holes appear in his bed
Holes through which stags with coral antlers can be seen in a glade
And naked women at the bottom of a mine
You remembered then you got up you got out of the train
Without glancing at the locomotive attacked by immense barometric roots
Complaining about its murdered boilers in the virgin forest
Its funnels smoking jacinths and moulting blue snakes
Then we went on, plants subject to metamorphosis
Each night making signs that man may understand
While his house collapses and he stands amazed before the singular
    packing-cases
Sought after by his bed with the corridor and the staircase
The staircase goes on without end
It leads to a millstone door it enlarges suddenly in a public square
It is made of the backs of swans with a spreading wing for banisters
It turns inside out as though it were going to bite itself
But no, it is content at the sound of our feet to open all its steps like
    drawers
Drawers of bread drawers of wine drawers of soap drawers of ice drawers
    of stairs
Drawers of flesh with handsfull of hair
Without turning round you seized the trowel with which breasts are
    made
We smiled at you you held us round the waist
And we took the positions of your pleasure
Motionless under our lids for ever as woman delights to see man
After having made love.

—DAVID GASCOYNE

## A BRANCH OF NETTLE ENTERS THROUGH THE WINDOW

The woman with the crepe paper body
The red fish in the fireplace
Whose memory is pieced together from a multitude of small watering
    places for distant ships
Who laughs like an ember fit to be set in snow

Et qui se voit grandir et diminuer la nuit sur des pas d'accordéon
La cuirasse des herbes la poignée de la porte des poignards
Celle qui descend des paillettes du sphinx
Celle qui met des roulettes au fauteuil du Danube
Celle pour qui l'espace et le temps se déchirent le soir quand le veilleur de
    son œil vacille comme un elfe
N'est pas l'enjeu du combat que se livrent mes rêves
Oiseau cassant
Que la nature tend sur les fils télégraphiques des transes
Et qui chavire sur le grand lac de nombres de son chant
Elle est le double cœur de la muraille perdue
A laquelle s'agrippent les sauterelles du sang
Qui traînent mon apparence de miroir mes mains de faille
Mes yeux de chenilles mes cheveux de longues baleines noires
De baleines cachetées d'une cire étincelante et noire

## LE GRAND SECOURS MEURTRIER

La statue de Lautréamont
Au socle de cachets de quinine
En rase campagne
L'auteur des Poésies est couché à plat ventre
Et près de lui veille l'héloderme suspect
Son oreille gauche appliquée au sol est une boite vitrée
Occupée par un éclair l'artiste n'a pas oublié de faire figurer au-dessus de
    lui
Le ballon bleu ciel en forme de tête de Turc
Le cygne de Montevideo dont les ailes sont déployées et toujours prêtes à
    battre
Lorsqu'il s'agit d'attirer de l'horizon les autres cygnes
Ouvre sur le faux univers deux yeux de couleurs différentes
L'un de sulfate de fer sur la treille des cils l'autre de boue diamantée
Il voit le grand hexagone à entonnoir dans lequel se crisperont bientôt les
    machines

And sees the night expand and contract like an accordion
The armor of the grass
Hilt of the dagger gate
Falling in flakes from the wings of the sphinx
Rolling the floor of the Danube
For which time and space destroy themselves
On the evening when the watchman of the inner eye trembles like an elf
Isn't this the stake of the battle to which my dreams surrender
Brittle bird
Rocked by the telegraph wires of trance
Shattering in the great lake created by the numbers of its song
This is the double heart of the lost wall
Gripped by grasshoppers of the blood
That drag my likeness through the mirror
My broken hands
My caterpillar eyes
My long whalebone hairs
Whalebone sealed under brilliant black wax

—DAVID ANTIN

LETHAL RELIEF

The statue of Lautréamont
Its plinth of quinine tabloids
In the open country
The author of the Poetical Works lies flat on his face
And near at hand the hiloderm a shady customer keeps vigil
His left ear is glued to the ground it is a glass case it contains
A prong of lightning the artist has not failed to figure aloft
In the form of a Turk's head the blue balloon
The Swan of Montevideo with wings unfurled ready to flap at a
    moment's notice
Should the problem of luring the other swans from the horizon arise
Opens upon the false universe two eyes of different hues
The one of sulphate of iron on vines of the lashes the other of sparkling
    mire
He beholds the vast funnelled hexagon where now in no time the
    machines

Que l'homme s'acharne à couvrir de pansements
Il ravive de sa bougie de radium les fonds du creuset humain
Le sexe de plumes le cerveau de papier huilé
Il préside aux cérémonies deux fois nocturnes qui ont pour but
    soustraction faite du feu d'intervertir les cœurs de l'homme et de
    l'oiseau
J'ai accès près de lui en qualité de convulsionnaire
Les femmes ravissantes qui m'introduisent dans le wagon capitonné de
    roses
Où un hamac qu'elles ont pris soin de me faire de leurs chevelures m'est
    réservé
De toute éternité
Me recommandent avant de partir de ne pas prendre froid dans la lecture
    du journal
Il paraît que la statue près de laquelle le chiendent de mes terminaisons
    nerveuses
Arrive à destination est accordée chaque nuit comme un piano

## LE MARQUIS DE SADE . . .

Le marquis de Sade a regagné l'intérieur du volcan en éruption
D'où il était venu
Avec ses belles mains encore frangées
Ses yeux de jeune fille
Et cette raison à fleur de sauve-qui-peut qui ne fut
Qu'à lui
Mais du salon phosphorescent à lampes de viscères
Il n'a cessé de jeter les ordres mystérieux
Qui ouvrent une brèche dans la nuit morale
C'est par cette brèche que je vois
Les grandes ombres craquantes la vieille écorce minée
Se dissoudre
Pour me permettre de t'aimer
Comme le premier homme aima la première femme
En toute liberté

By man in dressings rabidly swaddled
Shall lie a-writhing
With his radium bougie he quickens the dregs of the human crucible
With his sex of feathers and his brain of bull-paper
He presides at the twice nocturnal ceremonies whose object due
    allowance for fire having been made is the interversion of the hearts
    of the bird and the man
Convulsionary in ordinary I have access to his side
The ravishing women who introduce me into the rose-padded
    compartment
Where a hammock that they have been at pains to contrive with their
    tresses for
Me is reserved for
Me for all eternity
Exhort me before taking their departure not to catch a chill in the perusal
    of the daily
It transpires that the statue in whose latitude the squitch of my nerve
    terminals
Weighs anchor is tuned each night like a piano

—SAMUEL BECKETT


THE MARQUIS DE SADE . . .

The Marquis de Sade regained the interior of the erupting volcano
Whence he had come
With his beautiful hands still in ruffles
His eyes of a young girl
And that intelligence at the rim of panic that was
His alone
But from the salon phosphorescent with visceral lamps
He did not cease to hurl mysterious commands
That breached the moral night
Through that breach I see
The great creaking shadows the old sapped husk
Dissolve
So that I may love you
As the first man loved the first woman
In utter freedom

Cette liberté
Pour laquelle le feu même s'est fait homme
Pour laquelle le marquis de Sade défia les siècles de ses grands arbres
    abstraits
D'acrobates tragiques
Cramponnés au fil de la Vierge du désir


# SUR LA ROUTE DE SAN ROMANO

La poésie se fait dans un lit comme l'amour
Ses draps défaits sont l'aurore des choses
La poésie se fait dans les bois

*Elle a l'espace qu'il lui faut*
Pas celui-ci mais l'autre que conditionnent

    L'œil du milan
    La rosée sur une prèle
    Le souvenir d'une bouteille de Traminer embuée sur un plateau
      d'argent
    Une haute verge de tourmaline sur la mer
    Et la route de l'aventure mentale
    Qui monte à pic
    Une halte elle s'embroussaille aussitôt

Cela ne se crie pas sur les toits
Il est inconvenant de laisser la porte ouverte
Ou d'appeler des témoins

    Les bancs de poissons les haies de mésanges
    Les rails à l'entrée d'une grande gare
    Les reflets des deux rives
    Les sillons dans le pain
    Les bulles du ruisseau
    Les jours du calendrier
    Le millepertuis

This freedom
For which fire itself was made man
For which the Marquis de Sade defied the centuries with his great
  abstract trees
With his tragic acrobats
Caught in the gossamer of desire

—KEITH WALDROP

## ON THE ROAD TO SAN ROMANO

Poetry is made in bed like love
Its unmade sheets are the dawn of things
Poetry is made in a forest

*She has the space which she needs*
Not this one but the other

  Governed by the hawk's eye
  The dew on the spindle
  The memory of a moist bottle of Traminer on a silver platter
  A tall rod of tourmaline over the sea
  A road of mental adventure
  Which climbs abruptly
  One pause and it's instantly overgrown

Don't shout that from the roof tops
It's not fitting to leave the doors open
Or go around calling for witnesses

  The shoals of fishes the hedges of small birds
  The rails at the approach to the great station
  The glow of two river banks
  The furrows on a loaf of bread
  Bubbles in a brook
  The days of the calendar
  Hog-wart

L'acte d'amour et l'acte de poésie
Sont incompatibles
Avec la lecture du journal à haute voix

    Le sens du rayon de soleil
    La lueur bleue qui relie les coups de hache du bûcheron
    Le fil du cerf-volant en forme de cœur ou de nasse
    Le battement en mesure de la queue des castors
    La diligence de l'éclair
    Le jet de dragées du haut des vieilles marches
    L'avalanche

La chambre aux prestiges
Non messieurs ce n'est pas la huitième Chambre
Ni les vapeurs de la chambrée un dimanche soir

    Les figures de danse exécutées en transparence au-dessus des mares
    La délimitation contre un mur d'un corps de femme au lancer de
        poignards
    Les volutes claires de la fumée
    Les boucles de tes cheveux
    La courbe de l'éponge des Philippines
    Les lacés du serpent corail
    L'entrée du lierre dans les ruines
    *Elle a tout le temps devant elle*

L'étreinte poétique comme l'étreinte de chair
Tant qu'elle dure
Défend toute échappée sur la misère du monde

The act of love and the act of poetry
Are incompatible
With reading newspapers at the top of one's voice

    The way the sunlight falls
    The livid glitter which binds the ax-strokes of the woodcutter
    The string of a kite in the shape of a heart or a fish-trap
    The steady waving of the beaver's tail
    The perseverance of lightning
    The flinging down of sweets from the top of an old staircase
    An avalanche

The room of marvels
No gentlemen not the forbidden chamber
Nor the fumes of the barracks room on Sunday evenings

    The figure of the dance executed transparently above the
        marshes
    The body of a woman outlined by throwing knives
    The lucent rings of smoke
    The curls of your hair
    The twisting of a sponge from the Philippines
    The snakelike coils of coral
    The ivy's slitherings into the ruins
    *She has all of time ahead of her*

    The embrace of poetry like the embrace of the naked body
    Protects while it lasts
    Against all access by the misery of the world

—CHARLES SIMIC & MICHAEL BENEDIKT

## L'INVENTION

La droite laisse couler du sable
Toutes les transformations sont possibles.

Loin, le soleil aiguise sur les pierres sa hâte d'en finir.
La description du paysage importe peu,
Tout juste l'agréable durée des moissons.

Clair avec mes deux yeux,
Comme l'eau et le feu.

Quel est le rôle de la racine?
Le désespoir a rompu tous ses liens
Et porte les mains à sa tête.
Un sept, un quatre, un deux, un un.
Cent femmes dans la rue
Que je ne verrai plus.

L'art d'aimer, l'art libéral, l'art de bien mourir, l'art de penser, l'art incohé-
rent, l'art de fumer, l'art de jouir, l'art du moyen âge, l'art décoratif, l'art de
raisonner, l'art de bien raisonner, l'art poétique, l'art mécanique, l'art érotique,

# Paul Éluard
## 1895-1952

## THE INVENTION

The right hand winnows the sand
Every transformation is possible.

After the stones the sun whets his fever to have done
The description of the landscape is not very important
The pleasant space of harvesting and no longer

Clear with my two eyes
As water and fire.

What is the role of the root?
Despair has broken all his bonds
He carries his hands to his head
One seven one four one two one one
A hundred women in the street
Whom I shall never see again.

The art of living, liberal art, the art of dying well, the art of thinking,
incoherent art, the art of smoking, the art of enjoying, the art of the Middle
Ages, decorative art, the art of reasoning, the art of reasoning well, poetic art,

l'art d'être grand-père, l'art de la danse, l'art de voir, l'art d'agrément, l'art de caresser, l'art japonais, l'art de jouer, l'art de manger, l'art de torturer.

Je n'ai pourtant jamais trouvé ce que j'écris dans ce que j'aime.

## L'AMOUREUSE

Elle est debout sur mes paupières
Et ses cheveux sont dans les miens,
Elle a la forme de mes mains,
Elle a la couleur de mes yeux,
Elle s'engloutit dans mon ombre
Comme une pierre sur le ciel.

Elle a toujours les yeux ouverts
Et ne me laisse pas dormir.
Ses rêves en pleine lumière
Font s'évaporer les soleils,
Me font rire, pleurer et rire,
Parler sans avoir rien à dire.

## LE SOURD ET L'AVEUGLE

Gagnerons-nous la mer avec des cloches
Dans nos poches, avec le bruit de la mer
Dans la mer, ou bien serons-nous les porteurs
D'une eau plus pure et silencieuse?

L'eau se frottant les mains aiguise des couteaux.
Les guerriers ont trouvé leurs armes dans les flots

mechanic art, erotic art, the art of being a grandfather, the art of the dance, the art of seeing, the art of being accomplished, the art of caressing, Japanese art, the art of playing, the art of eating, the art of torturing.

Yet I have never found what I write in what I love.

—SAMUEL BECKETT

## LADY LOVE

She is standing on my lids
And her hair is in my hair
She has the colour of my eye
She has the body of my hand
In my shade she is engulfed
As a stone against the sky

She will never close her eyes
And she does not let me sleep
And her dreams in the bright day
Make the suns evaporate
And me laugh cry and laugh
Speak when I have nothing to say

—SAMUEL BECKETT

## THE DEAF AND BLIND

Do we reach the sea with clocks
In our pockets, with the noise of the sea
In the sea, or are we the carriers
Of a purer and more silent water?

The water rubbing against our hands sharpens knives.
The warriors have found their weapons in the waves

Et le bruit de leurs coups est semblable à celui
Des rochers défonçant dans la nuit les bateaux.

C'est la tempête et le tonnerre. Pourquoi pas le silence
Du déluge, car nous avons en nous tout l'espace rêvé
Pour le plus grand silence et nous respirerons
Comme le vent des mers terribles, comme le vent

Qui rampe lentement sur tous les horizons.


SECONDE NATURE
V

En l'honneur des muets des aveugles des sourds
A la grande pierre noire sur les épaules
Les disparitions du monde sans mystère

Mais aussi pour les autres à l'appel des choses par leur nom
La brûlure de toutes les métamorphoses
La chaîne entière des aurores dans la tête
Tous les cris qui s'acharnent à briser les mots

Et qui creusent la bouche et qui creusent les yeux
Où les couleurs furieuses défont les brumes de l'attente
Dressent l'amour contre la vie les morts en rêvent
Les bas-vivants partagent les autres sont esclaves
De l'amour comme on peut l'être de la liberté.

And the sound of their blows is like
The rocks that smash the boats at night.

It is the storm and the thunder. Why not the silence
Of the flood, for we have dreamt within us
Space for the greatest silence and we breathe
Like the wind over terrible seas, like the wind

That creeps slowly over every horizon.

—PAUL AUSTER

## SECOND NATURE
V

In honour of the dumb the blind the deaf
Shouldering the great black stone
The things of time passing simply away

But then for the others knowing things by their names
The sear of every metamorphosis
The unbroken chain of dawns in the brain
The implacable cries shattering words

Furrowing the mouth furrowing the eyes
Where furious colours dispel the mists of vigil
Set up love against life that the dead dream of
The low-living share the others are slaves
Of love as some are slaves of freedom

—SAMUEL BECKETT

# CONFECTIONS

1
La simplicité même écrire
Pour aujourd'hui la main est là.

2
Il faut voir de près
Les curieux
Quand on s'ennuie.

3
La violence des vents du large
Des navires de vieux visages
Une demeure permanente
Et des armes pour se défendre
Une plage peu fréquentée
Un coup de feu un seul
Stupéfaction du père
Mort depuis longtemps.

4
Tous ces gens mangent
Ils sont gourmands ils sont contents
Et s'ils rient ils mangent plus.

5
Par-dessus les chapeaux
Un régiment d'orfraies passe au galop
C'est un régiment de chaussures
Toutes les collections des fétichistes déçus
Allant au diable.

6
Des cataclysmes d'or bien acquis
Et d'argent mal acquis.

7
Les oiseaux parfument les bois
Les rochers leurs grands lacs nocturnes.

8
Gagner au jeu du profil
Qu'un oiseau reste dans ses ailes.

# CONFECTIONS

### 1

Simplicity yea even to write
To-day at least the hand is there

### 2

It is meet to scrutinize
The inquisitive
When one is weary

### 3

The violence of sea-winds
Ships old faces
A permanent abode
Weapons to defend one
A shot one only
Stupefaction of the father
Dead this long time

### 4

All these people eat
They are gluttonous they are happy
The more they laugh the more they eat

### 5

Above the hatwear
A regiment of ospreys gallops past
It is a regiment of footwear
All the disillusioned fetishists and their complete collections
Off to the devil

### 6

Cataclysms of gold well-gotten
And of silver ill-gotten

### 7

The birds perfume the woods
The rocks their great nocturnal lakes

### 8

Play at profile and win
Let a bird abide in its wings

9
Immobile
J'habite cette épine et ma griffe se pose
Sur les seins délicieux de la misère et du crime.

1 0
Pourquoi les fait-on courir
On ne les fait pas courir
L'arrivée en avance
Le départ en retard

Quel chemin en arrière
Quand la lenteur s'en mêle.

Les preuves du contraire
Et l'inutilité.

1 1
Une limaille d'or un trésor une flaque
De platine au fond d'une vallée abominable
Dont les habitants n'ont plus de mains
Entraîne les joueurs à sortir d'eux-mêmes.

1 2
Le salon à la langue noire lèche son maître
Il l'embaume il lui tient lieu d'éternité.

1 3
Le passage de la Bérésina par une femme rousse à grandes mamelles.

1 4
Il la prend dans ses bras
Lueurs brillantes un instant entrevues
Aux omoplates aux épaules aux seins
Puis cachées par un nuage.

Elle porte la main à son cœur
Elle pâlit elle frissonne
Qui donc a crié?

Mais l'autre s'il est encore vivant
On le retrouvera
Dans une ville inconnue.

9
Rapt
I dwell in this thorn and my claw alights
On the sweet breasts of poverty and crime


1 0
Why are they made to run
They are not made to run
Arriving underdue
Departing overdue

What a road back
When slowness takes a hand

Proofs of the contrary
And futility


1 1
Gold-filings a treasure a platinum
Puddle deep in a horrible valley
Whose denizens have lost their hands
It takes the players out of themselves


1 2
The drawing-room with its black tongue licks its master
Embalms him performs the office of eternity


1 3
The Beresina forded by a sandy jug-dugged woman


1 4
He takes her in his arms
Bright gleams for a second playing
On the shoulder-blades the shoulders and the breasts
Then hidden by a cloud

She carries her hand to her heart
She pales she quakes
Whose then was the cry

But he if he still lives
He shall be rediscovered
In a strange town

1 5

Le sang coulant sur les dalles
Me fait des sandales
Sur une chaise au milieu de la rue
J'observe les petites filles créoles
Qui sortent de l'école en fumant la pipe.

1 6

Il ne faut pas voir la réalité telle que je suis.

1 7

Toute la vie a coulé dans mes rides
Comme une agate pour modeler
Le plus beau des masques funèbres.

1 8

Les arbres blancs les arbres noirs
Sont plus jeunes que la nature
Il faut pour retrouver ce hasard de naissance
Vieillir.

1 9

Soleil fatal du nombre des vivants
On ne conserve pas ton cœur.


A PERTE DE VUE DANS LE SENS
DE MON CORPS

Tous les arbres toutes leurs branches toutes leurs feuilles
L'herbe à la base les rochers et les maisons en masse
Au loin la mer que ton œil baigne
Ces images d'un jour après l'autre
Les vices les vertus tellement imparfaits
La transparence des passants dans les rues de hasard
Et les passantes exhalées par tes recherches obstinées
Tes idées fixes au coeur de plomb aux lèvres vierges
Les vices les vertus tellement imparfaits

15

The blood flowing on the flags
Furnishes me with sandals
I sit on a chair in the middle of the street
I observe the little Creole girls
Coming out of school smoking pipes

16

Do not see reality as I am

17

All life even as an agate has poured itself
Into the seams of my countenance and cast
A death-mask of unrivalled beauty

18

The black trees the white trees
Are younger than nature
In order to recover this freak of birth one must
Age

19

Fatal sun of the quick
One cannot keep thy heart

—SAMUEL BECKETT

## OUT OF SIGHT IN THE DIRECTION OF MY BODY

All the trees all their boughs all their leaves
The grass at the base the rocks the massed houses
Afar the sea that thine eye washes
Those images of one day and the next
The vices the virtues that are so imperfect
The transparence of men that pass in the streets of hazard
And women that pass in a fume from thy dour questing
The fixed ideas virgin-lipped leaden-hearted
The vices the virtues that are so imperfect

La ressemblance des regards de permission avec les yeux que tu conquis
La confusion des corps des lassitudes des ardeurs
L'imitation des mots des attitudes des idées
Les vices les vertus tellement imparfaits

L'amour c'est l'homme inachevé.

## CHASSÉ

Quelques grains de poussière de plus ou de moins
Sur des épaules vieilles
Des mèches de faiblesse sur des fronts fatigués
Ce théâtre de miel et de roses fanées
Où les mouches incalculables
Répondent aux signes noirs que leur fait la misère
Poutres désespérantes d'un pont
Jeté sur le vide
Jeté sur chaque rue et sur chaque maison
Lourdes folies errantes
Que l'on finira bien par connaître par cœur
Appétits machinaux et danses détraquées
Qui conduisent au regret de la haine

Nostalgie de la justice.

## LIBERTÉ

Sur mes cahiers d'écolier
Sur mon pupitre et les arbres
Sur le sable sur la neige
J'écris ton nom

The eyes consenting resembling the eyes thou didst vanquish
The confusion of the bodies the lassitudes the ardours
The imitation of the words the attitudes the ideas
The vices the virtues that are so imperfect

Love is man unfinished.

—SAMUEL BECKETT

## HUNTED

A few grains of dust more or less
On ancient shoulders
Locks of weakness on weary foreheads
This theatre of honey and faded roses
Where incalculable flies
Reply to the black signs that misery makes to them
Despairing girders of a bridge
Thrown across space
Thrown across every street and every house
Heavy wandering madnesses
That we shall end by knowing by heart
Mechanical appetites and uncontrolled dances
That lead to the regret of hatred

Nostalgia of justice

—DAVID GASCOYNE

## LIBERTY

On my school notebooks
On my desk and the trees
On the sand on the snow
I write your name

Sur toutes les pages lues
Sur toutes les pages blanches
Pierre sang papier ou cendre
J'écris ton nom

Sur les images dorées
Sur les armes des guerriers
Sur la couronne des rois
J'écris ton nom

Sur la jungle et le désert
Sur les nids sur les genêts
Sur l'écho de mon enfance
J'écris ton nom

Sur les merveilles des nuits
Sur le pain blanc des journées
Sur les saisons fiancées
J'écris ton nom

Sur tous mes chiffons d'azur
Sur l'étang soleil moisi
Sur le lac lune vivante
J'écris ton nom

Sur les champs sur l'horizon
Sur les ailes des oiseaux
Et sur le moulin des ombres
J'écris ton nom

Sur chaque bouffée d'aurore
Sur la mer sur les bateaux
Sur la montagne démente
J'écris ton nom

Sur la mousse des nuages
Sur les sueurs de l'orage
Sur la pluie épaisse et fade
J'écris ton nom

Sur les formes scintillantes
Sur les cloches des couleurs
Sur la vérité physique
J'écris ton nom

On all the pages that have been read
On all the pages that are blank
Blood paper stone or ash
I write your name

On the gilded images
On the arms of the warriors
On the crown of the kings
I write your name

On the jungle and the desert
On the nests on the bushes of broom
On the echo of my childhood
I write your name

On the marvels of the nights
On the white bread of the days
On the betrothed seasons
I write your name

On all the rags of azure
On the pond that mouldy sun
On the lake that moon full of life
I write your name

On the fields on the horizon
On the wings of the birds
And on the mill of shadows
I write your name

On every breath of dawn
On the sea on the boats
On the demented mountain
I write your name

On the foam of clouds
On the sweat of the storm
On the thick tasteless rain
I write your name

On the sparkling forms
On the bells of the colors
On the truth of bodies
I write your name

Sur les sentiers éveillés
Sur les routes déployées
Sur les places qui débordent
J'écris ton nom

Sur la lampe qui s'allume
Sur la lampe qui s'éteint
Sur mes maisons réunies
J'écris ton nom

Sur le fruit coupé en deux
Du miroir et de ma chambre
Sur mon lit coquille vide
J'écris ton nom

Sur mon chien gourmand et tendre
Sur ses oreilles dressées
Sur sa patte maladroite
J'écris ton nom

Sur le tremplin de ma porte
Sur les objets familiers
Sur le flot du feu béni
J'écris ton nom

Sur toute chair accordée
Sur le front de mes amis
Sur chaque main qui se tend
J'écris ton nom

Sur la vitre des surprises
Sur les lèvres attentives
Bien au-dessus du silence
J'écris ton nom

Sur mes refuges détruits
Sur mes phares écroulés
Sur les murs de mon ennui
J'écris ton nom

Sur l'absence sans désir
Sur la solitude nue
Sur les marches de la mort
J'écris ton nom

On the wakened paths
On the unfurled roads
On the overflowing market-places
I write your name

On the lamp being lit
On the lamp going out
On my houses all together
I write your name

On the fruit cut in two
My mirror and my bedroom
On my bed empty shell
I write your name

On my dog greedy and tender
On his trained ears
On his clumsy paw
I write your name

On that springboard my door
On the familiar objects
On the flood of blessed fire
I write your name

On all flesh that says yes
On the forehead of my friends
On each hand that is held out
I write your name

On the window of surprises
On the attentive lips
Far above silence
I write your name

On my demolished refuges
On my crumbled lighthouses
On the walls of my boredom
I write your name

On the absence without desire
On the naked solitude
On the footsteps of death
I write your name

Sur la santé revenue
Sur le risque disparu
Sur l'espoir sans souvenir
J'écris ton nom

Et par le pouvoir d'un mot
Je recommence ma vie
Je suis né pour te connaître
Pour te nommer

Liberté.

## DU FOND DE L'ABÎME

I

La lumière et la chaleur
Piétinées dispersées

Le pain
Volé aux naïfs

Le fil de lait
Lancé aux bêtes enragées

Quelques profondes mares de sang
Quelques incendies pétulants
Pour égayer ceux qui vont vivre
Vivre vivre sur leur fumier.

II

Au milieu du délire
Gorges tumultueuses et ventres dévorants
La morsure est soleil et lune le crachat
La blessure un écrin la souillure une perle
Tiède le sein pourri
La légende pourrie du sein maternel

On health that has returned
On the risk that has vanished
On hope without memory
I write your name

And through the power of a word
I start my life over
I am born to know who you are
To give you your name

Liberty

—W. S. MERWIN

## FROM THE DEPTH OF THE ABYSS

I

The light and warmth
Trampled dispersed
The bread
Stolen from innocents
The thread of milk
Flung to ferocious beasts

Here and there deep pools of blood
Here and there impetuous fires
Sport for those who mean to live
Live live upon their midden-heaps.

II

In a delirious world
Throats in a tumult and devouring bellies
Their bites for us are sun their spittle moon
Our hurts a casket and our stains a pearl
The rotted breast luke-warm
Rotted the legend of the maternal breast
Of pink and verdigris our tongue
The lovely history of our speech spell-bound

Rose et verte la langue
La belle histoire de la langue changée en fée

III

Ils n'étaient pas fous les mélancoliques
Ils étaient conquis digérés exclus
Par la masse opaque
Des monstres pratiques
Avaient leur âge de raison les mélancoliques
L'âge de la vie

Ils n'étaient pas là au commencement
A la création
Ils n'y croyaient pas
Et n'ont pas su du premier coup
Conjuguer la vie et le temps

Le temps leur paraissait long
La vie leur paraissait courte

Et des couvertures tachées par l'hiver
Sur des cœurs sans corps sur des cœurs sans nom
Faissaient un tapis de dégoût glacé
Même en plein été.

IV

Le solitaire toujours premier
Comme un ver dans une noix
Réapparaît le long des sinuosités
De la plus fraîche des cervelles
Le solitaire apprend à marcher de côté
A s'arrêter quand il est ivre de solitude
Le solitaire tourne ses pieds dans tous les sens
Il vague il rompt esquive feint

Il bouge mais bientôt
Tout bouge et lui fait peur
Le solitaire quand on l'appelle
Petit petit petit petit
Fait celui qui n'entend pas

En pleine viande fraîche
Comme un couteau rouillé
Le solitaire s'éternise

I I I

These melancholics used not to be mad
They were subdued absorbed shut out
By the dense legions
Of efficient monsters

These melancholics had their age of reason
An age of life
They were not present when it all began
At the Creation
They had no faith in it
And from the first were at a loss to make
Life correspond with time

And bed-clothes winter-stained on hearts
Without a body and on nameless hearts
Spread out a covering of chill disgust
Even at summer's height

I V

Always the solitary will be first
Like a worm in a nut
To reappear along the convolutions
Even of the freshest brain
The solitary learns to sidle past
To stop when he is drunk with solitude
The solitary turns his steps all ways
He loiters pulls up short manoeuvres feints

He moves but then at once
Things move and frighten him
The solitary when they call to him
Come little one come little one Come here
Pretends he has not heard

Embedded in fresh meat
Left like a rusted knife
The solitary stops and stays for ever
The smell of carrion stops and stays for ever
The honeycomb of strength is stuffed with filth.

V

I speak from the bottom of the pit
I see to the bottom of the pit

Et l'odeur du cadavre monte et s'éternise
Le miel de la force est farci d'ordures.


### V

Je parle du fond de l'abîme
Et je vois le fond de l'abîme
L'homme creusé comme une mine
Comme un port sans vaisseaux
Comme un foyer sans feu

Pauvre visage sacrifié
Pauvre visage sans limites
Composé de tous les visages saccagés
Tu rêvais de balcons de voiles de voyages
Tu rêvais de printemps de baisers de bonté
Tu savais bien quels sont les droits et les devoirs
De la beauté mon beau visage dispersé

Il faudrait pour cacher ton horreur et ta honte
Des mains nouvelles des mains entières dans leur tâche
Mains travailleuses au présent
Et courageuses même en rêve.


### VI

Je parle du fond de l'abîme
Je parle du fond de mon gouffre
C'est le soir et les ombres fuient
Le soir m'a rendu sage et fraternel
Il ouvre partout ses portes lugubres
Je n'ai pas peur j'entre partout
Je vois de mieux en mieux la forme humaine
Sans visage encore et pourtant
Dans un coin sombre où le mur est en ruines
Des yeux sont là aussi clairs que les miens
Ai-je grandi ai-je un peu de pouvoir.


### VII

Nous sommes à nous deux la première nuée
Dans l'étendue absurde du bonheur cruel
Nous sommes la fraîcheur future
La première nuit de repos
Qui s'ouvrira sur un visage et sur des yeux nouveaux et purs

Nul ne pourra les ignorer.

A man hollowed out like a mine
Like a port without ships
Like a hearth with no fire

You poor sacrificed face
You poor face without form
A composite of every pillaged face
You dreamed of spring of kisses of good will
You dreamed of balconies of sails of journeys
And you knew well the rights and obligations
Of beauty beautiful dismembered face

To hide your shame and horror you will need
Hands that are new hands whole in their employment
Hands busy in the present
And brave even in dreams.

VI

I speak now from the bottom of the pit
The bottom of my chasm
Evening is here the shadows flee away
Evening has made me wise and brotherly
His gloomy doors are opened everywhere
I feel no fear I go in everywhere
And more and more I see the human form
Still without features yet
In a dark corner where the wall is down
Are eyes as clear as mine
Have I grown up Have I a little strength.

VII

We are for our two selves the first soft cloud
In the absurd expanse of cruel bliss

The future freshness
And the first night's rest
To open on a face and eyes made pure and new

These no one will be able to ignore.

—STEPHEN SPENDER & FRANCES CORNFORD

# HORIZON

*à Tristan Tzara*

Toute la ville est entrée dans ma chambre
les arbres disparaissaient
et le soir s'attache à mes doigts
Les maisons deviennent des transatlantiques
le bruit de la mer est monté jusqu'à moi
Nous arriverons dans deux jours au Congo
j'ai franchi l'Équateur et le Tropique du Capricorne
je sais qu'il y a des collines innombrables
Notre-Dame cache le Gaurisankar et les aurores boréales
la nuit tombe goutte à goutte
j'attends les heures

Donnez-moi cette citronnade et la dernière cigarette
je reviendrai à Paris

# Philippe Soupault
## 1897-

## HORIZON

*to Tristan Tzara*

The whole town has come into my room
the trees have disappeared
and evening clings to my fingers
The houses are turning into ocean liners
the sound of the sea has just reached me up here
In two days we'll arrive in the Congo
I've passed the Equator and the Tropic of Capricorn
I know there are innumerable hills
Notre-Dame hides the Gaurisankar and the Northern Lights
night falls drop by drop
I wait for the hours

Give me that lemonade and a last cigarette
I'm going back to Paris

—ROSMARIE WALDROP

GEORGIA

Je ne dors pas Georgia
je lance des flèches dans la nuit Georgia
j'attends Georgia
je pense Georgia
Le feu est comme la neige Georgia
La nuit est ma voisine Georgia
j'écoute les bruits tous sans exception Georgia
je vois la fumée qui monte et qui fuit Georgia
je marche à pas de loups dans l'ombre Georgia
je cours voici la rue les faubourgs Georgia
Voici une ville qui est la même
et que je connais pas Georgia
je me hâte voici le vent Georgia
et le froid silence et la peur Georgia
je fuis Georgia
je cours Georgia
les nuages sont bas ils vont tomber Georgia
j'étends les bras Georgia
je ne ferme pas les yeux Georgia
j'appelle Georgia
je crie Georgia
j'appelle Georgia
je t'appelle Georgia
Est-ce que tu viendras Georgia
bientôt Georgia
Georgia Georgia Georgia
Georgia
je ne dors pas Georgia
je t'attends
Georgia


SAY IT WITH MUSIC

Les bracelets d'or et les drapeaux
les locomotives les bateaux
et le vent salubre et les nuages

## GEORGIA

I do not sleep Georgia
I hurl spears in the night Georgia
I am waiting Georgia
I am thinking Georgia
The fire is like snow Georgia
The night is my neighbor Georgia
I hear each and every noise Georgia
I see the smoke that rises and wisps away Georgia
I walk like a wolf in the shadows Georgia
I am running here is a suburban street Georgia
Here is a city that is the same
and I've never seen it before Georgia
I hurry on and this is the wind Georgia
and cold and silence and fear Georgia
I escape Georgia
I am running Georgia
the clouds are low they will fall Georgia
I open my arms Georgia
I do not close my eyes Georgia
I call Georgia
I cry Georgia
I am calling Georgia
I call you Georgia
Would you come Georgia
soon Georgia
Georgia Georgia Georgia
Georgia
I do not sleep Georgia
I am waiting for you
Georgia

—PAUL AUSTER

## SAY IT WITH MUSIC

The golden bracelets and the flags
the locomotives the boats
and the salubrious wind and the clouds

je les abandonne simplement
mon cœur est trop petit
ou trop grand
et ma vie est courte
je ne sais quand viendra ma mort exactement
mais je vieillis
je descends les marches quotidiennes
en laissant une prière s'échapper de mes lèvres
A chaque étage est-ce un ami qui m'attend
est-ce un voleur
est-ce moi
je ne sais plus voir dans le ciel
qu'une seule étoile ou qu'un seul nuage
selon ma tristesse ou ma joie
je ne sais plus baisser la tête
est-elle trop lourde
Dans mes mains je ne sais pas non plus
si je tiens des bulles de savon ou des boulets de canon
je marche
je vieillis
mais mon sang rouge mon cher sang rouge
parcourt mes veines
en chassant devant lui les souvenirs du présent
mais ma soif est trop grande
je m'arrête encore et j'attends
la lumière
Paradis paradis paradis

## LE NAGEUR

Mille cris oiseaux
l'horizon trace une ligne de vie
Et les vagues visages perdus chuchotent
dans les golfes tendus comme des bras ouverts
Je suis sûr enfin d'être seul
est-ce le Nord est-ce l'Ouest
le soleil bourdonnant de lumière

I simply abandon them
my heart is too small
or too big
and my life is brief
I do not know exactly when my death will come
but I am growing old
I walk down the daily stairs
letting a prayer escape my lips
Is there on every floor a friend awaiting me
or a thief
Is it I
I can see nothing more in the sky
but a star or a cloud
according to my sadness or my joy
I can no longer bow my head
is it too heavy
Nor do I know if in my hands
I hold soap bubbles or cannon balls
I am walking
I am growing old
but my red blood my dear red blood
races through my veins
chasing before it the memories of the present
my thirst is too big
I stop and wait
for the light
Paradise paradise paradise

—EUGENE JOLAS

## THE SWIMMER

A thousand bird calls
the horizon traces a life line
And lost vague faces whisper
in gulfs held like open arms
I am certain at last of being alone
is this North is this West
the sun humming with light

rue du ciel et de la terre
je m'arrête pour savoir encore si l'été est rouge
dans mes veines
et mon ombre tourne autour de moi
dans le sens des aiguilles d'une montre
Le sommeil m'apporte les insectes et les reptiles
la douleur une grimace et le mensonge
le réveil
je flotte visage perdu au milieu d'une heure
sans secours sans appel
je descends sans conviction des marches sans but
et je continue sans regret jusqu'au sommeil
dans les yeux des miroirs et dans le rire du vent
je reconnais un inconnu qui est moi
je ne bouge plus
j'attends
et je ferme les yeux comme un verrou
Nous ne saurons jamais quand la nuit commence
et où elle finit
mais cela en somme n'a pas beaucoup d'importance
les nègres du Kamtchatka
s'endormiront ce soir près de moi
lorsque la fatigue se posera sur ma tête
comme une couronne

## COMRADE

Petits mois petites fumées
et l'oubli en robe de laine
une porte s'ouvre tendrement
près du mur où naît le vent
près du jardin bienheureux
où les saints et les anges
ont peur des saisons
Les allées n'ont pas de noms
ce sont les heures ou les années
je me promène lentement

street of sky and earth
I stop to ponder once more if the summer is red
in my veins
and my shadow turns around me
clock-wise
Sleep brings me insects and reptiles
pain a grimace and falsehood
waking
I float like a lost face in the midst of an hour
without help without a word
without conviction I go down the endless steps
and go on without regret until bedtime
in the eyes of mirrors and the laughter of wind
I recognize a stranger who is me
I do not move
I wait
and shut my eyes like a lock
We will never know when the night begins
or where it ends
but that hardly matters
the negroes of Kamtchatka
will sleep beside me this evening
when fatigue rests upon my head
like a crown

—PAUL AUSTER


COMRADE

Little months little smokes
and oblivion in a wool dress
a door opens tenderly
near a wall where the wind is born
near the jolly garden
where saints and angels
are afraid of the seasons
the alleys have no names
they are the hours or the years
I stroll leisurely

vêtu d'un paletot mastic
et coiffé d'un chapeau de paille noire
Je ne me souviens pas
s'il fait beau
je marche en fumant
et je fume en marchant
à pas lents
Quelquefois je me dis
Il est temps de s'arrêter
et je continue à marcher
Je me dis
Il faut prendre l'air
Il faut regarder les nuages
et respirer à pleins poumons
Il faut voir voler les mouches
et faire une promenade de santé
Il ne faut pas tant fumer
je me dis aussi
Calculons
je me dis encore
j'ai mal à la tête
Ma vie est une goutte d'eau sous ma paupière
et je n'ai plus vingt ans
Continuons
Les chansons sont des chansons
et les jours des jours
je n'ai plus aucun respect pour moi
mais je vois des voyous
qui fument les mêmes cigarettes que moi
et qui sont aussi bêtes que moi
Je suis bien content
sans vraiment savoir pourquoi
Il ne suffit pas de parler du soleil
des étoiles
de la mer et des fleuves
du sang des yeux des mains
Il est nécessaire bien souvent
de parler d'autres choses
On sait qu'il y a de très beaux pays
de très beaux hommes
de non moins charmantes femmes
mais tout cela n'est vraiment pas suffisant
Le vide étourdissant
qui sonne et qui aboie

dressed in a cement overcoat
and a hat of black straw
I don't remember
if it's nice out
I walk smoking
and I smoke walking
easily
every once in a while I tell myself
it's time to stop
and I continue walking
I tell myself
I have to get some air
I have to look at the clouds
and breathe in a lung full
I have to see the flys fly
and take a little exercise
I shouldn't smoke so much
I tell myself also
calculate
I tell myself again
I have a headache
my life is a drop of water on my eyelid
and I'm no longer twenty
continue
the songs are songs
and the days days
I no longer have one shred of respect for myself
but I see hoodlums
who smoke the same cigarettes as me
and who are just as stupid as me
I'm pretty content
without really knowing why
it doesn't suffice to speak of the sun
the stars
the sea and rivers
blood eyes hands
it is necessary quite often
to speak of other things
we know that there are very beautiful countries
with very handsome men
with no less charming women
but all that isn't really sufficient
the dizzying void
which rings and bays

fait pencher la tête
On regarde et on voit
encore beaucoup d'autres choses
qui sont toujours les mêmes
innombrables
identiques
Et là-bas simplement
quelqu'un passe
simple comme bonjour
et tout recommence encore une fois
je lis dans les astres la bonne volonté de mes amis
dans un fleuve j'aime une main
j'écoute les fleurs chanter
Il y a des adieux des oiseaux
Un cri tombe comme un fruit
Mon Dieu mon Dieu
je serai donc toujours le même
la tête dans les mains
et les mains dans la tête

## MÉDAILLE DE SAUVETAGE

Mon nez est long comme un couteau
et mes yeux sont rouges de rire
La nuit je recueille le lait et la lune
et je cours sans me retourner
Si les arbres ont peur derrière moi
Je m'en moque
Comme l'indifférence est belle à minuit

Où vont ces gens
orgueil des cités
musiciens de village
la foule danse à toute vitesse
et je ne suis que ce passant anonyme
ou quelqu'un d'autre dont j'ai oublié le nom

makes the head bow
we look and we see
again many other things
which are always the same
innumerable
identical
and over there simply
someone goes by
simple as hello
and everything starts all over once again
I read in the stars the good will of my friends
in a river I love one hand
I listen the flowers sing
there are the goodbyes of birds
a cry falls like a fruit
my God my God
I will be accordingly always the same
my head in my hands
and my hands in my head

—PAT NOLAN


## LIFE-SAVING MEDAL

My nose long like a knife
and my eyes red from laughing
At night I gather the milk and the moon
and run without turning around
If the trees are afraid behind me
I don't give a damn
How beautiful: indifference at midnight

Where are these people going
pride of the cities
village fiddlers
the crowd dances up a storm
and me just this anonymous passer-by
or somebody else whose name I forgot

—ROSMARIE WALDROP

# ARTICLES DE SPORT

Courageux comme un timbre-poste
il allait son chemin
en tapant doucement dans ses mains
pour compter ses pas
son cœur rouge comme un sanglier
frappait frappait
comme un papillon rose et vert
De temps en temps
il plantait un petit drapeau de satin
Quand il eut beaucoup marché
il s'assit pour se reposer
et s'endormit
Mais depuis ce jour il y a beaucoup de nuages dans le ciel
beaucoup d'oiseaux dans les arbres
et beaucoup de sel dans la mer
Il y a encore beaucoup d'autres choses

## SPORTING GOODS

Brave as a postage stamp
he went his way
gently clapping his hands
to count his steps
his heart red like a wild boar
beat and beat
like a pink and green butterfly
From time to time
he planted a small satin flag
When he had marched for a long time
he sat down to rest
and fell asleep
But from that day on there've been many clouds in the sky
many birds in the trees
much salt in the sea
And also many other things

—ROSMARIE WALDROP

## POÈME À CRIER DANS LES RUINES

Tous deux crachons tous deux
Sur ce que nous avons aimé
Sur ce que nous avons aimé tous deux
Si tu veux car ceci tous deux
Est bien un air de valse et j'imagine
Ce qui passe entre nous de sombre et d'inégalable
Comme un dialogue de miroirs abandonnés
A la consigne quelque part Foligno peut-être
Ou l'Auvergne la Bourboule
Certains noms sont chargés d'un tonnerre lointain
Veux-tu crachons tous deux sur ces pays immenses
Où se promènent de petites automobiles de louage
Veux-tu car il faut que quelque chose encore
Quelque chose
Nous réunisse veux-tu crachons
Tous deux c'est une valse
Une espèce de sanglot commode
Crachons crachons de petites automobiles
Crachons c'est la consigne
Une valse de miroirs
Un dialogue nulle part
Écoute ces pays immenses où le vent
Pleure sur ce que nous avons aimé

# Louis Aragon

1897-1982

---

## POEM TO SHOUT IN THE RUINS

Let's spit the two of us let's spit
On what we loved
On what we loved the two of us
Yes because this poem the two of us
Is a waltz tune and I imagine
What is dark and incomparable passing between us
Like a dialogue of mirrors abandoned
In a baggage-claim somewhere say Foligno
Or Bourboule in the Auvergne
Certain names are charged with a distant thunder
Yes let's spit the two of us on these immense landscapes
Where little rented cars cruise by
Yes because something must still
Some thing
Reconcile us yes let's spit
The two of us it's a waltz
A kind of convenient sob
Let's spit let's spit tiny automobiles
Let's spit that's an order
A waltz of mirrors
A dialogue in a void
Listen to these immense landscapes where the wind
Cries over what we loved

L'un d'eux est un cheval qui s'accoude à la terre
L'autre un mort agitant un linge l'autre
La trace de tes pas Je me souviens d'un village désert
A l'épaule d'une montagne brûlée
Je me souviens de ton épaule
Je me souviens de ton coude
Je me souviens de ton linge
Je me souviens de tes pas
Je me souviens d'une ville où il n'y a pas de cheval
Je me souviens de ton regard qui a brûlé
Mon cœur désert un mort Mazeppa qu'un cheval
Emporte devant moi comme ce jour dans la montagne
L'ivresse précipitait ma course à travers les chênes martyrs
Qui saignaient prophétiquement tandis
Que le jour faiblissait sur des camions bleus
Je me souviens de tant de choses
De tant de soirs
De tant de chambres
De tant de marches
De tant de colères
De tant de haltes dans des lieux nuls
Où s'éveillait pourtant l'esprit du mystère pareil
Au cri d'un enfant aveugle dans une gare-frontière
Je me souviens

Je parle donc au passé Que l'on rie
Si le cœur vous en dit du son de mes paroles
Aima Fut Vint Caressa
Attendit Epia les escaliers qui craquèrent
O violences violences je suis un homme hanté
Attendit attendit puits profonds
J'ai cru mourir d'attendre
Le silence taillait des crayons dans la rue
Ce taxi qui toussait s'en va crever ailleurs
Attendit attendit les voix étouffées
Devant la porte le langage des portes
Hoquet des maisons attendit
Les objets familiers prenaient à tour de rôle
Attendit l'aspect fantômatique Attendit
Des forçats évadés Attendit
Attendit Nom de Dieu
D'un bagne de lueurs et soudain
Non Stupide Non
Idiot

One of them is a horse leaning its elbow on the earth
The other a deadman shaking out linen the other
The trail of your footprints I remember a deserted village
On the shoulder of a scorched mountain
I remember your shoulder
I remember your elbow your linen your footprints
I remember a town where there was no horse
I remember your look which scorched
My deserted heart a dead Mazeppa whom a horse
Carries away like that day on the mountain
Drunkenness sped my run through the martyred oaks
Which bled prophetically while day
Light fell mute over the blue trucks
I remember so many things
So many evenings rooms walks rages
So many stops in worthless places
Where in spite of everything the spirit of mystery rose up
Like the cry of a blind child in a remote train depot

So I am speaking to the past Go ahead and laugh
At the sound of my words if you feel that way
He loved and Was and Came and Caressed
And Waited and Kept watch on the stairs which creaked
Oh violence violence I am a haunted man
And waited and waited bottomless wells
I thought I would die waiting
Silence sharpened pencils in the street
A coughing taxi drove off to die in the dark
And waited and waited smothered voices
In front of the door the language of doors
Hiccup of houses and waited
One after another familiar objects took on
And waited the ghostlike look And waited
Of convicts And waited
And waited God Damn
Escaped from a prison of half-light and suddenly
No Stupid No
Idiot
The shoe crushed the nap of the rug
I barely return
And loved loved loved but you cannot know how much
And loved it's in the past
Loved loved loved loved loved
Oh violence

La chaussure a foulé la laine du tapis
Je rentre à peine
Aima aima aima mais tu ne peux pas savoir combien
Aima c'est au passé
Aima aima aima aima aima
O violences

Ils en ont de bonnes ceux
Qui parlent de l'amour comme d'une histoire de cousine
Ah merde pour tout ce faux-semblant
Sais-tu quand cela devient vraiment une histoire
L'amour
Sais-tu
Quand toute respiration tourne à la tragédie
Quand les couleurs du jour sont ce que les fait un rire
Un air une ombre d'ombre un nom jeté
Que tout brûle et qu'on sait au fond
Que tout brûle
Et qu'on dit Que tout brûle
Et le ciel a le goût du sable dispersé
L'amour salauds l'amour pour vous
C'est d'arriver à coucher ensemble
D'arriver
Et après Ha ha tout l'amour est dans ce
Et après
Nous arrivons à parler de ce que c'est que de
Coucher ensemble pendant des années
Entendez-vous
Pendant des années
Pareilles à des voiles marines qui tombent
Sur le pont d'un navire chargé de pestiférés
Dans un film que j'ai vu récemment
Une à une
La rose blanche meurt comme la rose rouge
Qu'est-ce donc qui m'émeut à un pareil point
Dans ces derniers mots
Le mot dernier peut-être mot en qui
Tout est atroce atrocement irréparable
Et déchirant Mot panthère Mot électrique
Chaise
Le dernier mot d'amour imaginez-vous ça
Et le dernier baiser et la dernière
Nonchalance
Et le dernier sommeil Tiens c'est drôle

It's nothing but a joke to those
Who talk as if love were the story of a fling
Shit on all that pretence
Do you know when it truly becomes a story
Love
You know
When every breath turns into a tragedy
When even the day's colors are laughable
Air a shadow in shade a name thrown out
That everything burns and you know deep down
That eveything burns
And you say Let everything burn
And the sky is the taste of scattered sand
Love you bastards love for you
Is when you manage to sleep together
Manage to
And afterwards Ha ha all of love is in that
And afterwards
We manage to speak of what it is
To sleep together for years
Do you understand
For years
Just like a boat's sails toppling
Onto the deck of a ship loaded with lepers
In a film I saw recently
One by one
The white rose dies like the red rose
What is it then that stirs me up to such a pitch
In these last words
The word last perhaps a word in which
Everything is cruel cruelly irreparable
And torn to shreds Word panther Word electric
Chair
The last word of love imagine that
And the last kiss and the last
Nonchalance
And the last sleep No kidding it's comic
Thinking simply of the last night
Ah everything takes on this abominable meaning
I meant the last moment
The last goodbye the last gasp
Last look
Horror horror horror
For years now horror

Je pensais simplement à la dernière nuit
Ah tout prend ce sens abominable
Je voulais dire les derniers instants
Les derniers adieux le dernier soupir
Le dernier regard
L'horreur l'horreur l'horreur
Pendant des années l'horreur
Crachons veux-tu bien
Sur ce que nous avons aimé ensemble
Crachons sur l'amour
Sur nos lits défaits
Sur notre silence et sur les mots balbutiés
Sur les étoiles fussent-elles
Tes yeux
Sur le soleil fût-il
Tes dents
Sur l'éternité fût-elle
Ta bouche
Et sur notre amour
Fût-il
TON amour
Crachons veux-tu bien

*de* VALSE DU TCHELIABTRAKTROSTROI

C'est une valse ancienne
qui tournait pour les paresseux
Jadis on respirait à peine
quand les yeux
rencontraient
les yeux
Au son de la même rengaine
aujourdhui l'étrange boston
ce qui tourne sans perdre haleine
c'est le mélangeur de béton

Toute la ville ouvre ses grands yeux prolétariens sur la course insensée
Dans les fleurs un orchestre au milieu des rubans de paille

Yes let's spit
On what we loved together
Let's spit on love
On our unmade beds
On our silence and on our mumbled words
On the stars even if they are
Your eyes
On the sun even if it is
Your teeth
On eternity even if it is
Your mouth
And on our love
Even if it is
*Your* love
Yes let's spit

—GEOFFREY YOUNG

*from* TCHELIABTRAKTROSTROI WALTZ

    This is an ancient waltz
    That the idle danced amid sighs
    It would bring a catch in the breath
    When they gazed in each other's eyes
    To-day a peculiar boston
    Whirls to the stale elixir
    For what spins without losing breath
    Is the mortar and concrete mixer

The whole town opens wide proletarian eyes in amaze
At such crazy speeding
In a nest of flowers streamers and ribbons sits an orchestra
And plays mindless of the hour and the ceremony's import

oublie et l'heure et le sujet de la soirée et le ciel noir sur l'Europe et la
    sueur
formidable au dos puissant des travailleurs
La brigade
avec la solennité que tout ceci comporte a promis
de donner trois fois sa journée en un soir
Les petits enfants au lieu de dormir sont venus
voir

      L'orchestre reprend la romance
      qui grisait le monde aboli
      Dans mes bras Madame O démence
      Démon que vous êtes joli
      Au cœur même de la cadence
      qu'est-ce qui bat comme un tambour
      C'est cependant la même danse
      mais ce n'est plus le même amour

Celui qui vient de son village
et qui ne sait rien que les champs durs à la pioche et le long
    l'interminable
hiver
au premier rang s'étonne et rit sans comprendre et peut-être
prend peur devant la passion dont les flammes
mordent la fleur immense des mille regards
Celui qui vient de son village au premier rang se pose
toutes les questions de la philosophie
qui sont comme les poux sur la tête humaine tournée
vers les constellations
Les camarades
pour la centième fois chargent le mélangeur

      Camarades le passé craque
      au creux puissant de vos pas
      Emportons la vieille baraque
      dans les camions de nos bras
      Le canon contre nous se braque
      Mais malgré les feux et les fers
      le ciel des riches se détraque
      et leur soleil marche à l'envers

Quatre cents cinq cents six cents sept
cents mélangeurs crachés dans le délire Où sommes-nous
C'est le pays de la violence et des yeux bleus

And of the black night over Europe and the sweat
Massive on the workers' strong backs
While with all due solemnity that such things comport
The brigade has sworn to give three times a day's worth in one night
And the little children instead of sleeping have come to gaze

> The band strikes up again
> The romance of a world that's gone
> In my arms love ah what sweet folly
> Demon I am undone
> In the heart itself of the cadence
> A drum-beat seems to move
> Although surely the self-same dance
> It's no longer the same love

He who comes from his village
Knowing nothing but the hardness of fields in the hoeing
And the interminable span
Of winter
Sits in the front row amazed laughs without quite understanding
Uneasy too at this passionate flame
In the bouquet of a thousand eyes
Sits in the front row he who comes from his village
And all the philosophical questions assail him
That are like fleas on the head of humanity
Upturned searching the starry vault
And the comrades for the thousandth time now
Are feeding the mixer

> Comrades the past is cracking
> Where your powerful emblem stands
> Let us cart off the old wreckage
> In the wagon of our hands
> They train the cannon against us
> But despite the bullets and jail
> The sky of the rich is falling
> And their sun has begun to fail

Four five six and seven
Hundred mixings spat out in frenzy
Where is it we are
It's a land of violence a blue-eyed land
The immense perception of knees
Flexed under each shovelling

L'intelligence énorme des genoux
plie à chaque pelletée
sous l'effort révolutionnaire des bétonneurs
C'est le pays du Léninisme la main à la pelle
qui répond à l'appel de l'avenir cinq ans d'avance
C'est le Léninisme la pelle à la main le Léninisme
sur la brèche du siècle prenant
tout l'élan de la pioche et qui rit
sans essuyer son front splendide
et sans rejeter ses cheveux
à la terre docile et dure
à la nature fantasque et folle
aux hommes encore incertains
qui rit à l'électricité
sa fille esclave son enfant
le Léninisme au corps de flammes
aux pieds d'acier
aux mains de chair

    Mille la machine a par mille
    fois vidé son ventre tournant
    ainsi qu'une loterie agile
    au gré d'un éternel gagnant
    Tous les ouvriers de la ville
    debout criant hagards heureux
    comme une casquette inutile
    jettent le nombre mille aux cieux

## LES LILAS ET LES ROSES

O mois des floraisons mois des métamorphoses
Mai qui fut sans nuage et Juin poignardé
Je n'oublierai jamais les lilas ni les roses
Ni ceux que le printemps dans ses plis a gardés

Je n'oublierai jamais l'illusion tragique
Le cortège les cris la foule et le soleil
Les chars chargés d'amour les dons de la Belgique
L'air qui tremble et la route à ce bourdon d'abeilles
Le triomphe imprudent qui prime la querelle

Under the revolutionary urge of the concrete workers
It's the land of Leninism hand on shovel
That answers the future's call five years ahead
Leninism shovel in hand Leninism
In the breach of the century taking on
The swing of the pick itself
Careless of sweating brow
And tangled hair laughing
At earth both hard and docile
At nature mad and whimsical
At the uncertainty still in men laughing at electricity
Its child its vassal daughter
Leninism with its frame of fire
With its feet of steel
With its human hands

    Now from the bellying drum
    The thousandth emptying spins
    Like a nimble fortune-wheel
    To a player who always wins
    All the workers of the town
    Leap up and with frenzied eyes
    Like a cap torn from the head
    Hurl their thousand to the skies

—NANCY CUNARD


## THE LILACS AND THE ROSES

O months of blossoming, months of transfigurations,
May without a cloud and June stabbed to the heart,
I shall not ever forget the lilacs or the roses
Nor those the Spring has kept folded away apart.

I shall not ever forget the tragic sleight-of-hand,
The cavalcade, the cries, the crowd, the sun,
The lorries loaded with love, the Belgian gifts,
The road humming with bees, the atmosphere that spun,
The feckless triumphing before the battle,

Le sang que préfigure en carmin le baiser
Et ceux qui vont mourir debout dans les tourelles
Entourés de lilas par un peuple grisé

Je n'oublierai jamais les jardins de la France
Semblables aux missels des siècles disparus
Ni le trouble des soirs l'énigme du silence
Les roses tout le long du chemin parcouru
Le démenti des fleurs au vent de la panique
Aux soldats qui passaient sur l'aile de la peur
Aux vélos délirants aux canons ironiques
Au pitoyable accoutrement des faux campeurs

Mais je ne sais pourquoi ce tourbillon d'images
Me ramène toujours au même point d'arrêt
A Sainte-Marthe Un général De noirs ramages
Une villa normande au bord de la forêt
Tout se tait L'ennemi dans l'ombre se repose
On nous a dit ce soir que Paris s'est rendu
Je n'oublierai jamais les lilas ni les roses
Et ni les deux amours que nous avons perdus

Bouquets du premier jour lilas lilas des Flandres
Douceur de l'ombre dont la mort farde les joues
Et vous bouquets de la retraite roses tendres
Couleur de l'incendie au loin roses d'Anjou

## TAPISSERIE DE LA GRANDE PEUR

Le paysage enfant de la terreur moderne
A des poissons volants sirènes poissons-scies
Qu'écrit-il blanc sur bleu dans le ciel celui-ci
Hydre-oiseau qui fait songer à l'hydre de Lerne
Écumeur de la terre oiseau-pierre qui coud
L'air aux maisons oiseau strident oiseau-comète
Et la géante guêpe acrobate allumette
Qui met aux murs flambants des bouquets de coucous

The scarlet blood the scarlet kiss bespoke
And those about to die bolt upright in the turrets
Smothered in lilac by a drunken folk.

I shall not ever forget the flower-gardens of France—
Illuminated scrolls from eras more than spent—
Nor forget the trouble of dusk, the sphinx-like silence,
The roses all along the way we went;
Flowers that gave the lie to the soldiers passing
On wings of fear, a fear importunate as a breeze,
And gave the lie to the lunatic push-bikes and the ironic
Guns and the sorry rig of the refugees.

But what I do not know is why this whirl
Of memories always comes to the same point and drops
At Sainte-Marthe . . . a general . . . a black pattern . . .
A Norman villa where the forest stops;
All is quiet here, the enemy rests in the night
And Paris has surrendered, so we have just heard—
I shall never forget the lilacs nor the roses
Nor those two loves whose loss we have incurred:

Bouquets of the first day, lilacs, Flanders lilacs,
Soft cheeks of shadow rouged by death—and you,
Bouquets of the Retreat, delicate roses, tinted
Like far-off conflagrations: roses of Anjou.

—LOUIS MACNEICE


TAPESTRY OF THE GREAT FEAR

This landscape, masterpiece of modern terror
Has sharks and sirens, flying fish and swordfish
And hydra-headed birds like Lerna's hydra
What are they writing, white on blue, in the sky?
Skimmers of earth, steel birds that stitch the air
To the stone houses, strident comet-birds
Enormous wasps like acrobatic matchsticks
That deck the flaming walls with primroses

Ou si ce sont des vols de flamants qui rougissent
O carrousel flamand de l'antique sabbat
Sur un manche à balai de Messerschmitt s'abat
C'est la nuit en plein jour du nouveau Walpurgis
Apocalypse époque Espace où la peur passe
Avec son grand transport de pleurs et de pâleurs
Reconnais-tu les champs la ville et les rapaces
Le clocher qui plus jamais ne sonnera l'heure
Les chariots bariolés de literies
Un ours Un châle Un mort comme un soulier perdu
Les deux mains prises dans son ventre Une pendule
Les troupeaux échappés les charognes les cris
Des bronzes d'art à terre Où dormez-vous ce soir
Et des enfants juchés sur des marcheurs étranges
Des gens qui vont on ne sait où tout l'or des granges
Aux cheveux Les fossés où l'effroi vient s'asseoir
L'agonisant que l'on transporte et qui réclame
Une tisane et qui se plaint parce qu'il sue
Sa robe de bal sur le bras une bossue
La cage du serin qui traversa les flammes
Une machine à coudre Un vieillard C'est trop lourd
Encore un pas Je vais mourir va-t'en Marie
La beauté des soirs tombe et son aile marie
A ce Breughel d'Enfer un Breughel de Velours


ZONE LIBRE

Fading de la tristesse oubli
Le bruit du cœur brisé faiblit
Et la cendre blanchit la braise
J'ai bu l'été comme un vin doux
J'ai rêvé pendant ce mois d'août
Dans un château rose en Corrèze

Qu'était-ce qui faisait soudain
Un sanglot lourd dans le jardin
Un sourd reproche dans la brise

Or flights of pink flamingos in the sun
Kermess in Flanders, witches at their Sabbath
On a broomstick the Messerschmitt rides down
Darkness at noon, night of the new Walpurgis
Apocalyptic time. Space where fear passes
With all its baggage train of tears and trembling
Do you recognize the fields, the birds of prey?
The steeple where the bells will never ring
The farm carts draped with bedclothes. A tame bear
A shawl. A dead man dropped like an old shoe
Hands clutching the torn belly. A grandfather's clock
Roaming herds of cattle, carcasses, cries
Art bronzes by the roadside. Where will you sleep?
Children perched on the shoulders of strange men
Tramping off somewhere, while the gold of the barns
Gleams in their hair. Ditches where terror sits
The dying man in a cart who keeps asking
For herb tea, and complains of a cold sweat
A hunchbacked woman with a wedding dress
A birdcage that passed safely through the flames
A sewing machine. An old man. I can't walk
Just a step more. No, let me die here, Marie
Evening soars down with silent wingbeats, joining
A velvet Breughel to this Breughel of hell.

—MALCOLM COWLEY

THE UNOCCUPIED ZONE

Cross-fade of grief to nothingness,
The beat of the crushed heart grew less,
The coals grew white and lost their gleam;
Drinking the wine of summer's haze
In a rose-castle in Corrèze
I changed this August into dream.

What could it be that of a sudden
Brought an aching sob in the garden,
A voice of low reproach in the air?

Ah ne m'éveillez pas trop tôt
Rien qu'un instant le bel canto
Le déséspoir démobilise

Il m'avait un instant semblé
Entendre au milieu des blés
Confusément le bruit des armes
D'où me venait ce grand chagrin
Ni l'œillet ni le romarin
N'ont gardé le parfum des larmes

J'ai perdu je ne sais comment
Le noir secret de mon tourment
A son tour l'ombre se démembre
Je cherchais à n'en plus finir
Cette douleur sans souvenir
Quand parut l'aube de septembre

Mon amour j'étais dans tes bras
Au dehors quelqu'un murmura
Une vieille chanson de France
Mon mal enfin s'est reconnu
Et son refrain comme un pied nu
Troubla l'eau verte du silence

Ah not so soon, ah do not wake me;
This merest snatch of song must take me
Out of the barracks of despair.

I thought for a moment that I heard
In the middle of the corn a blurred
Noise of arms—a theme that scars.
Whence did this theme return to me?
Not carnations nor rosemary
Had thus retained the scent of tears.

By hook or crook I had got relief
From the dark secret of my grief
When lo—the shadows redivide;
My eyes were only on the track
Of apathy that looks not back
When September dawned outside.

My love, within your arms I lay
When someone hummed across the way
An ancient song of France; my illness
At last came clear to me for good—
That phrase of song like a naked foot
Rippled the green waters of stillness.

—LOUIS MACNEICE

## LÀ OÙ D'AUTRES...

Là où d'autres proposent des œuvres je ne prétends pas autre chose que de montrer mon esprit.

La vie est de brûler des questions.

Je ne conçois pas d'œuvre comme détachée de la vie.

Je n'aime pas la création détachée. Je ne conçois pas non plus l'esprit comme détaché de lui-même. Chacune de mes œuvres, chacun des plans de moi-même, chacune des floraisons glacières de mon âme intérieure bave sur moi.

Je me retrouve autant dans une lettre écrite pour expliquer le rétrécissement intime de mon être et le châtrage insensé de ma vie, que dans un essai extérieur à moi-même, et qui m'apparaît comme une grossesse indifférente de mon esprit.

Je souffre que l'Esprit ne soit pas dans la vie et que la vie ne soit pas l'Esprit, je souffre de l'Esprit-organe, de l'Esprit-traduction, ou de l'Esprit-intimida-tion-des-choses pour les faire entrer dans l'Esprit.

Ce livre je le mets en suspension dans la vie, je veux qu'il soit mordu par les choses extérieures, et d'abord par tous les soubresauts en cisaille, toutes les cillations *de mon moi à venir*.

Toutes ces pages traînent comme des glaçons dans l'esprit. Qu'on excuse ma liberté absolue. Je me refuse à faire de différence entre aucune des minutes de moi-même. Je ne reconnais pas dans l'esprit de plan.

Il faut en finir avec l'Esprit comme avec la littérature. Je dis que l'Esprit et la vie communiquent à tous les degrés. Je voudrais faire un Livre qui dérange les hommes, qui soit comme une porte ouverte et qui les mène où ils

# Antonin Artaud

## 1896-1948

---

## WHERE OTHERS . . .

Where others present their works, I claim to do no more than show my mind.

Life consists of burning up questions.

I cannot conceive of work that is detached from life.

I do not like detached creation. Neither can I conceive of the mind as detached from itself. Each of my works, each diagram of myself, each glacial flowering of my inmost soul dribbles over me.

I am as much myself in a letter written to explain the inner contraction of my being and the senseless castration of my life as in an essay which is external to myself and which appears to me as an indifferent pregnancy of my mind.

I suffer because the Mind is not in life and life is not the Mind: I suffer from the Mind as organ, the Mind as interpreter, the Mind as intimidator of things to force them to enter the Mind.

I suspend this book in life, I want it to be eaten away by external things, and above all by all the rending jolts, all the thrashings *of my future self.*

All these pages float around like pieces of ice in my mind. Excuse my absolute freedom. I refuse to make a distinction between any of the moments of myself. I do not recognize any structure in the mind.

We must get rid of the Mind, just as we must get rid of literature. I say that the Mind and life communicate on all levels. I would like to write a Book which would drive men mad, which would be like an open door leading them where they would never have consented to go, in short, a door that opens onto reality.

n'auraient jamais consenti à aller, une porte simplement abouchée avec la réalité.

Et ceci n'est pas plus une préface à un livre, que les poèmes par exemple qui le jalonnent ou le dénombrement de toutes les rages du mal-être.

Ceci n'est qu'un glaçon aussi mal avalé.

## DESCRIPTION D'UN ÉTAT PHYSIQUE

une sensation de brûlure acide dans les membres,

des muscles tordus et comme à vif, le sentiment d'être en verre et brisable, une peur, une rétraction devant le mouvement, et le bruit. Un désarroi inconscient de la marche, des gestes, des mouvements. Une volonté perpétuellement tendue pour les gestes les plus simples,

le renoncement au geste simple,

une fatigue renversante et centrale, une espèce de fatigue aspirante. Les mouvements à recomposer, une espèce de fatigue de mort, de la fatigue d'esprit pour une application de la tension musculaire la plus simple, le geste de prendre, de s'accrocher inconsciemment à quelque chose,

à soutenir par une volonté appliquée.

Une fatigue de commencement du monde, la sensation de son corps à porter, un sentiment de fragilité incroyable, et qui devient une brisante douleur,

un état d'engourdissement douloureux, une espèce d'engourdissement localisé à la peau, qui n'interdit aucun mouvement mais change le sentiment interne d'un membre, et donne à la simple station verticale le prix d'un effort victorieux.

Localisé probablement à la peau, mais senti comme la suppression radicale d'un membre, et ne présentant plus au cerveau que des images de membres filiformes et cotonneux, des images de membres lointains et pas à leur place. Une espèce de rupture intérieure de la correspondance de tous les nerfs.

Un vertige mouvant, une espèce d'éblouissement oblique qui accompagne tout effort, une coagulation de chaleur qui enserre toute l'étendue du crâne ou s'y découpe par morceaux, des plaques de chaleur qui se déplacent.

Une exacerbation douloureuse du crâne, une coupante pression des nerfs, la nuque acharnée à souffrir, des tempes qui se vitrifient ou se marbrent, une tête piétinée de chevaux.

Il faudrait parler maintenant de la décorporisation de la réalité, de cette espèce de rupture appliquée, on dirait, à se multiplier elle-même entre les

And this is no more the preface to a book than the poems which are scattered here and there, or the enumeration of all the rages of ill-being.

This is only a piece of ice which is also stuck in my throat.

—HELEN WEAVER

## DESCRIPTION OF A PHYSICAL STATE

a sharp burning sensation in the limbs,

muscles twisted, as if flayed, the sense of being made of glass and breakable, a fear, a recoiling from movement and noise. An unconscious confusion in walking, gestures, movements. A will that is perpetually strained to make the simplest gestures,

renunciation of the simple gesture,

a staggering and central fatigue, a kind of gasping fatigue. Movements must be recomposed, a sort of deathlike fatigue, a fatigue of the mind in carrying out the simplest muscular contraction, the gesture of grasping, of unconsciously clinging to something,

must be sustained by a constant effort of the will.

A fatigue as old as the world, the sense of having to carry one's body around, a feeling of incredible fragility which becomes a shattering pain,

a state of painful numbness, a kind of numbness localized in the skin which does not inhibit any movement but which changes the internal sensation of a limb and gives the simple act of standing up straight the value of a victorious effort.

Probably localized in the skin, but felt as the radical elimination of a limb, and presenting to the brain only images of limbs that are threadlike and woolly, images of limbs that are far away and not where they should be. A sort of internal fracturing of the whole nervous system.

A shifting vertigo, a sort of oblique bewilderment which accompanies every effort, a coagulation of heat which grips the entire surface of the skull or is cut into pieces, shifting patches of heat.

A painful exacerbation of the skull, a sharp pressure of the nerves, the nape of the neck straining after its pain, temples turning to glass or marble, a head trampled by horses.

One must speak now of the disembodiment of reality, of that sort of rupture that seems determined to multiply itself between things and the feeling they produce in our mind, the place they should take.

choses et le sentiment qu'elles produisent sur notre esprit, la place qu'elles
doivent prendre.

Ce classement instantané des choses dans les cellules de l'esprit, non pas
tellement dans leur ordre logique, mais dans leur ordre sentimental, affectif
(qui ne se fait plus):

les choses n'ont plus d'odeur, plus de sexe. Mais leur ordre logique aussi
quelquefois est rompu à cause justement de leur manque de relent affectif. Les
mots pourrissent à l'appel inconscient du cerveau, tous les mots pour n'im-
porte quelle opération mentale, et surtout celles qui touchent aux ressorts les
plus habituels, les plus actifs de l'esprit.


## VITRES DE SON

Vitres de son où virent les astres,
verres où cuisent les cerveaux
le ciel fourmillant d'impudeurs
dévore la nudité des astres.

Un lait bizarre et véhément
fourmille au fond du firmament;
un escargot monte et dérange
la placidité des nuages.

Délices et rages, le ciel entier
lance sur nous comme un nuage
un tourbillon d'ailes sauvages
torrentielles d'obscénités.


## IL ME MANQUE . . .

Il me manque une concordance des mots avec la minute de mes états.

« Mais c'est normal, mais à tout le monde il manque des mots, mais vous
êtes trop difficile avec vous-même, mais à vous entendre il n'y paraît pas, mais
vous vous exprimez parfaitement en français, mais vous attachez trop d'impor-
tance à des mots. »

This instantaneous classification of things in the cells of the mind, not so much in their logical order as in their emotional or affective order
(which no longer holds):
things have no more odor, no more sex. But their logical order is also sometimes broken precisely because of their lack of emotional aroma. Words rot at the unconscious summons of the brain, all the words for any kind of mental operation, and especially those operations which affect the most habitual, most active responses of the mind.

—HELEN WEAVER

## THE PANES OF SOUND

Panes of sound where stars swerve,
the glass where brains are cooking,
The sky, seething with immodesty,
eats the nakedness of the stars.

A strange and violent milk
Is seething deep in the sky,
a snail climbs and spoils
the calmness of the clouds.

Ecstacies and angers, the whole sky
hurls over us, like a cloud,
a whirlwind of savage winds
Pouring with obscenities.

—PAUL ZWEIG

## WHAT I LACK . . .

What I lack is words that correspond to each minute of my state of mind.
"But that's normal, everyone at times is at a loss for words, you're too hard on yourself, no one would think so to hear you, you express yourself perfectly in French, you attach too much importance to words."

Vous êtes des cons, depuis l'intelligent jusqu'au mince, depuis le perçant jusqu'à l'induré, vous êtes des cons, je veux dire que vous êtes des chiens, je veux dire que vous aboyez au dehors, que vous vous acharnez à ne pas comprendre. Je me connais, et cela me suffit, et cela doit suffire, je me connais parce que je m'assiste, j'assiste à Antonin Artaud.

—Tu te connais, mais nous te voyons, nous voyons bien ce que tu fais.

—Oui, mais vous ne voyez pas ma pensée.

A chacun des stades de ma mécanique pensante, il y a des trous, des arrêts, je ne veux pas dire, comprenez-moi bien, dans le temps, je veux dire dans une certaine sorte d'espace (je me comprends); je ne veux pas dire une pensée en longueur, une pensée en durée de pensées, je veux dire UNE pensée, une seule, et une pensée EN INTÉRIEUR; mais je ne veux pas dire une pensée de Pascal, une pensée de philosophe, je veux dire la fixation contournée, la sclérose d'un certain état. Et attrape!

Je me considère dans ma minutie. Je mets le doigt sur le point précis de la faille, du glissement inavoué. Car l'esprit est plus reptilien que vous-même, Messieurs, il se dérobe comme les serpents, il se dérobe jusqu'à attenter à nos langues, je veux dire à les laisser en suspens.

Je suis celui qui a le mieux senti le désarroi stupéfiant de sa langue dans ses relations avec la pensée. Je suis celui qui a le mieux repéré la minute de ses plus intimes, de ses plus insoupçonnables glissements. Je me perds dans ma pensée en vérité comme on rêve, comme on rentre subitement dans sa pensée. Je suis celui qui connaît les recoins de la perte.

## TOUTE L'ÉCRITURE . . .

Toute l'écriture est de la cochonnerie.

Les gens qui sortent du vague pour essayer de préciser quoi que ce soit de ce qui se passe dans leur pensée, sont des cochons.

Toute la gent littéraire est cochonne, et spécialement celle de ce temps-ci.

Tous ceux qui ont des points de repère dans l'esprit, je veux dire d'un certain côté de la tête, sur des emplacements bien localisés de leur cerveau, tous ceux qui sont maîtres de leur langue, tous ceux pour qui les mots ont un sens, tous ceux pour qui il existe des altitudes dans l'âme, et des courants dans la pensée, ceux qui sont esprit de l'époque, et qui ont nommé ces courants de pensée, je pense à leurs besognes précises, et à ce grincement d'automate que rend à tous vents leur esprit,

—sont des cochons.

You are asses, from the intelligent to the dimwitted, from the perceptive to the obtuse, you are asses, I mean that you are dogs. I mean that you bark in the streets, that you are determined not to understand. I know myself, and 'that is enough for me, and that should be enough. I know myself because I watch myself, I watch Antonin Artaud.

"You know yourself, but we see you, we see very well what you are doing."

"Yes, but you cannot see my thought."

At each of the stages of my thinking mechanism there are gaps, halts— understand me, I do not mean in time. I mean in a certain kind of space (I know what I mean); and I do not mean a series of thoughts. I do not mean a full sequence of thoughts, I mean a SINGLE thought, only one, and an INNER thought; I do not mean one of Pascal's thoughts, a philosopher's thought, I mean a contorted fixation, the sclerosis of a certain state. Take that!

I consider myself in my minutiae. I put my finger on the precise point of the fault, the unadmitted slide. For the mind is more reptilian than you yourselves, messieurs, it slips away snakelike, to the point where it damages our language, I mean it leaves it in suspense.

I am the man who has most felt the stupefying confusion of his speech in its relations with thought. I am the man who has most accurately charted the moment of his most intimate, his most imperceptible lapses. I lose myself in my thought, actually, the way one dreams, the way one suddenly slips back into one's thought. I am the man who knows the inmost recesses of loss.

—HELEN WEAVER

ALL WRITING . . .

All writing is garbage.

People who come out of nowhere to try to put into words any part of what goes on in their minds are pigs.

The whole literary scene is a pigpen, especially today.

All those who have points of reference in their minds, I mean on a certain side of their heads, in well-localized areas of their brains, all those who are masters of their language, all those for whom words have meanings, all those for whom there exist higher levels of the soul and currents of thought, those who represent the spirit of the times, and who have named these currents of thought, I am thinking of their meticulous industry and of that mechanical creaking which their minds give off in all directions,

—are pigs.

Ceux pour qui certains mots ont un sens, et certaines manières d'être, ceux qui font si bien des façons, ceux pour qui les sentiments ont des classes et qui discutent sur un degré quelconque de leurs hilarantes classifications, ceux qui croient encore à des « termes », ceux qui remuent des idéologies ayant pris rang dans l'époque, ceux dont les femmes parlent si bien et ces femmes aussi qui parlent si bien et qui parlent des courants de l'époque, ceux qui croient encore à une orientation de l'esprit, ceux qui suivent des voies, qui agitent des noms, qui font crier les pages des livres,

—ceux-là sont les pires cochons.

Vous êtes bien gratuit, jeune homme!

Non, je pense à des critiques barbus.

Et je vous l'ai dit: pas d'œuvres, pas de langue, pas de parole, pas d'esprit, rien.

Rien, sinon un beau Pèse-Nerfs.

Une sorte de station incompréhensible et toute droite au milieu de tout dans l'esprit.

Et n'espérez pas que je vous nomme ce tout, en combien de parties il se divise, que je vous dise son poids, que je marche, que je me mette à discuter sur ce tout, et que, discutant, je me perde et que je me mette ainsi sans le savoir à PENSER,—et qu'il s'éclaire, qu'il vive, qu'il se pare d'une multitude de mots, tous bien frottés de sens, tous divers, et capables de bien mettre au jour toutes les attitudes, toutes les nuances d'une très sensible et pénétrante pensée.

Ah ces états qu'on ne nomme jamais, ces situations éminentes d'âme, ah ces intervalles d'esprit, ah ces minuscules ratées qui sont le pain quotidien de mes heures, ah ce peuple fourmillant de données,—ce sont toujours les mêmes mots qui me servent et vraiment je n'ai pas l'air de beaucoup bouger dans ma pensée, mais j'y bouge plus que vous en réalité, barbes d'ânes, cochons pertinents, maîtres du faux verbe, trousseurs de portraits, feuilletonnistes, rez-de-chaussée, herbagistes, entomologistes, plaie de ma langue.

Je vous l'ai dit, que je n'ai plus ma langue, ce n'est pas une raison pour que vous persistiez, pour que vous vous obstiniez dans la langue.

Allons, je serai compris dans dix ans par les gens qui feront aujourd'hui ce que vous faites. Alors on connaîtra mes geysers, on verra mes glaces, on aura appris à dénaturer mes poisons, on décélera mes jeux d'âmes.

Alors tous mes cheveux seront coulés dans la chaux, toutes mes veines mentales, alors on percevra mon bestiaire, et ma mystique sera devenue un chapeau. Alors on verra fumer les jointures des pierres, et d'arborescents bouquets d'yeux mentaux se cristalliseront en glossaires, alors on verra choir des aérolithes de pierre, alors on verra des cordes, alors on comprendra la géométrie sans espaces, et on apprendra ce que c'est que la configuration de l'esprit, et on comprendra comment j'ai perdu l'esprit.

Alors on comprendra pourquoi mon esprit n'est pas là, alors on verra toutes les langues tarir, tous les esprits se dessécher, toutes les langues se racornir, les figures humaines s'aplatiront, se dégonfleront, comme aspirées par des

Those for whom certain words have meaning, and certain modes of being, those who are so precise, those for whom emotions can be classified and who quibble over some point of their hilarious classifications, those who still believe in "terms," those who discuss the ranking ideologies of the age, those whom women discuss so intelligently and the women themselves who speak so well and who discuss the currents of the age, those who still believe in an orientation of the mind, those who follow paths, who drop names, who recommend books,

—these are the worst pigs of all.

You are quite unnecessary, young man!

No, I am thinking of bearded critics.

And I have already told you: no works, no language, no words, no mind, nothing.

Nothing but a fine Nerve Meter.

A kind of incomprehensible stopping place in the mind, right in the middle of everything.

And do not expect me to name this everything, to tell you how many parts it is divided into, don't expect me to tell you its weight, don't think that you can get me to discuss it, and that while discussing I will forget myself and that I will thus begin, without realizing it, to THINK—and that it will be illuminated, that it will live, that it will deck itself in a multitude of words, all with well-polished meanings, all different, and able to express all the attitudes and nuances of a very sensitive and penetrating thought.

Ah, these states that are never named, these eminent positions of the soul, ah, these intermissions of the mind, ah, these minuscule failures which are the nourishment of my hours, ah, this population teeming with facts—I always use the same words and really I don't seem to advance very much in my thinking, but actually I am advancing more than you, bearded asses, pertinent pigs, masters of the false word, wrappers of portraits, serial writers, groundlings, cattle raisers, entomologists, plague of my speech.

I told you that I have lost my speech, but that is no reason for you to persist in speaking.

Enough, I shall be understood in ten years by people who will be doing what you do today. Then my geysers will be known, my ice floes will be seen, the secret of adulterating my poisons will have been learned, the games of my soul will be revealed.

Then all my hairs, all my mental veins will be buried in lime, then my bestiary will be perceived and my mystique will have become a hat. Then they will see the joints of the stones steam, and arborescent bouquets of mental eyes will be crystallized in glossaries, then they will see stone meteors fall, then they will see ropes, then they will understand a geometry without space, they will learn what is meant by the configuration of the mind, and they will understand how I lost my mind.

Then they will understand why my mind is not here, then they will see

ventouses desséchantes, et cette lubréfiante membrane continuera à flotter dans l'air, cette membrane lubréfiante et caustique, cette membrane à deux épaisseurs, à multiples degrés, à un infini de lézardes, cette mélancolique et vitreuse membrane, mais si sensible, si pertinente elle aussi, si capable de se multiplier, de se dédoubler, de se retourner avec son miroitement de lézardes, de sens, de stupéfiants, d'irrigations pénétrantes et vireuses,

    alors tout ceci sera trouvé bien,

    et je n'aurai plus besoin de parler.


# MANIFESTE EN LANGAGE CLAIR

*à Roger Vitrac.*

Si je ne crois ni au Mal ni au Bien, si je me sens de telles dispositions à détruire, s'il n'est rien dans l'ordre des principes à quoi je puisse raisonnablement accéder, le principe même en est dans ma chair.

Je détruis parce que chez moi tout ce qui vient de la raison ne tient pas. Je ne crois plus qu'à l'évidence de ce qui agite mes moelles, non de ce qui s'adresse à ma raison. J'ai trouvé des étages dans le domaine du nerf. Je me sens maintenant capable de départager l'évidence. Il y a pour moi une évidence dans le domaine de la chair pure, et qui n'a rien à voir avec l'évidence de la raison. Le conflit éternel de la raison et du cœur se départage dans ma chair même, mais dans ma chair irriguée de nerfs. Dans le domaine de l'impondérable affectif, l'image amenée par mes nerfs prend la forme de l'intellectualité la plus haute, à qui je me refuse à arracher son caractère d'intellectualité. Et c'est ainsi que j'assiste à la formation d'un concept qui porte en lui la fulguration même des choses, qui arrive sur moi avec un bruit de création. Aucune image ne me satisfait que si elle est en même temps *Connaissance*, si elle porte avec elle sa substance en même temps que sa lucidité. Mon esprit fatigué de la raison discursive se veut emporté dans les rouages d'une nouvelle, d'une absolue gravitation. C'est pour moi comme une réorganisation souveraine où seules les lois de l'Illogique participent, et où triomphe la découverte d'un nouveau Sens. Ce Sens perdu dans le désordre des drogues et qui donne la figure d'une intelligence profonde aux phantasmes contradictoires du sommeil. Ce Sens est une conquête de l'esprit sur lui-même, et, bien qu'irréductible par la raison, il existe, mais seulement à l'*intérieur de l'esprit*. Il est l'ordre, il est l'intelligence, il est la signification du chaos. Mais ce chaos, il ne

all language drain away, all minds run dry, all tongues shrivel up, human faces will flatten and deflate as if sucked in by hot-air vents, and this lubricating membrane will continue to float in the air, this lubricating caustic membrane, this double-thick, many-leveled membrane of infinite crevices, this melancholy and vitreous membrane, but so sensitive, so pertinent itself, so capable of multiplying, dividing, turning with a flash of crevices, senses, drugs, penetrating and noxious irrigations,

then all this will be accepted,

and I shall have no further need to speak.

—HELEN WEAVER

## MANIFESTO IN CLEAR LANGUAGE

*for Roger Vitrac*

If I believe neither in Evil nor in Good, if I feel such a strong inclination to destroy, if there is nothing in the order of principles to which I can reasonably accede, the underlying reason is in my flesh.

I destroy because for me everything that proceeds from reason is untrustworthy. I believe only in the evidence of what stirs my marrow, not in the evidence of what addresses itself to my reason. I have found levels in the realm of the nerve. I now feel capable of evaluating the evidence. There is for me an evidence in the realm of pure flesh which has nothing to do with the evidence of reason. The eternal conflict between reason and the heart is decided in my very flesh, but in my flesh irrigated by nerves. In the realm of the affective imponderable, the image provided by my nerves takes the form of the highest intellectuality, which I refuse to strip of its quality of intellectuality. And so it is that I watch the formation of a concept which carries within it the actual fulguration of things, a concept which arrives upon me with a sound of creation. No image satisfies me unless it is at the same time *Knowledge,* unless it carries with it its substance as well as its lucidity. My mind, exhausted by discursive reason, wants to be caught up in the wheels of a new, an absolute gravitation. For me it is like a supreme reorganization in which only the laws of Illogic participate, and in which there triumphs the discovery of a new Meaning. This Meaning which has been lost in the disorder of drugs and which presents the appearance of a profound intelligence to the contradictory phantasms of sleep. This Meaning is a victory of the mind over itself, and although it is irreducible by reason, it exists, but only *inside the mind.* It is order, it is intelligence, it is the signification of chaos. But it does not accept

l'accepte pas tel quel, il l'interprète, et comme il l'interprète, il le perd. Il est la logique de l'Illogique. Et c'est tout dire. Ma déraison lucide ne redoute pas le chaos.

Je ne renonce à rien de ce qui est l'Esprit. Je veux seulement transporter mon esprit ailleurs avec ses lois et ses organes. Je ne me livre pas à l'automatisme sexuel de l'esprit, mais au contraire dans cet automatisme je cherche à isoler les découvertes que la raison claire ne me donne pas. Je me livre à la fièvre des rêves, mais c'est pour en retirer de nouvelles lois. Je recherche la multiplication, la finesse, l'œil intellectuel dans le délire, non la vaticination hasardée. Il y a un couteau que je n'oublie pas.

Mais c'est un couteau à mi-chemin dans les rêves, et que je maintiens au dedans de moi-même, que je ne laisse pas venir à la frontière des sens clairs.

Ce qui est du domaine de l'image est irréductible par la raison et doit demeurer dans l'image sous peine de s'annihiler.

Mais toutefois il y a une raison dans les images, il y a des images plus claires dans le monde de la vitalité imagée.

Il y a dans le grouillement immédiat de l'esprit une insertion multiforme et brillante de bêtes. Ce poudroiement insensible et *pensant* s'ordonne suivant des lois qu'il tire de l'intérieur de lui-même, en marge de la raison claire et de la conscience ou raison *traversée*.

Dans le domaine surélevé des images l'illusion proprement dite, l'erreur matérielle, n'existe pas, à plus forte raison l'illusion de la connaissance; mais à plus forte raison encore le sens d'une nouvelle connaissance peut et doit descendre dans la réalité de la vie.

La vérité de la vie est dans l'impulsivité de la matière. L'esprit de l'homme est malade au milieu des concepts. Ne lui demandez pas de se satisfaire, demandez-lui seulement d'être calme, de croire qu'il a bien trouvé sa place. Mais seul le Fou est bien calme.

## CORRESPONDANCE DE LA MOMIE

Cette chair qui ne se touche plus dans la vie,
  cette langue qui n'arrive plus à dépasser son écorce,
  cette voix qui ne passe plus par les routes du son,
  cette main qui a oublié plus que le geste de prendre, qui n'arrive plus à déterminer l'espace où elle réalisera sa préhension,

this chaos as such, it interprets it, and because it interprets it, it loses it. It is the logic of Illogic. And this is all one can say. My lucid unreason is not afraid of chaos.

I renounce nothing of that which is the Mind. I want only to transport my mind elsewhere with its laws and its organs. I do not surrender myself to the sexual mechanism of the mind, but on the contrary within this mechanism I seek to isolate those discoveries which lucid reason does not provide. I surrender to the fever of dreams, but only in order to derive from them new laws. I seek multiplication, subtlety, the intellectual eye in delirium, not rash vaticination. There is a knife which I do not forget.

But it is a knife which is halfway into dreams, which I keep inside myself, which I do not allow to come to the frontier of the lucid senses.

That which belongs to the realm of the image is irreducible by reason and must remain within the image or be annihilated.

Nevertheless, there is a reason in images, there are images which are clearer in the world of image-filled vitality.

There is in the immediate teeming of the mind a multiform and dazzling insinuation of animals. This insensible and *thinking* dust is organized according to laws which it derives from within itself, outside the domain of clear reason or of *thwarted* consciousness or reason.

In the exalted realm of images, illusion properly speaking, or material error, does not exist, much less the illusion of knowledge; but this is all the more reason why the meaning of a new knowledge can and must descend into the reality of life.

The truth of life lies in the impulsiveness of matter. The mind of man has been poisoned by concepts. Do not ask him to be content, ask him only to be calm, to believe that he has found his place. But only the Madman is really calm.

—HELEN WEAVER

## CORRESPONDENCE OF THE MUMMY

This flesh no longer joined in life,
   this tongue that can no longer pass beyond its husk,
   this voice no longer keeping to the paths of sound,
   this hand that has forgotten more than the gesture of taking, and can no longer decide in which space it will achieve its grip,

cette cervelle enfin où la conception ne se détermine plus dans ses lignes, tout cela qui fait ma momie de chair fraîche donne à dieu une idée du vide où la nécessité d'être né m'a placé.

Ni ma vie n'est complète, ni ma mort n'est absolument avortée.

Physiquement je ne suis pas, de par ma chair massacrée, incomplète, qui n'arrive plus à nourrir ma pensée.

Spirituellement je me détruis moi-même, je ne m'accepte plus vivant. Ma sensibilité est au ras des pierres, et peu s'en faut qu'il n'en sorte des vers, la vermine des chantiers délaissés.

Mais cette mort est beaucoup plus raffinée, cette mort multipliée de moi-même est dans une sorte de raréfaction de ma chair. L'intelligence n'a plus de sang. La seiche des cauchemars donne toute son encre qui engorge les issues de l'esprit, c'est un sang qui a perdu jusqu'à ses veines, une viande qui ignore le tranchant du couteau.

Mais du haut en bas de cette chair ravinée, de cette chair non compacte circule toujours le feu virtuel. Une lucidité allume d'heure en heure ses braises, qui rejoignent la vie et ses fleurs.

Tout ce qui a un nom sous la voûte compacte du ciel, tout ce qui a un front, —ce qui est le nœud d'un souffle et la corde d'un frémissement, tout cela passe dans les girations de ce feu où se rebroussent les vagues de la chair même, de cette chair dure et molle et qui un jour monte comme le déluge d'un sang.

L'avez-vous vue la momie figée dans l'intersection des phénomènes, cette ignorante, cette vivante momie qui ignore tout des frontières de son vide, qui s'épouvante des pulsations de sa mort.

La momie volontaire est levée, et autour d'elle toute réalité bouge. Et la conscience, comme un brandon de discorde, parcourt le champ entier de sa virtualité obligée.

Il y a dans cette momie une perte de chair, il y a dans le sombre parler de sa chair intellectuelle tout un impouvoir à conjurer cette chair. Ce sens qui court dans les veines de cette viande mystique, dont chaque soubresaut est une manière de monde, et un autre genre d'enfantement, se perd et se dévore lui-même dans la brûlure d'un néant erroné.

Ah! être le père nourricier de ce soupçon, le multiplicateur de cet enfantement et de ce monde dans ses déduits, dans ses conséquences de fleur.

Mais toute cette chair n'est que commencements et qu'absences, et qu'absences, et qu'absences . . .

                                                        Absences.

this brain, at last, where thought can no longer clarify itself in its lines,

all these things which compose my mummy of live flesh give god a notion of the vacuum into which the need to be born has plunged me.

My life is not complete, my death not absolutely aborted.

Physically I do not exist, for my massacred, uncompleted body can no longer feed my thought.

Spiritually I destroy myself, I cannot accept myself alive. My sensibility is on a level with stones; a little more and there'll be worms coming out of it, the vermin of abandoned worksites.

But this death is much more refined; this magnified death of mine exists in a kind of rarefaction of my flesh. Intelligence now is bloodless. The cuttlefish of nightmares gives out all its ink, stuffing the outlets of the spirit; it is a blood that has lost everything, even its veins, a meat that knows nothing of the knife's sharp edge.

But from top to bottom of this gullied, loosened flesh, the potential fire still runs. From hour to hour a lucidity glows in its coals, reaching back toward life and the flowers of life.

All things named under the compact vault of the sky, all things having a brain—the knot of a breath and the cord of a quivering—all those things are dissolved in the whirling circles of this fire where even the waves of the flesh have been curled up: flesh, hard and soft, rising one day like some blood's deluge.

Have you seen that mummy frozen at the meeting point of these phenomena: that ignorant, living mummy, knowing nothing of the frontiers of its emptiness, terrified by the pulsing of its death.

The voluntary mummy is awake, and around it all reality moves. And consciousness, like a torch of discord, runs over the entire field of its required potentiality.

There is a loss of flesh in this mummy; in the dark speech of its mindly flesh, there is an incapacity to do away with this flesh. The meaning that flows in the veins of this mystical meat whose every jolt is a manner of world, and a new sort of birthgiving, loses and devours itself in the burn of an erroneous vacuum.

Ah! to be fosterfather to this suspicion, multiplier of this birthgiving, of this world in all its diversions, and its flowerly consequences.

But all this flesh is only beginnings, and absences, absences, absences . . .

Absences.

—PAUL ZWEIG

## CHANSON DE LA SÉCHERESSE

Va-t-il pleuvoir ciel de pendu
s'il pleut je mangerai du cresson
s'il ne pleut pas de la langouste

Va-t-il pleuvoir ciel de voyou
s'il pleut tu auras des frites
s'il ne pleut pas la prison

Va-t-il pleuvoir ciel d'andouille
s'il pleut tu auras un oignon
s'il ne pleut pas du vinaigre

Va-t-il pleuvoir ciel de gendarme
s'il pleut tu auras un âne
s'il ne pleut pas un putois

Va-t-il pleuvoir ciel de cocu
s'il pleut j'aurai ta femme
s'il ne pleut pas tes filles

Va-t-il pleuvoir ciel de curé
s'il pleut tu seras occis
s'il ne pleut pas tu seras brûlé

# Benjamin Péret

## 1899-1959

### SONG IN TIME OF DROUGHT

Sky of a hanged man, is it going to rain?
if it rains I'll eat watercress
unless it rains lobsters

Sky of a heel, is it going to rain?
if it rains you'll have fried potatoes
unless it rains jail

Pigs-gut sky, is it going to rain?
if it rains you'll have an onion
unless it rains vinegar

Policeman sky, is it going to rain?
if it rains you'll have a donkey
unless it rains skunks

Cuckold sky, is it going to rain?
if it rains I'll have a wife
unless it rains your girls

Parson sky, is it going to rain?
if it rains you'll be butchered
if it doesn't rain you'll be burned

Va-t-il pleuvoir ciel d'étable
s'il pleut tu auras des pierres
s'il ne pleut pas des mouches

Va-t-il pleuvoir ciel de sorcière
s'il pleut tu auras un peigne
s'il ne pleut pas une pelle

Va-t-il pleuvoir ciel d'égoût
s'il pleut tu auras un drapeau
s'il ne pleut pas un crucifix

Va-t-il pleuvoir ciel de cendre

## QUATRE À QUATRE

Meurtrie par les grandes grues électriques
la patte de mouche voyage cependant dans mon œil comme nul
    explorateur
Qu'il pleuve des sardines
ou vente à en tirebouchonner le mont Blanc
elle voyage sans se laisser arrêter par la tentation des parapluies fermés
vieux sabres de panoplies
qui ne savent plus que se moucher et éternuer
Se moucher et éternuer
en voilà une vie que n'envieraient pas les carottes à la sauce blanche
ni l'herbe qui pousse entre les pavés bordés de dentellières
sournoises comme un œil derrière un lorgnon
comme un signal de chemin de fer qui passe du rouge au vert
sans plus crier gare
qu'un jardin public où se cache un satyre
Mais la patte de mouche ne demande rien à personne
car les professeurs ne craignent que les escaliers branlants
où le gaz réussit parfois à tuer son ennemi le rat
à coups de pierres comme un flic chassé à courre
et les étoiles qui effraient les poissons rouges
ne sont ni à vendre ni à louer

Stable sky, is it going to rain?
if it rains you'll have stones
unless it rains flies

Sky of a witch, is it going to rain?
if it rains you'll get a comb
if not a shovel

Sewer sky, is it going to rain?
if it rains you'll have a flag
if it doesn't rain a crucifix

Is it going to rain, sky of ashes?

—JAMES LAUGHLIN

## ON ALL FOURS

Wiped out by the hugeness of the big electric crane
the fly's leg nevertheless goes traveling through my eye as no traveler
        ever managed to before
Though it may rain sardines
or blow hard enough to unscrew Mt. Blanc
it travels without stopping to consider the temptation of closed umbrellas
of ancient sabers hung from old suits of armor
which now only know how to blow their noses and sneeze
Sneeze and blow
it's a life no self-respecting carrot in white sauce would envy
nor the grass peeking from in between the pavement-cracks fringed by
        lace-making establishments
sly as an eye behind a pince-nez
as a railway signal which changes from red to green
without announcing a stop at the next station
like a metropolitan park in which a satyr is hiding
But still the fly's leg asks no questions of anyone
because the professors take only the rickety staircase seriously
where the gas at times succeeds in killing its enemy the rat
by throwing stones as if at a fleeing cop
and the stars that terrify goldfish

car à vrai dire ce ne sont pas des étoiles mais des tartes aux abricots
qui ont quitté la boutique du pâtissier
et errent comme un voyageur qui a perdu son train à minuit dans une
    ville déserte aux becs de gaz geignant à cause de leurs vitres cassées
Même si le voyageur rencontre une femme nue marchant sur le bord du
    trottoir
parce qu'entre les maisons et elle passe un troupeau silencieux
de crocodiles épouvantés par le feu de leurs pipes
et cherchant une église avec un large bénitier
même si le voyageur rencontre cette jeune femme
il n'évitera pas l'incendie d'un magasin de confections
d'où s'enfuiront des milliers de puces qui seront tenues pour responsables
    du désastre
mais si le magasin brûle comme une lampe Pigeon
le voyageur se sentira consolé
et attendra
paisiblement
bêtement
amoureusement
courageusement
tristement
ou paresseusement
que sa barbe pousse pour se raser
et se fera une large entaille près de l'oreille
par où sortira prudent et inquiet
un petit lézard de verre
qui ne réussira jamais à retrouver le lézard de son maître
et se perdra dans la cheminée
où l'attendent pour lui faire un mauvais parti
l'épingle à cheveux l'épingle à chapeau l'épingle de cravate l'épingle de
    nourrice
et cette brute de saladier écorné
qui serre déjà les poings

are neither for sale nor for lease
for the truth is they are not even stars but simply apricot tarts
which have forsaken the pastry shop
and now stroll along aimlessly like a traveler who's missed his train at
     midnight
in a deserted town where the gas lamps whine because their glass has all
     been smashed
Even if that same traveler should encounter a naked lady
walking along the furthermost edge of the pavement
because a silent procession is making its way between her and the houses
of old crocodiles terrified by the hellfires rising from their own pipes
each searching for a church with a vast supply of holy water
Even if that same traveler should meet this girl
he won't be able to escape the fumes of a burning candy-store
a million fleas jumping out of it will later be held responsible for the
     disaster
but if the stone burns like a lamp to guide the pigeons home
our traveler will feel consoled
and wait
contented
stupid
passionate
courageous
sad
or somewhat lazy
for his beard to grow long enough to be shaved
leaving a deep gash near the ear
a small troubled and cautious lizard
will creep out of it
which will have no luck at all in finding its master's lizard again
and will lose himself somewhere in the vicinity of the fireplace
There waiting to play a dirty trick on him
are the hair-pin the hat-pin the tie-pin the napkin-ring
and that brute of brutes the broken salad-bowl
clenching its fist

—CHARLES SIMIC & MICHAEL BENEDIKT

# FAIRE DES PIEDS ET DES MAINS

L'œil levé l'œil couché l'œil assis

Pourquoi s'égarer entre deux haies de rampes d'escalier
pendant que les échelles s'assoupissent
comme des nouveau-nés
comme les zouaves qui perdent leur patrie avec leurs chaussures
Pourquoi lever les bras au ciel
puisque le ciel s'est noyé
sans rime ni raison
pour passer le temps et faire pousser ses moustaches
Pourquoi mon œil s'assied-il avant de se coucher
parce que les bâts blessent les ânes
et que les crayons se brisent de la plus imprévisible façon
par tous les temps
à l'exception des jours d'orage
où ils se brisent en zigzags
et des jours de neige
où ils déchirent leur chandail
Mais les lunettes les vieilles lunettes débolies
chantent en cueillant du chiendent pour les chats
Les chats suivent la troupe
en portant des drapeaux
des drapeaux et des insignes
L'arête de poisson qui traverse un cœur battant
la gorge qui se soulève régulièrement pour imiter la mer qui l'entoure
et le poisson qui tourne autour d'un ventilateur
Il y a aussi des mains
de longues mains blanches avec des ongles de verdure fraîche
et des phalanges de rosée
des cils oscillants que contemplent des papillons
mélancoliques parce que le jour a fait un faux-pas dans l'escalier
Il y a aussi des sexes frais comme une eau vive
et qui bondissent dans la vallée
parce que le soleil les touche
Ils n'ont pas de barbe mais des yeux clairs
et poursuivent les libellules
sans se soucier du qu'en dira-t-on

# MAKING FEET AND HANDS

Eye standing up eye lying down eye sitting

Why wander about between two hedges of stair-rails
while the ladders become soft
as new-born babes
as zouaves who lose their homeland with their shoes
Why raise one's arms towards the sky
since the sky has drowned itself
without rhyme or reason
to pass the time and make its moustaches grow
Why does my eye sit down before going to bed
because saddles are making donkeys sore
and pencils break in the most unpredictable fashion
the whole time
except on stormy days
when they break into zigzags
and snowy days
when they tear their sweaters to pieces
But the spectacles the old tarnished spectacles
sing songs while gathering grass for cats
The cats follow the procession
carrying flags
flags and ensigns
The fish's tail crossing a beating heart
the throat regularly rising and falling to imitate the sea surrounding it
and the fish revolving about a ventilator
There are also hands
long white hands with nails of fresh greenery
and finger-joints of dew
swaying eyelashes looking at butterflies
saddened because the day made a mistake on the stairs
There are also sexes fresh as running water
which leap up and down in the valley
because they are touched by the sun
They have no beards but they have clear eyes
and they chase dragonflies
without caring what people will say

—DAVID GASCOYNE

## LOUIS XVI S'EN VA
## À LA GUILLOTINE

Pue pue pue
Qu'est-ce qui pue
C'est Louis XVI l'œuf mal couvé
et sa tête tombe dans le panier
sa tête pourrie
parce qu'il fait froid le 21 janvier
Il pleut du sang de la neige
et toutes sortes de saletés
qui jaillissent de sa vieille carcasse
de chien crevé au fond d'une lessiveuse
au milieu du linge sale
qui a eu le temps de pourrir
comme la fleur de lis des poubelles
que les vaches refusent de brouter
parce qu'elle répand une odeur de dieu
dieu le père des boues
qui a donné à Louis XVI
le droit divin de crever
comme un chien dans une lessiveuse

## LOUIS XVI GOES
## TO THE GUILLOTINE

Stink stink stink
What's that stink
It's Louis XVI that bad egg
and his head drops into the basket
his rotten head
since the cold is terrific this 21st of January
It rains blood it rains snow
and all sorts of other filth
that flourishes out of his ancient corpse
like a dog croaked on the bottom of a pail
in the midst of dirty laundry
who has had plenty of time to start decomposing
like the fleur-de-lys on the garbage can
which the cows refuse to nibble
for they give off an odor of true divinity
god the father of all mud
who gave to Louis XVI
the divine right to croak
like a dog in a laundry-pail

—CHARLES SIMIC

## J'AI TANT RÊVÉ DE TOI

J'ai tant rêvé de toi que tu perds ta réalité.

Est-il encore temps d'atteindre ce corps vivant et de baiser sur cette bouche la naissance de la voix qui m'est chère?

J'ai tant rêvé de toi que mes bras habitués, en étreignant ton ombre, à se croiser sur ma poitrine ne se plieraient pas au contour de ton corps, peut-être.

Et que, devant l'apparence réelle de ce qui me hante et me gouverne depuis des jours et des années, je deviendrais une ombre sans doute.

O balances sentimentales.

J'ai tant rêvé de toi qu'il n'est plus temps sans doute que je m'éveille. Je dors debout, le corps exposé à toutes les apparences de la vie et de l'amour et toi, la seule qui compte aujourd'hui pour moi, je pourrais moins toucher ton front et tes lèvres que les premières lèvres et le premier front venus.

J'ai tant rêvé de toi, tant marché, parlé, couché avec ton fantôme qu'il ne me reste plus peut-être, et pourtant, qu'à être fantôme parmi les fantômes et plus ombre cent fois que l'ombre qui se promène et se promènera allégrement sur le cadran solaire de ta vie.

# Robert Desnos

## 1900-1945

---

### I HAVE DREAMED OF YOU SO MUCH

I have dreamed of you so much that you are no longer real.

Is there still time for me to reach your breathing body, to kiss your mouth and make your dear voice come alive again?

I have dreamed of you so much that my arms, grown used to being crossed on my chest as I hugged your shadow, would perhaps not bend to the shape of your body.

For faced with the real form of what has haunted me and governed me for so many days and years, I would surely become a shadow.

O scales of feeling.

I have dreamed of you so much that surely there is no more time for me to wake up. I sleep on my feet, prey to all the forms of life and love, and you, the only one who counts for me today, I can no more touch your face and lips than touch the lips and face of some passerby.

I have dreamed of you so much, have walked so much, talked so much, slept so much with your phantom, that perhaps the only thing left for me is to become a phantom among phantoms, a shadow a hundred times more shadow than the shadow that moves and goes on moving, brightly, over the sundial of your life.

—PAUL AUSTER

# NON, L'AMOUR N'EST PAS MORT

Non, l'amour n'est pas mort en ce cœur et ces yeux et cette bouche qui proclamait ses funérailles commencées.

Écoutez, j'en ai assez du pittoresque et des couleurs et du charme.

J'aime l'amour, sa tendresse et sa cruauté.

Mon amour n'a qu'un seul nom, qu'une seule forme.

Tout passe. Des bouches se collent à cette bouche.

Mon amour n'a qu'un nom, qu'une forme.

Et si quelque jour tu t'en souviens

O toi, forme et nom de mon amour,

Un jour sur la mer entre l'Amérique et l'Europe,

A l'heure où le rayon final du soleil se réverbère sur la surface ondulée des vagues, ou bien une nuit d'orage sous un arbre dans la campagne, ou dans une rapide automobile,

Un matin de printemps boulevard Malesherbes,

Un jour de pluie,

A l'aube avant de te coucher,

Dis-toi, je l'ordonne à ton fantôme familier, que je fus seul à t'aimer davantage et qu'il est dommage que tu ne l'aies pas connu.

Dis-toi qu'il ne faut pas regretter les choses; Ronsard avant moi et Baudelaire ont chanté le regret des vieilles et des mortes qui méprisèrent le plus pur amour.

Toi, quand tu seras morte,

Tu seras belle et toujours désirable.

Je serai mort déjà, enclos tout entier en ton corps immortel, en ton image étonnante présente à jamais parmi les merveilles perpétuelles de la vie et de l'éternité, mais si je vis

Ta voix et son accent, ton regard et ses rayons,

L'odeur de toi et celle de tes cheveux et beaucoup d'autres choses encore vivront en moi,

En moi qui ne suis ni Ronsard ni Baudelaire,

Moi qui suis Robert Desnos et qui, pour t'avoir connue et aimée,

Les vaux bien

Moi qui suis Robert Desnos, pour t'aimer

Et qui ne veux pas attacher d'autre réputation à ma mémoire sur la terre méprisable.

# NO, LOVE IS NOT DEAD

No, love is not dead in this heart and these eyes and this mouth that proclaimed the beginning of its own requiem.

Listen, I've had enough of the picturesque, of colors and charm.

I love love, its tenderness and its cruelty.

The one I love has only a single name, a single form.

Everything goes. Mouths cling to this mouth.

The one I love has only one name, one form.

And some day if you remember it

O you, form and name of my love,

One day on the sea between America and Europe,

When the last ray of sun flashes on the undulating surface of the waves, or else one stormy night beneath a tree in the country, or in a speeding car,

One spring morning Boulevard Malesherbes,

One rainy day,

At dawn before putting yourself to bed,

Tell yourself, I summon your familiar ghost, that I was the only one to love you more and what a pity it is you didn't know it.

Tell yourself you shouldn't be sorry for anything: before me Ronsard and Baudelaire sang the sorrows of old women and dead women who despised the purest love.

You, when you die,

You will still be beautiful and desirable.

I'll already be dead, completely enclosed in your immortal body, in your astonishing image present forever among the perpetual wonders of life and eternity, but if I outlive you

Your voice and how it sounds, your gaze and how it shines,

The smell of you and of your hair and many other things will still go on living in me,

In me, and I'm no Ronsard or Baudelaire,

Just me Robert Desnos who, for having known and loved you,

Is as good as they are.

Just me Robert Desnos who, for loving you

Doesn't want to be remembered for anything else on this despicable earth.

—BILL ZAVATSKY

## LA VOIX DE ROBERT DESNOS

Si semblable à la fleur et au courant d'air
au cours d'eau aux ombres passagères
au sourire entrevu ce fameux soir à minuit
si semblable à tout au bonheur et à la tristesse
c'est le minuit passé dressant son torse nu au-dessus des beffrois et des
    peupliers
j'appelle à moi ceux-là perdus dans les campagnes
les vieux cadavres les jeunes chênes coupés
les lambeaux d'étoffe pourrissant sur la terre et le linge séchant aux
    alentours des fermes
j'appelle à moi les tornades et les ouragans
les tempêtes les typhons les cyclones
les raz de marée
les tremblements de terre
j'appelle à moi la fumée des volcans et celle des cigarettes
les ronds de fumée des cigares de luxe
j'appelle à moi les amours et les amoureux
j'appelle à moi les vivants et les morts
j'appelle les fossoyeurs j'appelle les assassins
j'appelle les bourreaux j'appelle les pilotes les maçons et les architectes
les assassins
j'appelle la chair
j'appelle celle que j'aime
j'appelle celle que j'aime
j'appelle celle que j'aime
le minuit triomphant déploie ses ailes de satin et se pose sur mon lit
les beffrois et les peupliers se plient à mon désir
ceux-là s'écroulent ceux-là s'affaissent
les perdus dans la campagne se retrouvent en me trouvant
les vieux cadavres ressuscitent à ma voix
les jeunes chênes coupés se couvrent de verdure
les lambeaux d'étoffe pourrissant dans la terre et sur la terre
claquent à ma voix comme l'étendard de la révolte
le linge séchant aux alentours des fermes habille d'adorables femmes que je
    n'adore pas
qui viennent à moi
obéissent à ma voix et m'adorent
les tornades tournent dans ma bouche
les ouragans rougissent s'il est possible mes lèvres
les tempêtes grondent à mes pieds
les typhons s'il est possible me dépeignent
je reçois les baisers d'ivresse des cyclones

# THE VOICE OF ROBERT DESNOS

So much like the flower and the current of air
like the waterway like the shadows passing everywhere
like the smile glimpsed this amazing evening at midnight
so much like everything happiness and sadness
it's yesterday's midnight lifting its naked torso above belfries and poplars
I'm calling those lost in the countryside
the old corpses the young oaks just cut down
the shreds of fabric rotting on the ground and linen drying in the
    farmyards
I'm calling tornadoes and hurricanes
tempests typhoons and cyclones
riptides
earthquakes
I'm calling the smoke of volcanoes and cigarettes
the smoke rings of fancy cigars
I'm calling loves and lovers
I'm calling the living and the dead
I'm calling the gravediggers I'm calling the murderers
I'm calling the executioners I'm calling the pilots the masons the
    architects
the murderers
I'm calling the flesh
I'm calling the one I love
I'm calling the one I love
I'm calling the one I love
triumphant midnight unfolds its satin wings and lands on my bed
belfries and poplars give in to my desires
those over there collapse and those fall back
those lost in the countryside find their bearings in finding me
the old corpses come back to life at my voice
the young oaks just cut down wrap themselves in greenery
the shreds of fabric rotting in the ground and on the ground
flap at my voice like the flag of rebellion
the linen drying in the farmyards clothes adorable women that I don't
    adore
who come to me
obey my voice and adore me
the tornadoes spin around in my mouth
the hurricanes redden my lips if they can do it
the tempests snarl at my feet
the typhoons rumple my hair if they can do it
I accept the kisses of cyclone drunkenness

les raz de marée viennent mourir à mes pieds
les tremblements de terre ne m'ébranlent pas mais font tout crouler à mon
    ordre
la fumée des volcans me vêt de ses vapeurs
et celle des cigarettes me parfume
et les ronds de fumée des cigares me couronnent
les amours et l'amour si longtemps poursuivis se réfugient en moi
les amoureux écoutent ma voix
les vivants et les morts se soumettent et me saluent
les premiers froidement les seconds familièrement
les fossoyeurs abandonnent les tombes à peine creusées et déclarent que
    moi seul puis commander leurs nocturnes travaux
les assassins me saluent
les bourreaux invoquent la révolution
invoquent ma voix
invoquent mon nom
les pilotes se guident sur mes yeux
les maçons ont le vertige en m'écoutant
les architectes partent pour le désert
les assassins me bénissent
la chair palpite à mon appel

celle que j'aime ne m'écoute pas
celle que j'aime ne m'entend pas
celle que j'aime ne me répond pas.


## MI-ROUTE

Il y a un moment précis dans le temps
Où l'homme atteint le milieu exact de sa vie,
Un fragment de seconde,
Une fugitive parcelle de temps plus rapide qu'un regard,
Plus rapide que le sommet des pâmoisons amoureuses,
Plus rapide que la lumière.
Et l'homme est sensible à ce moment.

De longues avenues entre des frondaisons
S'allongent vers la tour où sommeille une dame

the riptides come to die at my feet
the earthquakes don't shake me but make everything totter at my
     command
the smoke of volcanoes attires me in its vapors
and cigarette smoke perfumes me
and the smoke rings of fancy cigars crown me
the loved ones and the love pursued for so long find shelter in me
the lovers hear my voice
the living and the dead give in and wave to me
the former coolly the latter intimately
the gravediggers abandon partly dug graves and announce that I am the
     only one who can direct their nighttime labors
the murderers greet me
the executioners invoke the revolution
invoke my voice
invoke my name
the pilots use my eyes to navigate
the masons are seized with vertigo hearing me
the architects leave for the desert
the murderers bless me
the flesh quivers at my call

the one I love does not listen to me
the one I love does not hear me
the one I love does not answer me

—BILL ZAVATSKY

MIDWAY

There is a precise instant in time
When a man reaches the exact center of his life,
A fraction of a second,
A fugitive particle of time quicker than a glance,
More fleeting than lovers' bliss,
Faster than light,
And a man is awake to this moment.

Long roads strain thru green wreathes
to reach the tower where a Lady drowses

Dont la beauté résiste aux baisers, aux saisons,
Comme une étoile au vent, comme un rocher aux lames.

Un bateau frémissant s'enfonce et gueule.
Au sommet d'un arbre claque un drapeau.
Une femme bien peignée, mais dont les bas tombent sur les souliers
Apparaît au coin d'une rue,
Exaltée, frémissante,
Protégeant de sa main une lampe surannée et qui fume.

Et encore un débardeur ivre chante au coin d'un pont,
Et encore une amante mord les lèvres de son amant,
Et encore un pétale de rose tombe sur un lit vide,
Et encore trois pendules sonnent la même heure
A quelques minutes d'intervalle,
Et encore un homme qui passe dans une rue se retourne
Parce que l'on a crié son prénom,
Mais ce n'est pas lui que cette femme appelle,
Et encore, un ministre en grande tenue,
Désagréablement gêné par le pan de sa chemise coincé entre son pantalon
    et son caleçon,
Inaugure un orphelinat,
Et encore d'un camion lancé à toute vitesse
Dans les rues vides de la nuit
Tombe une tomate merveilleuse qui roule dans le ruisseau
Et qui sera balayée plus tard,
Et encore un incendie s'allume au sixième étage d'une maison
Qui flambe au cœur de la ville silencieuse et indifférente,
Et encore un homme entend une chanson
Oubliée depuis longtemps, et l'oubliera de nouveau,
Et encore maintes choses,
Maintes autres choses que l'homme voit à l'instant précis du milieu de sa
    vie,
Maintes autres choses se déroulent longuement dans le plus court des
    courts instants de la terre.
Il pressent le mystère de cette seconde, de ce fragment de seconde,

Mais il dit « Chassons ces idées noires »,
Et il chasse ces idées noires.
Et que pourrait-il dire,
Et que pourrait-il faire
De mieux?

Whose beauty defies all kisses, seasons,
As a star against wind, a stone against knives.

A shimmering boat sinks and shrieks.
At the top of a tree a flag flaps.
A woman—her hair stylish and stockings loose at the ankles—
Shows up at the corner
Impassioned, shimmering,
Her hand shielding an antiquated lamp billowing smoke.

And again a drunken dock-worker sings on a bridge,
And again a girl bites her lover's lips,
And again a rose-petal falls in an empty bed,
And again three clocks strike the same hour
A few minutes apart,
And again a man walking down the street turns back
Hearing his name called,
But it's not him she's calling,
And again a cabinet minister in full dress,
Irked by his shirt-tail caught between his trousers and his shorts,
Inaugurates an orphanage,
And again a truck barrelling flat-out
Thru empty streets at night
Drops a marvellous tomato that rolls in the gutter
To be swept away later,
And again a fire breaks out on the sixth floor of a building
Flaming in the heart of a silent, indifferent city,
And again a man hears a song—
Long forgotten—and soon to be forgotten all over,
And again many things,
Many other things that a man sees at the precise instant of the center of
    his life,
Many other things unfold at length in the shortest of earth's short
    instants.
He squeezes the mystery of this second, this fraction of a second,

But he says, "Get rid of these dark thoughts,"
And he gets rid of these dark thoughts.
And what could he say,
And what could he do
That's any better?

—GEORGE QUASHA

# COUCOU

Tout était comme dans une image enfantine.
La lune avait un chapeau claque dont les huit reflets se répercutaient à la
    surface des étangs,
Un revenant dans un linceul de la meilleure coupe
Fumait un cigare à la fenêtre de son logis,
Au dernier étage d'un donjon
Où la très savante corneille disait la bonne aventure aux chats.
Il y avait l'enfant en chemise perdue dans des sentiers de neige
Pour avoir cherché dans ses souliers l'éventail de soie et les chaussures à
    hauts talons,
Il y avait l'incendie sur lequel, immenses,
Se détachaient les ombres des pompiers,
Mais, surtout, il y avait le voleur courant, un grand sac sur le dos,
Sur la route blanchie par la lune,
Escorté par les abois des chiens dans les villages endormis
Et le caquet des poules éveillées en sursaut.
Je ne suis pas riche, dit le fantôme en secouant la cendre de son cigare, je
    ne suis pas riche
Mais je parie cent francs
Qu'il ira loin s'il continue.
Vanité tout n'est que vanité, répondit la corneille.
Et ta sœur? demandèrent les chats.
Ma sœur a de beaux bijoux et de belles araignées
Dans son château de nuit.
Une foule innombrable de serviteurs
Viennent chaque soir la porter dans son lit.
Au réveil, elle a du nanan, du chiendent, et une petite trompette
Pour souffler dedans.
La lune posa son chapeau haut de forme sur la terre.
Et cela fit une nuit épaisse
Où le revenant fondit comme un morceau de sucre dans du café.
Le voleur chercha longtemps son chemin perdu
Et finit par s'endormir
Et il ne resta plus au-delà de la terre
Qu'un ciel bleu fumée où la lune s'épongeait le front
Et l'enfant perdue qui marchait dans les étoiles.
Voici ton bel éventail
Et tes souliers de bal,
Le corset de ta grand-mère
Et du rouge pour tes lèvres.
Tu peux danser parmi les étoiles
Tu peux danser devant les belles dames

CUCKOO

It was all like a childhood picture.
The moon wore an opera hat whose eight glints were reflected on the
surface of ponds.
A ghost in a splendidly cut shroud
Smoked a cigar at the window of his lodging
On the upper story of a dungeon
Where a wise crow told the cats wonderful stories.
The child in pyjamas was lost in the snowy roads
Having searched in her slippers for the silk fan and the high-heeled shoes.
There was a fire on which the immense shadows of firemen stood out in
relief
But above all there was the running burglar, a huge pack on his back,
On the road whitened by the moon
Escorted by the barking of dogs in the sleeping villages
And by the cackle of the hens suddenly awakened.
I'm not rich, says the phantom, shaking the ashes off his cigar, I'm not
rich
But I'll bet a hundred dollars
That he'll go far if he continues.
Vanity, all is vanity, answered the crow.
And your sister? asked the cats.
My sister owns beautiful jewels and lovely spiders
In her nightcastle.
An innumerable crowd of servants
Arrive every night to bear her to bed.
When she gets up she's got goodies and a little trumpet
to blow in.
The moon laid her high hat on the earth
And that created a thick night
Into which the ghost melted like a sugar cube in coffee.
The burglar kept looking for his lost path
And ended up asleep
And beyond the earth
There was nothing but a blue sky smoke where the moon wiped her
forehead
And the lost child who walked in the stars.
Here is your beautiful fan
And your ballroom slippers
Your grandmother's corset
And lipstick.
You can dance among the stars
You can dance in front of the beautiful ladies

A travers les massifs de roses célestes
Dont l'une tombe chaque nuit
Pour récompenser le dormeur qui a fait le plus beau rêve.
Chausse tes souliers et lace ton corset
Mets une de ces roses à ton corsage
Et du rose à tes lèvres
Et maintenant balance ton éventail
Pour qu'il y ait encore sur la terre
Des nuits après les jours
Des jours après les nuits.

## COUCHÉE

A droite, le ciel, à gauche, la mer.
Et devant les yeux, l'herbe et ses fleurs.
Un nuage, c'est la route, suit son chemin vertical
Parallèlement à l'horizon de fil à plomb,
Parallèlement au cavalier.
Le cheval court vers sa chute imminente
Et cet autre monte interminablement.
Comme tout est simple et étrange.
Couchée sur le côté gauche,
Je me désintéresse du paysage
Et je ne pense qu'à des choses très vagues,
Très vagues et très heureuses,
Comme le regard las que l'on promène
Par ce bel après-midi d'été
A droite, à gauche,
De-ci, de-là,
Dans le délire de l'inutile.

Across the clumps of celestial roses
One of which falls every night
To reward the sleeper who's had the most beautiful dream.
Put on your shoes and lace your corset
Make a corsage of one of these roses
And put liprose on
And now balance your fan
So that on earth there again will be
Nights after days
Days after nights

—ARMAND SCHWERNER

## LYING DOWN

To the right, the sky, to the left, the sea.
And before your eyes, the grass and its flowers.
A cloud, the road, follows its vertical way
Parallel to the plumbline of the horizon,
Parallel to the rider.
The horse races toward its imminent fall
And the other climbs interminably.
How simple and strange everything is.
Lying on my left side
I take no interest in the landscape
And I think only of things that are very vague,
Very vague and very pleasant,
Like the tired look you walk around with
Through this beautiful summer afternoon
To the right, to the left,
Here, there,
In the delirium of uselessness.

—BILL ZAVATSKY

## L'ÉPITAPHE

J'ai vécu dans ces temps et depuis mille années
Je suis mort. Je vivais, non déchu mais traqué.
Toute noblesse humaine étant emprisonnée
J'étais libre parmi les esclaves masqués.

J'ai vécu dans ces temps et pourtant j'étais libre.
Je regardais le fleuve et la terre et le ciel,
Tourner autour de moi, garder leur équilibre
Et les saisons fournir leurs oiseaux et leur miel.

Vous qui vivez qu'avez-vous fait de ces fortunes?
Regrettez-vous les temps où je me débattais?
Avez-vous cultivé pour des moissons communes?
Avez-vous enrichi la ville où j'habitais?

Vivants, ne craignez rien de moi, car je suis mort.
Rien ne survit de mon esprit ni de mon corps.

# EPITAPH

I lived in those times. For a thousand years
I have been dead. Not fallen, but hunted;
When all human decency was imprisoned,
I was free amongst the masked slaves.

I lived in those times, yet I was free.
I watched the river, the earth, the sky,
Turning around me, keeping their balance,
The seasons provided their birds and their honey.

You who live, what have you made of your luck?
Do you regret the time when I struggled?
Have you cultivated for the common harvest?
Have you enriched the town I lived in?

Living men, think nothing of me. I am dead.
Nothing survives of my spirit or my body.

—KENNETH REXROTH

## MES OCCUPATIONS

Je peux rarement voir quelqu'un sans le battre. D'autres préfèrent le monologue intérieur. Moi, non. J'aime mieux battre.

Il y a des gens qui s'assoient en face de moi au restaurant et ne disent rien, ils restent un certain temps, car ils ont décidé de manger.

En voici un.

Je te l'agrippe, toc.

Je te le ragrippe, toc.

Je le pends au portemanteau.

Je le décroche.

Je le repends.

Je le redécroche.

Je le mets sur la table, je le tasse et l'étouffe.

Je le salis, je l'inonde.

Il revit.

Je le rince, je l'étire (je commence à m'énerver, il faut en finir), je le masse, je le serre, je le résume et l'introduis dans mon verre, et jette ostensiblement le contenu par terre, et dis au garçon: « Mettez-moi donc un verre plus propre. »

Mais je me sens mal, je règle promptement l'addition et je m'en vais.

# Henri Michaux

1899-

## MY OCCUPATIONS

I can rarely see anyone without fighting him. Others prefer the internal monologue. Not me. I like fighting best.

There are people who sit down in front of me at the restaurant and say nothing, they stay on a while, for they have decided to eat.

Here is one of them.

See how I grab him, boom!

See how I re-grab him, boom!

I hang him on the coat hook.

I unhook him.

I hang him up again.

I re-unhook him.

I put him on the table, I push him together and choke him.

I foul him up, I flood him.

He revives.

I rinse him off, I stretch him out (I'm beginning to get worked up, I must finish off), I bunch him together, I squeeze him, I sum him up and introduce him into my glass, and ostentatiously throw the contents to the ground, and say to the waiter: "Let me have a cleaner glass."

But I feel ill, I pay the check quickly and go off.

—RICHARD ELLMANN

## LA SIMPLICITÉ

Ce qui a manqué surtout à ma vie jusqu'à présent, c'est la simplicité. Je commence à changer petit à petit.

Par exemple, maintenant, je sors toujours avec mon lit, et quand une femme me plaît, je la prends et couche avec aussitôt.

Si ses oreilles sont laides et grandes ou son nez, je les lui enlève avec ses vêtements et les mets sous le lit, qu'elle retrouve en partant; je ne garde que ce qui me plaît.

Si ses dessous gagneraient à être changés, je les change aussitôt. Ce sera mon cadeau. Si cependant je vois une autre femme plus plaisante qui passe, je m'excuse auprès de la première et la fais disparaître immédiatement.

Des personnes qui me connaissent prétendent que je ne suis pas capable de faire ce que je dis là, que je n'ai pas assez de tempérament. Je le croyais aussi, mais cela venait de ce que je ne faisais pas tout *comme il me plaisait*.

Maintenant j'ai toujours de bonnes après-midi. (Le matin, je travaille.)

## INTERVENTION

Autrefois, j'avais trop le respect de la nature. Je me mettais devant les choses et les paysages et je les laissais faire.

Fini, maintenant *j'interviendrai*.

J'étais donc à Honfleur et je m'y ennuyais. Alors résolument j'y mis du chameau. Cela ne paraît pas fort indiqué. N'importe, c'était mon idée. D'ailleurs je la mis à exécution avec la plus grande prudence. Je les introduisis d'abord les jours de grande affluence, le samedi sur la place du Marché. L'encombrement devint indescriptible et les touristes disaient: « Ah! ce que ça pue! Sont-ils sales les gens d'ici!» L'odeur gagna le port et se mit à terrasser celle de la crevette. On sortait de la foule plein de poussières et de poils d'on ne savait quoi.

Et la nuit il fallait entendre les coups de pattes des chameaux quand ils essayaient de franchir les écluses, gong! gong! sur le métal et les madriers!

L'envahissement par les chameaux se fit avec suite et sûreté.

## SIMPLICITY

What has been particularly lacking in my life up to now is simplicity. Little by little I am beginning to change.

For instance, I always go out with my bed now and when a woman pleases me, I take her and go to bed with her immediately.

If her ears are ugly and large, or her nose, I remove them along with her clothes and put them under the bed, for her to take back when she leaves; I keep only what I like.

If her underthings would improve by being changed, I change them immediately. This is my gift. But if I see a better-looking woman go by, I apologize to the first and make her disappear at once.

People who know me claim that I am incapable of doing what I have just described, that I haven't enough spunk. I once thought so myself, but that was because I was not then doing everything *just as I pleased.*

Now I always have excellent afternoons. (Mornings I work.)

—RICHARD ELLMANN

## INTERVENTION

In the old days I had too much respect for nature. I put myself in front of things and landscapes and let them alone.

No more of that, now *I will intervene.*

I was then at Honfleur and was getting bored. So I resolutely brought in some camels there. That didn't seem to be called for. Never mind. It was my idea. Besides, I put it into execution with the greatest prudence. I introduced them first on the days of great crowds, on Saturdays at the market place. The confusion became indescribable and the tourists said: « Oh, how it stinks! How dirty the people here are!» The smell reached the port and began to outdo that of the shrimp. You emerged from the crowd full of dust and the hairs of nobody knew what.

And at night you couldn't help hearing the pounding of camels' feet when they were trying to cross the dikes, gong! gong! on the metal and the joists!

The camel invasion took place with regularity and sureness.

On commençait à voir les Honfleurais loucher à chaque instant avec ce regard soupçonneux spécial aux chameliers, quand ils inspectent leur caravane pour voir si rien ne manque et si on peut continuer à faire route; mais je dus quitter Honfleur le quatrième jour.

J'avais lancé également un train de voyageurs. Il partait à toute allure de la Grand'Place, et résolument s'avançait sur la mer sans s'inquiéter de la lourdeur du matériel; il filait en avant, sauvé par la foi.

Dommage que j'ai dû m'en aller, mais je doute fort que le calme renaisse tout de suite en cette petite ville de pêcheurs de crevettes et de moules.

## L'AVENIR

Quand les mah,
Quand les mah,
Les marécages,
Les malédictions,
Quand les mahahahahas,
Les mahahaborras,
Les mahahamaladihahas,
Les matratrimatratrihahas,
Les hondregordegarderies,
Les honcucarachoncus,
Les hordanoplopais de puru para puru,
Les immoncéphales glossés,
Les poids, les pestes, les putréfactions,
Les nécroses, les carnages, les engloutissements,
Les visqueux, les éteints, les infects,
Quand le miel devenu pierreux,
Les banquises perdant du sang,
Les Juifs affolés rachetant le Christ précipitamment,
L'Acropole, les casernes changées en choux,
Les regards en chauve-souris, ou bien en barbelés, en boîte à clous,
De nouvelles mains en raz de marée,
D'autres vertèbres faites de moulins à vent,
Le jus de la joie se changeant en brûlure,
Les caresses en ravages lancinants, les organes du corps les mieux unis en
     duels au sabre,

You began to see the Honfleurians squint every minute with the suspicious look peculiar to camel-drivers when they are inspecting their caravans to see if anything is missing and if they can proceed; but I had to leave Honfleur on the fourth day.

I had launched in the same way a train of travellers. It left Main Square at full speed, and went resolutely forward along the water without worrying about the heaviness of the material; it sped onwards, saved by faith.

A pity that I had to go away, but I doubt very much that calm will immediately reappear in that little city of shrimp and mussel fishers.

—RICHARD ELLMANN


TOMORROW

when the mar
               when the mar
                             the marshymorasswamps
the maledictions
when the mahahahahas
the mahahatorrors
the mahagonorrhyphilohahas
the matratrimatratrihahas
the rancywitherwatcheries
the bungholecockroachogrebuggers
the carbofecalfungorators of pus-y pissy pus-y
the voyeurisibled putrocephalics
the fat the plagues the maggofactions
the necroses the carnages the engulpings
the viscid the snuffed-out the foul
when the honey become stony
the icebergs leaking blood
the maddened Jews precipitously ransoming Christ
the Acropolis
the barracks turned into cabbages
the glances into bats or mailboxes
fresh hands into eagres
other vertebrae made of windmills
joyjuice shifting to burns
caresses into twinging ravages

Le sable à la caresse rousse se retournant en plomb sur tous les amateurs
de plage,
Les langues tièdes, promeneuses passionnées, se changeant soit en
couteaux, soit en durs cailloux,
Le bruit exquis des rivières qui coulent se changeant en forêts de
perroquets et de marteaux-pilons,
Quand l'*Épouvantable-Implacable* se débondant enfin,
Assoira ses mille fesses infectes sur ce Monde fermé, centré, et comme
pendu au clou,
Tournant, tournant sur lui-même sans jamais arriver à s'échapper,
Quand, dernier rameau de l'Être, la souffrance pointe atroce, survivra
seule, croissant en délicatesse,
De plus en plus aiguë et intolérable . . . et le Néant têtu tout autour qui
recule comme la panique . . .
Oh! Malheur! Malheur!
Oh! Dernier souvenir, petite vie de chaque homme, petite vie de chaque
animal, petites vies punctiformes!
Plus jamais.
Oh! Vide!
Oh! Espace! Espace non stratifié . . . Oh! Espace, Espace!

the best articulated organs into saberduels
the sand with its russet caress into lead to crush sunbathers
the tepid tongues, passionate promenaders, changing themselves into
    knives or rocks
the exquisite sound of coursing rivers into forests of parrots or piledrivers
when the *Implacable-Indescribable* will sit his 1000 foetid buttocks on this
              closed
              concentred
              nailhung
                    World
  turning, turning in
        upon himself without hope of escape
when anguish, last
        twig of Being, atrocious point,
        will alone survive, growing in fragility,
        sharper and increasingly intolerable
                       and the
        obdurate Nothing all around
        drawing back like panic
        Oh


              Misery

        oh
final memory
        minute life of each man
        tiny life of every animal
                  little
        punctiform
        lives

never again

        Oh        emptiness
        space, unstratified

                space

        Space

        Space

—ARMAND SCHWERNER

## REPOS DANS LE MALHEUR

Le Malheur, mon grand laboureur,
Le Malheur, assois-toi,
Repose-toi,
Reposons-nous un peu toi et moi,
Repose,
Tu me trouves, tu m'éprouves, tu me le prouves.
Je suis ta ruine.

Mon grand théâtre, mon havre, mon âtre.
Ma cave d'or.
Mon avenir, ma vraie mère, mon horizon.
Dans ta lumière, dans ton ampleur, dans mon horreur,
Je m'abandonne.

## << JE VOUS ÉCRIS D'UN PAYS LOINTAIN >>

I

Nous n'avons ici, dit-elle, qu'un soleil par mois, et pour peu de temps. On se frotte les yeux des jours à l'avance. Mais en vain. Temps inexorable. Soleil n'arrive qu'à son heure.

Ensuite on a un monde de choses à faire, tant qu'il y a de la clarté, si bien qu'on a à peine le temps de se regarder un peu.

La contrariété, pour nous, dans la nuit, c'est quand il faut travailler, et il le faut: il naît des nains continuellement.

II

Quand on marche dans la campagne, lui confie-t-elle encore, il arrive que l'on rencontre sur son chemin des masses considérables. Ce sont des montagnes, et il faut tôt ou tard se mettre à plier les genoux. Rien ne sert de résister, on ne pourrait plus avancer, même en se faisant du mal.

Ce n'est pas pour blesser que je le dis. Je pourrais dire d'autres choses, si je voulais vraiment blesser.

# REPOSE IN CALAMITY

Calamity, my great laborer,
Sit down, Calamity,
Take it easy,
Let's take it easy for a minute, both of us,
Easy.
You find me, you get the hang of me, you try me out,
I'm the ruin of you.

My big theater, my harbor, my hearth,
My golden cave,
My future, my real mother, my horizon,
In your light, in your great spaces, in your horror,
I let myself go.

—W. S. MERWIN

# "I AM WRITING TO YOU FROM A FAR-OFF COUNTRY"

I

We have here, she said, only one sun in the month, and for only a little while. We rub our eyes days ahead. But to no purpose. Inexorable weather. Sunlight arrives only at its proper hour.

Then we have a world of things to do, so long as there is light, in fact we hardly have time to look at one another a bit.

The trouble is that nighttime is when we must work, and we really must: dwarfs are born constantly.

II

When you walk in the country, she further confided to him, you may chance to meet with substantial masses on your road. These are mountains and sooner or later you must bend the knee to them. Resisting will do no good, you could go no farther, even by hurting yourself.

I do not say this in order to wound. I could say other things if I really wanted to wound.

III

L'aurore est grise ici, lui dit-elle encore. Il n'en fut pas toujours ainsi. Nous ne savons qui accuser.

Dans la nuit le bétail pousse de grands mugissements, longs et flûtés pour finir. On a de la compassion, mais que faire?

L'odeur des eucalyptus nous entoure: bienfait, sérénité, mais elle ne peut préserver de tout, ou bien pensez-vous qu'elle puisse réellement préserver de tout?

IV

Je vous ajoute encore un mot, une question plutôt.

Est-ce que l'eau coule aussi dans votre pays? (je ne me souviens pas si vous me l'avez dit) et elle donne aussi des frissons, si c'est bien elle.

Est-ce que je l'aime? Je ne sais. On se sent si seule dedans, quand elle est froide. C'est tout autre chose quand elle est chaude. Alors? Comment juger? Comment jugez-vous, vous autres, dites-moi, quand vous parlez d'elle sans déguisement, à cœur ouvert?

V

Je vous écris du bout du monde. Il faut que vous le sachiez. Souvent les arbres tremblent. On recueille les feuilles. Elles ont un nombre fou de ner-vures. Mais à quoi bon? Plus rien entre elles et l'arbre, et nous nous dispersons, gênées.

Est-ce que la vie sur terre ne pourrait pas se poursuivre sans vent? Ou faut-il que tout tremble, toujours, toujours?

Il y a aussi des remuements souterrains, et dans la maison comme des colères qui viendraient au-devant de vous, comme des êtres sévères qui voudraient arracher des confessions.

On ne voit rien, que ce qu'il importe si peu de voir. Rien, et cependant on tremble. Pourquoi?

VI

Nous vivons toutes ici la gorge serrée. Savez-vous que, quoique très jeune, autrefois j'étais plus jeune encore, et mes compagnes pareillement. Qu'est-ce que cela signifie? Il y a là, sûrement, quelque chose d'affreux.

Et autrefois quand, comme je vous l'ai déjà dit, nous étions encore plus jeunes, nous avions peur. On eût profité de notre confusion. On nous eût dit: « Voilà, on vous enterre. Le moment est arrivé.» Nous pensions: « C'est vrai, nous pourrions aussi bien être enterrées ce soir, s'il est avéré que c'est le moment.»

Et nous n'osions pas trop courir: essoufflées, au bout d'une course, arriver devant une fosse toute prête, et pas le temps de dire mot, pas le souffle.

Dites-moi, quel est donc le secret à ce propos?

III

The dawn is grey here, she went on to tell him. It was not always like this. We do not know whom to accuse.

At night the cattle make a great bellowing, long and flutelike at the end. We feel compassionate, but what can we do?

The smell of eucalyptus surrounds us: a blessing—serenity, but it cannot protect us from everything, or else do you think that it really can protect us from everything?

IV

I add one further word to you, a question rather.

Does water flow in your country too? (I don't remember whether you've told me so) and it gives chills too, if it is the real thing.

Do I love it? I don't know. One feels so alone when it is cold. But quite otherwise when it is warm. Well then? How can I decide? How do you others decide, tell me, when you speak of it without disguise, with open heart?

V

I am writing to you from the end of the world. You must realize this. The trees often tremble. We collect the leaves. They have a ridiculous number of veins. But what for? There's nothing between them and the tree any more, and we go off troubled.

Could not life continue on earth without wind? Or must everything tremble, always, always?

There are subterranean disturbances, too, in the house as well, like angers which might come to face you, like stern beings who would like to wrest confessions.

We see nothing, except what is so unimportant to see. Nothing, and yet we tremble. Why?

VI

We women here all live with tightened throats. Do you know, although I am very young, in other days I was still younger, and my companions were too. What does that mean? There is surely something horrible in it.

And in other days when, as I have already told you, we were younger still, we were afraid. Someone might have taken advantage of our confusion. Someone might have said to us: « You see, we're going to bury you. The moment has arrived. » We were thinking: « It's true, we might just as well be buried this evening, if it is definitely stated that this is the moment. »

And we did not dare run too much: Out of breath, at the end of a race, arriving in front of a ditch all prepared, and no time to say a word, no breath.

Tell me, just what is the secret in regard to this?

VII

Il y a constamment, lui dit-elle encore, des lions dans le village, qui se promènent sans gêne aucune. Moyennant qu'on ne fera pas attention à eux, ils ne font pas attention à nous.

Mais s'ils voient courir devant eux une jeune fille, ils ne veulent pas excuser son émoi. Non! aussitôt ils la dévorent.

C'est pourquoi ils se promènent constamment dans le village où ils n'ont rien à faire, car ils bâilleraient aussi bien ailleurs, n'est-ce pas évident?

. . . .

XI

Elle lui écrit encore:

« Vous n'imaginez pas tout ce qu'il y a dans le ciel, il faut l'avoir vu pour le croire. Ainsi, tenez, les . . . mais je ne vais pas vous dire leur nom tout de suite. »

Malgré des airs de peser très lourd et d'occuper presque tout le ciel, ils ne pèsent pas, tout grands qu'ils sont, autant qu'un enfant nouveau-né.

Nous les appelons des nuages.

Il est vrai qu'il en sort de l'eau, mais pas en les comprimant, ni en les triturant. Ce serait inutile, tant ils en ont peu.

Mais, à condition d'occuper des longueurs et des longueurs, des largeurs et des largeurs, des profondeurs aussi et des profondeurs et de faire les enflés, ils arrivent à la longue à laisser tomber quelques gouttelettes d'eau, oui, d'eau. Et on est bel et bien mouillé. On s'enfuit furieuses d'avoir été attrapées; car personne ne sait le moment où ils vont lâcher leurs gouttes; parfois ils demeurent des jours sans les lâcher. Et l'on resterait en vain chez soi à attendre.

XII

L'éducation des frissons n'est pas bien faite dans ce pays. Nous ignorons les vraies règles et quand l'événement apparaît, nous sommes prises au dépourvu.

C'est le Temps, bien sûr. (Est-il pareil chez vous?) Il faudrait arriver plus tôt que lui; vous voyez ce que je veux dire, rien qu'un tout petit peu avant. Vous connaissez l'histoire de la puce dans le tiroir? Oui, bien sûr. Et comme c'est vrai, n'est-ce pas! Je ne sais plus que dire. Quand allons-nous nous voir enfin?

VII

There are constantly, she told him further, lions in the village, who walk about without any hindrance at all. On condition that we pay no attention to them, they pay no attention to us.

But if they see a young woman running in front of them, they have no desire to apologize for her anxiety. No! They devour her at once.

That is why they constantly walk about the village where they have nothing to do, for quite obviously they might yawn just as well elsewhere.

. . . .

XI

She writes to him again:

« You cannot imagine all that there is in the sky, you would have to see it to believe it. So now, the . . . but I'm not going to tell you their name at once.

In spite of their air of weighing a great deal and of occupying almost all the sky, they do not weigh, huge though they are, as much as a newborn baby.

We call them clouds.

It is true that water comes out of them, but not by compressing them, or by pounding them. It would be useless, they have so little.

But, by reason of their occupying lengths and lengths, widths and widths, deeps also and deeps, and of puffing themselves up, they succeed in the long run in making a few droplets of water fall, yes, of water. And we are good and wet. We run off furious at having been trapped; for nobody knows the moment when they are going to release their drops; sometimes they rest for days without releasing them. And one would stay home waiting for them in vain.

XII

The education regarding chills is not well handled in this country. We are ignorant of the true rules and when the event appears, we are taken unawares.

It is Time, of course. (Is it the same with you?) One must arrive a little sooner than it does; you see what I mean, only a tiny little bit ahead. You know the story of the flea in the drawer? Yes, of course. And how true it is, don't you think! I don't know what more to say. When are we going to see each other at last?

—RICHARD ELLMANN

# PLUIE

La pluie, dans la cour où je la regarde tomber, descend à des allures très diverses. Au centre c'est un fin rideau (ou réseau) discontinu, une chute implacable mais relativement lente de gouttes probablement assez légères, une précipitation sempiternelle sans vigueur, une fraction intense du météore pur. A peu de distance des murs de droite et de gauche tombent avec plus de bruit des gouttes plus lourdes, individuées. Ici elles semblent de la grosseur d'un grain de blé, là d'un pois, ailleurs presque d'une bille. Sur des tringles, sur les accoudoirs de la fenêtre la pluie court horizontalement tandis que sur la face inférieure des mêmes obstacles elle se suspend en berlingots convexes. Selon la surface entière d'un petit toit de zinc que le regard surplombe elle ruisselle en nappe très mince, moirée à cause de courants très variés par les imperceptibles ondulations et bosses de la couverture. De la gouttière attenante où elle coule avec la contention d'un ruisseau creux sans grande pente, elle choit tout à coup en un filet parfaitement vertical, assez grossièrement tressé, jusqu' au sol où elle se brise et rejaillit en aiguillettes brillantes.

Chacune de ses formes a une allure particulière; il y répond un bruit particulier. Le tout vit avec intensité comme un mécanisme compliqué, aussi précis que hasardeux, comme une horlogerie dont le ressort est la pesanteur d'une masse donnée de vapeur en précipitation.

La sonnerie au sol des filets verticaux, le glou-glou des gouttières, les minuscules coups de gong se multiplient et résonnent à la fois en un concert sans monotonie, non sans délicatesse.

# Francis Ponge

1899-

## RAIN

In the yard where I watch it fall, the rain comes down at several different speeds. In the middle it is a delicate and threadbare curtain (or a net), an implacable but relatively slow descent of quite small drops, a sempiternal precipitation lacking vigor, an intense fragment of the pure meteor. A little away from the walls on each side heavier drops fall separately, with more noise. Some look the size of a grain of corn, others a pea, or almost a marble. On the parapets and balustrades of the window the rain runs horizontally, and on the inside of these obstacles it hangs down in convex loops. It streams in a thin sheet over the entire surface of a zinc roof straight below me—a pattern of watered silk, in the various currents, from the imperceptible bosses and undulations of the surface. In the gutter there, it flows with the contention of a deep but only slightly inclined stream, until suddenly it plunges in a perfectly vertical thread, quite thickly platted, to the ground, where it breaks and scatters in shining needles.

Each of these forms has its own particular manner of moving; each elicits a particular sound. The whole thing is intensely alive in the manner of a complicated mechanism, both precise and precarious, like a piece of clock-work in which the activating force is the weight of a mass precipitated from vapor.

The ringing of the vertical threads on the pavement, the gurgling from the gutters, the miniature gong-chimes, multiply and resonate together in a consort which avoids monotony, and is not without delicacy.

Lorsque le ressort s'est détendu, certains rouages quelque temps continuent à fonctionner, de plus en plus ralentis, puis toute la machinerie s'arrête. Alors si le soleil reparaît tout s'efface bientôt, le brillant appareil s'évapore: il a plu.

## LA BOUGIE

La nuit parfois ravive une plante singulière dont la lueur décompose les chambres meublées en massifs d'ombre.

Sa feuille d'or tient impassible au creux d'une colonnette d'albâtre par un pédoncule très noir.

Les papillons miteux l'assaillent de préférence à la lune trop haute, qui vaporise les bois. Mais brûlés aussitôt ou vannés dans la bagarre, tous frémissent aux bords d'une frénésie voisine de la stupeur.

Cependant la bougie, par le vacillement des clartés sur le livre au brusque dégagement des fumées originales encourage le lecteur,—puis s'incline sur son assiette et se noie dans son aliment.

## LES PLAISIRS DE LA PORTE

Les rois ne touchent pas aux portes.

Ils ne connaissent pas ce bonheur: pousser devant soi avec douceur ou rudesse l'un de ces grands panneaux familiers, se retourner vers lui pour le remettre en place,—tenir dans ses bras une porte.

... Le bonheur d'empoigner au ventre par son nœud de porcelaine l'un de ces hauts obstacles d'une pièce: ce corps à corps rapide par lequel un instant la marche retenue, l'œil s'ouvre et le corps tout entier s'accommode à son nouvel appartement.

And when the pressure is relaxed, some of the clockwork continues to function for a while, getting slower and slower, until the whole machine stops. Then, if the sun comes out again, the whole thing is quite soon effaced —the shiny apparatus evaporates: it has been raining.

—PETER RILEY

## THE CANDLE

Night sometimes revives a curious plant whose light decomposes furnished rooms into clumps of shadows.

Its golden leaf, held by a very black peduncle, stands unconcerned in the hollow of a little column of alabaster.

Shabby moths attack it, preferably at high moon which disolves the woods. But quickly burnt or beaten in the scuffle, all of them shudder on the edge of a frenzy close to stupor.

Yet the candle, by the flickering of its brightness on the book with abrupt eruptions of original smoke, encourages the reader to go on—but then bends over its plate and drowns in its own nourishment.

—RAYMOND FEDERMAN

## THE PLEASURES OF THE DOOR

Kings do not touch doors.

They do not know that happiness: to push before them with kindness or rudeness one of these great familiar panels, to turn around towards it to put it back in place—to hold it in one's arms.

... The happiness of grabbing by the porcelain knot of its belly one of these huge single obstacles; this quick grappling by which, for a moment, progress is hindered, as the eye opens and the entire body fits into its new environment.

D'une main amicale il la retient encore, avant de la repousser décidément et s'enclore,—ce dont le déclic du ressort puissant mais bien huilé agréablement l'assure.

## FAUNE ET FLORE

La faune bouge, tandis que la flore se déplie à l'œil.

Toute une sorte d'êtres animés est directement assumée par le sol.

Ils ont au monde leur place assurée, ainsi qu'à l'ancienneté leur décoration.

Différents en ceci de leurs frères vagabonds, ils ne sont pas surajoutés au monde, importuns au sol. Ils n'errent pas à la recherche d'un endroit pour leur mort, si la terre comme des autres absorbe soigneusement leurs restes.

Chez eux, pas de soucis alimentaires ou domiciliaires, pas d'entre-dévoration: pas de terreurs, de courses folles, de cruautés, de plaintes, de cris, de paroles. Ils ne sont pas les corps seconds de l'agitation, de la fièvre et du meurtre.

Dès leur apparition au jour, ils ont pignon sur rue, ou sur route. Sans aucun souci de leurs voisins, ils ne rentrent pas les uns dans les autres par voie d'absorption. Ils ne sortent pas les uns des autres par gestation.

Ils meurent par dessication et chute au sol, ou plutôt affaissement sur place, rarement par corruption. Aucun endroit de leur corps particulièrement sensible, au point que percé il cause la mort de toute la personne. Mais une sensibilité relativement plus chatouilleuse au climat, aux conditions d'existence.

Ils ne sont pas . . . Ils ne sont pas . . .
*Leur enfer est d'une autre sorte.*

Ils n'ont pas de voix. Ils sont à peu de chose près paralytiques. Ils ne peuvent attirer l'attention que par leurs poses. Ils n'ont pas l'air de connaître les douleurs de la non-justification. Mais ils ne pourraient en aucune façon échapper par la fuite à cette hantise, ou croire y échapper, dans la griserie de la vitesse. Il n'y a pas d'autre mouvement en eux que l'extension. Aucun geste, aucune pensée, peut-être aucun désir, aucune intention, qui n'aboutisse à un monstrueux accroissement de leur corps, à une irrémédiable *excroissance*.

Ou plutôt, et c'est bien pire, rien de monstrueux par malheur: malgré tous leurs efforts pour « s'exprimer », ils ne parviennent jamais qu'à répéter un

With a friendly hand he holds it a while longer before pushing it back decidedly thus shutting himself in—of which, he, by the click of the powerful and well-oiled spring, is pleasantly assured.

—RAYMOND FEDERMAN

## FAUNA AND FLORA

Fauna move about, whereas flora unfold themselves to the eye.

The ground has taken directly upon itself a whole class of animated creatures.

Their position in the world is assured, and, by right of seniority, their decorations.

Differing in this respect from their vagabond fellows, they are not superadded to the earth, intruders upon the ground. They need not wander seeking a place to die, though the earth carefully consumes their remains, as those of others.

No need for them to worry about provisions or shelter; in their societies, no dog-eat-dog: no terrors, nor wild running, no cruelties, lamentations, cries, words. They are no abettors of restlessness, confusion and murder.

From the moment they see the light, they have settled down. Perfectly unconcerned about their neighbours, they do not enter into each others' lives by means of mutual consumption. They do not issue from each other by gestation.

They die by desiccation and falling to the ground, or rather by sinking in their tracks; rarely by rotting. No area of their bodies is peculiarly sensitive, to the degree that, were it wounded, it would cause the death of the whole individual. Their sensibility, however, is by comparison more subtly susceptible to the climate, to the conditions of existence.

They are not . . . They are not . . .
*Their hell is of another sort.*

They have no voices. They are all but paralytic. They can attract attention only by their postures. They do not give the impression of knowing the pain of not being able to justify themselves. But they could in no manner escape by flight from that obsession, did they have it; or even think to escape it, in the intoxication of speed. They are capable of no movement save extension. They know no gesture, no thought, perhaps no desire or intention, which

million de fois la même expression, la même feuille. Au printemps, lorsque, las de se contraindre et n'y tenant plus, ils laissent échapper un flot, un vomissement de vert, et croient entonner un cantique varié, sortir d'eux-mêmes, s'étendre à toute la nature, l'embrasser, ils ne réussissent encore que, à des milliers d'exemplaires, la même note, le même mot, la même feuille.

*L'on ne peut sortir de l'arbre par des moyens d'arbre.*

« Ils ne s'expriment que par leurs poses.»

Pas de gestes, ils multiplient seulement leurs bras, leurs mains, leurs doigts, —à la façon des bouddhas. C'est ainsi qu'oisifs, ils vont jusqu'au bout de leurs pensées. Ils ne sont qu'une volonté d'expression. Ils n'ont rien de caché pour eux-mêmes, ils ne peuvent garder aucune idée secrète, ils se déploient entièrement, honnêtement, sans restriction.

Oisifs, ils passent leur temps à compliquer leur propre forme, à parfaire dans le sens de la plus grande complication d'analyse leur propre corps. Où qu'ils naissent, si cachés qu'ils soient, ils ne s'occupent qu'à accomplir leur expression: ils se préparent, ils s'ornent, ils attendent qu'on vienne les lire.

Ils n'ont à leur disposition pour attirer l'attention sur eux que leurs poses, que des lignes, et parfois un signal exceptionnel, un extraordinaire appel aux yeux et à l'odorat sous forme d'ampoules ou de bombes lumineuses et parfumées, qu'on appelle leurs fleurs, et qui sont sans doute des plaies.

Cette modification de la sempiternelle feuille signifie certainement quelque chose.

Le temps des végétaux: ils semblent toujours figés, immobiles. On tourne le dos pendant quelques jours, une semaine, leur pose s'est encore précisée, leurs membres multipliés. Leur identité ne fait pas de doute, mais leur forme s'est de mieux en mieux réalisée.

La beauté des fleurs qui fanent: les pétales se tordent comme sous l'action du feu: c'est bien cela d'ailleurs: une déshydratation. Se tordent pour laisser apercevoir les graines à qui ils décident de donner leur chance, le champ libre.

C'est alors que la nature se présente face à la fleur, la force à s'ouvrir, à s'écarter: elle se crispe, se tord, elle recule, et laisse triompher la graine qui sort d'elle qui l'avait préparée.

Le temps des végétaux se résout à leur espace, à l'espace qu'ils occupent peu à peu, remplissant un canevas sans doute à jamais déterminé. Lorsque c'est fini, alors la lassitude les prend, et c'est le drame d'une certaine saison.

Comme le développement de cristaux: une volonté de formation, et une impossibilité de se former autrement que *d'une manière.*

does not culminate in a monstrous enlargement of their bodies, in an irremediable *excrescence.*

Or rather, what is very much worse, they are unhappily incapable of monstrosity: despite all their efforts to "express themselves," they never succeed in doing more than repeating the same expression, the same leaf, a million times over. When, in the spring, weary of constraint and no longer able to bear it, they give vent to a flood, an explosion of green, and think to break into an altered chant, to get out of themselves, to stretch out to all nature and embrace it, they still succeed only in producing, thousands of times reduplicated, the same note, the same word, the same leaf.

*The tree may not be escaped from by means of the tree.*

"They express themselves solely by their postures."

No gestures, only the multiplication of their arms, their hands, their fingers —like Buddhas. And so, indolently, they follow their thoughts out to the end. They are nothing but a will to expression. They hold nothing hidden and to themselves, they are unable to keep secret a single idea, they display themselves entirely, honestly, unreservedly.

Being indolent, they spend their days in complicating their own shapes, in pushing to the limit—in the direction of the greatest possible analytical complexity—their own bodies. Wherever they are born, however hidden they may be, they concern themselves only with the achievement of their self-expression: they dispose themselves, they adorn themselves, they wait for someone to come and read them.

For the purpose of attracting attention, they have at their disposal only their postures, their lines, and occasionally an exceptional signal, an extraordinary appeal to the eye and the sense of smell, in the shape of bulbs or luminous and odorous balls, which are said to be their flowers, but are probably wounds.

This modification of the everlasting leaf surely must signify something.

Time among the plants: they seem always frozen, immobile. One turns one's back for a few days, for a week, and their postures are all the more definite, while their members have multiplied. Of their identities there is never any question, but their forms are constantly more and more fulfilled.

The beauty of fading flowers: the petals twist as if under the effect of fire: and of course that's what it really is: a dehydration. They twist so as to expose the seeds to whom they now decide to give their chance, to whom they leave the field free.

This is the season when nature confronts the flower, forcing it to lay itself open to change, to discard itself: it shrivels up, and twists, it shrinks, and gives the victory to the seed which it has made ready, and which emerges from it.

Parmi les êtres animés on peut distinguer ceux dans lesquels, outre le mouvement qui les fait grandir, agit une force par laquelle ils peuvent remuer tout ou partie de leur corps, et se déplacer à leur manière par le monde,—et ceux dans lesquels il n'y a pas d'autre mouvement que l'extension.

Une fois libérés de l'obligation de grandir, les premiers *s'expriment* de plusieurs façons, à propos de mille soucis de logement, de nourriture, de défense, de certains jeux enfin lorsqu'un certain repos leur est accordé.

Les seconds, qui ne connaissent pas ces besoins pressants, l'on ne peut affirmer qu'ils n'aient pas d'autres intentions ou volonté que de s'accroître mais en tout cas toute volonté d'expression de leur part est impuissante, sinon à développer leur corps, comme si chacun de nos désirs nous coûtait l'obligation désormais de nourrir et de supporter un membre supplémentaire. Infernale multiplication de substance à l'occasion de chaque idée! Chaque désir de fuite m'alourdit d'un nouveau chaînon!

Le végétal est une analyse en acte, une dialectique originale dans l'espace. Progression par division de l'acte précédent. L'expression des animaux est orale, ou mimée par gestes qui s'effacent les uns les autres. L'expression des végétaux est écrite, une fois pour toutes. Pas moyen d'y revenir, repentirs impossibles: pour se corriger, il faut ajouter. Corriger un texte écrit, et *paru*, par des appendices, et ainsi de suite. Mais, il faut ajouter qu'ils ne se divisent pas à l'infini. Il existe à chacun une borne.

Chacun de leurs gestes laisse non pas seulement une trace comme il en est de l'homme et de ses écrits, il laisse une présence, une naissance irrémédiable, *et non détachée d'eux.*

Leurs poses, ou « tableaux-vivants » :
muettes instances, supplications, calme fort, triomphes.

L'on dit que les infirmes, les amputés voient leurs facultés se développer prodigieusement: ainsi des végétaux: leur immobilité fait leur perfection, leur fouillé, leurs belles décorations, leurs riches fruits.

Aucun geste de leur action n'a d'effet en dehors d'eux-mêmes.

La variété infinie des sentiments que fait naître le désir dans l'immobilité a donné lieu à l'infinie diversité de leurs formes.

Un ensemble de lois compliquées à l'extrême, c'est-à-dire le plus parfait hasard, préside à la naissance, et au placement des végétaux sur la surface du globe.

La loi des *indéterminés déterminants*.

Time among the plants is expressed in terms of space, in the space which the plants occupy little by little, filling out patterns which are probably forever determined . . .

Like the development of crystals: a will to formation, coupled with an absolute inability to form oneself in any other fashion but the *one*.

Among living beings one may make a distinction between those in whom, in addition to the movement which makes them grow, there operates a force whereby they may move all, or some part, of their bodies, and each in his own way move about in the world—and those in whom there is no other movement than extension.

Once free of the obligation to grow, the first *express themselves* in various fashions, in regard to the thousand problems of shelter and food and defence, and finally—once they have achieved a certain degree of security—in certain pastimes.

Of the second class, who are not confronted with these pressing necessities, one cannot say that they have no other urge or purpose than to increase in size, but in any case, whatever wishes for expression they may possess are powerless to accomplish anything, unless it is the development of their own bodies—as if each of one's desires were to cost one the obligation thenceforward to nourish and support an additional member. An infernal multiplication of one's substance, occasioned by the slightest thought! Each dream of flight adds another link to my heavy chain!

The plant is an analysis in action, a peculiar dialectic in space. Development by the subdivision of the preceding operation. Among animals, expression is oral, or is pantomimed by gestures which cancel one another out. But the self-expression of vegetable life is a written thing, and once done it is done. No chance of going back and changing it, no possibility of revisions or repentances: in order to correct, one must append. Like correcting an essay already written, and which has already *appeared,* by means of appendices, and so on. However, it must be added that plants cannot infinitely subdivide themselves. For each one there is a set limit.

Each one of their movements leaves not only a mark, as do men in writing, but leaves also a presence, something irremediably begotten, and *not separate from themselves.*

Their postures, or "tableaux-vivants":
mute entreaties, supplications, unruffled strength, triumphs.

They say the crippled and the amputated find that their faculties develop prodigiously: likewise the plants: to their immobility they owe their perfection, their intricate profusion, their lovely decorations, their rich fruits.

Les végétaux la nuit.

L'exhalaison de l'acide carbonique par la fonction chlorophyllienne, comme un soupir de satisfaction qui durerait des heures, comme lorsque la plus basse corde des instruments à cordes, le plus relâchée possible, vibre à la limite de la musique, du son pur, et du silence.

BIEN QUE L'ÊTRE VÉGÉTAL VEUILLE ÊTRE DÉFINI PLUTÔT PAR SES CONTOURS ET PAR SES FORMES, J'HONORERAI D'ABORD EN LUI UNE VERTU DE SA SUBSTANCE: CELLE DE POUVOIR ACCOMPLIR SA SYNTHÈSE AUX DÉPENS SEULS DU MILIEU INORGANIQUE QUI L'ENVIRONNE. TOUT LE MONDE AUTOUR DE LUI N'EST QU'UNE MINE OÙ LE PRÉCIEUX FILON VERT PUISE DE QUOI ÉLABORER CONTINÛMENT SON PROTOPLASME, DANS L'AIR PAR LA FONCTION CHLOROPHYLLIENNE DE SES FEUILLES, DANS LE SOL PAR LA FACULTÉ ABSORBANTE DE SES RACINES QUI ASSIMILENT LES SELS MINÉRAUX. D'OÙ LA QUALITÉ ESSENTIELLE DE CET ÊTRE, LIBÉRÉ À LA FOIS DE TOUS SOUCIS DOMICILIAIRES ET ALIMENTAIRES PAR LA PRÉSENCE À SON ENTOUR D'UNE RESSOURCE INFINIE D'ALIMENTS: *L'immobilité.*

RHÉTORIQUE

Je suppose qu'il s'agit de sauver quelques jeunes hommes du suicide et quelques autres de l'entrée aux flics ou aux pompiers. Je pense à ceux qui se suicident par dégoût, parce qu'ils trouvent que « *les autres* » ont trop de part en eux-mêmes.

Not a single gesture, out of all their actions, has any effect outside themselves.

Their immobility has translated the infinite variety of feelings generated by desire into the infinite diversity of their forms.

A set of the most extremely complicated laws, that is to say the most absolute chance, governs the birth of plants, and their placement upon the surface of the globe.
The law of *indeterminate determinants*.

Plants at night.
The exhalation of carbonic acid by the reaction of the chlorophyll, is as a sigh of satisfaction lasting for hours, or as if the lowest string of all the stringed instruments, slackened as far as possible, vibrated at the very limits of music, of pure sound, and of silence.

ALTHOUGH THE VEGETABLE BEING HAD RATHER BE DEFINED BY ITS CONTOURS AND BY ITS FORMS, I SHALL FIRST PAY IT HONOUR FOR A VIRTUE PERTAINING TO ITS SUBSTANCE: THAT OF BEING ABLE TO ACCOMPLISH ITS OWN SYNTHESIS AT THE EXPENSE OF NOTHING BUT THE INORGANIC ENVIRONMENT WHICH SURROUNDS IT. ALL THE WORLD ABOUT IT IS BUT A MINE WHENCE THE PRECIOUS GREEN VEIN BORROWS WHAT IT NEEDS FOR THE CONTINUAL ELABORATION OF ITS PROTO-PLASM, DRAWING FROM THE AIR BY THE PHOTOSYNTHETIC FUNCTION OF ITS LEAVES, FROM THE EARTH BY THE ABSORBENT ACTION OF ITS ROOTS IN THE ASSIMILATION OF MINERAL SALTS. THENCE COMES THE ESSENTIAL CHARACTER OF THIS BEING, FREED OF DOMICILIARY WORRIES, AND OF ALIMENTARY CARES AS WELL, BY THE PRESENCE ABOUT IT OF AN INFINITE SOURCE OF SUSTENANCE: *Immobility*.

—RICHARD WILBUR

# RHETORIC

I assume that we are talking about saving a few young men from suicide and a few others from becoming cops or firemen. I have in mind those who commit suicide out of disgust, because they find that *others* own too large a share of them.

On peut leur dire: donnez tout au moins *la parole* à la minorité de vous-mêmes. Soyez poètes. Ils répondront: mais c'est là surtout, c'est là encore que je sens les autres en moi-même, lorsque je cherche à m'exprimer je n'y parviens pas. Les paroles sont toutes faites et s'expriment: elles ne m'expriment point. Là encore j'étouffe.

C'est alors qu'enseigner l'art de *résister aux paroles* devient utile, l'art de ne dire que ce que l'on veut dire, l'art de les violenter et de les soumettre. Somme toute fonder une rhétorique, ou plutôt apprendre à chacun l'art de fonder sa propre rhétorique, est une oeuvre de salut public.

Cela sauve les seules, les rares personnes qu'il importe de sauver: celles qui ont la conscience et le souci et le dégoût des autres en eux-mêmes.

Celles qui peuvent faire avancer l'esprit et à proprement parler changer la face des choses.

## INTRODUCTION AU GALET

Comme après tout si je consens à l'existence c'est à condition de l'accepter pleinement, en tant qu'elle remet tout en question; quels d'ailleurs et si faibles que soient mes moyens comme ils sont évidemment plutôt d'ordre littéraire et rhétorique; je ne vois pas pourquoi je ne commencerais pas, arbitrairement, par montrer qu'à propos des choses les plus simples il est possible de faire des discours infinis entièrement composés de déclarations inédites, enfin qu'à propos de n'importe quoi non seulement tout n'est pas dit, mais à peu près tout reste à dire.

Il est tout de même à plusieurs points de vue insupportable de penser dans quel infime manège depuis des siècles tournent les paroles, l'esprit, enfin la réalité de l'homme. Il suffit pour s'en rendre compte de fixer son attention sur le premier objet venu: on s'apercevra aussitôt que personne ne l'a jamais observé, et qu'à son propos les choses les plus élémentaires restent à dire. Et j'entends bien que sans doute pour l'homme il ne s'agit pas *essentiellement* d'observer et de décrire des objets, mais enfin cela est un signe, et des plus nets. A quoi donc s'occupe-t-on? Certes à tout, sauf à changer d'atmosphère intellectuelle, à sortir des poussiéreux salons où s'ennuie à mourir tout ce qu'il y a de vivant dans l'esprit, à progresser—enfin!—non seulement par les pensées, mais par les facultés, les sentiments, les sensations, et somme toute à accroître *la quantité de ses qualités.* Car des millions de sentiments, par exemple, aussi différents du petit catalogue de ceux qu'éprouvent actuellement les hommes les plus sensibles, sont à connaître, sont à éprouver. Mais non! L'homme se contentera longtemps encore d'être « fier» ou « humble» , « sincere» ou

To them one should say: at least let the minority within you have the right to *speak*. Be poets. They will answer: but it is especially there, it is always there that I feel others within me; when I try to express myself, I am unable to do so. Words are ready-made and express themselves: they do not express me. Once again I find myself suffocating.

At that moment, teaching the art of *resisting words* becomes useful, the art of saying only what one wants to say, the art of doing them violence, of forcing them to submit. In short, it is a matter of public safety to found a rhetoric, or rather, to teach everyone the art of founding his own rhetoric.

This saves those few, those rare individuals who must be saved: those who are aware, and who are troubled and disgusted by the others within them.

Those individuals who make the mind progress, and who are, strictly speaking, capable of changing the reality of things.

—SERGE GAVRONSKY

## INTRODUCTION TO THE PEBBLE

If I admit existence at all, it is on condition of complete acceptance of it, inasmuch as everything is involved by it; besides, however feeble my powers may be, since they are obviously directed towards the pursuits of rhetoric and literature, I see no reason why I should not begin arbitrarily by showing that à propos of even the simplest things one can evolve endless and elaborate diatribes entirely composed of new and unforeseen statements. In other words, no matter what the subject, not only has all not been said, but practically everything still remains to be said.

From several points of view it is unbearable to think of the abject little merry-go-round which has been carrying around the words, the spirit, the very reality of mankind for centuries. To be conscious of this it is sufficient to focus one's attention upon the first object that comes to hand. One will quickly realize that no one else has ever really observed it, and that the most elementary things remain to be said about it. And I quite understand that mankind's essential function is not that of observing and describing objects. Still, the fact that we have not done it is significant. And in place of it what do we do? Certainly we are not busy changing the intellectual atmosphere, or saving whatever part of the spirit is still alive by dragging it out of the dusty parlor of mortal boredom, or progressing—at last!—not alone by means of thought but through all the faculties, the feelings, the sensations; in other words, by increasing the *quantity of our qualities*. Yet millions of feelings, for instance, utterly different from those to be found in the slim lists of even the most sensitive persons of today, remain to be discovered and experienced. But,

« hypocrite » , « gai » ou « triste » , « malade » ou « bien portant » , « bon » ou « méchant » , « propre » ou « sale » , « durable » ou « éphémère » , etc., avec toutes les combinaisons possibles de ces pitoyables qualités.

Eh bien! Je tiens à dire quant à moi que je suis bien autre chose, et par exemple qu'en dehors de toutes les qualités que je possède en commun avec le rat, le lion, et le filet, je prétends à celles du diamant, et je me solidarise d'ailleurs entièrement aussi bien avec la mer qu'avec la falaise qu'elle attaque et avec le galet qui s'en trouve par la suite créé, et dont l'on trouvera à titre d'exemple ci-dessous la description essayée, sans préjuger de toutes les qualités dont je compte bien que la contemplation et la nomination d'objets extrêmement différents me feront prendre conscience et jouissance effective par la suite.

A tout désir d'évasion, opposer la contemplation et ses ressources. Inutile de partir: se transférer aux choses, qui vous comblent d'impressions nouvelles, vous proposent un million de qualités inédites.

Personnellement ce sont les distractions qui me gênent, c'est en prison ou en cellule, seul à la campagne que je m'ennuierais le moins. Partout ailleurs, et quoi que je fasse, j'ai l'impression de perdre mon temps. Même, la richesse de propositions contenues dans le moindre objet est si grande, que je ne conçois pas encore la possibilité de rendre compte d'aucune autre chose que des plus simples: une pierre, une herbe, le feu, un morceau de bois, un morceau de viande.

Les spectacles qui paraîtraient à d'autres les moins compliqués, comme par exemple simplement le visage d'un homme sur le point de parler, ou d'un homme qui dort, ou n'importe quelle manifestation d'activité chez un être vivant, me semblent encore de beaucoup trop difficiles et chargés de significations inédites (à découvrir, puis à relier dialectiquement) pour que je puisse songer à m'y atteler de longtemps. Dès lors, comment pourrais-je décrire une scène, faire la critique d'un spectacle ou d'une œuvre d'art? Je n'ai là-dessus aucune opinion, n'en pouvant même conquérir la moindre impression un peu juste, ou complète.

Tout le secret du bonheur du contemplateur est dans son refus de considérer *comme un mal* l'envahissement de sa personnalité par les choses. Pour éviter que cela tourne au mysticisme, il faut: 1° se rendre compte précisément, c'est-à-dire expressément de chacune des choses dont on a fait l'objet de sa contemplation; 2° changer assez souvent d'objet de contemplation, et en somme garder une certaine mesure. Mais le plus important pour la santé du contemplateur est la *nomination*, au fur et à mesure, de toutes les qualités qu'il découvre; il ne faut pas que ces qualités, qui le TRANSPORTENT le transportent plus loin que leur expression mesurée et exacte.

Je propose à chacun l'ouverture de trappes intérieures, un voyage dans l'épaisseur des choses, une invasion de qualités, une révolution ou une subver-

no! Man will go on for a good while yet, satisfied with being "proud," "humble," "sincere," "hypocritical," "happy," "sad," "lasting," "ephemeral," together with all the possible combinations of these wretchedly insufficient states.

Well! I for one should like to say that I am different, and that for instance, in addition to all those qualities I share in common with the rat, the lion and the trout, I also lay claim to those of the diamond, and I make myself a part of the sea with no greater ease than I do of the cliff she attacks, or of the pebble formed thereby, the pebble whose attempted description is to follow here as an example. And I have no foreknowledge of the qualities which I expect to discover and savor by examining and naming objects quite different from the pebble.

To all desire for escape you must oppose contemplation and its resources. It is useless to leave; you must move across to things that overwhelm you with new impressions, things that suggest an endless flow of unsuspected considerations.

Personally I am bored by amusement. I should be the least bored in prison or alone in the country. Besides, no matter where I am I have the feeling that I am wasting my time. The infinity of propositions contained in the least worthy objects is so manifest that I am as yet unable to report on anything but the simplest ones: a stone, a blade of grass, a block of wood, a piece of meat.

Sights which might seem eminently uncomplicated to others, as, let us say, the face of a man about to speak, or another man asleep, or any manifestation of activity in a living person, strike me as being still much too difficult, and too full of unfamiliar meanings (first to be discovered and then to be bound together dialectically) for me to dream of attacking them for a long time to come. And once I have reached that point, how shall I be able to describe a scene, or criticize a play or a work of art? I have no ideas on that score, since I cannot summon up the slightest impression that could be called at all accurate or complete.

The entire secret of happiness for the contemplator lies in his refusal to *object* to the taking over of his personality by things. To keep all this from becoming mysticism, one must first of all be quite conscious, that is, purposely and precisely so, of each thing he has made the object of his contemplation. Also one must change objects fairly often, and in general show a certain moderation. But most important for the health of the contemplator is the *naming*, as he goes along, of every quality he discovers; these qualities that "send" him must not send him any further than their measured and exact expression would warrant.

I suggest that every person open an interior trapdoor, that he negotiate a trip into the thickness of things, that he make an invasion of their characteristics, a revolution, a turning-over process comparable to that accomplished by

sion comparable à celle qu'opère la charrue ou la pelle, lorsque, tout à coup et pour la première fois, sont mises au jour des millions de parcelles, de paillettes, de racines, de vers et de petites bêtes jusqu'alors enfouies. O ressources infinies de l'épaisseur des choses, *rendues* par les ressources infinies de l'épaisseur sémantique des mots!

La contemplation d'objets précis est aussi un repos, mais c'est un repos privilégié, comme ce repos perpétuel des plantes adultes, qui porte des fruits. Fruits spéciaux, empruntés autant à l'air ou au milieu ambiant, au moins pour la forme à laquelle ils sont limités et les couleurs que par opposition ils en prennent, qu'à la personne qui en fournit la substance; et c'est ainsi qu'ils se différencient des fruits d'un autre repos, le sommeil, qui sont nommés les rêves, uniquement formés par la personne, et, par conséquence, indéfinis, informes, et sans utilité: c'est pourquoi ils ne sont pas véritablement des fruits.

Ainsi donc, si ridiculement prétentieux qu'il puisse paraître, voici quel est à peu près mon dessein: je voudrais écrire une sorte de *De natura rerum*. On voit bien la différence avec les poètes contemporains: ce ne sont pas des poèmes que je veux composer, mais une seule cosmogonie.

Mais comment rendre ce dessein possible? Je considère l'état actuel des sciences: des bibliothèques entières sur chaque partie de chacune d'elles . . . Faudrait-il donc que je commence par les lire, et les apprendre? Plusieurs vies n'y suffiraient pas. Au milieu de l'énorme étendue et quantité des connaissances acquises par chaque science, du nombre accru des sciences, nous sommes perdus. Le meilleur parti à prendre est donc de considérer toutes choses comme inconnues, et de se promener ou de s'étendre sous bois ou sur l'herbe, et de reprendre tout du début.

Exemple du peu d'épaisseur des choses dans l'esprit des hommes jusqu'à moi: du *galet*, ou de la pierre, voici ce que j'ai trouvé qu'on pense, ou qu'on a pensé de plus original:
*Un coeur de pierre* (Diderot);
*Uniforme et plat galet* (Diderot);
*Je méprise cette poussière qui me compose et qui vous parle* (Saint-Just);
*Si j'ai du goût ce n'est guère*
*Que pour la terre et les pierres* (Rimbaud).
Eh bien! Pierre, galet, poussière, occasion de sentiments si communs quoique si contradictoires, je ne te juge pas si rapidement, car je désire te juger à ta valeur: et tu me serviras, et tu serviras dès lors aux hommes à bien d'autres expressions, tu leur fourniras pour leurs discussions entre eux ou avec eux-mêmes bien d'autres arguments; même, si j'ai assez de talent, tu les armeras de quelques nouveaux proverbes ou lieux communs: voilà toute mon ambition.

the plough or the spade, when suddenly millions of particles of dead plants, bits of roots and straw, worms and tiny crawling creatures, all hitherto buried in the earth, are exposed to the light of day for the first time. O infinite resources of the thickness of things, *restored* to us by the infinite resources in the semantic thickness of words!

The contemplation of precise objects is also a relaxation, but it is a privileged one, akin to that relaxation enjoyed by adult plants which bear fruit. This however is very special fruit, borrowed as much from the air or the surrounding atmosphere (at least as to the form to which it is limited and the colors it takes on in contrast) as from the person who furnishes its substance by creating it. And it is thus that this fruit is distinguished from the fruits of another, different, relaxation: sleep,—called dreams. These are exclusively formed by the person, and as a result they are indefinite, amorphous, useless. That is why dreams are not true fruits.

And so, however ridiculous and pretentious it may seem, here is the sum and substance of my plan: I should like to write a kind of *De natura rerum*. It is easy to see the difference between this desire and that of the contemporary poets: it is not *poems* I want to write, but *one* single cosmogony.

But how to make this plan work? I think of the present state of the sciences: whole libraries on each part of each science. Must I begin by reading the books, and learn them by heart? Several lives would not be long enough. Surrounded by the vast expanse and quantity of the knowledge acquired by each science, by the growing number of sciences, we are lost. The best procedure is to consider all things as unknown, to stroll or stretch out among the shrubs or on the grass, and start all over again from the beginning.

As an example of the paucity of feeling for the thickness of things in the mind of man up until now: of the pebble, or of the stone, here are the remarks that have been made; these are the most original thoughts men have had:
*A heart of stone . . .*
*Uniform and flat pebble . . .* (Diderot)
*I scorn this dust of which I am made, and which speaks to you . . .* (Saint-Just)
*If I have a taste for anything,*
*It is for little more than the earth and the stones.* (Rimbaud)
Well! Stone, pebble, dust; you who furnish the occasion for such common if contradictory sentiments . . . I shall not form such a swift judgment of you, for I hope to judge you in your own terms. You shall be useful to me, and to other men, in many ways, you shall supply them with material for their discussions with each other and for their arguments with themselves; and, if my talent is great enough, you shall even arm them with a few new proverbs and commonplaces: there in a nutshell is my ambition.

—PAUL BOWLES

## LES ZIAUX

les eaux bruns, les eaux noirs, les eaux de merveille
les eaux de mer, d'océan, les eaux d'étincelles
nuitent le jour, jurent la nuit
chants de dimanche à samedi

les yeux vertes, les yeux bleues, les yeux de succelle
les yeux de passante au cours de la vie
les yeux noires, yeux d'estanchelle
silencent les mots, ouatent le bruit

eau de ces yeux penché sur tout miroir
gouttes secrets au bord des veilles
tout miroir, toute veille en ces ziaux bleues ou vertes
les ziaux bruns, les ziaux noirs, les ziaux de merveille

# Raymond Queneau

## 1903-1976

THE SEYES

brown seas, black seas, seas of marvel
seas of springs, seas of salt, seas of sparkle
they night the day and daze the night
singing from dusk to daylight

green eyes, blue eyes, eyes of marble
eyes of passing women throughout life
dark eyes, eyes of periwinkle
they silence words and muffle strife

seas of eyes poring over every mirror
secret droplets edging every vigil
every mirror, every vigil in green-blue seas-eyes
sighs of brown, sighs of black, sighs of marvel

—TEO SAVORY

CYGNES

Quand Un fit l'amour avec Zéro
Les sphères embrassèrent les tores
Et les nombres premiers s'avancèrent
Tendant leurs mains vers les frais sycomores
Et les fractions continues blessées à mort
Dans le torrent des décimales muettes se couchèrent

Quand B fit l'amour avec A
Les paragraphes s'embrasèrent
Les virgules s'avancèrent
Tendant leur cou par-dessus les ponts de fer
Et l'alphabet blessé za mort
S'évanouit dans les bras d'une interrogation muette

PAUVRE TYPE

Toto a un nez de chèvre et un pied de porc
Il porte des chaussettes
en bois d'allumette
et se peigne les cheveux
avec un coupe-papier qui a fait long feu
S'il s'habille les murs deviennent gris
S'il se lève le lit explose
S'il se lave l'eau s'ébroue
Il a toujours dans sa poche
un vide-poche

Pauvre type

SINES

When One made love to Zero
spheres embraced their arches
and prime numbers caught their breath
holding out their hands to fresh larches
simple fractions fractured to death
lay down in the torrent of silent decimals

When B made love to A
the paragraphs caught fire
the commas caught their breath
holding their necks over a bridge's arc
and the alphabet fractured to death
vanished into the arms of a silent question-mark

—TEO SAVORY

POOR FELLOW

Toto has a goat's nose and the foot of a pig
He carries his socks
in a matchbox
and he combs his hair
with a hung-up paper-cutter
If he gets dressed the walls turn grey
If he gets up the bed explodes
If he washes the water snorts
In his button-hole
he always has a button-hook

Poor fellow

—TEO SAVORY

# POUR UN ART POÉTIQUE

I

Un poème c'est bien peu de chose
à peine plus qu'un cyclone aux Antilles
qu'un typhon dans la mer de Chine
un tremblement de terre à Formose

Une inondation du Yang Tse Kiang
ça vous noie cent mille Chinois d'un seul coup
vlan
ça ne fait même pas le sujet d'un poème
Bien peu de chose

On s'amuse bien dans notre petit village
on va bâtir une nouvelle école
on va élire un nouveau maire et changer les jours de marché
on était au centre du monde on se trouve maintenant près du fleuve océan
      qui ronge l'horizon

Un poème c'est bien peu de chose

# L'ESPÈCE HUMAINE

L'espèce humaine m'a donné
le droit d'être mortel
le devoir d'être civilisé
la conscience humaine
deux yeux qui d'ailleurs ne fonctionnent pas très bien
le nez au milieu du visage
deux pieds deux mains
le langage
l'espèce humaine m'a donné
mon père et ma mère
peut-être des frères on ne sait

# TOWARD A POETIC ART

I

A poem's just a little thing
Hardly more than a cyclone in the Antilles
a typhoon in the China Seas
an earthquake in Nanking

A flood in the Yang-tse Kiang
at one fell swoop drowns you a thousand Chinese
bang
that's not even the subject for a poem
Nothing much

We keep busy in our village
going to build a better school
going to vote for a new mayor
 and change our market days

we used to be the hub of the universe but now
 we find we're near the ocean current that
 the horizon gnaws at

A poem's just a little thing

—TEO SAVORY

# THE HUMAN SPECIES

The human species has given me
the right to be mortal
the duty to be civilized
a conscience
2 eyes that don't always function very well
a nose in the middle of my face
2 feet 2 hands
speech

the human species has given me
my father and mother

des cousins à pelletées
et des arrière-grands-pères
l'espèce humaine m'a donné
ses trois facultés
le sentiment l'intelligence et la volonté
chaque chose de façon modérée
l'espèce humaine m'a donné
trente-deux dents un cœur un foie
d'autres viscères et dix doigts
l'espèce humaine m'a donné
de quoi se dire satisfait

## SI TU T'IMAGINES

Si tu t'imagines
si tu t'imagines
fillette fillette
si tu t'imagines
xa va xa va xa
va durer toujours
la saison des za
la saison des za
saison des amours
ce que tu te goures
fillette fillette
ce que tu te goures

Si tu crois petite
si tu crois ah ah
que ton teint de rose
ta taille de guêpe
tes mignons biceps
tes ongles d'émail
ta cuisse de nymphe
et ton pied léger
si tu crois petite
xa va xa va xa

some brothers maybe who knows
a whole mess of cousins
and some great-grandfathers
the human species has given me
its 3 faculties
feeling intellect and will
each in moderation
32 teeth and 10 fingers a liver
a heart and some other viscera
the human species has given me
what I'm supposed to be satisfied with

—TEO SAVORY

## IF YOU IMAGINE

If you imagine
if you imagine
little sweetie little sweetie
if you imagine
this will this will this
will last forever
this season of
this season of
season of love
you're fooling yourself
little sweetie little sweetie
you're fooling yourself

If you think little one
if you think ah ah
that that rosy complexion
that waspy waist
those lovely muscles
the enamel nails
nymph thigh
and your light foot
if you think little one
that will that will that

va durer toujours
ce que tu te goures
fillette fillette
ce que tu te goures

les beaux jours s'en vont
les beaux jours de fête
soleils et planètes
tournent tous en rond
mais toi ma petite
tu marches tout droit
vers que tu vois pas
très sournois s'approchent
la ride véloce
la pesante graisse
le menton triplé
le muscle avachi
allons cueille cueille
les roses les roses
roses de la vie
et que leurs pétales
soient la mer étale
de tous les bonheurs
allons cueille cueille
si tu le fais pas
ce que tu te goures
fillette fillette
ce que tu te goures

will last forever
you're fooling yourself
little sweetie little sweetie
you're fooling yourself

The lovely days disappear
the lovely holidays
suns and planets
go round in a circle
but you my little one
you go straight
toward you know not what
very slowly draw near
the sudden wrinkle
the weighty fat
the triple chin
the flabby muscle
come gather gather
the roses the roses
roses of life
and may their petals
be a calm sea
of happinesses
come gather gather
if you don't do it
you're fooling yourself
little sweetie little sweetie
you're fooling yourself

—MICHAEL BENEDIKT

## PATER NOSTER

Notre Père qui êtes aux cieux
Restez-y
Et nous nous resterons sur la terre
Qui est quelquefois si jolie
Avec ses mystères de New York
Et puis ses mystères de Paris
Qui valent bien celui de la Trinité
Avec son petit canal de l'Ourcq
Sa grande muraille de Chine
Sa rivière de Morlaix
Ses bêtises de Cambrai
Avec son océan Pacifique
Et ses deux bassins aux Tuileries
Avec ses bons enfants et ses mauvais sujets
Avec toutes les merveilles du monde
Qui sont là
Simplement sur la terre
Offertes à tout le monde
Éparpillées
Émerveillées elles-mêmes d'être de telles merveilles
Et qui n'osent se l'avouer
comme une jolie fille nue qui n'ose se montrer
Avec les épouvantables malheurs du monde

# Jacques Prevert
## 1900-1977

PATER NOSTER

Our Father who art in heaven
Stay there
And we'll stay here on earth
Which is sometimes so pretty
With its mysteries of New York
And its mysteries of Paris
At least as good as that of the Trinity
With its little canal at Ourcq
Its great wall of China
Its river of Morlaix
Its candy canes
With its Pacific Ocean
And its two basins in the Tuileries
With its good children and bad people
With all the wonders of the world
Which are here
Simply on the earth
Offered to everyone
Strewn about
Wondering at the wonder of themselves
And daring not avow it
As a naked pretty girl dares not show herself
With the world's outrageous misfortunes

Qui sont légion
Avec leurs légionnaires
Avec leurs tortionnaires
Avec les maîtres de ce monde
Les maîtres avec leurs prêtres leurs traîtres et leurs
reîtres
Avec les saisons
Avec les années
Avec les jolies filles et avec les vieux cons
Avec la paille de la misère pourrissant dans l'acier des
canons.

## LE CANCRE

Il dit non avec la tête
mais il dit oui avec le cœur
il dit oui à ce qu'il aime
il dit non au professeur
il est debout
on le questionne
et tous les problèmes sont posés
soudain le fou rire le prend
et il efface tout
les chiffres et les mots
les dates et les noms
les phrases et les pièges
et malgré les menaces du maître
sous les huées des enfants prodiges
avec des craies de toutes les couleurs
sur le tableau noir du malheur
il dessine le visage du bonheur

Which are legion
With legionaries
With torturers
With the masters of this world
The masters with their priests their traitors and their troops
With the seasons
With the years
With the pretty girls and with the old bastards
With the straw of misery rotting in the steel
of cannons.

—LAWRENCE FERLINGHETTI

## THE DUNCE

He says no with his head
but he says yes with his heart
he says yes to what he loves
he says no to the teacher
he stands
he is questioned
and all the problems are posed
sudden laughter seizes him
and he erases all
the words and figures
names and dates
sentences and snares
and despite the teacher's threats
to the jeers of infant prodigies
with chalk of every color
on the blackboard of misfortune
he draws the face of happiness.

—LAWRENCE FERLINGHETTI

## LA CÈNE

Ils sont à table
Ils ne mangent pas
Ils ne sont pas dans leur assiette
Et leur assiette se tient toute droite
Verticalement derrière leur tête.

## ET LA FÊTE CONTINUE

Debout devant le zinc
Sur le coup de dix heures
Un grand plombier zingueur
Habillé en dimanche et pourtant c'est lundi
Chante pour lui tout seul
Chante que c'est jeudi
Qu'il n'ira pas en classe
Que la guerre est finie
Et le travail aussi
Que la vie est si belle
Et les filles si jolies
Et titubant devant le zinc
Mais guidé par son fil à plomb
Il s'arrête pile devant le patron
Trois paysans passeront et vous paieront
Puis disparaît dans le soleil
Sans régler les consommations
Disparaît dans le soleil tout en continuant sa chanson.

# THE LAST SUPPER

They are at table
They eat not
Nor touch their plates
And their plates stand straight up
Behind their heads.

—LAWRENCE FERLINGHETTI

# AND THE FETE CONTINUES

Standing before the bar
At the stroke of ten
A tall plumber
Dressed for sunday on monday
Sings for himself alone
Sings that it's thursday
That there's no school today
That the war is over
And work too
That life is so beautiful
And the girls so pretty
And staggering by the bar
But guided by his plumb-line
He stops dead before the proprietor
Three peasants will pass and pay you
Then disappears in the sun
Without settling for the drinks
Disappears in the sun all the while singing his song.

—LAWRENCE FERLINGHETTI

# BARBARA

Rappelle-toi Barbara
Il pleuvait sans cesse sur Brest ce jour-là
Et tu marchais souriante
Épanouie ravie ruisselante
Sous la pluie
Rappelle-toi Barbara
Il pleuvait sans cesse sur Brest
Et je t'ai croisée rue de Siam
Tu souriais
Et moi je souriais de même
Rappelle-toi Barbara
Toi que je ne connaissais pas
Toi qui ne me connaissais pas
Rappelle-toi
Rappelle-toi quand même ce jour-là
N'oublie pas
Un homme sous un porche s'abritait
Et il a crié ton nom
Barbara
Et tu as couru vers lui sous la pluie
Ruisselante ravie épanouie
Et tu t'es jetée dans ses bras
Rappelle-toi cela Barbara
Et ne m'en veux pas si je te tutoie
Je dis tu à tous ceux que j'aime
Même si je ne les ai vus qu'une seule fois
Je dis tu à tous ceux qui s'aiment
Même si je ne les connais pas
Rappelle-toi Barbara
N'oublie pas
Cette pluie sage et heureuse
Sur ton visage heureux
Sur cette ville heureuse
Cette pluie sur la mer
Sur l'arsenal
Sur le bateau d'Ouessant
Oh Barbara
Quelle connerie la guerre
Qu'es-tu devenue maintenant
Sous cette pluie de fer
De feu d'acier de sang
Et celui qui te serrait dans ses bras

# BARBARA

Remember Barbara
It rained all day on Brest that day
And you walked smiling
Flushed enraptured streaming-wet
In the rain
Remember Barbara
It rained all day on Brest that day
And I ran into you in Siam Street
You were smiling
And I smiled too
Remember Barbara
You whom I didn't know
You who didn't know me
Remember
Remember that day still
Don't forget
A man was taking cover on a porch
And he cried your name
Barbara
And you ran to him in the rain
Streaming-wet enraptured flushed
And you threw yourself in his arms
Remember that Barbara
And don't be mad if I speak familiarly
I speak familiarly to everyone I love
Even if I've seen them only once
I speak familiarly to all who are in love
Even if I don't know them
Remember Barbara
Don't forget
That good and happy rain
On your happy face
On that happy town
That rain upon the sea
Upon the arsenal
Upon the Ushant boat
Oh Barbara
What shitstupidity the war
Now what's become of you
Under this iron rain
Of fire and steel and blood
And he who held you in his arms

Amoureusement
Est-il mort disparu ou bien encore vivant
Oh Barbara
Il pleut sans cesse sur Brest
Comme il pleuvait avant
Mais ce n'est plus pareil et tout est abîmé
C'est une pluie de deuil terrible et désolée
Ce n'est même plus l'orage
De fer d'acier de sang
Tout simplement des nuages
Qui crèvent comme des chiens
Des chiens qui disparaissent
Au fil de l'eau sur Brest
Et vont pourrir au loin
Au loin très loin de Brest
Dont il ne reste rien.

Amorously
Is he dead and gone or still so much alive
Oh Barbara
It's rained all day on Brest today
As it was raining before
But it isn't the same anymore
And everything is wrecked
It's a rain of mourning terrible and desolate
Nor is it still a storm
Of iron and steel and blood
But simply clouds
That die like dogs
Dogs that disappear
In the downpour drowning Brest
And float away to rot
A long way off
A long long way from Brest
Of which there's nothing left.

—LAWRENCE FERLINGHETTI

## TRISTE PETIT TRAIN DE VIE

Celle qui pourrit dans mon cœur
c'est la lueur qui se nourrit des peurs
qui rôdent chantant le malheur,
en haut, en bas, toujours.

Nuit sur la nuit, c'est fête, enfonçons la détresse
sous l'ouate d'une joie épaisse;
nuit sur la nuit, c'est la faiblesse
du cœur brisé par de trop beaux visages, sur la route.

La pourriture est dans mon souffle et ce vent
c'est le siffleur fascinant, c'est la dent,
c'est le goût de saumure de ce gouffre avant
la fuite en bas, la tête sous la nuit des trop douces larmes.

Plaie du jour à mon flanc!
la nuit, c'est mon sang
qui s'enfuit par ce trou blanc,
soleil qui me baigne jusqu'au petit matin,
　　　　m'ôte la faim
　　　　　au petit matin de ma fin,

# René Daumal

## 1908-1944

SAD LITTLE ROUND OF LIFE

What rots in my heart
Is the glimmer which feeds on fears
Which prowl around singing evil
High low all the time.

Night after night it's a holiday
Let's swathe the pain
In wads of thick joy
Night after night, it's the weak
Heart broken by too many
Beautiful faces along the way.

My breath is rotten and the wind
Is a charming whistler, is a tooth,
Is the taste of brine, of the gulf before
The plunge to the depths, the head
Under the night of mawkish tears.

Wound of day on my thigh
At night it's my blood
Which runs away through a white hole—
This sun which bathes me at dawn.

personne n'entend, personne,
personne ne tend la main,
je suis l'aiguille,
l'aiguille dans le tas de foin,
le foin sans fin, l'étouffeur à la fin . . .

personne ne vient, personne ne pleure,
sauf toujours la même, la terreur.

## LA PEAU DE LUMIÈRE . . .

La peau de lumière vêtant ce monde est sans épaisseur et moi je vois la nuit
profonde de tous les corps identique sous le voile varié et la lumière de
moi-même c'est cette nuit que même le masque solaire ne peut plus me cacher.
Je suis le voyant de la nuit l'auditeur du silence car le silence aussi s'habille
d'une peau sonore et chaque sens a sa nuit comme moi-même je suis ma nuit
je suis le penseur du non-être et sa splendeur je suis le père de la mort. Elle
en est la mère elle que j'évoque du parfait miroir de la nuit je suis l'homme
à l'envers ma parole est un trou dans le silence. Je connais la désillusion je
détruis ce que je deviens je tue ce que j'aime.

## LA RÉVOLUTION EN ÉTÉ

La lumière est excessive. Les hommes courent acheter des foulards, et ce
n'est pas pour se moucher.
Dernier recours: l'éclipse, acrobatie céleste.
Dans le carnaval cosmique, cet homme qui prend au sérieux son rôle de
planète. On brûle le soleil en effigie, ironie du sort, plaisanterie d'esclaves.
Qu'on n'en rie pas trop. Les esclaves tournent maintenant autour de la
meule qui moud du vide. Leur sueur enivre les astres, le soleil pansu se traîne
dans la poussière des routes, un œil crevé s'ouvre dans le ciel et les esclaves
rient, les épaules luisantes.

I put away my hunger
On the dawn of my end
Nobody understands, nobody,
Nobody gives me a hand.
I am a needle
A needle in a haystack
Of infinite hay.
Nobody comes, nobody weeps,
Only the same thing, the terror.

—KENNETH REXROTH

## THE SKIN OF LIGHT . . .

The skin of light enveloping this world lacks depth and I can actually see the black night of all these similar bodies beneath the trembling veil and light of myself it is this night that even the mask of the sun cannot hide from me I am the seer of night the auditor of silence for silence too is dressed in sonorous skin and each sense has its own night even as I do I am my own night I am the conceiver of non-being and of all its splendor I am the father of death she is its mother she whom I evoke from the perfect mirror of night I am the great inside-out man my words are a tunnel punched through silence I understand all disillusionment I destroy what I become I kill what I love

—MICHAEL BENEDIKT

## REVOLUTION IN SUMMERTIME

Too much light. Men run around buying scarves, and it's not to blow their noses in.

Last recourse: eclipse, celestial acrobatics.

In the cosmic carnival, this man who takes his role as planet seriously. They're burning the sun in effigy, irony of fate, a slave's joke.

Hold back on the laughter. Now the slaves are turning around the millstone that grinds the void. Their sweat makes the stars drunk, the potbellied sun crawls in the dust of roads, a shattered eye opens in the sky and the slaves laugh, their shoulders shining.

—ARMAND SCHWERNER

## LE PAYS DES MÉTAMORPHOSES

Me voici encore au carrefour, avec cette terreur blanche qui m'attend. Mes conquêtes me coulent des doigts, mes belles conquêtes sages, folles, rouges, vertes, tournant comme un sémaphore maintenant inutile. Et la peur blanche luit sur la falaise, une gelée vivante tremble sur le sol. Les étincelles des anciens désastres s'éteignent sur mes mains de charbon. Ah! pour cette fois cela n'ira pas sans que je crie, sans que je casse quelque chose, et voilà, voilà, mes plus précieux bijoux je les brise sous mon talon et c'est pour ton œil de folie claire, lune de craie qui me défend l'accès des océans. Pour ton œil que rien n'aveugle, pour en finir plus vite—et pour recommencer—ah! ton éternelle ruse! Tu me dictes même ma fureur, et la voici déjà écroulée. Les glaçons filent sur le fleuve limoneux et l'éclair silencieux ne luit que sur des morts.

Je reviens à ma situation humaine, que veux-je dire? Ah! il s'agit donc de moi? Ces accidents brisent ma voix, faut-il donc renverser les murs pour se faire comprendre? et ce ne serait encore rien.

Un maître impitoyable au sourire de glace lumineuse me propose un autre corps, et me voici, ayant accepté l'épouvantable marché, devant toujours la même gelée tremblante sur la falaise blanche; devant ce corps sans forme que je ne sais comment animer. C'est le terrible amour qui m'est réservé, celui que j'ai choisi, hélas! Je suis stupide comme un adolescent devant la première femme, avec des yeux qui certainement me sortent peu à peu de la tête, en calculant mentalement le nombre de secondes renfermées dans une année, pour tenter de ne pas croire à cela. Il faut me tailler là-dedans des yeux, des oreilles, une bouche, des narines, des membres et tout un corps comme je le désire, mais la vie est traître, elle ne voulait pas me quitter et se collait à mes os; maintenant elle m'a laissé, non, je n'aurais pas la force d'entrer dans cette mer, je n'engendre que des cadavres. Les lueurs tournant encore sur les dunes, elles sont devenues grises. Oh! c'est vrai, non, ce n'est pas la peine de se cacher, dans les boues, des cadavres, des cadavres seulement, plus vite et plus vite; à chaque tour du sang de peur au sémaphore des dunes, il tombe un nouveau cadavre. Voilà. Mon désespoir ne ferait plus bouger un brin d'herbe, et j'ai la voix blanche des mourants—non je n'ai plus ni voix ni souffle, je ne sais pas, qu'est-ce que ça peut faire? Une ombre, les vivants ne la connaissent plus; mais reconnaîtront-ils un jour son reflet dans le sourire cruel des morts solitaires?

## THE COUNTRY OF METAMORPHOSES

Here I am again at the crossroads, with this white terror waiting for me. My conquests run from my fingers, my pretty conquests—wise, insane, red, green—turning like a now useless semaphore. And the white fear shines on the cliff, a living frost trembles on the ground. The sparks of old disasters extinguish themselves on my charcoal hands. This time it won't all go by without my crying out, without my breaking something, and look—my most precious jewels: I crush them under my heel and it's for your eye of clear madness, chalk moon which forbids me ocean access. For your eye nothing can blind, for a quicker end—and for a new beginning—ah your eternal ruse! You even dictate my fury, and it's already crumbled. The icicles spin on the silty river and the noiseless lightning shines only on the dead.

I come back to my human situation, meaning what? Ah, is it about me? These accidents shatter my voice, do I have to break down walls to make myself understood? and yet it would still mean nothing.

A pitiless teacher with a smile like luminous ice offers me another body and here I am, having accepted the appalling deal, still facing the same trembling frost on the white cliff, facing this formless body I don't know how to quicken. It's the terrible love set aside for me, the one I chose. I'm as stupid as an adolescent with his first woman, my eyes certainly popping out of my head, figuring the number of seconds in a year, in order not to believe all this. I've got to carve out eyes, ears, a mouth, nostrils, limbs, the body I want, but life betrays, she wouldn't leave me and stuck to my bones; now she's left me, no, I wouldn't have the strength to enter into that sea, I give birth only to corpses. The lights still turning on the dunes have turned grey. Oh, it's true, no, no point in hiding. In the mud, corpses only corpses, faster and faster; at every turning of the blood of terror in the dunes' semaphore a new corpse falls. That's it. My desperation wouldn't stir one blade of grass and I've got the white voice of the dying—no I have neither voice nor breath any more, I don't know, so what? A shadow the living no longer recognize; but will they one day recognize its reflection in the cruel smile of the solitary dead?

—ARMAND SCHWERNER

# JÉSUS DEVANT PILATE

*(Matthieu, 27)*

Jésus devant Pilate ne répondait pas un mot. Et le gouverneur s'en émerveillait grandement.—Il se dit: « Voici un homme comme on n'en voit pas tous les jours. Quel plaisir j'aurais eu à philosopher avec lui, si mes fonctions ne me l'interdisaient! » Il dévore Jésus des yeux. Mais sa main droite se cramponne à la boule de l'accoudoir, qui lui rappelle le globe symbolique de l'Empire, dont il est un fonctionnaire fidèle et sans doute bien payé. Et puis, il y a Caïphe, bouffi de haine sous ses habits épiscopaux, qui ne veut pas manquer cette occasion de réconcilier contre le Fils de l'Homme le sarcasme sadducéen et l'hypocrisie pharisienne. Et enfin, il y a la foule, qui réclame Barabbas, ce brave garçon, qui a déjà le pied droit hors de la geôle, tandis que les menuisiers préparent la croix. L'Administration, le Clergé, la Populace: devant ces trois pouvoirs, Pilate n'a plus qu'à se laver les mains. Chacun, ici, est prisonnier de sa fonction, de son déguisement, et chacun regarde avec son masque le seul qui soit sans masque, le seul qui soit un et qui regarde au centre de lui-même la vérité vivante: cette vérité dont le nom seul préoccupe tant le pauvre Ponce Pilate.

# LE MOT ET LA MOUCHE

Un magicien avait coutume de divertir son monde du petit tour que voici. Ayant bien ventilé la chambre et fermé les fenêtres, il se penchait sur une grande table d'acajou et prononçait attentivement le mot « mouche ». Et aussitôt une mouche trottinait au milieu de la table, tâtant le vernis de sa petite trompe molle et se frottant les pattes de devant comme n'importe quelle mouche naturelle. Alors, de nouveau, le magicien se penchait sur la table et prononçait encore le mot « mouche ». Et l'insecte tombait raide sur le dos, comme foudroyé. En regardant son cadavre à la loupe, on ne voyait qu'une carcasse vide et sèche, ne renfermant aucun viscère, aucune humeur, aucune lueur dans les yeux à facettes. Le magicien regardait alors ses invités avec un sourire modeste, quêtant les compliments, qu'on lui accordait comme il se doit.

J'ai toujours trouvé ce tour assez misérable. A quoi aboutissait-il? Au commencement, il n'y avait rien, et à la fin il y avait un cadavre de mouche. La

# JESUS BEFORE PILATE

*(Matthew, 27)*

Jesus before Pilate said nothing. And the governor marvelled greatly. He says to himself: "One does not meet up with this kind of man everyday. What pleasure it would have given me to discuss ideas with him, if my official duties did not preclude such things!" He eyes Jesus with longing. But his right hand clasps the knob of the armrest, a reminder of the sphere of the Empire whose faithful and no doubt well-payed official he is. And then, there is Caiaphas, swollen with hatred under his priestly robes, unwilling to let pass this opportunity to unite the skepticism of the Sadducees with the hypocrisy of the Pharisees against the Son of Man. And last of all, there is the mob, calling for Barabbas, that good fellow who already has one foot outside the prison while the carpenters are finishing the cross within. Government, Clergy, Populace: before these three powers, Pilate has only to wash his hands. Everyone here is the prisoner of his office, of his facade, and everyone looks through his mask at the only one who wears no mask, the only one who in fact is one, who looks into the center of his being and sees the living truth: that truth whose name alone so utterly absorbs poor Pontius Pilate.

—KATHARINE WASHBURN

# POETRY AND THOUGHT

A magician was in the habit of amusing his public with the following little trick. Having well aired the room and closed the windows, he would lean over a large mahogany table and carefully pronounce the word "fly." And immediately a fly would be trotting about in the middle of the table, testing the polish with its soft little proboscis and rubbing its front legs together like any natural fly. Then the magician would lean over the table again, and once again pronounce the word "fly." And the insect would fall flat on its back, as if struck by lightning. Looking at the corpse through a magnifying glass, one could see only a dry and empty carcass, no innards, no life, no light in the facetted eyes. The magician would then look at his guests with a modest smile, seeking compliments which were duly paid him.

I have always thought this was a pretty pathetic trick. Where did it lead? At the beginning there was nothing, and at the end there was the corpse of a fly. Such progress. And one still had to get rid of the corpses—although

belle avance! Il fallait encore se débarrasser des cadavres—encore qu'une vieille admiratrice du magicien les collectionnât, quand elle pouvait les ramasser à la dérobée. Cela faisait mentir la règle: « jamais deux sans trois ». On attendait une troisième profération du mot « mouche », qui eût fait disparaître sans traces le cadavre de l'insecte; ainsi toutes choses à la fin eussent été comme au commencement, sauf dans nos mémoires, déjà bien assez encombrées sans cela.

Je dois préciser que c'était un assez médiocre magicien, un raté qui, après s'être essayé avec aussi peu de bonheur à la poésie et à la philosophie, avait transporté ses ambitions dans l'art des prestiges; et même là, il lui manquait encore quelque chose.

there was an aging lady admirer of the magician who collected them, whenever she could pick them up unnoticed. It disproved the rule: where there's two there's always three. One expected a third utterance of the word "fly" which would have made the insect's corpse disappear without a trace; in that way things would have been the same at the end as they were at the beginning, except in our memories, which are quite cluttered enough without that.

I must add that he was a fairly mediocre magician, a failure who, having tried his hand at poetry and philosophy without much luck, transferred his ambitions to the art of wonders; and even there he didn't really come up to scratch.

—MICHAEL WOOD

## FACE

Pays de rocaille, pays de broussaille—rocs
Agacés de sécheresse.

Terre
Comme une gorge irritée
Demandant du lait,
Femme sans mâle, colline
Comme une fourmilière ébouillantée,
Terre sans ventre, musique de cuivre:
Face
De juge.

# Eugène Guillevic
1907-

---

FACE

Country of rubble, country of brush—rocks
Rasped by drought.

Earth
Like an inflamed throat
Calling for milk,
Woman without man, hill
Like a scalded antheap,
Earth without womb, music of brass:
Judge-face.

—TEO SAVORY

## QUE DÉJÀ JE ME LÈVE . . .

Que déjà je me lève en ce matin d'été
Sans regretter longtemps la nuit et le repos,

Que déjà je me lève
Et que j'aie cette envie d'eau froide
Pour ma nuque et pour mon visage,

Que je regarde avec envie
L'abeille en grand travail
Et que je la comprenne,

Que déjà je me lève et voie le buis,
Qui probablement travaille autant que l'abeille,
Et que j'en sois content,

Que je me sois levé au-devant de la lumière
Et que je sache: la journée est à ouvrir,

Déjà, c'est victoire.

## LA MER . . .

La mer comme un néant
Qui se voudrait la mer,

Qui voudrait se donner
Des attributs terrestres

Et la force qu'elle a
Par référence au vent.

LET ME GET UP EARLY . . .

Let me get up early on this summer morning,
without regretting a longer night for repose,

Let me get up early
and let me desire this cold water
for my neck and my face.

Let me watch the bee with envy
in his ceaseless work,
and let me understand it.

Let me get up early and see the boxwood
that probably works as hard as the bee,
and let me be satisfied with that.

Let me get up before the light
and let me know: the day is beginning.

Already, this is victory.

—TEO SAVORY

THE SEA . . .

The sea, a nothingness
Which longs to be the sea

Which longs to lend itself
Earthliness

And the drive she
Derives from the wind.

—JOHN MONTAGUE

## SOYONS JUSTES . . .

Soyons justes: sans toi
Que nous serait l'espace
Et que seraient les rocs?

Ta peur de n'être pas
Te fait copier les bêtes

Et ta peur de rater
Les mouvements des bêtes,
Leurs alarmes, leurs cris,
Te les fait agrandir.

Quelquefois tu mugis
Comme aucune d'entre elles

## L'ÉTERNITÉ . . .

L'éternité
ne fut jamais perdue.

Ce qui nous a manqué
Fut plutôt de savoir

La traduire en journées,
En ciels, en paysages,

En paroles pour d'autres,
En gestes vérifiables.

Mais la garder pour nous
N'était pas difficile

Et les moments étaient présents
Où nous paraissait clair
Que nous étions l'éternité.

BE FAIR . . .

Be fair: if you weren't there
What would space
And the rocks be?

Your fear of not being
Makes you imitate the beasts

And your fear of missing
The movement of beasts,
Their alarm, their cries,
Makes you magnify them.

Sometimes you moan
Like nobody's business.

—JOHN MONTAGUE

ETERNITY . . .

Eternity
never was lost.

What we did not know

was how to translate it into days,
skies, landscapes,

into words for others,
authentic gestures.

But holding on to it for ourselves,
that was not difficult,

and there were moments
when it seemed clear to us
we ourselves were eternity.

—DENISE LEVERTOV

UN BAHUT

Je t'ai ciré,
Je t'ai frotté,

J'ai pris plaisir
A te donner ma peine,

A sentir mon pouvoir
Sur ton gros bois de chêne.

Presque tu ronronnais
Sur ton linge et ton creux.

Je te regarde maintenant,
Je me sens net.

LA FLAMME

J'ai vu la flamme. Elle est partout,

Dans ce que je regarde
Quand pour de bon je le regarde.

Elle y demeure et bouge
A peine plus qu'un mot,

Dans le morceau de zinc, le panneau de l'armoire,
Le crayon, la pendule et le vin dans les verres,
Dans le pot de tabac, dans l'émail du réchaud,
Le papier sur la table et le linge lavé,
Dans le fer du marteau, dans la conduite en cuivre,
Dans ton genou plié, dans tes lieux plus cachés.

Parfois dans l'âtre la voilà
Qui se dévoile, se proclame
Et va périr.

## A CABINET

I've waxed you,
I've rubbed you.

I've taken pleasure
in giving you my pain,

In feeling my power
over your thick oakwood.

You were almost purring
over your linen and your hollowness.

I look at you now
and I feel clean.

—TEO SAVORY

## THE FLAME

I have seen the flame. It is everywhere,

In whatever I look at,
whenever I look for something good.

It lives and moves there,
scarcely more than a word,

In the piece of zinc, the cupboard door,
the pencil, the clock, and the wine in the glass,
in the tobacco-jar, in the stove's enamel,
the paper on the table and the clean clothes,
in the iron of the hammer, in the copper piping,
in your crossed knees, your most hidden places.

Sometimes it's there on the hearth,
revealing itself, proclaiming itself,
and going on to perish.

Ailleurs, tout comme d'autres,
Elle cherche sa place,
Elle cherche son chant
Dans la chair du silence,

Brûle du temps qui vient,
Refuse le sommeil,
Fait son travail de flamme,
Nous sauve et veut sourire.

## UN MARTEAU

Fait pour ma main,
Je te tiens bien.
Je me sens fort
De notre force.

Tu dors longtemps,
Tu sais le noir,
Tu as sa force.

Je te touche et te pèse,
Je te balance,
Je te chauffe au creux de ma main.

Je remonte avec toi
Dans le fer et le bois.

Tu me ramènes,
Tu veux
T'essayer,
Tu veux frapper.

Elsewhere it, like all others,
seeks its place,
looks for its song,
in the flesh of silence,

Burning the time to come,
refusing sleep,
going on with its work of flame,
saving us and wanting to smile.

—TEO SAVORY

## A HAMMER

You're made for my hand,
I get a firm grip on you,
and feel
strong in our strength.

You sleep a lot,
you know what black is,
its force is your force.

I touch you, weigh you, balance you,
warm you in the hollow of my hand.

I return with you
into iron and wood.

But you pull me back:
you want
to try yourself,
to strike.

—DENISE LEVERTOV

# ESPAGNE

*à Maria Théresa Leon et à Rafael Alberti*

Un silence, Espagne, un silence et rien
Que ce trou noir et froid dans un coin de mémoire.

Espagne, il y en a
Qui n'ont pas don pour écouter.

Il y en a qui ne croient pas
Et c'est les mêmes.

Ils ne croient qu'au malheur
Et ça les mène loin,

Jusqu'à des routes
Où tu n'es pas.

Il y en a qui ont été
Jusqu'à confondre, c'est leur crime,
Ton silence avec ton secret.

## SPAIN

A silence, Spain, a silence and nothing
but this black, cold hole in a corner of memory.

Spain, there are people
with no gift for listening.

There are people without belief
and they are the same ones.

They believe only in sorrow,
and that leads them far away,

away to roads
where you are not.

There are some who have been
so far away they confound—and that's their crime—
your silence with your secret.

—DENISE LEVERTOV

## ÉPITAPHE

Quand je remettrai mon ardoise au néant
un de ces prochains jours,
il ne me ricanera pas à la gueule.
Mes chiffres ne sont pas faux,
ils font un zéro pur.
Viens mon fils, dira-t-il de ses dents froides,
dans le sein dont tu es digne.
Je m'étendrai dans sa douceur.


## MAISON À VENDRE

Tant de gens ont vécu là, qui aimaient
l'amour, le réveil et enlever la poussière.
Le puits est sans fond et sans lune,
les anciens sont partis et n'ont rien emporté.
Bouffe le lierre sous le soleil d'hier,
reste la suie, leur marc de café.
Je m'attelle aux rêves éraillés.

# André Frénaud

1907-

## EPITAPH

When I put my slate back in the void
one of these days,
the void will not sneer in my face.
My figures are not wrong,
they add up to a round 0.
Come my son, it will say with its cold teeth,
into the bosom you are worthy of.
I shall stretch out in its sweetness.

—KEITH BOSLEY

## HOUSE FOR SALE

So many have lived here, who loved
love, waking up and raising the dust.
The well is bottomless and moonless,
the previous folk have left and taken nothing away.
The ivy bulges in yesterday's sunlight,
the soot, their coffee-grounds remain.
I settle down to frayed dreams.

J'aime la crasse de l'âme des autres,
mêlée à ces franges de grenat,
le suint des entreprises manquées.
Concierge, j'achète, j'achète la baraque.
Si elle m'empoisonne, je m'y flambe.
On ouvrira les fenêtres . . . Remets la plaque.
Un homme entre, il flaire, il recommence.


## IL N'Y A PAS DE PARADIS

*à Dylan Thomas*

Je ne peux entendre la musique de l'être
Je n'ai reçu le pouvoir de l'imaginer
Mon amour s'alimente à un non-amour
Je n'avance qu'attisé par son refus
Il m'emporte dans ses grands bras de rien
Son silence me sépare de ma vie

Être sereinement brûlant que j'assiège
quand enfin je vais l'atteindre dans les yeux
sa flamme a déjà creusé les miens m'a fait cendres
Qu'importe après le murmure misérable du poème
C'est néant cela non le paradis.

Je venais d'apprendre par une personne amie de Dylan
Thomas qu'au cours d'une conversation celui-ci,
imaginant et rêvant, s'était écrié: « Je voudrais faire
entendre la musique du Paradis. »


## MACHINE INUTILE

Une machine à faire du bruit
qui s'ébroue et supplie et proclame
pas seulement pour vous faire taire
peut-être pas pour m'amuser

I love the muck from others' souls,
mixed with these garnet fringes,
the grease of failed undertakings.
Caretaker, I'll buy, I'll buy the shack.
If it poisons me, I'll go to blazes.
We'll open the windows . . . Put away the sign.
A man is moving in, sniffing, starting again.

—KEITH BOSLEY

# THERE IS NO PARADISE

*for Dylan Thomas*

I cannot hear the music of existence
I have not been given the power to imagine it
My love feeds on non-love
I cannot move unless stirred by its refusal
It carries me away in its huge arms of nothing
Its silence separates me from my life

Being serenely burning that I besiege
when finally I have reached its eyes
its flame has already hollowed mine made me ashes
What matters after the poor murmur of the poem
Is nothingness—not paradise.

—SERGE GAVRONSKY

# USELESS MACHINE

A machine to make noise
that snorts and begs and proclaims
not only to keep you quiet
perhaps not to amuse me

construite en mots dépaysés
pour se décolorer l'un par l'autre
pour entrer dans l'épais du grain
pour y trouer tous les grains
pour y passer par les trous
pour y pomper l'eau imprenable
dont le courant gronde sans bruit
machine à capter ce silence
pour vous en mettre dans l'oreille
à grands coups d'ailes inutiles.

## POUR BOIRE AUX AMIS

Je boirai en souvenir de la blancheur des montagnes.
Je tirerai du vin du bouillonnement de la source
par-delà les hauts lieux glacés.
Pour offrir le meilleur aux amis pour les réjouir,
il faut n'avoir eu peur de rien,
il faut s'être avancé très haut.
Pour m'inviter à boire, moi aussi,
comme si j'étais devenu mon ami
par la grâce de la blancheur de la source,
pour devenir mon ami droit dans les yeux.

## HAINEUSEMENT MON AMOUR LA POÉSIE

Comme un serpent qui remonte les rivières
comme une épée qui tombe reparaît sans mot dire
comme une grosse femme qui bout
comme une paire de haricots qui débouche
par-dessus la terre râtissée

built out of alien words
to discolor one by the other
to enter the depth of the grain
to pierce all the grains
to pass through the holes
to draw the impregnable water
whose course roars without noise
a machine to capture this silence
to put some of it in your ear
with a great fluttering of useless wings.

—SERGE GAVRONSKY

## TO DRINK TO FRIENDS

I will drink in remembrance of the whiteness of mountains.
I will draw wine from the bubbling of the spring
beyond the frozen high places.
To offer the best to friends to cheer them,
we need to have been afraid of nothing,
we need to have come a long way up.
To invite myself to drink also,
as if I had become my friend
by the grace of the whiteness of the spring,
to become my friend straight in the eye.

—KEITH BOSLEY

## HATEFULLY POETRY MY LOVE

Like a serpent that ascends the rivers
like a sword that fallen reappears without a word
like a fat woman that boils over
like a pair of stringbeans that appear
above the raked earth

comme sur un mur qu'éboule l'ardeur de la salamandre
seul feu elle traverse étincelante le vide
comme le temps travaillé par la nuit
obscure comme un ver luisant
branchue comme une étoile longuement éteinte
qui tout à coup reprend lumière
haineusement mon amour la poésie.

## JE NE T'AI JAMAIS OUBLIÉE

Sans nom maintenant, sans visage,
sans plus rien de tes yeux ni de ta pâleur.

Dénoué de l'assaut de mon désir
dans ton égarante image,
dénué par les faux aveux du temps,
par les fausses pièces de l'amour racheté,
par tous ces gains perdu,
libéré de toi maintenant,
libre comme un mort,
vivant de seule vie moite,
enjoué avec les pierres et les feuillages.

Quand je glisse entre les seins des douces mal aimées
je gis encore sur ton absence,
sur la vivante morte que tu fais
par ton pouvoir ordonné à me perdre
jusqu'au bout de mon silence.

like a wall that crumbles under the heat of the salamander
casting sparks into the void when it crosses fire
like time worked over by night
obscure like a firefly
branched like a long extinguished star
that suddenly lights up again
hatefully poetry my love.

—SERGE GAVRONSKY

# I HAVE NEVER FORGOTTEN YOU

No more your name, not your face,
No more your eyes, nor your pallor.

Loosed from the assaults of my desire
                    by your lost image,
Stripped by the false vows of time,
By the counterfeit money of redeemed love,
By all that lost profit—
Free of you now,
Free as the dead,
Living my lonely sodden life,
Playing with stones and leaves.

When I slip between kind, unloved breasts,
I lie once again on your absence,
On the living corpse you have made
By your power to destroy me
To the very end of my silence.

—KENNETH REXROTH

## MUTILATION VOLONTAIRE

Pour s'éviter de servir
aux armées de l'empereur,
un beau soir avec la hache
le maître se mutila
de deux grands doigts de sa main,
sa jeune et blonde épouse
pansa la plaie tendrement
et les pensées à cœur jaune
tremblèrent dans le parterre
les deux chiens du maître hurlèrent
quand on le porta au lit
alors charbonnaient les lampes
entourées de papillons;
mais les femmes assemblées
sur la place du village
devant la rougeur des nuages
disaient que ce qu'elles voyaient
était le sang des soldats.

# Jean Follain

## 1903-1971

### VOLUNTARY MUTILATION

Rather than have to serve
in the emperor's armies
one fine evening the master
took the axe to himself
cut from his hand two great fingers,
his young blonde wife
gently bandaged the place
and the yellow-hearted
pansies shook in the border
the master's two dogs howled
as he was carried to bed
then the lamps smoked
surrounded by moths
but the women who gathered
on the village square
facing the red clouds said
that what they saw was the blood
of soldiers.

—W. S. MERWIN

## PAYSAGE DE L'ENFANT ALLANT
## CHEZ LES RÉGENTS

Ce grand silence liquide
habitant les tonneaux
ces minuscules insectes
s'essayant en vain à dévorer la peau des vierges
les charrons buvant près du chardon bleu
les frelons fabriquant leur miel blanc
l'abeille distillant son miel blond
les chaudrons fulgurants
que l'on frotte de cendre mouillée
les bruits de fin d'orage
l'âcre fumée
de la mauvaise herbe brûlée
en tas dans les jardins à buis
et le portrait d'un roi
au mur de la cuisine
et l'argile et le plâtre
dans les royaumes humides,
Tout est Courrier d'une impossible aurore;
voilà qu'elle est déjà tout en haut de la côte
la veuve
qui conduit par la main jusqu'au lointain collège
l'enfant à tignasse rouge.

## SOIRS D'ENCRE

Obsédant souvenir des contacts
premiers,
c'était le frémissement des tiges
et des feuilles dans le jardin
aux sournois jours de cendre.
Taches d'encre
dans les soirs rouges
alors que tremblaient les bêtes;
taches qui s'étoilaient
sur le maigre papier des cahiers froids.

## LANDSCAPE OF A CHILD ON HIS WAY
## TO THE PLACE OF THE REGENTS

This great liquid silence
inhabiting the barrels
these tiny insects
trying in vain to devour the skin of virgins
the wheelwrights drinking near the blue thistle
the hornets making their white honey
the bees distilling their blond honey
the flashing cauldrons
that are rubbed with wet ashes
the sounds of the storm's end
the rank smoke
of weeds burning in piles
in box-hedged gardens
and the portrait of a king
on the kitchen wall
and the clay and plaster
in the damp kingdoms:
All of it is the Messenger of an impossible dawn:
there she is already at the top of the hill
the widow
leading by the hand to the distant school
the child with the wild red hair.

—W. S. MERWIN

## EVENINGS OF INK

Obsessive memory of first
contacts,
it was the rustling of twigs
and leaves in the garden
in the sullen days of ash.
Spots of ink
in the red evenings
while the beasts trembled;
spots that ran into stars
on the thin paper of cold notebooks.

Immenses brumes autour des femmes,
elles allaient
saluant les croix rougées.
Encre dont il revoit les sels verts,
quand ses yeux se fatiguent,
quand sa gorge est amère.
Encre d'apparat
dans le bourg envieux.


NOIR D'UNE ENFANCE

Lampes éteintes
ses parents partis au spectacle
un enfant se bute aux armoires énormes
aux courbes des consoles
aucun vase n'est pourtant brisé;
en habit noir le père
s'endort au vieux théâtre
la femme éloignant toute image de mort
montre une gorge reposée
qu'ornent des bijoux froids.


L'ŒUF

La vieille dame essuie un œuf
avec son tablier d'usage
œuf couleur ivoire et lourd
que nul ne lui revendique
puis elle regarde l'automne
par la petite lucarne
et c'est comme un tableau fin
aux dimensions d'une image
rien n'y est

Immense fogs around women,
they went
greeting the gnawed crosses.
Ink whose green salts he sees again
when his eyes grow tired,
when his throat is bitter.
Sumptuous ink
in the envious town.

—W. S. MERWIN


## CHILD'S BLACKNESS

Lights out
his parents gone to the play
a child runs against great wardrobes
against the legs of tables
but no vase is broken:
dressed in black the father
dozes in the old theatre
as his wife putting off every image of death
displays an impassive throat
adorned with cold gems.

—KEITH WALDROP


## THE EGG

The old woman dried an egg
with her working apron
heavy egg the color of ivory
which nobody claims from her
then she looks at the autumn
through the little dormer
and it is like a fine painting
the size of a picture book
nothing is

hors de saison
et l'œuf fragile
que dans sa paume elle tient
reste le seul objet neuf.


## PENSÉES D'OCTOBRE

On aime bien
ce grand vin
que l'on boit solitaire
quand le soir illumine les collines cuivrées
plus un chasseur n'ajuste
les gibiers de la plaine
les sœurs de nos amis
apparaissent plus belles
il y a pourtant menace de guerre
un insecte s'arrête
puis repart.


## CHIEN AUX ÉCOLIERS

Les écoliers par jeu brisent la glace
dans un sentier
près du chemin de fer
on les a lourdement habillés
d'anciens lainages sombres
et ceinturés de cuirs fourbus
le chien qui les suit
n'a plus d'écuelle où manger tard
il est vieux
car il a leur âge.

out of season
and the fragile egg
that she holds in her palm
remains the one thing that is new.

—W. S. MERWIN

## OCTOBER THOUGHTS

How one loves
this great wine
that one drinks all alone
when the evening illumines its coppered hills
not a hunter now
stalks the lowland game
the sisters of our friends
seem more beautiful
at the same time there is a threat of war
an insect pauses
then goes on.

—W. S. MERWIN

## DOG WITH SCHOOLBOYS

For fun the schoolboys crack the ice
along a path
next to the railroad
they are heavily clothed
in dark old woolens
belted with beat leather
The dog that follows them
no longer has a bowl to eat from
he is old
for he is their age.

—KEITH WALDROP

VIE

Il naît un enfant
dans un grand paysage
un demi-siècle après
il n'est qu'un soldat mort
et c'était là cet homme
que l'on vit apparaître
et puis poser par terre
tout un lourd sac de pommes
dont deux ou trois roulèrent
bruit parmi ceux d'un monde
où l'oiseau chantait
sur la pierre du seuil.

FIN DE SIÈCLE

Une mouche marchait sur l'initiale
d'un drap lourd de silence
on éveilla l'enfant
un trente et un décembre
pour qu'il pût voir la fin d'un siècle
des visages épuisés
s'en adoucirent aux lueurs des flammes;
fronces, guipures, tresses
résisteraient des mois encore
l'avare ayant ouvert son coffre
avait rassasié son regard
mille ans après
tombe toujours la pluie
sur un village.

LIFE

A child is born
into a great landscape
Half a century later
he's nothing but a dead soldier
This was the man we saw appear
and then set on the ground
a heavy sack of apples
two or three of which rolled out
sound among a world's sounds
where birds sang
on the stone threshold.

—KEITH WALDROP

END OF A CENTURY

A fly walked on the initial
of a sheet heavy with silence
they woke the child
a thirty-first of December
to see the end of a century
worn out faces
softened in the glimmer of flames;
gathers, laces, braids
would last for a few months yet
the miser had opened his coffer
and feasted his eyes
a thousand years later
the rain still falls
on a village.

—W. S. MERWIN

## LE COSTUME DU SOIR

Sur le sol raviné
d'un paysage rafraîchi
un intrépide marcheur
pourvu par la charité
d'un vieux costume du soir
sent venir la mort
pour assez tard encore,
un fil s'est dépris de l'étoffe.
Donateur du vêtement noir
l'architecte va mener son pont
jusqu'à l'achèvement,
museau contre terre à ses pieds
un animal se repose
inconscient d'être né.

## ÈVE

Un livre déclare Ève
venir de la racine hayah
voulant dire vivre
cependant que des créatures
certaines d'exister
font apprendre aux filles
les passions humaines
mais la plus jeune
tient une pomme blonde
sur un seuil creusé
ne faisant rien d'autre
avant son sommeil.

## THE EVENING SUIT

Over the eroded earth
of a cooled landscape
an intrepid walker
whom charity has provided
with an old evening suit
feels death on the way
but not for some time yet,
a thread has pulled loose from the cloth.
Donor of the black garment
the architect will bring
his bridge to completion;
muzzle to earth at his feet
an animal rests
unaware of having been born.

—W. S. MERWIN

## EVE

One book has it that Eve
came from the haya root
meaning live
and at the same time creatures
sure of their existence
pass on to girls knowledge
of human passions
but the youngest
holds a blond apple
on a worn sill
and does nothing else
before she sleeps.

—W. S. MERWIN

## LES SEIGNEURS DE MAUSSANE

L'un après l'autre, ils ont voulu nous prédire un avenir heureux,
Avec une éclipse à leur image et toute l'angoisse conforme à nous!
Nous avons dédaigné cette égalité,
Répondu non à leurs mots assidus.
Nous avons suivi l'empierrement que notre cœur s'était tracé
Jusqu'aux plaines de l'air et l'unique silence.
Nous avons fait saigner notre amour exigeant,
Lutter notre bonheur avec chaque caillou.

Ils disent à présent qu'au delà de leur vue,
La grêle les effraie plus que la neige des morts!

# René Char

1907-

## THE LORDS OF MAUSSANE

One after the other, they wished to predict a happy future for us,
With an eclipse in their image and all the anguish befitting us!
We disdained this equality,
Answered no to their assiduous words.
We followed the stony way the heart traced for us
Up to the plains of the air and the unique silence.
We made our demanding love bleed,
Our happiness wrestle with each pebble.

They say at this moment that, beyond their vision,
The hail terrifies them, more than the snow of the dead!

—JAMES WRIGHT

## TOUTE VIE . . .

Toute vie qui doit poindre
achève un blessé.
Voici l'arme,
rien,
vous, moi, réversiblement
ce livre,
et l'énigme
qu'à votre tour vous deviendrez
dans le caprice amer des sables.

## A * * *

Tu es mon amour depuis tant d'années,
Mon vertige devant tant d'attente,
Que rien ne peut vieillir, froidir;
Même ce qui attendait notre mort,
Ou lentement sut nous combattre,
Même ce qui nous est étranger,
Et mes éclipses et mes retours.

Fermée comme un volet de buis
Une extrême chance compacte
Est notre chaîne de montagnes,
Notre comprimante splendeur.

Je dis chance, ô ma martelée;
Chacun de nous peut recevoir
La part de mystère de l'autre
Sans en répandre le secret;
Et la douleur qui vient d'ailleurs
Trouve enfin sa séparation
Dans la chair de notre unité,
Trouve enfin sa route solaire
Au centre de notre nuée
Qu'elle déchire et recommence.

EVERY LIFE . . .

Every life, as it dawns,
kills one of the injured.
This is the weapon:
nothing,
you, me, interchangeably
with this book,
and the riddle
that you, too, will become
in the bitter caprice of the sands.

—JAMES WRIGHT

TO . . .

You have been my love for so many years,
My giddiness before so much waiting,
Which nothing can age or cool;
Even that which awaited our death,
Or slowly learned how to fight us,
Even that which is strange to us,
Both my eclipses and my returns.

Closed like a box-wood shutter,
An extreme and compact chance
Is our chain, our mountain-range,
Our compressing splendour and glow.

I say chance, O my hammered one;
Either of us can receive
The mysterious part of the other
While keeping its secret unshed;
And the pain that comes from elsewhere
Finds its separation at last
In the flesh of our unity,
Finds its solar orbit at last
At the centre of our own cloud
Which it rends and starts once more.

Je dis chance comme je le sens.
Tu as élevé le sommet
Que devra franchir mon attente
Quand demain disparaîtra.

## A LA SANTÉ DU SERPENT

I

Je chante la chaleur à visage de nouveau-né, la chaleur désespérée.

II

Au tour du pain de rompre l'homme, d'être la beauté du point du jour.

III

Celui qui se fie au tournesol ne méditera pas dans la maison. Toutes les pensées de l'amour deviendront ses pensées.

IV

Dans la boucle de l'hirondelle un orage s'informe, un jardin se construit.

V

Il y aura toujours une goutte d'eau pour durer plus que le soleil sans que l'ascendant du soleil soit ébranlé.

VI

Produis ce que la connaissance veut garder secret, la connaissance aux cent passages.

VII

Ce qui vient au monde pour ne rien troubler ne mérite ni égards ni patience.

VIII

Combien durera ce manque de l'homme mourant au centre de la création parce que la création l'a congédié?

IX

Chaque maison était une saison. La ville ainsi se répétait. Tous les habi-

As I feel it, I say chance.
You have raised up the mountain-peak
Which my waiting will have to clear
When tomorrow disappears.

—MICHAEL HAMBURGER

# TO THE HEALTH OF THE SERPENT

I
I sing the heat that is like a newborn babe, desperate heat.

II
It is bread's turn to break man, to be the beauty of daybreak.

III
He who believes in the sunflower will not meditate in the house. All
thoughts of love will become his thoughts.

IV
Within the swallow's loop a storm is instructed, a garden formed.

V
There will always be a drop of water to outlast the sun, without shaking
the sun's ascendancy.

VI
Bring out that which knowledge would keep secret, knowledge with its
hundred corridors.

VII
That which comes into the world to disturb nothing deserves neither
respect nor patience.

VIII
How long will this failure last—man dying at the center of creation because
creation has dismissed him?

IX
Each house was a season. So the town revolved. Together all the inhabi-

tants ensemble ne connaissaient que l'hiver, malgré leur chair réchauffée, malgré le jour qui ne s'en allait pas.

x

Tu es dans ton essence constamment poète, constamment au zénith de ton amour, constamment avide de vérité et de justice. C'est sans doute un mal nécessaire que tu ne puisses l'être assidûment dans ta conscience.

x i

Tu feras de l'âme qui n'existe pas un homme meilleur qu'elle.

x i i

Regarde l'image téméraire où se baigne ton pays, ce plaisir qui t'a longtemps fui.

x i i i

Nombreux sont ceux qui attendent que l'écueil les soulève, que le but les franchisse, pour se définir.

x i v

Remercie celui qui ne prend pas souci de ton remords. Tu es son égal.

x v

Les larmes méprisent leur confident.

x v i

Il reste une profondeur mesurable là où le sable subjugue la destinée.

x v i i

Mon amour, peu importe que je sois né: tu deviens visible à la place où je disparais.

x v i i i

Pouvoir marcher, sans tromper l'oiseau, du cœur de l'arbre à l'extase du fruit.

x i x

Ce qui t'accueille à travers le plaisir n'est que la gratitude mercenaire du souvenir. La présence que tu as choisie ne délivre pas d'adieu.

x x

Ne te courbe que pour aimer. Si tu meurs, tu aimes encore.

tants knew only winter, despite their well-warmed bodies, despite the day-light that would not go.

X

In your essence you are always a poet, always at the height of your love, always hungry for truth and justice. It is no doubt a necessary evil that you cannot be one steadily in your conscience.

XI

You will make of the soul, which does not exist, a man better than she is.

XII

Look how your country glows in the light of daring; this pleasure has not been yours for a long time.

XIII

Many there are who wait till they are lifted by the reef, reached by the goal, before they take a stand.

XIV

Be grateful to the man who cares nothing for your remorse. You are his equal.

XV

Tears despise their sympathizer.

XVI

The depth remains measurable when the sands subdue destiny.

XVII

My love, it matters little that I was born: you come into sight where I disappear.

XVIII

Would I could walk, without deceiving the bird, from the heart of the tree to the ecstasy of the fruit.

XIX

That which beckons to you from beyond pleasure is only the mercenary gratitude of memory. The presence you have chosen bids no farewells.

XX

Stoop only to love. If you die, you still love.

**XXI**

Les ténèbres que tu t'infuses sont régies par la luxure de ton ascendant solaire.

**XXII**

Néglige ceux aux yeux de qui l'homme passe pour n'être qu'une étape de la couleur sur le dos tourmenté de la terre. Qu'ils dévident leur longue remonstrance. L'encre du tisonnier et la rougeur du nuage ne font qu'un.

**XXIII**

Il n'est pas digne du poète de mystifier l'agneau, d'investir sa laine.

**XXIV**

Si nous habitons un éclair, il est le cœur de l'éternel.

**XXV**

Yeux qui, croyant inventer le jour, avez éveillé le vent, que puis-je pour vous, je suis l'oubli.

**XXVI**

La poésie est de toutes les eaux claires celle qui s'attarde le moins aux reflets de ses ponts.

Poésie, la vie future à l'intérieur de l'homme requalifié.

**XXVII**

Une rose pour qu'il pleuve. Au terme d'innombrables années, c'est ton souhait.

XXI

The glooms in which you steep yourself are subject to the lustiness of your solar ascendant.

XXII

Have nothing to do with those in whose eyes man is merely a passing shade of the color on earth's tormented back. Let them reel off their long protestation. The glow of the poker and the blush of the cloud are but one.

XXIII

It is unworthy of the poet to mystify the lamb, to invest himself in its fleece.

XXIV

If we live in a lightning flash, it is the heart of eternity.

XXV

Eyes that thought to create the day but woke the wind, what can I do for you? I am oblivion.

XXVI

Poetry is of all clear streams the one that lingers least about its reflected bridges.
Poetry: life's future held in requalified man.

XXVII

A rose that it may rain. At the end of innumerable years, that is your wish.

—JACKSON MATHEWS

## VERS L'ARBRE-FRÈRE
## AUX JOURS COMPTÉS

Harpe brève des mélèzes,
Sur l'éperon de mousse et de dalles en germe
—Façade des forêts où casse le nuage—,
Contrepoint du vide auquel je crois.


## VICTOIRE ÉCLAIR

L'oiseau bêche la terre,
Le serpent sème,
La mort améliorée
Applaudit la récolte.
Pluton dans le ciel!

L'explosion en nous.
Là seulement dans moi.
Fol et sourd, comment pourrais-je l'être davantage?

Plus de second soi-même, de visage changeant, plus de saison pour la
      flamme et de saison pour l'ombre!

Avec la lente neige descendent les lépreux.

Soudain l'amour, l'égal de la terreur,
D'une main jamais vue arrête l'incendie, redresse le soleil, reconstruit
      l'Amie.

Rien n'annonçait une existence si forte.

# TO FRIEND-TREE
# OF COUNTED DAYS

Brief harp of the larches
On mossy spur of stone crop
—Façade of the forest,
Against which mists are shattered—
Counterpoint of the void in which
   I believe.

—WILLIAM CARLOS WILLIAMS


# LIGHTNING VICTORY

The bird tills the soil,
The serpent sows,
Death, enriched,
Praises the harvest.
Pluto in the sky!

In ourselves the explosion.
There in myself only.
Mad and deaf, how could I be more so?

No more second self, nor changing face, no more season of flame and
    season of shadow!

The lepers come down with the slow snow.

Suddenly love, the equal of terror,
With a hand I had never seen, puts an end to the fire, straightens the sun,
    reshapes the beloved.

Nothing had heralded so strong an existence.

—W. S. MERWIN

## LA CHAMBRE DANS L'ESPACE

Tel le chant du ramier quand l'averse est prochaine—l'air se poudre de
pluie, de soleil revenant—, je m'éveille lavé, je fonds en m'élevant; je
vendange le ciel novice.

Allongé contre toi, je meus ta liberté. Je suis un bloc de terre qui réclame
sa fleur.

Est-il gorge menuisée plus radieuse que la tienne? Demander c'est mourir!

L'aile de ton soupir met un duvet aux feuilles. Le trait de mon amour
ferme ton fruit, le boit.

Je suis dans la grâce de ton visage que mes ténèbres couvrent de joie.

Comme il est beau ton cri qui me donne ton silence!

## LUTTEURS

Dans le ciel des hommes, le pain des étoiles me sembla ténébreux et durci,
mais dans leurs mains étroites je lus la joute de ces étoiles en invitant d'autres:
émigrantes du pont encore rêveuses; j'en recueillis la sueur dorée, et par moi
la terre cessa de mourir.

## SEPTENTRION

—Je me suis promenée au bord de la Folie.—

Aux questions de mon cœur,
S'il ne les posait point,
Ma compagne cédait,

# ROOM IN SPACE

Such is the wood-pigeon's song when the shower approaches—the air is
    powdered with rain, with ghostly sunlight—
I awake washed, I melt as I rise, I gather the tender sky.

Lying beside you, I move your liberty.
I am a block of earth reclaiming its flower.

Is there a carved throat more radiant than yours? To ask is to die!

The wing of your sigh spreads a film of down on the leaves. The arrow
    of my love closes your fruit, drinks it.

I am in the grace of your countenance which my darkness covers with
    joy.

How beautiful your cry that gives me your silence!

—W. S. MERWIN

# FIGHTERS

    In the sky of men the bread of stars seemed to me shadowy and hardened
but in their narrow hands I read the jousting of these stars, inviting others:
still dreaming emigrants from the deck; I gathered up their golden sweat and
because of me the earth stopped dying.

—THOMAS MERTON

# SEPTENTRION

I went walking (said the girl)
on the edge of madness.

She, my companion, gave way
to the questions of my heart

Tant est inventive l'absence.
Et ses yeux en décrue comme le Nil violet
Semblaient compter sans fin leurs gages s'allongeant
Dessous les pierres fraîches.

La Folie se coiffait de longs roseaux coupants.
Quelque part ce ruisseau vivait sa double vie.
L'or cruel de son nom soudain envahisseur
Venait livrer bataille à la fortune adverse.

## FACTION DU MUET

Les pierres se serrèrent dans le rempart et les hommes vécurent de la mousse des pierres. La pleine nuit portait fusil et les femmes n'accouchaient plus. L'ignominie avait l'aspect d'un verre d'eau.

Je me suis uni au courage de quelques êtres, j'ai vécu violemment, sans vieillir, mon mystère au milieu d'eux, j'ai frissonné de l'existence de tous les autres, comme une barque incontinente au-dessus des fonds cloisonnés.

## CONVERGENCE DES MULTIPLES

Cet homme n'était pas généreux parce qu'il voulait se voir généreux dans son miroir. Il était généreux parce qu'il venait des Pléiades et qu'il se détestait.

La même ombre prodigue, aux phalanges des doigts relevés, nous joignit lui et moi. Un soleil qui n'était point pour nous s'en échappa comme un père en faute ou mal gratifié.

when my heart did not ask
any questions:
Such is the inventiveness of absence.
Then her eyes, at ebbtide like the violet Nile
Seemed to count their wages endlessly
Reaching under the cool stones.

Madness dressed her hair
With long and cutting rushes.
Somewhere this stream lives its double life.
The cruel gold of its invading name
Came to give battle to unfriendly fortune.

—THOMAS MERTON

## FACTION DU MUET

The stones huddled together on the ramparts and men lived off the moss
of the stones. Deep night carried a gun and the women did not give birth.
Disgrace had the look of a glass of water.

I joined up with the courage of a few beings, lived violently, growing no
older, my mystery in their midst, I shuddered for the existence of all the others
like an unchaste vessel riding over cloistered deeps.

—THOMAS MERTON

## CONVERGENCE OF THE MANY

This man was generous not because he wanted to see himself as generous
in his own looking-glass. He was generous because he came from the Pleiades
and abhorred himself.

One same prodigal shadow with phalanxes of upraised fingers joined us
together. Him and me. A sun which was not for us broke away from it like
a guilty or unsatisfied father.

—THOMAS MERTON

# LA CHUTE ET L'EXIL

1

*(« Ma prière est celle du grain de poussière à la montagne, de la goutte d'eau à l'océan, du souffle de feu au soleil.*

*Tu es le versant et la cime. Tu es le pourtour. Tu es la vague reprise et l'écume. Tu es le sel. Tu es l'aurore et le crépuscule.*

*C'est pourquoi ma prière est, chaque fois, une autre prière; c'est pourquoi Tu n'es jamais Toi, étant successivement Toi engendré de Toi, parfois contre Toi.*

*Mon Dieu, je dois être une créature méprisable puisque je ne sais pas prier. »*

—REB BOHOR.

*« Au centre de toute méditation, disait Reb Akri, il y a la mer; ses menaces et ses menottes. As-tu jamais été conduit en prison par la mer ou par la nuit? Quelle aventure. Et personne à prévenir. On coule, droit; on expire, aveugle; mais on respire, poisson; mais on scintille, étoile. Et c'est le pire.*

*Être vivant au sein de la mort. Être debout où l'air et l'eau sont un même rythme couché. »* )

2

« Je n'avais de regard que pour l'infini. J'avais tendance à laisser passer les jours. Ils m'ont puni. »

—REB ALBEN.

« La part féminine de l'homme est le sommeil. Toute demeure est le lieu de prédilection du repos. L'espace est compagnon du soleil. »

—REB BAHARA.

# Edmond Jabès
## 1912-

## FALL AND EXILE

### I

("*My prayer is that of a grain of dust on the mountain, a drop of water in the sea, a breath of fire in the sun.*

"*You are the slope and the summit. You are the circumference. You are the wave taken back and the foam. You are the salt. You are dawn and dusk.*

"*Therefore my prayer is different every time. Therefore You are never You, but successive You's engendered by You, sometimes against You.*

"*My God, I must be a contemptible creature because I do not know how to pray.*"

—REB BOHOR.

"*At the core of any meditation,*" *said Reb Akri,* "*there is the sea, its menace and its manacles. Have you ever been taken prisoner by the sea or the night? What an adventure. And nobody to give warning. You go straight down. You expiate, blindly. But you breathe—a fish, you glitter—a star. And that is the worst.*

"*To be alive at the bosom of death. To stand where air and water are the same horizontal rhythm.*")

### 2

"I only had eyes for the infinite. I tended to let the days pass by. They punished me."

—REB ALBEN

"Sleep is the female part of man. Any dwelling is a preferred spot for rest. Space is companion to the sun."

—REB BAHARA

« Après la mort, j'en suis sûr, je serai là pour me lire; car mon nom est dans le livre et la mort est l'apothéose du nom.»  —REB BETTIT.

3

« Plus un mot. Dieu me parle. Je lui réponds. Plus un son; mais le silence qui écoute le silence.»  —REB SAFIR.

« Le passé luit; l'avenir vécu luira. Le ciel de tous les astres est le livre du passé.»  —REB ARIAD.

« Les yeux levés, tu contemples le passé. Quel avenir l'égalera en fureur?»  —REB DOMANAS.

« Demain est ton avenir; mais, à peine apparu, le soleil réclame son bien.»  —REB ARBEH.

« Le monde se consume avec le jour.»  —REB ARGY.

« Quelques larmes et c'est déjà une échelle vers Toi.»  —REB KARAB.

4

### Chanson

Sur le bord de la route,
il y a des feuilles
si fatiguées d'être feuilles,
qu'elles sont tombées.

Sur le bord de la route,
il y a des Juifs
si fatigués d'être juifs,
qu'ils sont tombés.

Balayez les feuilles.
Balayez les Juifs.

Les mêmes feuilles repoussent-elles au printemps?
Y a-t-il un printemps pour les Juifs piétinés?

5

(« *Tu appelles la chute, un exil. Ainsi, tu survis.* »  —REB TADIÉ)

"I am sure I will be there after my death to read myself. For my name is in the book, and death is the apotheosis of the name." —REB BETTIT

3

"Not another word. God is speaking to me. I answer. Not another sound: silence listens to silence." —REB SAFIR

"The past glimmers; the lived future will shine. The sky of all the stars is the book of the past." —REB ARIAD

"You are looking up to contemplate the past. What future could equal its fury?" —REB DOMANAS

"Tomorrow is your future. But no sooner has it come than the sun claims it as its own." —REB ARBEH

"The world consumes itself with the day." —REB ARGY

"A few tears—already a ladder toward You." —REB KARAB

4

Song

By the wayside
leaves
so tired of being leaves
they fell.

By the wayside
Jews
so tired of being Jews
they fell.

Sweep up the leaves.
Sweep up the Jews.

Will the same leaves regrow in spring?
Is there a spring for trampled Jews?

5

(*"You call falling an exile. Hence you survive."* —REB TADIÉ)

—ROSMARIE WALDROP

# RÉPONSE À UNE LETTRE

*Dieu est né de l'immortel désir de mourir de Dieu.*

Tu me poses de nombreuses questions. Faute de pouvoir répondre directement à toutes, je tâcherai d'en aborder quelques-unes par le biais; interrogations qui me mèneront à emprunter certaines voies obscures que j'ai suivies, solitaire, et qui m'ont abandonné à l'aube, au carrefour de mes chemins; comme si le départ était après la route, comme si indéfiniment l'on se préparait à partir, sachant que l'on ne ferait que parcourir cette distance qui nous sépare du point écartelé du départ.

Toute poussée en avant est terreur et épreuve du premier pas. Ainsi, avec chaque lettre dans le mot, avec chaque vocable dans la phrase, commence le Livre.

Intimes chemins donc que je n'aurais épuisés qu'en moi-même et qui m'auraient conduit au bord de l'être où toute présence est livrée à la soif: une quête de la pauvreté, dirais-je, dans un labyrinthe, tels ceux de verre qui font recette dans les foires et autour desquels un public amusé vous épie en vous désignant du doigt; un labyrinthe où l'on est vu et où l'on ne voit pas. La sortie, après tant de tâtonnements, sera, bien sûr, trouvée; mais elle ne nous aura donné que la mesure du labyrinthe. Combien y en a-t-il que l'on ne quitte pas?

J'éprouve une grande difficulté à écrire, contrairement à ce que tu en penses. Lorsque je prends ma plume, toute issue devant moi se ferme. Le pays, le monde se replient sur eux-mêmes. Dans cet univers clos, chaque vocable est alors le verrou que je tire en le formant. Prisonnier, je ne sais plus où frapper.

Je suis, chaque fois, entré dans mes livres avec l'impression très nette de ne pas être attendu ou plutôt d'avoir été attendu depuis si longtemps que l'on avait fini par désespérer de ma venue; comme si le livre, n'appartenant vraiment qu'aux vocables, ceux-ci étaient prêts—ou ne l'étaient plus—à s'engager dans une aventure que j'allais fatalement leur proposer. D'où ces inévitables instants d'incertitude, ces hésitations au seuil de l'ouvrage où la preuve est sans cesse réclamée de l'importance d'une quête—peut-être, dans son essence, illusoire—dont il appartient à l'écrivain, en dépit de ses inquiétudes et de ses angoisses, d'affirmer le bien-fondé. En fait, il s'agit pour lui davantage d'en évaluer les risques que de chercher à attirer les mots dans un guet-apens dont il serait la première victime. Aller à la mort, faire sa mort comme on cherche, ailleurs, à faire sa vie, voilà, je crois, la tâche qu'il lui incombe d'accomplir dans le livre. Pour cela, il s'identifiera aux vocables après s'être mesuré à eux. Dans un univers peuplé de syllabes, il assumera un nom multiple, ayant appris que chaque lettre est un nom. Lorsque l'initiative lui échappera, lorsque sa voix cessera, tout à coup, d'être prépondérante, il saura enfin qu'il écrit, qu'il a été écrit et qu'il représente, désormais, une infime partie du livre qui s'ébranle et

ANSWER TO A LETTER

*God is born of his immortal desire to die.*

You ask me many questions. As I cannot answer them all directly I will approach at least some in a roundabout way. This questioning will take me over certain obscure routes which I had followed alone and which abandoned me at dawn at the parting of my ways. As if departure came after the journey. As if we forever prepared to leave, knowing we could only reach the torturous point of departure.

Any advance is terror and trial of the first step. So with each letter in the word, with each word in the sentence, the Book begins.

Intimate ways, therefore, which I could not exhaust except inside myself. Ways leading me to the brink of being where all presence is surrendered to thirst: a quest of poverty, I would say, in a labyrinth like the glass ones at fairs, which draw crowds who gather around you, watching you, pointing their fingers at you. A labyrinth where one is seen but does not see. After much groping, the exit, to be sure, will be found. But it has given us only the measure of the labyrinth. How many are there that we never leave?

I find it very difficult to write, contrary to what you seem to think. When I take my pen all doors close in front of me. The country, the world folds shut. In this closed universe, each word—even while I form it—becomes the lock I turn the key in. Imprisoned, I no longer know where to knock.

I have entered each book of mine with the very clear impression that I was not expected or, rather, that I had been expected so long they finally despaired of my coming. As if the book belonged really only to the words and they were —or were no longer—ready to let themselves in for an adventure I could not help proposing. Hence these inevitable moments of uncertainty, these hesitations at the threshold of the work, which constantly require proof of the importance of the quest—perhaps illusory in its essence. A quest whose merits the author must affirm in spite of his misgivings and distress. In fact, it is much more a matter of sizing up the danger than of trying to snare the words in traps into which the author would fall first. To go towards death, to make a death for himself as one would make a life, this is, I think, his task in the book. He will, then, identify with the words after measuring himself against them. In a universe filled with syllables, he will assume a manifold name, having learned that each letter is a name. When the initiative escapes him, when his voice suddenly stops taking the lead, he knows he is finally writing, he has been written, and he represents from now on a tiny part of the book which is surging forward and will destroy him as it breaks. Drowned where the ocean roars, he will, for a moment of eternity, lift his head. But only in passing, to salute the sky which no passion and no suffering can wrinkle.

The book is engulfed by the book. But the word is innocent wherever it gave in to the urgent promptings of an unknown force, a voice more sonorous

qui l'anéantira dans son déferlement. Noyé, où gronde l'océan, il lèvera, un instant d'éternité, la tête; mais ce sera pour saluer au passage le ciel qu'aucune passion, qu'aucune souffrance ne viennent rider.

Le livre est englouti par le livre, mais la parole est innocente où elle s'est rendue aux pressantes injonctions d'une puissance inconnue; voix plus sonore que la sienne, absence augurale de voix qui la fascine et la fait trembler. La mort, à son plus bel âge, s'enivre des cris de notre mort. Nous émergeons et sombrons d'une même audace partagée.

Avant le livre que nous nous apprêtons à cerner, des dizaines de livres s'épanouissent et périssent sans nous, dans un espace oublié que le vocable effleure à peine. De sorte que chaque mot, outre sa vie propre tissée de tant de vies vécues et qui, pour tout autre, demeure étrangère, en répondant à nos sollicitations se soustrait à d'innombrables existences rêvées, imaginées, autrefois, par nous et que nous lui aurions fait entrevoir comme pouvant être la sienne. Il ne faut pas croire que le mot soit sans mémoire. Là où nous avons tout effacé, il est présent pour nous rappeler notre passé dans ce qu'il eût pu être et dans ce qu'il fut, d'un éclair, d'une unique lumière.

Avant le livre donc, où nous nous débattons sans souvenirs, d'insaisissables moments du livre s'inscrivent dans son projet et dans son attente. De sorte que l'on ne sait jamais si le livre n'est pas déjà dans cet avant-livre plein de questions qui ne s'adressent qu'au livre et auxquelles celui-ci, comme en dehors de nous, s'efforce de répondre.

Entre nos interrogations et celle que, de son côté, se pose le livre, l'œuvre se fait et se défait avec notre concours. Nous sommes, face à l'ouvrage, à l'écoute d'une vérité qui ne se livre jamais que dans ses sentiers sinueux et ses humiliants retours au vide que comblera l'océan. La vérité du livre est la fraction du temps où il s'arrache à sa totalité pour retrouver la page, la phrase, le signe qu'il a fait, dès l'abord, saigner.

Ah! Savons-nous combien, à sa suite, nous sommes sans idée, sans besoin, sans image?

Innocence innée du verbe pareille à la naïveté d'une foule que l'espoir ou le désespoir attire en un lieu déterminé où son avenir se joue. Le verbe étale son innocence jusqu'au moment où, gagné par le vertige, il se déclare possesseur de la vérité.

Le péché originel se perpétuerait-il à travers une vérité dont nous nous glorifierions d'être les tenants? Sur qui affirme la détenir, elle se venge sans pitié. Combien de nos semblables ont péri de ses lances; combien d'ouvrages elle a, d'une arme adaptée, éteints.

Intransmissible vérité, sœur du gouffre et du silence. La page blanche en serait-elle la détentrice privilégiée? Toute blancheur est violence, comme le mur l'est par son obstination muette à nous barrer la route. Toute blancheur est couleur de Dieu qui, dans le silence d'une infinie vérité, nous troue les yeux et nous broie. La lutte de l'écrivain ne réside-t-elle pas dans son effort insensé, à proximité de la plage, de planter une fois ses mains dans le sable avant de

than its own, augural absence of a voice which fascinates and makes it tremble. Death, in his prime, gets drunk on the screams of our own deaths. We rise and founder from the same shared daring.

Before the book that we are closing in on, dozens of books blossom and die without us, in a forgotten space hardly touched by the word. So that each word, beside its own life woven of so many lived lives, which to others will always be unknown—each word, when it responds to our entreaties, eludes innumerable existences which we have formerly dreamed or imagined, and of which we let it catch a glimpse: possibilities it could have had. You must not think the word is without memory. Where we have erased everything, it is present to remind us of our past, in what it could have been and what it was, in a stroke of lightning, in a single light.

Before the book, then, where we struggle without memories, elusive moments of the book inscribe themselves in its scheme and in its expectation. So that you never know but what the book is already in this pre-book full of questions asked only of the book and which it tries to answer, as if independent.

Between our questions and those the book asks on its own, the work is done and undone with our help. Facing the task, we are listening to a truth which never surrenders except in its winding paths and humiliating returns to the void, which only the ocean will fill. The book's truth is that fraction of time when it breaks from its totality to meet the page, the phrase, the sign, which from the very first it has made bleed.

Ah, do we know how much, while we pursue it, we are without idea, without need, without image?

Innate innocence of the verb matching the naiveté of a crowd which hope or despair draws to a fixed place where their future is at stake. The verb displays its innocence to the moment of dizziness, when it claims to possess the truth.

Is it perhaps that original sin persists, within a truth we preen ourselves on championing? On those who assert they own it, truth takes ruthless revenge. How many of our fellows have died of its spears; how many works it has extinguished with the proper weapon.

Truth impossible to pass on, a sister of silence and the abyss. Is the blank page perhaps its preferred repository? All whiteness is violence, like the wall's mute determination to block our road. All whiteness is God's color, which in the silence of an infinite truth pierces our eyes and crushes us. Is the writer's struggle not this mad effort once to plant his hands into the sand of the beach before the wave takes him back? White page, tormented, strong in its will from beyond the sea whose wave, raging to devour the port, with unwearying effort hollows out the bottom. God is in the wall. God is in the wave. Our arms, our complaints will henceforth try only to mitigate his violence until we are forced to give in.

The convict in his tower will eventually scream to escape the cruelest

se laisser reprendre par les flots? Page blanche, tourmentée, forte de sa volonté d'outre-mer dont la vague, ivre de dévorer le port, creuse inlassablement le fond. Dieu est dans le mur. Dieu est dans la mer. Nos bras, nos plaintes ne vont plus chercher qu'à atténuer sa violence jusqu'à l'abandon.

Le condamné dans sa tour se met un jour à hurler pour échapper au plus cruel des châtiments: l'étouffement dans la parole, dans l'absence de parole. Ainsi l'écrivain et le vocable qu'une distance sépare toujours de leur vie brève. Il n'y a pas un geôlier, un lecteur tant soit peu attentif qui n'aient entendu leurs pathétiques appels à la vie.

Cris devenus gerbes, devenus aurore. Terres étrangères dont nous avons salué la survivance, voix mortes qui montrent le chemin à l'intérieur du chemin et que l'on ne peut plus ignorer; dures étapes jusqu'à la paix promise.

Écrire, est-ce, dans son ingénuité, se dresser contre le silence, sursaut de vie dans la mort, pour enfin mourir, avec lui, d'une ardeur qui nous surprend soudain par sa perte d'énergie tel un soleil déclinant? O nuit, vaste tombeau d'oubli. Et ce n'est pas vulgaire coïncidence si l'on peut voir, au milieu des ombres, scintiller nos paroles refoulées pareilles à des épitaphes figées dans leur ordre éternel; mais la paix totale, inviolable nous sera-t-elle octroyée? Le songe trahit la violence du silence et l'inconscient qui nous trouble et perturbe n'est, en définitive, qu'une parole tue. Y aurait-il une fin qui serait un sommeil sans rêves ni rives obsédantes? Certes pas dans le livre.

Autour de ce qui n'est pas exprimé, de ce que nous ne saurons jamais formuler, nous parlons comme des sourds, nous écrivons en aveugles, hors du temps; mais la vie est là qui nous talonne, la vie venue à notre rencontre, où nous avons su stoïquement nous passer d'elle. Que nous veut-elle? Et d'abord quelle emprise exerce-t-elle sur le livre? O prestige du prélude. Toute démarche est placée sous son signe; mais elle porte la mort en son sein et c'est de cette mort que nous nous sommes nourris.

Le silence, où la parole abdique, c'est aussi la mort exemplaire de Dieu dont témoigne chaque racine séchée avec nos larmes au cœur du désert.

Parler, est-ce alors tenter de combler le vide laissé par la mort de Dieu? On parle à Dieu, comme on parle à l'envers du silence; c'est-à-dire à l'ombre d'une ombre qui va s'éclaircir puis nous expulser.

M'accuseras-tu d'être un écrivain de la mort? Tu me reproches mon effacement au nom du livre, comme si l'écrivain n'avait d'autre alternative que celle qui consiste, après en avoir pris conscience, à proclamer son impossibilité d'être? « Ne pouvant être qui je suis, que le livre désormais soit. J'aurai, par lui, une chance de durer. » Impossibilité d'être, non pas en tant qu'individu, mais comme « intervenant » dans l'embrasement d'un instant accordé à sa défaite; mais comme « participant » à l'éclosion d'un astre dont nous nous mettrons ensuite à dénombrer les taches sombres. Rien, de l'homme aux prises avec la page blanche, ne capte notre attention. Qu'il soit puissant ou pauvre, séduisant ou laid, doux ou tyrannique, il est ce qu'il devient et ce qu'il devient

punishment: suffocation in the word, in the absence of the word. Likewise the writer, and also the word, both always at a distance from their short lives. There is no jailer, no reader no matter how inattentive, who has not heard their touching appeals to life.

Screams that have turned into sheaves, turned into dawn. Strange lands whose survival we have saluted, dead voices which show the way within the way and which you can no longer ignore. Hard stages before the promised peace.

Is writing, in its simplicity, to rise up against silence, a twitch of life within death, and finally die of its pain? Die with its pain, a death which catches us unaware with its loss of energy like a setting sun? Oh night, vast tomb of oblivion. And it is no common coincidence if we can see our words shine in the dark, held like epitaphs frozen in their eternal order. But will we be allowed a total, inviolable peace? The dream betrays the violence of silence. And the unconscious, which troubles and disturbs us, is finally nothing but a silenced word. Could there be an end which would be sleep without haunting dreams or shores? Certainly not in the book.

Around what is not expressed, around what we will never know how to formulate, we talk like the deaf and write blindly, outside time. But life is there, on our heels, life come to meet us where we were stoically able to do without. What does it want from us? And, first of all, what hold does it have on the book? Oh weight of prelude. All steps are under its sign. But life carries death in its womb; and we have eaten of this death.

Silence, where the word abdicates, is also the exemplary death of God. Each root dried with our tears in the heart of the desert bears witness.

Is speaking, then, the attempt to fill the void left by the death of God? One speaks to God as one speaks to the far side of silence, that is to say, to the shadow of a shadow which will brighten, then turn us out.

Will you accuse me of being a writer of death? You reproach me for effacing myself in the book's name, as if the writer had no alternative but to proclaim, once he is aware of it, his impossibility to be? "Unable to be who I am, let the book henceforward be. I have, through it, my chance to endure." Impossibility to be, not as an individual, but as a "partaker" in the burning of an instant granted to his defeat; as a "participant" in the birth of a star whose dark spots we will afterwards start to count. Nothing in the man who grapples with the white page catches our attention. He may be powerful or poor, engaging or ugly, gentle or a tyrant, he is what he becomes, and what he becomes does not recognize him. And yet this creature of absence lives; and his life is a sketch of mysteries. In bending over it he loses his reality. Thus he is separated from his name by the naming itself.

Is speaking, perhaps, at this point, pledging one's being to a series of metamorphoses across a space modified by the hour, but where time is powerless? Could it be, further, silencing within the word all toying with allegiance

ne le reconnaît pas. Et, pourtant, cette créature de l'absence vit et sa vie est un tracé d'énigmes. De se pencher sur elle, il perd sa réalité. Ainsi est-il écarté de son nom par cela même qui le nomme.

Parler, à ce point du discours, serait-ce engager son être dans une série de métamorphoses à travers un espace modifié par l'heure, mais où le temps est sans pouvoir? Serait-ce, en outre, faire taire dans la parole toute velléité d'allégeance à l'univers, où elle est veillée aux limites de son aire et portée tel un oiseau dans l'infini fleurissant?

A son dernier envol, la parole se ferait visible et inventerait une écriture, à la fois secrète et gigantesque, que nous revendiquerions pour l'avoir, dans ses évolutions, contemplée de la terre;

mais est-ce nous, en fin de compte, qu'elle compromet? Si oui, cela reviendrait à prétendre que nous portons la responsabilité de l'escarpement d'une falaise ou du fougueux bondissement de l'onde. N'est-ce pas, cependant, par nous qu'océan et falaise se définissent; n'est-ce pas à travers nous qu'ils communiquent?

Trait d'union par excellence, l'écrivain pour retrouver son lieu, se veut lien indissoluble. Son lien est ce nœud coulant au-dessus de l'abîme où la parole captive le substitue à elle. D'abord un cercle, puis l'écrivain de moins en moins à l'aise dans ce cercle jusqu'à ne plus pouvoir remuer. Au matin, le nœud lâche et il retrouve le vide, meurtri jusqu'à l'âme par une vérité dont il a perdu le visage.

Consumées depuis des milliards d'années, certaines étoiles continuent de briller pour nous. L'éloignement nous leurre au-delà de la mort qui est solennel accès à l'éloignement.

Écrire, est-ce tout simplement cette manière, dans ce qui s'exprime sans nous, de s'exprimer à travers ce qui nous a été rapporté de nos origines et que le vocable nous fait découvrir?

Je n'ai de regard que pour ce que je ne vois pas et qui va bientôt, je le sais, m'éblouir. La route s'étend entre ses deux commencements. Le soleil brûle dans la nuit au lieu de battre, ou bat peut-être en brûlant, bat sûrement. La mort est complice de la création. La mort est le lieu absent où se tient, pour son accomplissement, le livre.

to the universe where it is watched over at the limits of its space and carried like a bird into the infinite in flower?

And does the word, perhaps, in its last flight, become visible and invent a script at the same time secret and monumental which we will claim as our own for having watched its evolutions from the ground?

But is it in the long run we who are implicated? To answer yes would mean holding ourselves responsible for the steep of the cliff or the impetuous heave of the wave. Is it not through us, however, that ocean and cliff define themselves, through us that they communicate?

Link par excellence, the writer, in order to recapture his place, wishes to be an unbreakable bond. His bond is a noose above the abyss where the word escapes, leaving him caught. A circle at first, then the writer less and less at ease in this circle, until he can no longer move. In the morning, the knot gives, and he finds again the void, bruised to the soul by a truth whose visage he has lost.

Burnt out millions of years ago, certain stars continue to shine for us. Absence lures us beyond death which is the formal access to absence.

Is writing simply the way in which that which expresses itself without us, nevertheless expresses itself through what has been handed down to us from our origins and which the word has made us discover?

I have eyes only for what I do not see and what, I know, will soon dazzle me. The road stretches between its two beginnings. The sun burns in the night instead of pulsing, or perhaps pulses while burning. It is certainly a pulse. Death is an accomplice of creation. Death is the absent place where the book waits for its fulfilment.

—ROSMARIE WALDROP

# N'AYEZ POINT PITIÉ

Fumez marais

les images rupestres de l'inconnu
vers moi détournent le silencieux crépuscule
de leur rire

Fumez ô marais cœur d'oursin
les étoiles mortes apaisées par des mains merveilleuses
jaillissent
de la pulpe de mes yeux
Fumez fumez
l'obscurité fragile de ma voix craque de cités
flamboyantes
et la pureté irrésistible de ma main appelle
de loin de très loin du patrimoine héréditaire
le zèle victorieux de l'acide dans la chair
de la vie—marais—

telle une vipère née de la force blonde de l'éblouissement.

# Aimé Césaire
## 1913-

HAVE NO MERCY

Keep smoking swamp

the rupestral images of the unknown
turn the silent dusk of their laughter
toward me

Keep smoking oh swamp sea urchin core
dead stars calmed by marvelous hands gush
from the pulp of my eyes
Smoke smoke
the frail darkness of my voice crackles with blazing cities
and the irresistible purity of my hand summons
out of vast distance from a genetic inheritance
the victorious zeal of the acid in the flesh of life—swamp—

like a viper born from the blonde force of resplendence.

—CLAYTON ESHLEMAN & ANNETTE SMITH

# SOLEIL SERPENT

Soleil serpent œil fascinant mon œil
et la mer pouilleuse d'îles craquant aux doigts des roses
lance-flamme et mon corps intact de foudroyé
l'eau exhausse les carcasses de lumière perdues dans le couloir sans pompe
des tourbillons de glaçons auréolent le cœur fumant des corbeaux
nos cœurs
c'est la voix des foudres apprivoisées tournant sur leurs gonds de lézarde
transmission d'anolis au paysage de verres cassés c'est
les fleurs vampires à la relève des orchidées
élixir du feu central
feu juste feu manguier de nuit couvert d'abeilles mon
désir un hasard de tigres surpris aux soufres mais l'éveil
stanneux se dore des gisements enfantins
et mon corps de galet mangeant poisson mangeant
colombes et sommeils
le sucre du mot Brésil au fond du marécage.

# PHRASE

Et pourquoi pas la haie de geysers les obélisques des heures le cri lisse des
    nuages la mer en écart vert pâle fienté d'oiseaux vauriens et l'espérance
    roulant ses billes sur les faîtes et entrefaîtes des maisons et les déchirures
    en dorades des surgeons bananiers

dans les hautes branches du soleil sur le cœur heurté des matins sur le tableau
    âcre du ciel un jour de craie de faucon de pluie et d'acacia sur un portulan
    d'îles premières secouant leurs cheveux de sel interjetés de doigts de mâts
    en toute main à toute fin sous le battement de cil du hasard aux délices
    chantées d'ombre un assassin vêtu d'étamines riches et calmes comme un
    chant de vin dur

# SERPENT SUN

Serpent sun eye bewitching my eye
and the sea flea-ridden with islands cracking in the fingers of
    flame-thrower roses and my intact body of one thunderstruck
the water raises the carcasses of light lost in the pompless corridor
whirlwinds of the ice-floes halo the steaming hearts of ravens
our hearts
it is the voice of tamed thunderbolts turning on their crack hinges
a transfer of anolis to the landscape of broken glasses it is the vampire
    flowers relaying the orchids
elixir of the central fire
fire just fire night mango tree swarming with bees
my desire a throw of tigers caught in the sulphurs
but the stannous
awakening gilds itself with infantine deposits
and my pebble body eating fish eating
doves and slumbers
the sugar in the word Brazil deep in the marsh

—CLAYTON ESHLEMAN & ANNETTE SMITH

# SENTENCE

And why not the hedge of geysers the obelisk of hours the smooth scream
    of clouds the sea's quartered pale green spattered by good-for-nothing
    birds and hope playing marbles on the beams and between of houses and
    the dolphin-like rips of banana tree suckers.

in the top branches of the sun on the stubbed heart of mornings on the acrid
    canvas of the sky a day of chalk of falcons of rain and acacia on a portulan
    of primeval islands shaking their saline hair interposed by fingers of masts
    handwritten for any purpose under the blink of chance with its shadow sung
    delights an assassin clad in rich and calm muslins like a chant of hard
    wine

—CLAYTON ESHLEMAN & ANNETTE SMITH

## PERDITION

nous frapperons l'air neuf de nos têtes cuirassées
nous frapperons le soleil de nos paumes grandes ouvertes
nous frapperons le sol du pied nu de nos voix
les fleurs mâles dormiront aux criques des miroirs
et l'armure même des trilobites
s'abaissera dans le demi-jour de toujours
sur des gorges tendres gonflées de mines de lait
et ne franchirons-nous pas le porche
le porche des perditions?
un vigoureux chemin aux veineuses jaunissures
tiède
où bondissent les buffles des colères insoumises
court
avalant la bride des tornades mûres
aux balisiers sonnants des riches crépuscules

## AU DELÀ

d'en bas de l'entassement furieux des songes épouvantables
les aubes nouvelles
montaient
roulant leurs têtes de lionceaux libres
le néant niait ce que je voyais à la lumière
plus fraîche de mes yeux naufragés
mais—des sirènes sifflant de puissance sourde—
la faim des heures manquées agaça l'aigle farouche
du sang
les bras trop courts s'allongèrent de flammes
les désirs éclatèrent en grisou violent dans la ténèbre
des cœurs lâches
le poids du rêve bascula dans le vent des flibustes
—merveille de pommes douces pour les oiseaux des branches—
et des bandes réconciliées se donnèrent richesse dans
la main d'une femme assassinant le jour

# PERDITION

we will strike the new air with our armor-plated heads
we will strike the sun with our wide open palms
we will strike the soil with the bare feet of our voices
the male flowers will sleep in the coves of mirrors
and even the armor of trilobites
will sink in the half-light of forever
over the tender breasts swollen with lodes of milk
and will we not cross the porch
the porch of perditions?
a vigorous road with veiny jaunders
tepid
where the buffaloes of irrepressible angers bound
runs
full-tilting the ripe tornadoes
in the tolling balisiers of crepuscular riches

—CLAYTON ESHLEMAN & ANNETTE SMITH

# BEYOND

from the bottom of the furious piling up of appalling dreams
new dawns were
rising
rolling their free lion-cub heads
nothingness denied what I was seeing by the fresher
light of my shipwrecked eyes
but—sirens hissing from a secret power—
the hunger of botched hours vexed the fierce eagle of blood
arms too short lengthened into flames
desires exploded like violent pit-gas in the dark of cowardly hearts
the weight of the dream teetered in the freebooting wind
—wonder of sweet apples for birds of the branches—
and reconciled bands shared riches in
the hand of a woman assassinating the day

—CLAYTON ESHLEMAN & ANNETTE SMITH

# PROPHÉTIE

là où l'aventure garde les yeux clairs
là où les femmes rayonnent de langage
là où la mort est belle dans la main comme un oiseau saison de lait
là où le souterrain cueille de sa propre génuflexion un luxe de prunelles
    plus violent que des chenilles
là où la merveille agile fait flèche et feu de tout bois

là où la nuit vigoureuse saigne une vitesse de purs végétaux

là où les abeilles des étoiles piquent le ciel d'une ruche plus ardente que la
    nuit
là où le bruit de mes talons remplit l'espace et lève à rebours la face du
    temps
là où l'arc-en-ciel de ma parole est chargé d'unir demain à l'espoir et
    l'infant à la reine,

    d'avoir injurié mes maîtres mordu les soldats du sultan
d'avoir gémi dans le désert
d'avoir crié vers mes gardiens
d'avoir supplié les chacals et les hyènes pasteurs de caravanes

je regarde
la fumée se précipite en cheval sauvage sur le devant de la scène ourle un
    instant la lave de sa fragile queue de paon puis se déchirant la
    chemise s'ouvre d'un coup la poitrine et je la regarde en îles
    britanniques en îlots en rochers déchiquetés se fondre peu à peu dans
    la mer lucide de l'air
où baignent prophétiques
ma gueule
        ma révolte
            mon nom.

# PROPHECY

there where adventure stays clear-sighted
where women radiate language
where death in the hand is beautiful like a milk season bird
where the tunnel gathers from its own genuflexion a profusion of
    wild plums fiercer than caterpillars
where the agile wonder leaves no stone or fire unturned

there where the vigorous night bleeds a speed of pure vegetation

where the bees of the stars sting the sky with a hive more ardent
    than the night
where the noise of my heels fills space and raises the face of time
    backwards
where the rainbow of my speech is charged to unite tomorrow with
    hope and the infante with the queen,

for having insulted my masters bitten the sultan's men
for having cried in the wilderness
for having screamed at my jailers
for having begged from the jackals and the hyenas shepherds of caravans

I watch
the smoke rushes like a mustang to the front of the stage briefly hems its lava
    with its fragile peacock tail then tearing its shirt suddenly opens its chest
    and I watch it dissolve little by little into British Isles into islets into
    jagged rocks in the limpid sea of the air
where my mug
my revolt
      my name
          prophetically bathe.

—CLAYTON ESHLEMAN & ANNETTE SMITH

## GRAND LIVRE

On te dira qu'après la pluie vient le beau temps; on te dira
Qu'un tiens vaut mieux que deux tu l'auras.
    Ne le crois pas.
Il est bon qu'après la pluie vienne le déluge; il est excellent
Qu'un tiens fasse sortir deux loups du bois; il est nécessaire
Que pour ne pas aller assez souvent à la fontaine
    La cruche soit cassée.

Efface et recommence. On te dira qu'après deux 9 souvent vient le 36
Et qu'à Évian l'été dernier le zéro sortit trois fois de suite.
    C'est vrai.
Un colonel polytechnicien joua trois fois le maximum sur le zéro;
Cent cinq mille francs; merci pour les employés, merci monsieur pour les
Comptables du grand livre où sont inscrits depuis toujours vos
    États de service.

Campagnes sous Charles dit le Sage, sous Pyrrhus, sous Ramsès II,
Sous Hamourabi; blessures neuf; deux morts à l'échafaud,
    Un suicide,
Une vie ratée comme femme de magistrat. Comme décorations
Un enfant élevé contre tous, une parole tenue en dépit du bon sens,
Trois défaites par obstination contre l'évidence,
    Déshonneur et fidélité.

# Jean-Paul de Dadelsen

## 1914-1957

THE GREAT BOOK

They'll tell you, after the rain, the sun comes out—
They'll tell you, a bird in hand is worth more than two in the bush
    —don't you believe them.
It is good that the rain is followed by flood. It is excellent
That a bird in hand calls forth two wolves from the woods.
It is necessary that the jar should break, so it won't have to go
    to the well
        any more.

Erase. Start over. They'll tell you, after two nines
Thirty-six tends to come up
And at Évian last summer, zero came up three times in a row.
Some colonel in the Engineers bet maximum on that zero,
    three times in a row:
One hundred and five thousand francs. Thank you,
On behalf of the employees, thank you, sir, on behalf of
The great book in which are inscribed, forever, your
    ranks of service.

Campaigns, under Charles the Wise, Pyrrhus, Rameses the Second,
Hammurabi. Wounded nine times. Two deaths on the scaffold.
One suicide.
One life wasted, as a magistrate's wife. Decorations:

Il lui dit: Et alors, tu es restée avec lui? Eh bien oui, elle est
Restée avec lui, s'est fait sauter trois, dont la première fut
 Ratée pour elle
Et la troisième ratée par lui. Mais qui sait à quel titre
Cela faisait partie de son service à elle. Et de quel droit
Se serait-il senti si généreux, si magnanime, pour avoir pardonné?
 Elle n'est à personne.

Je ne suis pas à moi. Je ne sais d'où je viens, je ne sais
Ce qui est marqué à mon compte ou contre moi
 Dans le grand livre.
Je ne suis pas mon oubli et ne suis pas ma paresse et ne suis pas
Ma pesanteur. Mais j'ai honte du plus profond de ma mémoire
J'ai honte de n'avoir pas crié contre toi
 Éternel.

L'Éternel est en moi qui me regarde moi, plus futile
Qu'un souffle de brise au soir sur une eau calme
 Et sans mémoire.
Il regarde du plus intérieur de moi mes pensées, mes idoles,
Mon besoin puéril d'un Dieu qui ait un prénom,
Mon désir insensé d'une femme qui n'aime
 Que moi.

La femme est sage. Jamais elle n'aime qu'à travers nous, n'aime
Que l'imbécile, le porc et le poltron caché en nous, n'aime que
 Notre mort
Que nous contenons comme la prune son noyau. Jamais ne tient parole,
Jamais n'est chose cadastrable, jamais n'amasse mousse, jamais
Ne récompense l'insensé qui prétend oublier qu'elle est
 En service.

La maquerelle qui sut que la politesse est une forme de la charité
Sera l'aïeule d'un romancier d'une rare
 Élévation de pensée.
Le sperme de Saint Louis chaque jour coule à flots
Dans les paillasses de Bourgogne et de Basse-Bretagne.
Rien n'a ni rime ni raison, rien n'est pour notre usage,
 Après nous le beau temps.

A child raised in the face of general disapproval,
A word kept in spite of all common sense,
Three cases lost due to bucking the evidence—
    fidelity
        and disgrace.

So he said to her: so you stayed with him nevertheless. Oh yes,
She stayed with him, though she skipped him thrice.
The first one she fucked up,
The third one, he managed to waste. But who knows,
    it was probably written
That this was part of her service contract. What right did he have
To feel so generous, magnanimous, *forgiving* her?
        She is no one's property.

I am not my own property. I don't know where I come from,
I don't know what the credits are, or the debits, on my account
    in the great book.
I'm not what I forget. I'm not my sluggishness. I'm not
    my drag-ass brain.
But I am shamed, from the depths of my memory, ashamed
Never to have cried out against *you*,
        the Eternal.

The Eternal's inside me, staring at me, more useless
Than an evening breeze on calm water, total amnesia.
From my innermost places it looks at my thoughts, my idols,
My childish need of a God with a first name,
My insane longing for a woman who loves no one
        but me.

Woman is sensible. Never loves but she loves *across*—
Loves only the imbecile, the pig, the poltroon within us,
Loves only our death
Which we contain as the plum
        contains its progeniture.
Never keeps her word, is never censused & mapped,
Never gathers moss, never rewards the maniac
Who tries to forget
    that she is
        in service.

The brothel madam who knew, politeness is a form of charity:
The ancestress of a novelist of rare elevation of thought:

## PEUPLIERS ET TREMBLES

Peupliers et trembles. Dans la dernière clarté horizontale
    à cette heure où la feuille la plus haute, qui tout le jour
    était prise dans la rivière de brise invisible
        soudain se fige en un miel de silence.

Pourquoi toujours ai-je reconnu le soir?
    Le soir n'arrête rien
    —si ce n'est ce court instant irrésolu où la terre,
    ayant cessé d'inspirer, retient son souffle
    avant sa longue expiration nocturne—
    et tout à l'heure la chasse sera ouverte de toute dent,
    de tout œil, de toute griffe contre tout poil, contre tout sang.

    L'Éternel
    est un grand hibou au plumage de silence.
    L'Éternel est une martre.
    L'Éternel tue l'Éternel et se nourrit de son propre sang.
    L'Éternel est ce qui n'a pas de sens,
    n'a point de lieu, de nom, de temps—

Peupliers, trembles du soir,
    que j'ai aimé ces feuilles à deux couleurs
    entraînées pâle et sombre dans le courant de l'ample rivière invisible!

Tout à l'heure, la recherche de la chaleur, les grottes,
    les profondeurs de la nuit créée, la plongée
        vers les eaux souterraines, mais maintenant
    ce court arrêt, la largeur à peine d'un fuseau horaire,
        ailleurs meuglent les usines, les rotatives,
    ici même aux fenêtres de grands express européens
        la matrone hollandaise entre Colmar et Mulhouse regarde
    Bolwiller tout éperdu dans un miel solennel.

The spunk of St. Louis, every day, flows in abundance
Over straw pallets in Burgundy and Lower Brittany.
There *is* no rhyme, no reason. Nothing is simply used.
      After us, some nice weather.

—ANSELM HOLLO


## POPLARS AND ASPENS

Poplars and aspens. In the last horizontal
    clarity of the moment when the highest-up leaf
    caught all day in invisible river of air
        suddenly dips into honeyed stillness—

Why is it I've always been friends with evening?
    Evening's no stop
    —only this brief, unresolved moment
    when earth stops breathing, holds it back
    before night's long exhalation—
    and instantly, open season:
    tooth, eye, claw
    against all skin, all blood . . .

    The Eternal
    's a great owl, plumed with silence.
    The Eternal's a marten.
    The Eternal slays the Eternal and drinks its own blood.
    The Eternal's what has no sense,
    no point of view, no name, no time—

Poplars, aspens of evening.
    How I've loved those two-tone leaves,
    floating away, light and dark
    on great invisible current . . .

Now, then—search for warmth, for caves—
    nocturnal depths of creation: a plunge
        into subterranean waters
    stopped by a sudden thin space
    no wider than a time-zone—

Rien de réglé, rien de promis, le soir n'apporte rien.
O confitures du quiétisme! miel vénéneux à l'âme, et pourtant
le soir est l'image du pays natal
le soir nous ouvre un pays ancien.

## PSAUME

La baleine, dit Jonas, c'est la guerre et son black-out.
La baleine, c'est la ville et ses puits profonds et ses casernes
La baleine, c'est la campagne et son enlisement dans la terre et l'épicerie
et la main morte et le cul mal lavé et l'argent.
La baleine, c'est la société, et ses tabous, et sa vanité, et son ignorance.
La baleine, c'est (dans bien des cas, mes frères, mes sœurs) le mariage.
La baleine, c'est l'amour de soi. Et d'autres choses encore que je vous
dirai
Plus tard quand vous serez un peu moins obtus (à partir de la page x).
La baleine, c'est la vie incarnée.
La baleine, c'est la création, en fin de compte superflue, mais indispensable
pour cette expérience gratuite et d'ailleurs quasiment inintelligible.
La baleine est toujours plus loin, plus vaste; croyez-moi, on n'échappe
guère, on échappe difficilement, à la baleine.
La baleine est nécessaire.

Et ne croyez pas que vous allez tout comprendre comme cela d'un coup.
Car enfin,
Bien sûr la guerre est emmerdante
Bien sûr la société
Bien sûr le mariage
Mais on n'a pas encore trouvé d'autre école
De sorte qu'en fin de compte
Il ne reste en dernière analyse, comme cause d'emmerdement
Que l'amour de soi-même.

factories, rotary presses roaring—
yet even here, in window of great European train
    Dutch matron in transit from Colmar to Mulhouse
gazes out at Bolwiller in calm honeyed light.

No rule. No promise. The evening's just that.
    Oh, candy of quietism! Honey, soul poison, and yet—
        evening's image of native land:
            gate to ancient location.

—ANSELM HOLLO

# PSALM

The whale, says Jonah, is the war and its black-outs.
The whale is the city, and its deep pits, and its high-rise slums.
The whale is the country, bogged-down in the fields, and the
    general store, the dead hand, the none-too-clean asshole, and
    money.
The whale is society, and its taboos, its vanity, its ignorance.
The whale is (in many cases, dear brothers, dear sisters)
    marriage.
The whale is self-love. And still other things which I'll tell
    you about
Later, when you have become a little smarter (from page x on).
The whale is life incarnate.
The whale is creation, that finally superfluous event, which
    nevertheless is indispensable for this gratuitous and
    otherwise well-nigh unintelligible experience.
The whale is always farther away, and vaster; believe me, one
    never escapes from the whale, or only with great difficulty.
The whale is necessary.

And don't you believe that you are going to understand everything
    just like that, all at once.
Because, finally,
It is true that war is a load of shit,
        true that society—
        true that marriage—

Car il faut savoir: l'on regarde au-dedans ou au dehors
(Comme moi quand elle ouvrit la bouche—ou à travers moi).

Ainsi justement: la guerre,
La société, le mariage . . . il y en
A qui se servent comme
De tremplin pour sauter plus loin qu'eux-mêmes . . .

## CANTIQUE DE JONAS

Nous avons passé l'âge de nous plaindre;
De quoi au fait nous plaindrions-nous?
Il y a beau temps qu'on est sevré de la baleine maternelle.
Nous avons été dans la gueule de la baleine guerre
Et elle nous a recraché sur le rivage.
Geignards ou glorieux, nous avons passé l'âge.

Moi, dit Jonas, à la fin d'une phrase je mets un point.
Et les majuscules au début de chaque ligne c'est uniquement parce que
Ça fait plus joli à l'œil, chaque imprimeur vous dira ça.
Évidemment pour celui qui écoute un autre lui lire ce n'est pas pareil
Et lui ça lui est égal qu'il y ait des majuscules.

Pourtant, Seigneur—et certes, ce que j'en dis,
Ce n'est pas pour élever ma voix contre l'Éternel.
Plutôt contre moi et pour remâcher ma folie
Dont le goût dans ma bouche qui s'édente est amer.
Contre ma folie et contre ce vide de moi
Qui de moi-même fait comme
Une baleine de vanité, une baudruche de vent.

Mais en l'absence du Seigneur je m'assieds et m'attriste.

But no one has yet found another school
So that, when all is said and done,
In the final analysis, the only reason for the shitty state
 of things
Remains the love of self.
Keep in mind: one sees the whale either from within or from
 without
(Like me, when it opens its maw—or through me).

And thus—war,
Society, marriage . . . there
Are those who use them like
A springboard, to leap beyond themselves . . .

—ANSELM HOLLO

## JONAH'S CANTICLE

We have grown too old to complain:
What, as a matter of fact, is there to complain about?
It is high time we were severed from the maternal whale.
We have been stuck in the craw of the whale named war,
And it has spit us back onto the shore.
Whiners or braggarts, we have grown too old to complain.

Me, says Jonah, at the end of a sentence, I put a period.
And the capital letters at the beginning of each line are there
Only because it pleases the eye more; any printer will tell you that.
It seems that for someone listening to someone else read
This isn't so, and he won't give a damn if there are capitals or not.

Nevertheless, my Lord—and believe me, what I say
I do not say in order to raise my voice against the Eternal.
Rather, it is raised against myself, to chew the cud of my folly
Whose taste is bitter in my increasingly toothless mouth.
Against my folly, against this void in me
Which turns myself into a whale of vanity, a windbag.

But in the absence of the Lord I sit down and weep.

De quoi pourtant, de quoi Jonas se plaindrait-il?
Je suis vivant, dit Jonas, pas très vivant
Puisque l'Esprit si rarement si brièvement me visite
Mais je suis vivant la bouche encore pleine
De mer et des humeurs âcres de la bête
Et pas très remis encore du mal de mer
Mais au total il n'y a pas à dire ça va
Et quand ça ne va pas, on fait aller.

Palmes, dans le ciel vert des oiseaux de passage
Au bord de l'eau, le soir encore brûlant
Échoué sur la côte du Brésil j'ai levé les yeux
et remercie l'Éternel qui me tient dans le creux de sa main.

Ce n'est pas tellement que je m'accuse
Ni d'ailleurs que j'essaie de me justifier.
Quoi! J'ai peu menti, j'avais tué en fait et
Presque jamais en pensée; pour le reste, c'est entendu,
Flemmard et peloteur et parfois geignard
Personne au total de particulièrement, de bien intéressant.
O liquéfaction métaphysique, noyade bouddhique
O dispense de composer une personne superflue
O lassitude et secret désir d'enfin se perdre pour de bon
Dans les ténèbres internes de quelque baleine définitive.

Sentinelle, dis-nous la fin de la nuit.

Bonne affaire, bon aloi, bonnes fortunes
Bon usage de mon bon droit,
Bon air, bonne à tout faire, bon enfant,
Bonne vie, bonne à rien faire,
Quand ça ne va pas, on fait aller.

Ah l'époque est intéressante, notez bien
ah, le moi est intéressant
mais celui qui est établi, celui qui vit dans l'entre-deux
celui qui n'aime assez ni son Moi ni Dieu
celui qui a été craché des ténèbres de la baleine personnelle
sur un rivage vide où il n'a pas su parler à Dieu
celui-là, que fera-t-il?

Yet what, what was Jonah complaining about?
I am alive, says Jonah, not very much alive
Since the Spirit visits me so rarely, so briefly,
But I am alive, my mouth still full of brine
And the bitter humors of the beast,
Still not quite recovered from the sickness of the sea.
But generally speaking, things are not going so well,
And when they're not going, it's time to go.

Palm trees, in the green sky, migrant birds
At the water's edge, the evening still hot:
Cast up on the shore of Brazil, I have raised my eyes
And thanked the Eternal One who holds me cupped in his hand.

Really, I am not accusing
Nor trying to justify myself.
Why should I! I haven't lied much, I have killed, in fact
And almost never in my thoughts; as for the rest, it is true,
I have procrastinated, and flattered, and sometimes whined,
Been a person, in short, of no particular interest.
Oh, metaphysical liquefaction, oh, Buddhist drowning,
Oh, respite from having to constitute a superfluous person,
Oh, lassitude and secret desire to finally lose oneself for good
In the internal darkness of some definitive whale.

Watchman, tell us the end of the night.

Good business, good stuff, good fortune,
Good use of my good right,
Good air, good housekeeper, good child,
Good life, good lay;
When it doesn't go, it's time to go.

Ah, the epoch is interesting, take note,
ah, the self is interesting,
but the one who has settled, who lives in the inbetween,
who does not love his Self nor his God enough—
who has been spit out of the darkness of the personal whale
onto an empty shore, where he has not known how to speak to God—
that one, what will he do?

—ANSELM HOLLO

## VRAI NOM

Je nommerai désert ce château que tu fus,
Nuit cette voix, absence ton visage,
Et quand tu tomberas dans la terre stérile
Je nommerai néant l'éclair qui t'a porté.

Mourir est un pays que tu aimais. Je viens
Mais éternellement par tes sombres chemins.
Je détruis ton désir, ta forme, ta mémoire,
Je suis ton ennemi qui n'aura de pitié.

Je te nommerai guerre et je prendrai
Sur toi les libertés de la guerre et j'aurai
Dans mes mains ton visage obscur et traversé,
Dans mon cœur ce pays qu'illumine l'orage.

# Yves Bonnefoy

1923-

TRUE NAME

I will name wilderness the castle which you were,
Night your voice, absence your face,
And when you fall back into sterile earth
I will name nothingness the lightning which bore you.

Dying is a country which you loved. I approach
Along your dark ways, but eternally.
I destroy your desire, your form, your trace in me,
I am your enemy who shows no mercy.

I will name you war and I will take
With you the liberties of war, and I will have
In my hands your dark-crossed face,
In my heart this land which the storm lights.

—GALWAY KINNELL

## QUELLE PAROLE . . .

Quelle parole a surgi près de moi,
Quel cri se fait sur une bouche absente?
A peine-si j'entends crier contre moi,
A peine si je sens ce souffle qui me nomme.

Pourtant ce cri sur moi vient de moi,
Je suis muré dans mon extravagance.
Quelle divine ou quelle étrange voix
Eût consenti d'habiter mon silence?

## UNE VOIX

J'ai porté ma parole en vous comme une flamme,
Ténèbres plus ardues qu'aux flammes sont les vents.
Et rien ne m'a soumise en si profonde lutte,
Nulle étoile mauvaise et nul égarement.
Ainsi ai-je vécu, mais forte d'une flamme,
Qu'ai-je d'autre connu que son recourbement
Et la nuit que je sais qui viendra quand retombent
Les vitres sans destin de son élancement?
Je ne suis que parole intentée à l'absence,
L'absence détruira tout mon ressassement.
Oui, c'est bientôt périr de n'être que parole,
Et c'est tâche fatale et vain couronnement.

# WHAT WORD SPRINGS . . .

What word springs up beside me,
What cry is forming on an absent mouth?
I hardly hear this cry against me,
I hardly feel that breath saying my name.

And yet the cry comes from myself,
I am walled up in my extravagance,
What divine or what strange voice
Would have agreed to live in my silence?

—GALWAY KINNELL

# A VOICE

I have carried my word in you like a flame,
A darkness more brutal than winds are to flames.
And nothing has quelled me in such deep struggle,
No bad star, no straying from the path.
In this way have I lived, yet strong with a flame.
What have I known but its bending,
And the night, which I know will come when the windows
Fall again, cut from the fate of its yearning?
I am only word, acting against absence.
Absence will destroy my endless returning.
Yes, soon it will perish for having been but word,
A fatal task, a futile crowning.

—PAUL AUSTER

# TAIS-TOI . . .

Tais-toi puisqu'aussi bien nous sommes de la nuit
Les plus informes souches gravitantes,
Et matière lavée et retournant aux vieilles
Idées retentissantes où le feu s'est tari,
Et face ravinée d'une aveugle présence
Avec tout feu chassée servante d'un logis,
Et parole vécue mais infiniment morte
Quand la lumière enfin s'est faite vent et nuit.


# LIEU DE LA SALAMANDRE

La salamandre surprise s'immobilise
Et feint la mort.
Tel est le premier pas de la conscience dans les pierres,
Le mythe le plus pur,
Un grand feu traversé, qui est esprit.

La salamandre était à mi-hauteur
Du mur, dans la clarté de nos fenêtres.
Son regard n'était qu'une pierre,
Mais je voyais son cœur battre éternel.

O ma complice et ma pensée, allégorie
De tout ce qui est pur,
Que j'aime qui resserre ainsi dans son silence
La seule force de joie.

Que j'aime qui s'accorde aux astres par l'inerte
Masse de tout son corps,
Que j'aime qui attend l'heure de sa victoire,
Et qui retient son souffle et tient au sol.

# QUIET . . .

Quiet, for we too are of the night,
The most shapeless, gravitating stumps,
Cleansed matter, returning to the old
Ideas, resounding where the fire falters,
The ravaged face of a blind presence
With all hunted fire serving a home,
And the word, alive, but infinitely dead
When at last the light is made nocturnal wind.

—PAUL AUSTER

# PLACE OF THE SALAMANDER

The startled salamander freezes
And feigns death.
This is the first step of consciousness among the stones,
The purest myth,
A great fire passed through, which is spirit.

The salamander was halfway up
The wall, in the light from our windows.
Its gaze was merely a stone,
But I saw its heart beat eternal.

O my accomplice and my thought, allegory
Of all that is pure,
How I love that which clasps to its silence thus
The single force of joy.

How I love that which gives itself to the stars by the inert
Mass of its whole body,
How I love that which awaits the hour of its victory
And holds its breath and clings to the ground.

—GALWAY KINNELL

## L'IMPERFECTION EST LA CIME

Il y avait qu'il fallait détruire et détruire et détruire,
Il y avait que le salut n'est qu'à ce prix.

Ruiner la face nue qui monte dans le marbre,
Marteler toute forme toute beauté.

Aimer la perfection parce qu'elle est le seuil,
Mais la nier sitôt connue, l'oublier morte,

L'imperfection est la cime.

## LE RAVIN

Il y a qu'une épée était engagée
Dans la masse de pierre.
La garde était rouillée, l'antique fer
Avait rougi le flanc de la pierre grise.
Et tu savais qu'il te fallait saisir
A deux mains tant d'absence, et arracher
A sa gangue de nuit la flamme obscure.
Des mots étaient gravés dans le sang de la pierre,
Ils disaient ce chemin, connaître puis mourir.

Entre dans le ravin d'absence, éloigne-toi,
C'est ici en pierrailles qu'est le port.
Un chant d'oiseau
Te le désignera sur la nouvelle rive.

# IMPERFECTION IS THE SUMMIT

There was this:
You had to destroy, destroy, destroy.
There was this:
Salvation is only found at such a price.

To ruin the naked face that rises in the marble,
To hammer at every beauty every form.

Love perfection because it is the threshold
But deny it once known, once dead forget it,

Imperfection is the summit.

—ANTHONY RUDOLF

# THE RAVINE

And so a sword was driven
Into the mass of stone.
The hilt was rusted, the ancient blade
Had reddened the flank of the grey stone.
And you had, you knew, to seize
So much absence in both hands, and tear
The dark flame from its vein of night.
Words were engraved in the blood of the stone,
They spoke this road: to know and then to die.

Enter the ravine of absence, move away,
The harbour is here, in rubble.
A bird song
Will point it out to you on the new shore.

—ANTHONY RUDOLF

## LA MÊME VOIX, TOUJOURS

Je suis comme le pain que tu rompras,
Comme le feu que tu feras, comme l'eau pure
Qui t'accompagnera sur la terre des morts.

Comme l'écume
Qui a mûri pour toi la lumière et le port.

Comme l'oiseau du soir, qui efface les rives,
Comme le vent du soir soudain plus brusque et froid.

## L'ARBRE, LA LAMPE

L'arbre vieillit dans l'arbre, c'est l'été.
L'oiseau franchit le chant de l'oiseau et s'évade.
Le rouge de la robe illumine et disperse
Loin, au ciel, le charroi de l'antique douleur.

O fragile pays,
Comme la flamme d'une lampe que l'on porte,
Proche étant le sommeil dans la sève du monde,
Simple le battement de l'âme partagée.

Toi aussi tu aimes l'instant où la lumière des lampes
Se décolore et rêve dans le jour.
Tu sais que c'est l'obscur de ton cœur qui guérit,
La barque qui rejoint le rivage et tombe.

## THE SAME VOICE, STILL

I am like the bread you will break,
Like the fire you will make, like the pure water
That will go with you on the earth of the dead.

Like the foam
That ripened the harbor and the light for you.

Like the evening bird that blots the shores.
Like the colder, brusquer, sudden evening wind.

—PAUL AUSTER

## THE TREE, THE LAMP

The tree ages in the tree, it is summer.
The bird passes through the bird's song and escapes.
The red of the dress illumines and disperses
Far, in the sky, the ancient grief's procession.

Oh fragile country,
Like the flame of a lamp that one carries,
Sleep, near in the world's sap,
And the thudding of the shared soul, simple.

You too you love the moment when the light of lamps
Loses its color, and dreams in the day.
You know it is the dark in your heart that heals,
The boat that reaches the shore again, and falls.

—ANTHONY RUDOLF

## LE SANG, LA NOTE SI

Longues, longues journées.
Le sang inapaisé heurte le sang.
Le nageur est aveugle.
Il descend par étages pourpres dans le battement de ton cœur.

Quand la nuque se tend
Le cri toujours désert prend une bouche pure.

Ainsi vieillit l'été. Ainsi la mort
Encercle le bonheur de la flamme qui bouge.
Et nous dormons un peu. La note si
Résonne très longtemps dans l'étoffe rouge.


## HEURE . . .

Heure
Retranchée de la somme, maintenant.
Présence
Détrompée de la mort. Ampoule
Qui s'agenouille en silence
Et brûle
Déviée, secouée
Par la nuit qui n'a pas de cime.

Je t'écoute
Vibrer dans le rien de l'œuvre
Qui peine de par le monde.
Je perçois le piétinement
D'appels
Dont le pacage est l'ampoule qui brûle.
Je prends la terre à poignées
Dans cet évasement aux parois lisses
Où il n'est pas de fond
Avant le jour.
Je t'écoute, je prends

## BLOOD, THE NOTE *B*

Long, long days.
Unslaked blood is hitting blood.
The swimmer is blind.
He descends the purple steps
Into the beating of your heart.

When the nape is taut
The cry, that desert, catches a pure mouth.

Thus summer does grow old. Thus death
Surrounds the joy of the moving flame.
And we sleep a little. The note *B*
Reverberates a long time in the red cloth.

—ANTHONY RUDOLF

## UTMOST HOUR . . .

Utmost hour
Cut off from everything, now.
The no longer questioned
Presence of death. Light bulb
That kneels in silence
And burns,
Refracted, shaken,
By the darkness that has no summit.

I listen to you
Vibrating in the null of the work
That makes its way through the world.
I hear the stamping
Of cries
Whose pasture is the burning bulb.
I take up the earth in handfuls
Within this widening of naked walls
That is fathomless
Before the beginning of day.
I listen to you, I take

Dans ton panier de corde
Toute la terre. Dehors,
C'est encore le temps de la douleur
Avant l'image.
Dans la main de dehors, fermée,
A commencé à germer
Le blé des choses du monde.

All the earth
From your rope-basket. Outside,
The moment of grief endures
Before every image.
The hand of the outside is shut,
And within it has begun to grow
The wheat
Of the things of the world.

—PAUL AUSTER

# LE MOTEUR BLANC

I

J'ai vite enlevé
cette espèce de pansement arbitraire

je me suis retrouvé
libre
et sans espoir

comme un fagot
ou une pierre

je rayonne

avec la chaleur de la pierre

qui ressemble à du froid
contre le corps du champ

mais je connais la chaleur et le froid

la membrure du feu

le feu

# André du Bouchet
## 1924-

================

## THE WHITE MOTOR

I

I quickly removed
this sort of arbitrary bandage

I found myself
free
and without hope

like knotted sticks
or stone

I radiate

with the heat of stone

which resembles the cold
against the body of the field

but I know the heat and cold

the frame of the fire

the fire

dont je vois
la tête

les membres blancs.


II

Le feu perce en plusieurs points le côté sourd du ciel, le côté que je n'avais
jamais vu.

Le ciel qui se hisse un peu au-dessus de la terre. Le front noir. Je ne sais pas
si je suis ici ou là,
                    dans l'air ou dans l'ornière. Ce sont des morceaux d'air que
je foule comme des mottes.

Ma vie s'arrête avec le mur ou se met en marche là où le mur s'arrête, au ciel
éclaté. Je ne cesse pas.


III
                Mon récit sera la branche noire qui fait un coude dans le ciel.


IV

Ici, il ouvre sa bouche blanche. Là, il se défend sur toute la ligne, avec ces
arbres retranchés, ces êtres noirs. Là encore, il prend la forme lourde et chaude
de la fatigue, comme des membres de terre écorchés par une charrue.

Je m'arrête au bord de mon souffle, comme d'une porte, pour écouter son cri.

Ici, dehors, il y a sur nous une main, un océan lourd et froid, comme si on
accompagnait les pierres.


V
Je sors
dans la chambre

comme si j'étais dehors

parmi des meubles
immobiles

dans la chaleur qui tremble

in which I see
the head

the white limbs.


I I

At several points the fire pierces the sky, the deaf side, which I have never seen.

The sky that heaves a bit above the earth. The black brow. I don't know if I am here or there,
                            in the air or in a rut. They are scraps of air, which I crush like clumps of earth.

My life stops with the wall, or begins to walk where the wall stops, in the shattered sky. I do not stop.


I I I
        My telling will be the black branch that forms an elbow in the sky.


I V

Here, its white mouth opens. There, it defends itself along the whole line, with these entrenched trees, these black beings. There again, it takes the hot, heavy form of fatigue, like limbs of earth, scorched by a plow.

I stop at the edge of my breath, as if beside a door, to listen to its cry.

Here, outside, a hand is upon us, a cold, heavy sea, as if, as the stones walk, we were walking with stones.


V
I go out
inside the room

as if outside

among the still
furnishings

in the shuddering heat

toute seule

hors de son feu

il n'y a toujours
rien

le vent.


VI

Je marche, réuni au feu, dans le papier vague confondu avec l'air, la terre
désamorcée. Je prête mon bras au vent.

Je ne vais pas plus loin que mon papier. Très loin au-devant de moi, il comble
un ravin. Un peu plus loin dans le champ, nous sommes presque à égalité. A
mi-genoux dans les pierres.

A côté, on parle de plaie, on parle d'un arbre. Je me reconnais. Pour ne pas
être fou. Pour que mes yeux ne deviennent pas aussi faibles que la terre.


VII

Je suis dans le champ
comme une goutte d'eau
sur du fer rouge

lui-même s'éclipse

les pierres s'ouvrent

comme une pile d'assiettes
que l'on tient
dans ses bras

quand le soir souffle

je reste
avec ces assiettes blanches et froides

comme si je tenais la terre
elle-même

dans mes bras.

alone

outside its fire

there is not yet
anything

the wind.


VI

I walk, joined with fire, in the uncertain paper, mingled with air, the un-
primed earth. I lend my arm to the wind.

I go no farther than my paper. Far before me, it fills a ravine. A bit farther,
in the field, we are almost level. Half knee-deep in stones.

Nearby they speak of wounds, of a tree. I see myself in what they speak. That
I not be mad. That my eyes not become as weak as the earth.


VII

I am in the field
like a drop of water
on a red-hot iron

the field itself
eclipsed

the stones open

like a stack of plates
held
in the arms

when evening breathes

I stay
with these cold white plates

as if I held the earth
itself

in my arms.

VIII

Déjà des araignées courent sur moi, sur la terre démembrée. Je me lève droit au-dessus des labours, sur les vagues courtes et sèches,

                                         d'un champ accompli

et devenu bleu, où je marche sans facilité.


IX

Rien ne me suffit. Je ne suffis à rien. Le feu qui souffle sera le fruit de ce jour-là, sur la route en fusion qui réussit à devenir blanche aux yeux heurtés des pierres.


X

Je freine pour apercevoir le champ vide, le ciel au-dessus du mur. Entre l'air et la pierre, j'entre dans un champ sans mur. Je sens la peau de l'air, et pourtant nous demeurons séparés.

Hors de nous, il n'y a pas de feu.


XI

                Une grande page blanche palpitante dans la lumière dévastée dure jusqu'à ce que nous nous rapprochions.


XII

En lâchant la porte chaude, la poignée de fer, je me trouve devant un bruit qui n'a pas de fin, un tracteur. Je touche le fond d'un lit rugueux, je ne commence pas. J'ai toujours vécu. Je vois plus nettement les pierres, surtout l'ombre qui sertit, l'ombre rouge de la terre sur les doigts quand elle est fragile, sous ses tentures, et que la chaleur ne nous a pas cachés.


XIII

Ce feu, comme un mur plus lisse en prolongement vertical de l'autre et violemment heurté jusqu'au faîte où il nous aveugle, comme un mur que je ne laisse pas se pétrifier.

La terre relève sa tête sévère.

Ce feu comme une main ouverte auquel je renonce à donner un nom. Si la réalité est venue entre nous comme un coin et nous a séparés, c'est que j'étais trop près de cette chaleur, de ce feu.

VIII

Already the spiders are running over me, on the dismembered earth. I rise above the plowing, on the clipped and arid runnels,

of a finished field, now blue, where I walk without ease.

IX

Nothing satisfies me. I satisfy nothing. The bellowing fire will be the fruit of that day, on the fusing road, reaching whiteness in the battered eyes of stones.

X

I brake to see the vacant field, the sky above the wall. Between air and stone, I enter an unwalled field. I feel the skin of the air, and yet we remain divided.

Beyond us, there is no fire.

XI

A large white page, palpitating in the ruined light, lasts until we get closer to one another.

XII

In releasing the warm door, the iron knob, I find myself before a noise that has no end, a tractor. I touch the base of a gnarled bed. I do not begin. I have always lived. I see the stones more clearly. The enclosing shadow, the earth's red shadow on my fingers, in its weakness, beneath its draping, which the heat has not hidden from us.

XIII

This fire, like a smoother wall, built on top of another, and struck, violently, up to its peak, where it blinds us, like a wall I do not allow to petrify.

The earth lifts its harsh head.

The fire, like an open hand, which I no longer wish to name. If reality has come between us, like a wedge, and divided us, it was because I was too close to this heat, to this fire.

XIV

Alors, tu as vu ces éclats de vent, ces grands disques de pain rompu, dans le pays brun, comme un marteau hors de sa gangue qui nage contre le courant sans rides dont on n'aperçoit que le lit rugueux, la route.

Ces fins éclats, ces grandes lames déposées par le vent.

Les pierres dressées, l'herbe à genoux. Et ce que je ne connais pas de profil et de dos, dès qu'il se tait: toi, comme la nuit.

Tu t'éloignes.

Ce feu dételé, ce feu qui n'est pas épuisé et qui nous embrase, comme un arbre, le long du talus.

XV

Ce qui demeure après le feu, ce sont les pierres disqualifiées, les pierres froides, la monnaie de cendre dans le champ.

Il y a encore la carrosserie de l'écume qui cliquette comme si elle rejaillissait de l'arbre ancré dans la terre aux ongles cassés, cette tête qui émerge et s'ordonne, et le silence qui nous réclame comme un grand champ.

AJOURNEMENT

J'occupe seul cette demeure
blanche

où rien ne contrarie le vent

si nous sommes ce qui a crié
et le cri

qui ouvre ce ciel
de glace

XIV

So, you have seen these burstings of the wind, these great discs of broken bread, in this brown country, like a hammer out of its matrix that swims against the unrippled current, of which nothing can be seen but the gnarled bed, the road.

These keening bursts, these great blades, left by the wind.

The raised stone, the grass on its knees. What I don't know of the back and profile, since the moment of soundlessness: you, like the night.

You recede.

This unharnessed fire, this unconsumed fire, igniting us, like a tree, along the slope.

XV

What remains after the fire are disqualified stones, frigid stones, the change of ashes in the field.

The carriage of the foam still remains, rattling, as if it had rushed forth again from the tree, anchored to the earth with broken nails, this head, that emerges and falls into place, and the silence that claims us, like a vast field.

—PAUL AUSTER

POSTPONEMENT

> Alone I inhabit this white
> place
>
> where nothing thwarts the wind
>
> if we are what cried
> and the cry
>
> that opens this sky
> of ice

ce plafond blanc

nous nous sommes aimés sous ce plafond.

――――

Je vois presque,
à la blancheur de l'orage, ce qui se fera sans moi.

Je ne diminue pas. Je respire au pied de la lumière aride.

――――

S'il n'y avait pas la force
de la poussière
qui coupe jambes et bras

mais seul le blanc
qui verse

je tiendrais le ciel

profonde ornière
avec laquelle nous tournons

et qui donne contre l'air.

――――

Dans cette lumière que le soleil
abandonne, toute chaleur résolue en feu, j'ai couru, cloué à la lumière des
routes, jusqu'à ce que le vent plie.

――――

Où je déchire l'air,
tu as passé avec moi. Je te retrouve dans la chaleur. Dans
l'air, encore plus loin, qui s'arrache, d'une secousse, à la chaleur.

La poussière illumine. La montagne,
faible lampe, apparaît.

this white ceiling

we have loved under this ceiling

=======

                                              I almost see,
in the whiteness of the storm, what will come to pass without me.

I do not diminish. I breathe at the foot of arid light.

=======

If there were not the force
of dust
that severs arms and legs

but only the white
that spills

I would hold the sky

deep rut
with which we turn

and which knocks against the air.

=======

                                      In this light that sun
abandons, all heat resolved in fire, I ran, nailed to the light of roads, till wind
buckles under.

=======

Where I rend the air,
                        you have come through with me. I find you in the heat.
In the air, even farther, which uproots itself, with a single jolt, away from the
heat.

                                  The dust lights up. The mountain,
frail lamp, appears.

—PAUL AUSTER

## LA LUMIÈRE DE LA LAME

Ce glacier qui grince

pour dire
la fraîcheur de la terre

sans respirer.

=====

                  Comme du papier à plat sur cette terre,
ou un peu au-dessus de la terre,
            comme une lame je cesse de respirer. La nuit
je me retourne, un instant, pour le dire.

                A la place de l'arbre.
                    A la clarté des pierres.

                J'ai vu, tout le long du jour,
la poutre sombre et bleue qui barre le jour se soulever pour nous rejoindre
dans la lumière immobile.

=====

                Je marche dans les éclats de la poussière
qui nous réfléchit.

Dans le souffle court
et bleu
      de l'air qui claque

loin du souffle

l'air tremble et claque.

# THE LIGHT OF THE BLADE

This glacier that creaks

to utter
the cool of the earth

without breathing.

═══════

      Like paper flat against this earth,
or a bit above the earth,
    like a blade I stop breathing. At night I return to
myself, for a moment, to utter it.

    In place of the tree.
       In the light of the stones.

       I saw, all along the day,
the dark blue rafter that bars the day rise up to reach us in the motionless light.

═══════

      I walk in the gleams of dust
that mirror us.

In the short blue
breath
  of the clattering air

far from breath

the air trembles and clatters.

—PAUL AUSTER

## LA VEILLÉE FUNÈBRE

On ne fait pas de bruit
dans la chambre des morts:
on lève la bougie
et les voit s'éloigner.

J'élève un peu la voix
sur le seuil de la porte
et je dis quelques mots
pour éclairer leur route.

Mais ceux qui ont prié
même de sous la neige,
l'oiseau du petit jour
vient leur voix relayer.

# Philippe Jaccottet
## 1925-

## THE VIGIL

One makes no noise
in the room of the dead:
one lifts up the candle
and sees them depart.

At the threshold I raise
my voice a little
and say a few words
to light up their way.

But those who have prayed
even beneath
snow—the dawn bird
comes to relay their voices.

—ANTHONY RUDOLF

UNE SEMAISON . . .

Une semaison de larmes
sur le visage changé,
la scintillante saison
des rivières dérangées:
chagrin qui creuse la terre

L'âge regarde la neige
s'éloigner sur les montagnes

LUNE D'HIVER

Pour entrer dans l'obscurité
prends ce miroir où s'éteint
un glacial incendie:

atteint le centre de la nuit,
tu n'y verras plus reflété
qu'un baptême de brebis

LÀ OÙ LA TERRE . . .

Là où la terre s'achève
levée au plus près de l'air
(dans la lumière où le rêve
invisible de Dieu erre)

entre pierre et songerie

cette neige: hermine enfuie

## A SOWING OF TEARS . . .

A sowing of tears
on the changed face,
the glittering season
of rivers gone wild:
grief that hollows the earth

Age watches the snow
receding on the mountains

—W. S. MERWIN

## WINTER MOON

To enter the dark
take this mirror where
a glacial fire
is dying out:

once you are deep
at night's center you'll see
reflected
just a baptism of sheep.

—CHARLES TOMLINSON

## WHERE EARTH . . .

Where earth ends
lofted nearest to air
(in the light where the invisible
dream of God wanders)

between stone and revery

this snow: vanished ermine

—PAUL AUSTER

JE MARCHE . . .

Je marche
dans un jardin de braises fraîches
sous leur abri de feuilles

un charbon ardent sur la bouche


LA PARFAITE . . .

La parfaite douceur est figurée au loin
à la limite entre les montagnes et l'air:

distance, longue étincelle
qui déchire, qui affine


POIDS DES PIERRES . . .

Poids des pierres, des pensées

Songes et montagnes
n'ont pas même balance

Nous habitons encore un autre monde
Peut-être l'intervalle

# I WALK . . .

I walk
in a garden of cool embers
under their shelter of leaves

a burning coal against my mouth

—PAUL AUSTER

# PERFECT . . .

Perfect calm sketched afar
at the limit between mountains and air:

distance, long spark
that tears apart, that hones

—PAUL AUSTER

# WEIGHT OF STONES . . .

Weight of stones, weight of thoughts

Dreams and mountains
do not even balance

We still inhabit another world
Perhaps the interval

—PAUL AUSTER

## FLEURS . . .

Fleurs couleur bleue
bouches endormies
sommeil des profondeurs

Vous pervenches
en foule
parlant d'absence au passant

## AUBE

Heure où la lune s'embue
à l'approche de la bouche
qui murmure un nom caché

au point qu'on y distingue à peine
le peigne et la chevelure

## CASCADE NOIRE . . .

Cascade noire suspendue
Chose mystérieuse, chevaline
Plumage
Chose à tordre
`Brûlant tout près de notre centre
Toison, tison, torche inversée
Flamme de la nuit dans le jour
Fer dans notre cœur

FLOWERS . . .

Flowers colored blue
mouths asleep
slumber of depths

You periwinkles
a horde
speaking of absence to the passer-by

—PAUL AUSTER

DAWN

Hour when the moon mists over
at the approach of a mouth
murmuring a hidden name

so that one can scarcely make out
the comb and the hair

—W. S. MERWIN

BLACK CASCADE . . .

Black cascade suspended
Mysterious thing, horselike
Plumage
A thing to twist
Burning close to our centre
Fleece, brand, inverted torch
Flame of night by day
Iron in our hearts

—MICHAEL HAMBURGER

## MÉTAMORPHOSE DES AMANTS

De partout la nuit craque et se fend
Et les amants se retrouvent couverts de plume
Avec un peu de sable sur les doigts.

Les amants ont soif dans leur lit desséché
Car toute l'eau est partie se noyer dans la mer:
Et les coqs à la fenêtre se poussent du jabot
Picorant dans la vitre les dernières étoiles.

Amants qui portez des panaches blancs et des couteaux
Saignez ces coqs et dans un plat de faïence
Répandez leur sang: qu'ils dorment, qu'ils dorment
Dans le cercle de craie où vos bras les ont clos.

## LÀ-BAS

L'horloge sur des tas de coquilles décalque
Le temps. Le foin bleuit. Nous allons vers la mer

# Robert Marteau

1925-

## THE METAMORPHOSIS OF LOVERS

On all sides the night cracks & splinters
And lovers find themselves covered in feathers
With grains of salt between the fingers.

Lovers are thirsty in their drained beds
For all the moisture has left for the sea
And in the window the roosters are pouting,
Pecking in the glass the last stars.

Lovers who carry white plumes and knives
Bleed these cocks in an earthenware bowl
Spread the blood that they may sleep,
Sleep in the chalk circle your arms seal.

—JOHN MONTAGUE

## DOWN THERE

Time transcribes its passage on seashell piles.
The hay turns blue. Towards the sea we march

Et soudain il n'y a plus d'arbres mais des bœufs
Qui tirent des charrois de varech sur le sable.

Une bande d'étourneaux s'égraine dans les vignes.
Un cri comme une noix! Des touffes de méduses
(Leur ventre violet éclate sous le fer)
A la crête du flux font d'énormes rosées

De pleurs et de poisons. La carcasse d'un chien
(Les crabes ont mangé la viande), cage d'os
Ensablée, oscille au rythme de la marée.

O pays de tristesse où la tourbe mûrit,
Tu saignes lentement comme un faisceau d'entrailles,
Ou bien comme un oiseau que le vent a cassé.


## BANDERILLES NOIRES

Quelle bête de suif et salive a mouillé
Mes os que me voilà tout de nocturnes linges
Tatoué? Dans mon dos qui navigue? Je feins,
Je décide l'oubli. Son mufle m'a fouillé

Les épaules, un lys maintenant me marque, un
Gel précoce qui déploie au-dessus de mes reins
Je sais quelle toile où la coutume a taillé
Son manteau de limon, un drap où le noyé

Dégorge son eau, un lambeau de brumes, un
Jeu de flèches (fuseaux noirs qu'on m'aurait plantés
Pour descendre aux Enfers!) Tout cri qui monte en vain,

Fumée, image, peu de sang pour ces vérités
Qui lèchent des parois d'astres morts, et sans fin
Raclent dans le cuveau l'amertume du vin.

And suddenly there are no trees, only oxen
Drawing carts of kelp along the strand.

A flock of starlings scatter among the vines.
A cry, a nut falling! Tufts of jellyfish
(Their bellies burst violet under the rim)
On the cresting tide form enormous dews

Of tears and poison. A dog's carcass
(The crabs have eaten the flesh) oscillates
To the sea's rhythm its silted cage of bones.

O sad land where the turf matures,
You bleed slowly, a knot of entrails,
Like a bird the wind has broken.

—JOHN MONTAGUE


## BLACK BANDERILLAS

What beast of saliva and suet has moistened my bones
That I am tattooed all over with this
Nocturnal linen? Who's sailing my back? I dissemble,
Decide on oblivion. His muzzle has rummaged

My shoulders, I'm marked with a lily now, an early
Frost unfurls across my loins the remembered
Cloth from which custom has cut
Its cloak of silt, its sheet where the drowned man

Coughs up his water, a tatter of haze,
An archery (black spindles planted in me for
The descent to the Underworld)! Every cry that goes up

In vain, smoke or image, little blood for these
Truths that lick the shells of dead stars, and forever
Scrape up in the vat the wine's bitter lees.

—ANNE WINTERS

SALAMANDRE

Salamandre, ce nid d'écumes et de joncs,
Ce Parnasse de poudre où la hache tournoie,
C'est comme dans Paros: quand la muse se noie
Il faut que les dauphins la tirent des filons.

Il faut dans les filets trouver le loup de soie
Qui tombe avec la nuit; il faut courir au long
Des grèves, prévenir par cris, à coups de gong
Que sel est la statue où l'aube se déploie.

Rincez ce trou, massacrez ces pigeons, tendez
Sur le bois d'olivier la flanelle écarlate,
Que le pourrissement des mouches qui éclatent

(En quels lointains secrets maintenant dégradés)
Serve à notre salut. De votre chair d'abeilles,
O Vierge, j'ai dit les guérisons, les merveilles.

STÈLE

pour l'âne dont les cartilages
fleurissent le fossé
pour le chien, pour l'enfant
qui refroidit sous ma paume
dans l'herbe rase de l'Europe
je revois tes pieds nus
qu'un peu de sang tache
et ta robe gitane

et ton épaule tachée de framboise
où l'aile lentement pousse son duvet noir

ainsi la beauté de l'oiseau et celle de la renarde
ici succombent
dans le chuintement de la gomme sur l'asphalte

aucun dieu ne vient

# SALAMANDER

Salamander, this nest of rushes and foam,
This powder Parnassus and whirling axe,
Remind me of Paros: the dolphins must drag
The drowning muse from the buried lodes.

We must take the black silken mask in our nets
When it falls with the night; we must cry, run down
The beaches, give warning with blows of our gong
That salt is the statue unfurling the dawn.

Kill these pigeons, rinse out this fissure, and spread
Scarlet flannel out on the olive wood,
That the blaze and bursting of rotting flies

(Now sunk to what secret depths) may serve
Our salvation. And now, great Virgin, I've named
Your bees' flesh, and told of its marvels and cures.

—ANNE WINTERS

# STELE

for the ass whose gristle
flowers the ditch
for the dog, for the child
grown cold beneath my palm
in the smooth grass of Europe
again I see your bare feet
stained with a little blood
and your gypsy dress

and the raspberry stain of your shoulder, where slowly
the wing puts forth its dark down

so the beauty of birds and vixens
perishes here
in the screeching of rubber on asphalt

and no god comes

notre Père qui êtes aux cieux
que vôtre règne arrive
seulement la brute habillée de vinyl
qui disperse à coups de mâchoires
le chœur lamentable
nul sacre ni sacrement
le monde n'est qu'un tas de faits divers
la mort au visage de chevrotines
s'avance parmi nous
incognito, saccageant en nuits de noces
la lingerie des motels

les pauvres n'ont plus de larmes
depuis qu'on gouverne en leur nom

privés de parole, absents de toute prière
ils vont
nippés de surplus, persuadés
de n'être rien d'autre que ce qu'ils sont.

Je dis: rien n'est tragique
depuis que le crâne de l'homme
a perdu la forme du ciel
je dis
et vous me maudissez
bénédiction d'Ève sur le trésor

je dis à l'ange
tu es Thot, tu es Hermès
les serpents t'obéissent—et le calame.

INNOMMÉ TOUJOURS . . .

Innommé toujours est le monde, hors de nous
la vasque où le saule prend racine, où le cerf
vient boire, hors de nous l'axe qui joint les vertèbres,
hors de nous la glande florale, et la chevelure
qui tombe du miroir au sommet.

our Father which art in heaven
thy kingdom come
only the brute dressed in vinyl
whose jawing scatters
the sorrowful choir
no consecration, no sacrament
the world is only a pile of tabloid news
the buckshot face of death
moves among us
incognito, ransacking on wedding nights
the motel linen

the poor have no more tears
since we govern in their name

wordless, absent from all prayer
they go about
decked out in surplus, persuaded
they're nothing more than what they are.

I say: nothing is tragic
since the skull of man
has lost the form of heaven
I say
and you curse me
Eve's blessing on the treasure

I say to the angel
you are Thoth, you are Hermes
the serpents obey you—and the reed.

—ANNE WINTERS

## UNNAMED ALWAYS . . .

Unnamed always is the world, outside of us
the basin where the willow takes root, where the stag
comes to drink, outside of us the axis that joins the vertebrae,
outside of us the floral gland and the long hair
that falls from the mirror at the zenith.

—LOUIS SIMPSON

## LE RÈGNE MINÉRAL

Dans ce pays la foudre fait germer la pierre.

Sur les pitons qui commandent les gorges
Des tours ruinées se dressent
Comme autant de torches mentales actives
Qui raniment les nuits de grand vent
L'instinct de mort dans le sang du carrier.

Toutes les veines du granit
Vont se dénouer dans ses yeux.

Le feu jamais ne guérira de nous,
Le feu qui parle notre langue.

# Jacques Dupin
## 1927-

MINERAL KINGDOM

In this country lightning quickens stone.

On the peaks that dominate the gorges
Ruined towers rise up
Like nimble torches of the mind
That revive the nights of high wind
The instinct of death in the quarryman's blood.

Every granite vein
Will unravel in his eyes.

The fire that will never be cured of us.
The fire that speaks our language.

—PAUL AUSTER

## LA SOIF

J'appelle l'éboulement
(Dans sa clarté tu es nue)
Et la dislocation du livre
Parmi l'arrachement des pierres.

Je dors pour que le sang qui manque à ton supplice,
Lutte avec les arômes, les genêts, le torrent
De ma montagne ennemie.

Je marche interminablement.

Je marche pour altérer quelque chose de pur,
Cet oiseau aveugle à mon poing
Ou ce trop clair visage entrevu
A distance d'un jet de pierres.

J'écris pour enfouir mon or,
Pour fermer tes yeux.

## RESTE LE SEUL . . .

Reste le seul battement
D'une minuscule agonie désirable
Dans les hauts jardins refermés.

La scansion de l'affreux murmure te dégrade:
Écourte ta journée, enterre tes outils.

## THIRST

I summon the landslide
(In its clarity you are naked)
And the dismemberment of the book
Among the uprooting of stones.

I sleep so the blood your torture lacks
Will struggle with scents, the gorse, the torrent
Of my enemy mountain.

I walk endlessly.

I walk to alter something pure,
This blind bird upon my fist
Or this too clear face, glimpsed
At a stone's throw.

I write to bury my gold,
To close your eyes.

—PAUL AUSTER

## THE ONLY BEATING . . .

The only beating remains
Of a small desirable agony
In the high gardens that have shut again.

The scansion of the hideous murmur degrades you:
Shorten your day, bury your tools.

—PAUL AUSTER

## MON CORPS . . .

Mon corps, tu n'occuperas pas la fosse
Que je creuse, que j'approfondis chaque nuit.

Comme un sanglier empêtré dans les basses branches
Tu trépignes, tu te débats.

Le liseron du parapet se souvient-il d'un autre corps
Prostré sur le clavier du gouffre?

Jette tes vêtements et tes vivres,
Sourcier de l'ordinaire éclat.

Le glissement de la colline
Comblera la profondeur fourbe,
L'excavation secrète sous le pas.

Le calme s'insinue avec l'air de la nuit
Par les pierres disjointes et le cœur criblé

A la seconde où tu as disparu
Comme une écharde dans la mer.

## OUVERTE . . .

Ouverte en peu de mots,
comme par un remous, dans quelque mur,
une embrasure, pas même une fenêtre

pour maintenir à bout de bras
cette contrée de nuit où le chemin se perd,

à bout de forces une parole nue

# MY BODY . . .

My body, you will not fill the ditch
That I am digging, that I deepen each night.

Like a wild boar caught in the underbrush
You leap, you struggle.

Does the vine on the rampart remember another body
Prostrate on the keyboard of the void?

Throw off your clothes, throw away your food,
Diviner of water, hunter of lowly light.

The sliding of the hill
Will overflow the false depth,
The secret excavation underfoot.

Calm wriggles into the night air
Through disjointed stones and the riddled heart

At the instant you disappear,
Like a splinter in the sea.

—PAUL AUSTER

# OPENED . . .

Opened in few words
as if by an eddy, in some wall,
an embrasure, not even a window

to hold at arm's length
this night country where the path is lost

at the limit of strength a naked word

—PAUL AUSTER

## LA VAGUE . . .

La vague de calcaire et la blancheur du vent
traversent la poitrine du dormeur

dont les nerfs inondés vibrent plus bas
soutiennent les jardins en étages
écartent les épines et prolongent
les accords des instruments nocturnes
vers la compréhension de la lumière
—et de son brisement

sa passion bifurquée sur l'enclume
il respire
comme le tonnerre
sans vivres et sans venin parmi les genévriers
de la pente, et le ravin lui souffle
un air obscur
pour compenser la violence des liens

## IL M'EST INTERDIT . . .

Il m'est interdit de m'arrêter pour voir. Comme si j'étais condamné à voir
en marchant. En parlant. A voir ce dont je parle et à parler justement parce
que je ne vois pas. Donc à donner à voir ce que je ne vois pas, ce qu'il m'est
interdit de voir. Et que le langage en se déployant heurte et découvre. La
cécité signifie l'obligation d'inverser les termes et de poser la marche, la parole,
avant le regard. Marcher dans la nuit, parler sous la rumeur, pour que le rayon
du jour naissant fuse et réplique à mon pas, désigne la branche, et détache le
fruit.

# THE WAVE . . .

The wave of limestone and the white of wind
cross the sleeper's chest

whose flooded nerves are shaking below
propping the gardens in tiers
parting the thorns and prolonging
the harmonies of nocturnal instruments
toward comprehension of the light
—and its breaking

his forked passion on the anvil
he breathes
like thunder
without food without venom among the junipers
on the slope, and the ravine makes him breathe
a dark air
to compensate for the violence of his chains

—PAUL AUSTER

# I AM FORBIDDEN . . .

I am forbidden to stop to see. As if I were condemned to see while walking.
While speaking. To see what I speak, and to speak precisely because I do not
see. Thus to show what I do not see, what I am forbidden to see. What
language, unfolding, strikes and discovers. Blindness signifies the obligation
to invert the terms, and to posit walking and word before the eyes. To walk
in the night, to speak through din and confusion, so that the shaft of the rising
day fuses and answers my step, designates the branch, and picks the fruit.

—PAUL AUSTER

## SALUONS . . .

Saluons ce qui nous délivre, le bulldozer jaune flamme, le scarabée géant au thorax secoué de fièvre, les reins en porte-à-faux pour un monstrueux cambrement. Il est venu déraciner le palais et les ruines, renverser les images et la pierre, coucher les colombiers et les dômes, extirper les vieilles passions érectiles des hommes, et leur syntaxe verticale, et la prison en dernier lieu, tout ce qui reste de la ville. Clairière désormais pure de toute ombre malsaine. Table rase. Table dressée pour un festin sans nourritures et sans convives. Je salue sa candeur enragée qui s'apprête à combler notre attente, à signer notre ouvrage.

C'est alors que je te vois grandir, étoile. Que je te vois grandir et briller dans ma main minuscule, pierre taillée contre la famine.

## DANS L'ATTENTE . . .

Dans l'attente à voix basse
De quelque chose de terrible et de simple
—Comme la récolte de la foudre
Ou la descente des gravats . . .

C'est la proximité du ciel intact
Qui fait la maigreur des troupeaux,
Et cet affleurement de la roche brûlante,
Et le regain d'odeurs de la montagne défleurie . . .

Sommets de vent et de famine,
Motet insipide, fureur des retours,
Je redoute moins la déchéance qui m'est due
Que cette immunité
Qui m'entrave dans ses rayons.

Terre promise, terre de l'éboulement,
Malgré les colonnes, malgré le tambour.

## LET US SALUTE . . .

Let us salute what delivers us, the flame yellow bulldozer, the giant beetle with fever-shaken thorax, the small of its back twisted for a monstrous arching. It has come to uproot the palace and its ruins, to overturn images and stone, to fold up the domes and dovecots, to rip out the old erectile passions of men, their vertical syntax, and last of all, the prison, all that remains of the city. From now on, a clearing free from all diseased shadow. Bare table. A table adorned for a feast without food, without guests. I salute its enraged candor, preparing to redeem our waiting, to sign our work.

It is then that I see you grow, star. That I see you grow and shine in my tiny hand, a stone, girded against famine.

—PAUL AUSTER

## WAITING . . .

Waiting with lowered voice
For something terrible and simple
—Like the harvest of the lightning
Or the crumbling of the plaster . . .

It is the nearness of the intact sky
That emaciates the flocks,
This jut of burning rock,
And the revival of smells from the flowerless mountain . . .

Summits of wind and famine,
Insipid motet, fury of returns,
I dread the ruin which is due to me
Less than this immunity
That fetters me in its rays.

Promised land, land that crumbles,
Despite the columns, despite the drum.

—PAUL AUSTER

# SOUS LA FRAYEUR . . .

Sous la frayeur du récit
inarticulé

le soleil
la signification de l'octroi

aphasique moyeu
ton règne
depuis que la roue me broie
je le nie

quelle que soit l'odeur putride des quartiers neufs
et les instruments de déclin étalés à nos pieds

nous dévorons le mâchefer
ce qui s'écrit sans nous
en contrebas

l'éraflure et la saveur
contiguës et désaccordées
ce qui s'écrit obliquement sournoisement
établissant le calme

comme une pyramide sur sa pointe

# GRIPPED BY THE DREAD . . .

Gripped by the dread of the unspoken
telling

the sun
the meaning
of giving in

aphasiac hub
your kingdom
since the wheel crushed me
I have denied it

Whatever the putrid smell of new neighborhoods
the instruments of decline spread out at our feet

we devour the slag
what is written without us
downwards

abrasion and aroma
contiguous and discordant
what is written obliquely and with cunning
building calm

like a pyramid on its point

—PAUL AUSTER

## LA LIGNE SINUEUSE . . .

La ligne sinueuse et boisée d'une colline. Trois maisons où l'on se repose, le soir. L'espace d'une rivière que bordent des jardins. Puis le ciel, presque blanc.

Et tel est mon exil: cette page où s'impriment les pas d'un géant qui sommeille.


## ET PEUT-ÊTRE . . .

Et peut-être les mots sont-ils de pures apparences
Entre le ciel et mon visage . . .

Il neige,
Hors du spectre.
Et mes yeux n'osent plus respirer.

# Roger Giroux

## 1925-1973

THE SINUOUS . . .

The sinuous, wooded outline of a hill. Three houses, peaceful, at evening. The space of a river, bordered by gardens. Then the sky, almost white. Such is my exile: this page, darkened by the steps of a slumbering giant.

—PAUL AUSTER

AND PERHAPS . . .

And perhaps words are pure appearances
Between the sky and my face . . .

It snows,
Beyond this ghostly presence,
And my eyes
Dare not breathe anymore.

L'âme perd toute connaissance,
Et la mesure de ce pays.

Et je me désunis.

## UN OISEAU . . .

Un oiseau, lorsqu'il va, sur la mer,
Porter mémoire de la terre à la limite de ce jour
De lumière et d'amour, un oiseau . . .

Comment dire cela sans défaire l'ouvrage
Des yeux, des mains, et de tout le visage,
Et sans briser en nous l'oiseau et le langage . . .
Comment dire cela sans rougir, et se taire?

Toute œuvre est étrangère, toute parole absente,
Et le poème rit et me défie de vivre
Ce désir d'un espace où le temps serait nul.
Et c'est don du néant, ce pouvoir de nommer

Un oiseau, lorsqu'il va, sur la mer, comme on respire,
Cet instant qui ne dure que pour mourir, là-bas,
Depuis le commencement du monde jusqu'au dernier naufrage,
Et peut-être plus loin, vers la dernière étoile,
La première parole, ô comment dire cela . . .

## LE CENTRE . . .

Le centre est noir,
Et la parole n'éteint pas la lèpre du visage.

The soul is emptied,
And loses all measure of this land.

I separate myself
From myself.

—PAUL AUSTER


A BIRD . . .

A bird, when it moves out to sea,
To carry memory of land to the far end of this day
Of light and love, a bird . . .

How say that and not unmake all
The work of eyes, of hands, and of one's whole
Face, and not kill
In us the bird and language . . . How say it
And not blush and fall silent . . .

Every work is alien, each word absent,
This poem laughs in my face, defies me
To live this passion for a space where time would be
Null. And it is a nulling gift, this power of naming

A bird, when it moves out to sea, like someone breathing,
This instant which endures only to die, out there,
From world's beginning to the last ship's wreck,
And maybe further, toward the last star,
The first word, O how say that . . .

—JONATHAN GRIFFIN


THE CENTER . . .

The center is black,
And speech does not quell

Son pouvoir s'étiole, hors du cercle,
Et s'échoue, au bord d'un astre sans chaleur.

Et c'est la nuit, la chute vague.
Et le ciel tourne dans la main qui s'éloigne
Du cœur.

( L E   T E M P S  . . .

(Le temps s'éloigne encore,
me déliant du souvenir
des grandes marges solitaires
et me laisse en lieu pur
en un jardin forclos
lieu de fougère et de perdition
où je suis, où je vis, contemplé
(en un espace nul)
du fond de l'air inanimé,
irrespirable, délétère . . . )

( R E I N E   D ' A L L E R  . . .

(Reine d'aller, jadis
Et, plus proche que toutes,
Être soi-même le désir,
Elle disait je viens,
Comme on dresse les fleurs,
Par soudaine clarté:

Cette chambre où je suis,
D'un matin idéal . . . )

The leprous crumbling of the face.
Outside the circle, its power wanes
And vanishes at the edge of a cold star.

Night: the slide into chaos.
The sky turns in the hand
That draws away from the heart.

—PAUL AUSTER

(ONCE MORE . . .

(Once more time withdraws,
releasing me from the memory
of wide solitary margins
and leaving me where it is pure
in a foreclosed garden
place of fern and perdition
where I am, living, gazed at
(in a non space)
from the depths of inanimate air,
irrespirable, noxious . . . )

—ANTHONY BARNETT

(QUEEN OF GOING . . .

(Queen of going, long ago
And, closer than all,
Being herself desire,
She was saying I come,
Like placing flowers
In a sudden shaft of light:

This room where I am,
One perfect morning . . . )

—ANTHONY BARNETT

NUE . . .

Nue,
Frileusement venue,
Devenue elle sans raison, ne sachant
Quel simulacre de l'amour appeler en image
(belle d'un doute inachevé
vague après vague,
et comme inadvenue aux lèvres), ici
d'une autre qui n'est plus
que sa feinte substance nommée

Miroir, abusive nacelle,
eau de pur silex.

BEAUTÉ PERDUE . . .

Beauté perdue ne désespère
D'une parole défendue.
D'un ange qui s'est tu
Elle fait une voile
A la mer.

VISAGE . . .

Visage de nul bruit: la mouette, le bouleau,
Les convoitises dans le ciel et, plus haut,
Entre les arbres et la musique,
De grands lacs bleus d'incertitude.

# NAKED . . .

Naked,
Come shivering,
Become this without reason, not knowing
What pretence of love to summon in image
(beautiful with an unrealized doubt
wave after wave,
and as if uncome at the lips) here
from another no more
than the name of its sham substance

Mirror, unseemly skiff,
water of pure silex.

—ANTHONY BARNETT

# LOST BEAUTY . . .

Lost beauty does not despair
Of a forbidden word.
Out of an angel who kept silent
A sail is set
Upon the sea.

—ANTHONY BARNETT

# SURFACE . . .

Surface of no sound: seabird, birch,
Cupidity in the sky and, higher still,
Between trees and music,
Great blue lakes of uncertainty.

—ANTHONY BARNETT

C'ÉTAIT . . .

C'était avant les choses dites.
Connaissant l'astre et le moment.
La lampe nue dans son royaume.

(SA MÉMOIRE . . .

(Sa mémoire chemine entre les jours.

Elle est comme un vieux livre des secrets
Dans le vent nu des choses, âme laissée
Qu'elle sait sans écho.
                    Qu'elle sait,
Ne sachant quelle image a tenu son image
Captive, aux pieds d'un astre.)

LOIN . . .

loin
    comme un fil

comme si quelque chose de soi allait
fleuve parmi le fleuve
rose que nulle rose
n'achève

## IT WAS . . .

It was before spoken things.
Knowing the star and the moment.
The naked lamp in its kingdom.

—PAUL AUSTER

## (THIS MEMORY . . .

(This memory moves among the days.

Like an old book of secrets
In the naked wind of things, abandoned soul
Known without an echo.
                        Known
Unknown what image has held this image
Captive, at the foot of a star.)

—ANTHONY BARNETT

## FAR . . .

far
   like a thread

as if part of me were leaving
river amid the river
rose no rose
perfects

—ANTHONY BARNETT

## DES LÈVRES . . .

des lèvres elle a touché
le mouvement de la lumière
l'épine blanche sur la vitre
qui fût elle
        sans elle

           sans le cri

# TOUCHED . . .

touched with the lips
the passage of the light
the white thorn on the pane
that was this
         without this

            without a sound

—ANTHONY BARNETT

## O LA GRANDE APPOSITION . . .

O la grande apposition du monde

un champ de roses près d'un
champ de blé et deux enfants rouges dans le champ voisin du champ de roses
et un champ de maïs près du champ de blé et deux saules vieux à la jointure;
le chant de deux enfants roses dans le champ de blé près du champ de roses
et deux vieux saules qui veillent les roses les blés les enfants rouges et le maïs

Le bleu boit comme tache
L'encre blanche des nuages
Les enfants sont aussi mon
Chemin de campagne

# Michel Deguy
## 1930-

## O GREAT APPOSITION . . .

O great apposition of the world

a rose field near a wheat field and
two red children in the field bordering on the rose field and a corn field near
the wheat field and two old willows where they join; the song of two rose
children in the wheat field near the rose field and two old willows keeping
watch over the roses the wheat the red children and the corn

The blue blots like a spot
The white ink of clouds
Children are also my
Country path

—CLAYTON ESHLEMAN

TOI

Si près de moi, là où je ne veux pas être, tu te tiens trop souvent.

C'est par la peur que tu n'es pas au monde, et moi par l'insouciance et la hardiesse.

Laisse-moi! Je me rassemble dans la fuite, trouve mon lieu dans l'accident, et je hais le tort réciproque.

La nuit le cœur comme un boiteux le cœur veut errer seul,

Le revenant fondamental.

LES YEUX

Cri de corbeau des yeux qu'enfoncent les poings en deuil:
Le même bruit sous les paupières closes, où le même hiver pâle attend
Tes yeux longeaient mes yeux; ils rampaient jusqu'aux miens
Cherchant la mire invisible où j'eusse aimé paraître
Puis tes yeux se cabraient
La bête agile des prunelles, toute la violence de l'autre espèce s'y résume;
mais les yeux encerclés de mémoire, rapides comme l'oiseau, les yeux sont
retenus captifs aux menottes des os
Cri de corbeau le même cri sous les paupières closes où le pâle hiver de
mémoire sommeille

C'EST ENTRE NOUS . . .

C'est entre nous
L'air entre les mains salut
Et la main entre les saluts

## YOU

Too often you keep so near me, where I do not want to stand.

It's through fear that you are not in the world; and me, through unconcern and effrontery.

Leave me! I pull myself together in flight, find my place in accident; I hate the reciprocal wrong.

At night the heart like a lame man the heart wants to wander alone.

The fundamental ghost.

—ANTHONY RUDOLF

## THE EYES

   Crow cry of eyes that fists in mourning grind into:
   The same sound under closed eyelids, where the same pale winter waits
   Your eyes walked along mine: crawled up to mine
   Seeking the invisible aim where I should have loved to appear
Then your eyes were rearing
   The agile beast of pupils, all the violence of the other species is summed up there; but the eyes encircled with memory, quick as a bird, the eyes are held captive by bone handcuffs
   Crow cry the same cry under closed eyelids where the pale winter of memory dozes

—CLAYTON ESHLEMAN

## IT'S BETWEEN OURSELVES . . .

It's between ourselves
Air between our hands salutation
And hand between salutations

Et le salut pur intervalle
Rien avec rien jouant à
S'envoyer la belle apparition


ALLUVION . . .

Alluvion des cris Minerai d'hirondelles
Dans le delta du vent les plissements du vent
    La trembleraie bleuit
Le pouls de l'étang bat
      Toutes les trois heures un poème
      Devient nouveau puis se ternit
      Sous la lecture Recroît dans le silence


QUAND LE VENT . . .

Quand le vent pille le village
    Tordant les cris
      L'oiseau
S'engouffre dans le soleil

    Tout est ruine
    Et la ruine
Un contour spirituel

And salutation pure interval
Nothing with nothing playing at
Sending back and forth
The beautiful visitation

—ANTHONY RUDOLF


ALLUVIUM . . .

Alluvium of cries Ore of swallows
In the delta of wind the foldings of wind
    The aspen grove turns blue
The pond's pulse beats
      Every three hours a poem
      Becomes new then tarnishes
      Under the reading Grows again in the silence

—CLAYTON ESHLEMAN


WHEN THE WIND . . .

When the wind sacks the village
      Twisting the cries
        The bird
    Engulfs itself in the sun

      All is ruin
      And the ruin
    A spiritual contour

—CLAYTON ESHLEMAN

# LE MUR . . .

Le mur est massif, de pierre pleine, dur, fini; pourtant il suinte Le mur est lisse, neuf et vieux, durable, et pourtant il est lézardé, et par la faille sourd et glisse une goutte, une bête, une mousse Le mur accomplit son rôle, il borde, il bouche, il sépare, il dérobe, il obstrue, et pourtant est-ce à lui de le faire, il protège, il soutène l'insecte à 100%, il se lamente, il adosse la décision, il est compté jusqu'à l'os, il transperce les eaux, il vient de laisser passer la main qui inscrivait, il met mortel en tête

Ici est tombé

Ici a vécu

Ici est mort

Ici a passé

# THE WALL . . .

The wall is massive, of solid stone, hard, finished; yet it oozes The wall is smooth, new and old, durable, and yet it is cracked, and through the fault welling and sliding a drop, a beast, a moss The wall performs its role, it borders, it blocks, it separates, it conceals, it obstructs, and yet it must do it, it protects, it breast walls the insect at 180°, it wails, it puts the decisions back against, it is counted to the bone, it pierces the waters, it has just allowed the inscribing hand to pass through, it makes one mortal in one's mind

| Here | fell |
| --- | --- |
| Here | lived |
| Here | died |
| Here | passed |

—CLAYTON ESHLEMAN

## LE MIEUX SERAIT . . .

le mieux serait de changer de lumière    de vivre dans l'œil de deux grains de sable qui s'écartent    d'être un seul banc vert dans plutôt le désert printemps central    à toujours cinq heures du matin

le mieux    si du moins il peut exister un mieux    pour l'approfondissement du désert toujours le même    (autruche rapetissée jusqu'à être l'œuf du pigeon ou goutte d'eau étirée jusqu'à l'infinité du rail)

le mieux serait alors résolument immobile    fixer la pierre quand elle trempe l'acier de l'eau    (une bouche va s'ouvrir et vibrer jusqu'au désordre)


si l'on pouvait aliéné absolu    durer    prendre pied en un point comme Loth pétrifié dans trois mémoires de sel blanc

# Jacques Roubaud
## 1932-

## THE BEST THING . . .

the best thing would be to change    light to live in the eye of two wandering
grains of sand    to be a solitary green bench in the desert above all in the heart
of spring    at five o'clock in the morning forever

best to be    if at least a best could exist    to plunge deep into a desert always
the same    (ostrich shrunk down to the size of a pigeon's egg    or a drop of
water stretched to the infinite distance of a railroad track)

it would be best to be then resolutely motionless    to hold the whetstone
steady as it tempers the sword with water    (a mouth will open and tremble
until confusion)

if one could be absolutely insane    to hold out    take root in one place like Lot
turned to stone in three white salt memories

—NEIL BALDWIN

## PETIT TAMIS . . .

petit tamis pour pépites petit    petit remous dans la grande eau blanche    petit
  menu foin menus celliers    fontaine devant les chutes    petit cahier où se
lira petit morceau de craie petite fable    petit marbre sous petit if taillé bas
petite histoire pauvrement

malheur    pas malin    bouche cousue    pauvreté confusion pierres    petite
morale d'agneau bâté    petits habitants de polenta de panurgie petits ports
d'anchois et d'ail    petite porte des lionnes à Mycènes

pentes de l'or et pentes du vin    petits sous tassés petitement    légère mousse
d'un autrement    d'un ailleurs    petit argent de la jeunesse petit plomb de la
fatigue

presque pas    peu à peu    à peine    par hasard    parcelle    hôpital    corridor
  mots petits    presque-mots    paille    plainte    peureux    petits désastres
petits    petit monde

## SOLEIL BRUIT . . .

soleil bruit    soleil chaud
mains autour de nos cous
nous vivons contre ton mur
et nous t'aimons assis
seuls et fermant les yeux
les pieds dans tes eaux blanches

on voit or et violet
on devient bourdonnant
de la fumée des voix
et ce ne pourrait être mieux
s'il n'y avait aussi le soir
et l'absence armée et la mort

## SMALL SIEVE . . .

small sieve for nuggets small    small eddy in a great foamy wake small    small
harvest small grain cellars    fountain before waterfalls    small notebook
where a little piece of chalk will be read a little story    small gravestone
beneath a small yew tree trimmed low    small story poorly

bad luck    not evil    hold your tongue    poverty disorder stones    small
moral of the burdened lamb    small dwellers of Polenta of Panurge small
harbors with anchovies and garlic    small doorway of lionesses at Mycenae

hills of gold and hills of wine    small pennies cheaply pinched    light froth of
an otherwise    of an elsewhere    small silver of youth small lead weight of
weariness

almost not    little by little    scarcely    by chance    fragment    hospital    cor-
ridor    small words    almost-words    straw    moan    fearful    small tragedies
   small children    small world

—NEIL BALDWIN

## SUN NOISE . . .

sun noise    sun hot
hands around our necks
we live up against your wall
and we love you sitting
alone or closing our eyes
feet in your white waters

one sees gold and violet
one becomes the humming
of smoke of voices
and it couldn't be better
if it weren't for evening
and armed absence and death

—ROBERT KELLY

## TU ES SAUF . . .

tu es sauf dans la mort tu ne verras pas
moisir les jours, rompre la fête illusoire
l'amour s'abriter, fléchir la mémoire
le silence cerner de son court compas

la petite forêt ouverte à nos pas
sauf et mort je suis enfin prêt à te croire
mon frère enserré dans le si lourd noir
dont tu te raidis, hier, dont tu nous frappas

j'ai renoncé à soumettre ce langage
que tu sais, tu as raison, c'était bouffon
le bon troubadour, capuchonné de nuages
a glissé dans la fosse, se noie au fond

j'achève un vrai bilan d'ombres on va rire
alors, quelle raison de vivre, qui dure?

## LE TEMPS . . .

le temps fuit le temps, le temps est comme larve
le temps est l'inconscient de la terre étale
le temps est regard le temps est transparence
aux morts à la passion aux fausses épreuves
durée d'homme seul durée de femme seule
lumières de la lumière de l'absence
l'alliance n'est que toute petite écume
véloce ensuite les vagues se séparent
le temps est rougeoiement le temps est de l'ombre
le temps est cette écriture qui s'allume
sur les pages sur les langues de hasard
le temps le temps est fourmi le temps est nombre
rapproche les reflets les bouge les mêle
efface l'homme et la femme, les enfances

## YOU ARE SAFE . . .

you are safe inside death you never will see
the days mildew, the illusory feast break up,
love take shelter, memory sag
silence surround with its brief precinct

the little forest open to our footsteps
safe and dead I am finally ready to trust you
my brother locked in such heavy blackness
where you stiffen, yesterday, where you hit us

I have refused to submit this language
that you know, you're right, it's a clown,
this bonny troubadour monk-hooded with cloud
has slid into the ditch, drowns at the bottom

I achieve a true balance of shades, you'll laugh
so what's the sense of living, who ever endures?

—ROBERT KELLY

## TIME . . .

time flees time, time is like a larva
time is the unconscious of the slack earth
time is glance time is being transparent
to the dead to passion to false tests
lived through by man alone lived through by woman alone
lights of the light of absence
being together is only a tiny bit of foam
quick then the waves part company
time is turning red time is of shadow
time is this writing that lights up
on pages on the tongues of chance
time time is ant time is number
brings reflections close stirs them mingles them
erases man and woman, childhoods

—ROBERT KELLY

## JE RÊVE . . .

je rêve que tu souris
que je te parle à ma porte
des livres que tu as lus
du temps comme tu le sens
c'est une nuit à Paris
puis il pleut dans notre vin
je rêve un jardin mouillé
puis nous marchons dans la rue
comme au retour de l'école
au devant de notre chien
adieu adieu l'âge des jeux
l'âge des vents est fini
et tout pouvait être mieux
tout pouvait être différent
je m'éveille dans les cris
un fou avec dérision
appelle Marie Marie
et moi je suis dans ce noir
et je sais que tu es mort
et personne ne t'attend

## ( NOYADE )

Je suis un homme sans enfance
moitié remords moitié fumées
dans ma tête dansent les nombres
et je blanchis comme un été
sur les crêtes du sable sombre

Je suis un homme du silence
gris rangé sous les lois du temps
la mer mortelle offre ses chances
et je me hâte dans le vent
nageant vers l'insignifiance

Je suis un homme solitaire
que la douleur a dévié

# I DREAM . . .

I dream you're smiling
that I'm talking to you at my door
about books you've read
about weather how you feel it
it is a night in Paris
later it rains in our wine
I dream of a moist garden
later we walk down the street
like coming home from school
with our dog behind us
goodbye goodbye age of games
the age of winds is over
and everything could have been better
everything could have been different
I wake up among screams
a man mad with mockery
is calling Marie Marie
and I am in this blackness
and I know that you're dead
and no one is waiting for you.

—ROBERT KELLY

# (DROWNING)

I am a man without childhood
half remorse half smoke
numbers dance in my head
and I turn white like summer
over the crests of dark sand

I am a man of the gray silence
ordered by the laws of time
the mortal sea offers its chances
and I hurry in the wind
swimming toward the meaningless

I am a solitary man
detoured by pain

les vagues montent à la terre
et moi je sombre décrié
sous les mouettes qui délibèrent

sœur la mort ô sœur difficile
tu m'attends couche de la mer
oubliez les ainsi soit il
j'étais un rire du désert

j'étais une bouche inutile

## JARDIN DE ROSES À OAKLAND

*Pour M et E. Granich*

Des années de roses ont abouti
à cet air de fontaine de Provence
étrange en la ville de Jack London
le vingtième siècle semble une ortie

Qui griffe la terre mais on pardonne
à cause de ces allées de silence
où marchent les roses   Amérique je

ne sais s'il te sera compté beaucoup
dans la stupide balance des âges

Mais
que ceux qui dans ce jardin m'accompagnent

que je regarde marcher près des doux
wagons de roses puissent voir un signe
dans les milliards d'yeux à travers le monde
que tout n'ira pas danser dans les cendres

the waves climb up the land
and I sink down discredited
beneath the parleying gulls

sister death o difficult sister
you wait for me bed of the sea
forget them amen amen
I was a smile in the desert

I was a useless mouth.

—ROBERT KELLY

## OAKLAND ROSE GARDEN

*for M. & E. Granich*

Years and years of roses have burst forth here
around a Provençal fountain's breathing
out of place in Jack London's town
the twentieth century like a thorn

Scratching the earth but we forgive it
because of these silent pathways
where roses stroll   America I

do not know if you'll add up to very much
in the idiotic reckoning of the ages

But
     may those who accompany me in this garden

who I watch as they walk by the sweet-smelling
wheelbarrows of roses find a sign
in the billions of eyes throughout the world
that everything will not go up in smoke

—NEIL BALDWIN

## NOIR

savoir de ne plus tenir
chant

A la vérité
agacement inouï
les serviettes lui frôlant encore
    le nez
dans un temps
où les matinaux se laissent
dans ne plus voir
regarder
et caresser les pères

vous aviateurs

et vous fermés
patte marelle trainée derrière les
    hôpitaux
brodeuse de drapeaux
homme trop pâle pour aimer les femmes
dans les lits qu'have les confessions barbières
rieuses avec le bleu du ciel des draps vers
le foutre nuage
                    voilà
jamais un œil

# Marcelin Pleynet

## 1933-

BLACK

to know how not to hang on any more song

In truth
incredible irritation
the towels still graze his nose
in a time
when the early risers leave themselves
in no more see
look at
and caress the fathers

you aviators

and you closed
paw hopscotch behind the hospitals
embroiderer of flags
man too pale to like women in
the beds undercut by the barber confessions
merry with the blue of the sky of the
     sheets toward
the come cloud
            that's it
never an eye

—JOHN ASHBERY

## DE CHARBON

*A James Bishop*

seulement nous ne pensons pas que vous puissiez un
jour ou l'autre retenir la mer d'ordure qui s'accroche au
balcon en soirée pour le bonheur du monde pour un
musée de chair

> Certes à l'heure les éléphants emplissent la page
> A l'heure la nuit couvre le troupeau
> Comme une terre gorgée de lait

avec vous des hommes qui refusent de parler jamais
de dire oui de dire publiquement orageux l'avenir
pendu aux balcons pour mémoire « cadavre esquis »
de la parole series of blankets beasts and tables

## LA NOUVELLE RÉPUBLIQUE

Card of licence A B C aussi le vice-roi des Indes était une tante dans la majorité
des cas les collines soulevèrent les grisailles du sexe simplement faisant l'amour
comme des tourteaux revenus d'Ulysse et vers l'est bleu quelqu'éther énivrant
la morte non pas qu'il crache sur l'amour mais alors ce soulèvement ce profil
de vague alors toute porte close comme un assassinat

une femme sans doute autre chose les lois morales réminiscence d'un tabac
plus divin ainsi que je vous dis entre nous sa blessure de géante et les otages
gardés à vue sous la pluie qui passait entre les mailles

sans doute l'anarchie des mâles la solitude d'un bibliothécaire condamné aux
forceps et mangeur d'alcool sain derrière les vitres blanches un été sans vous
perdant dans les cabarets du territoire les filles malades qui le battent fumant
d'un corps les plus féroces curiosités avant de vivre au bal.

NOUS MANGEONS LE MÊME POISON pendu au profit des veuves qui
rêvent sur la page

## OF COAL

only we don't think that you will be able some day or
other to hold back the sea of garbage that attaches itself
to the balcony in the evening for the happiness of the
world for a flesh museum

Certainly the elephants fill up the page on time
On time night covers the flock
Like a land gorged with milk

with you men who refuse ever to speak to say yes
to say publicly the future threatening hung from the
balconies as a reminder "exquisite corpse" of the word
*series of blankets beasts and tables*

—JOHN ASHBERY

## THE NEW REPUBLIC

*Card of licence* A B C the viceroy of India was a queen in the majority of cases
the hills stirred up the grisailles of the genitals simply making love like crabs
come back from Ulysses and toward the east blue some ether intoxicating the
dead woman not that he spits on love but then that upheaval that profile of
a wave then every door shut like an assassination

a woman no doubt something else the moral laws reminiscence of a diviner
tobacco as I'm telling you just between us his giantess' wound and the hos-
tages watched closely in the rain which came through the coats of mail

no doubt the anarchy of males the solitude of a librarian condemned to the
forceps and eater of alcohol healthy behind the white panes a summer without
you losing in the cabarets of the territory the sick girls who beat him smoking
with a body the most ferocious curiosities before living at the dance

WE EAT THE SAME POISON hung for the benefit of widows dreaming
on the page

—JOHN ASHBERY

## CES MATINÉES . . .

ces matinées
voici la vraie couleur
comme un rideau derrière les vitres
elle garde et s'élève ces temples qui ne parlent pas

autant se soucier de cette urne grise
qu'ils tiennent à la main
ce qui tourne est exactement du style des couleurs

« on dirait un paradoxe et aussi bien c'en est un en ce qui
concerne le sentiment, mais non en ce qui concerne l'esprit. »

autant dire que ceux qu'ils trouvent
souffrent de ce défaut de la vue
qui les rend aveugles

ces trois dimensions dans un édifice quelconque
s'ajourent et ne livrent rien
que la répétition
la vraie couleur qu'ils voient

## C'EST TOUJOURS . . .

C'est toujours le même mot
mais pas ce qu'ils disent
ce qui nous inquiète
ainsi c'est toujours le même mot
et de temps en temps se lève une distance égale
non pas ailleurs non plus dans le regard
pourtant et comme la pensée les nomme
avec ces jambages / déployés dans l'apparence
où fuit et commence la pensée
alors si nous nous retournons tu passes près d'elle
et comme quatre murs dessinent la vallée
le matin et le soir s'encombrent

# THESE MORNINGS . . .

these mornings
here is a true color
like a curtain behind windowpanes
she keeps and soars these temples that do not speak

as well worry about the gray urn
held in their hands
what revolves is of a style that is exactly the colors'

"one could call it a paradox and indeed it is one where feeling
is concerned but not where sense is concerned"

as well say that those they find
suffer from that defect of vision
which makes them blind

these three dimensions in a commonplace structure
let light through and furnish nothing
but repetition
the true color that they see

—HARRY MATHEWS

# IT'S ALWAYS . . .

It's always the same word
but not what they say
that troubles us
thus it is always the same word
and from time to time an equal distance occurs
not elsewhere nor in the glance
yet and as the mind names them
with these strokes / placed in the appearance
where thought flees and begins
then if we turn around you pass close to her
and as four walls define a valley
morning and evening get in each other's way

les murs dressés l'un près de l'autre
les passages dressés
tout ce qu'il faut connaître pour être là
souhaitant qu'un mur les sépare

ils n'imaginent pas comme c'est écrit


OÙ LA LUMIÈRE . . .

où la lumière se pose et dans la chair elle avive les herbes
qu'elle mord et ouverte appelle l'air humide qui la tient nue
glacée peut-être sur la rive
par la trop violente lumière seule ou blessée
quand passe et s'arrache violemment
s'écrase sur l'herbe

si je la regarde où la lumière se posent autant de taches bleues

walls raised one next to the other
raised paths
everything that needs to be known to be there
wanting a wall to keep them apart

they cannot imagine how it is written

—SERGE GAVRONSKY

# WHERE THE LIGHT . . .

where the light comes to rest and in the flesh they brighten the grasses
that she bites and readily calls the damp air that keeps it naked
chilled perhaps on the bank
by the overviolent light alone or wounded
when there passes and tears itself violently away
crashes on the grass.

if I look at her where the light comes to rest so many blue flecks

—HARRY MATHEWS

# THÉÂTRE DES AGISSEMENTS D'ÉROS

1

*Théâtral acte d'Amour: I^{re} chance*

hors du bouillonnnement de l'instrument, sem-
blable à cette phrase mal tournée de notre suicide
Ensemble, à l'Épée-de-rose—enseigne verte, on
Voit un peu de verdure de Sologne au travers—,
. . . n'osant donner de l'héroïne aux vers afin que
Nul ne meure d'une telle agronomique erreur:

Une jupe fleurie qui crée un Amour à chaque pas,
Dérobe à nos yeux de ravissants appas; et cette
Cuisse comme à Vénus potelée . . . A mille beautés,
A mille appas vivants, atours, vous ne substituez que
Des empêchements! . . . Et ce soulier mignon, qui
Couvre un pied d'Hébé, de Vénus, tout provocant qu'il
Est, vaut-il ses charmes nus? . . .
Tu en as menti, ô fleur de mes lèvres, les
Haricots et les bulles des folles, ton cul bien
Droit fait vers moi quelques périphrases (inuti-
les aujourd'hui) en forme de tire-bouchons.

# Denis Roche

1937-

## EROS POSSESSED

1

*Demonstrative act of Love: 1st chance*

out of the seething of the tool, which re-
sembles this ill-fated sentence of our suicide
Together, at The Rose Sword—green sign, you
See a little Sologne greenery in it—,
. . . not daring to give heroin to the worms lest
Any die of such an error of husbandry:

*A flower'd gown that raises a Love at each step*
*Ravishes delectable charms from our eyes; and this*
*Thigh as round as Venus' . . . A thousand beauties,*
*A thousand living charms, and ornaments, you replace but with*
*Hindrances! . . . And this darling slipper, that*
*Encloses a foot like Hebe's or Venus', alluring as it*
*Is, can it match her naked grace? . . .*
You lied about it, naked flower of my mouth, the
Beans and the crazy women's bubbles, your ass perfectly
Upright performs toward me a number of circumlocutions
(useless today) having the shape of corkscrews.

2
*en face de la parenthèse:*

L'Amour est une affection
Qui, par les yeux, dans le cœur entre,
Et, par forme de fluxion,
S'escoule par le bas du ventre.

en même temps—c'est une surimpression dans le
temps—, Agrippa d'Aubigné écrit les *Aventures du
baron de Foeneste.* C'est-à-dire:
   "Il y a force choses que le poëte n'a pas interprétées,
ce que l'œil descouvre c'est une grande multitude de
soldats des Alpes bien empeschez au soleil à recoudre
toutes les balafres de leurs pourpoints faits à la mode,
à déglacer leurs doubles moustaches—là vous voyez
des laquais botez, une damoiselle qui a la ceinture entre
le nombril et les tétins."

Fiction double: l'écrivain et son époque. La preuve est
que tout le monde l'a déjà écrit. Retours à la fiction
simple.

3
*Théâtral acte d'Amour: 2ᵉ chance*

                      que
Des bords d'une nappe de coton j'essuyai
L'arme encore coupante de ta puanteur:

   (ici la citation de Mathurin Régnier)

Le blé plus facile des peintres était tout-
à-fait saccagé quand nous nous sommes relevés.
Quelle poésie enfin enfoncée dans un trou de
Glaise n'aime pas les jupes dont on fait les
Bouchons?—« Voudriez-vous me faire un
Plaisir, Mademoiselle?—Oui, oui, oui.—
De donner ces deux-là . . . —Je sais, je sais . . .»
J'ai beau y mettre des ronds-de-jambe, des
Sphères, des Pulcinelles, au besoin la balan-
çoire même en signe de puritaine sentine,
La poésie, d'une crémière, ou du bond qu'un
Augustin ferait sur icelle, n'en revêtira jamais

2

facing the parenthesis:

*For Love is an affection*
*That finds the heart through th' eyes,*
*Then, by a way of fluxion,*
*Runs out between the thighs.*

at the same time— —,
Agrippa d'Aubigné wrote *Les Aventures du baron Foeneste.*
That is:

*Scarce can the Poet interprete euerie thinge, what the eie*
*discouers is a greate multitude of alpine Souldiers sorely*
*busyed under the sunne with sewing up the slashes in their*
*doublets made after the fashion, with thawing their double*
*mustachios—here you see uarlets shooing a Damsel who hath*
*her girdle twixt nauel and teates.*

Double fiction: the writer and his time. The proof is that it
has already been written by everyone. Back to the single fiction.

3

*Demonstrative act of Love: 2nd chance*

————————————————————————that
With the edges of a cotton cloth I wiped
The still-sharp weapon of your stink:

(here the quotation from Mathurin Régnier)

The more accessible wheat of the painters was thor-
oughly pillaged when we stood up again.
What poetry, finally shoved into a hole of
Clay, dislikes the skirts from which cork-
screws are made?—*"Would you grant me one*
*Delight, milady?" "Oh yes, oh yes."*
*"To yield that pair . . ." "I know, I know . . ."*
It doesn't matter if I add court manners,
Spheres, Pulcinellas, or if needed the
Swing itself as a token of puritan bilge,
Poetry, concerning a dairymaid, or the leap that
A friar would make upon her, would never for all that

Pour autant l'habit que je te passe quand il ne
Tient qu'à moi de remettre l'assaut *(sic).*

4

*Théâtral acte d'Amour: immédiatement après la 2ᵉ chance*

Quand on vient d'écrire des phrases comme celles
De la page précédente je suis avec des brindilles
Ma compagne la plus avancée pensant amasser mon
Doute comme le prétexte d'un moulin dans une
Dans une campagne ancienne (si tu peux te faire à l'idée
Du papier et de l'encre de l'empire chinois
Dans un siècle encore plus ancien que ne l'aurait
Été le moulin) J'emplis l'appareil de ce phénomè
ne d'un grand nombre de ressorts communs à mon
Imagination. Comme le pied posé précautionneuse-
ment sur le rebord de la baignoire la main gauche
Rabattant le gant de toilette vers les plis qui sont
Au niveau de son estomac. Etc. Bien sûr, sinon
Quelle importance, de la verdure ou de la fontaine?
Rien n'emporterait plus ce que j'avais à te dire
En t'entourant les jambes. Conseil enfin: continuer
Par le titre suivant

5

*Interlude dans les chances: des voyelles et de l'érosion*

« J'avoue le 20 que je me trouve dans un état
mort.» *Des mets divins du poème charmant,* comme
Le bagage dont s'apprête à disposer l'aubergiste,
Prennent en plein quelque reflet. Le tonnerre
Est à peine venu. Je reconsidère l'avancée
Brutale cette fois de la terre, celle en fri-
Che celle dont les gens sont morts où restent
Des abricotiers où la mort mais pas la leur tombe
Creusée dans les pois lieu des arrestations fos-
Et ainsi de suite la parole n'étant rien.
La fatigue pourrait-elle n'être qu'une sorte de
Discipline? Qui me rendrait aveugle quand j'
Écris? Les jeunes voisines de ta beauté
Pourraient en rire de notre colloque ne voyant
Pas ce que nos mains font des mets divins du
Poème charmant —————————

Be adorned with the raiment I lent you when it's
Entirely up to me to resume the attack *(sic).*


4

*Demonstrative act of Love: immed. after the 2nd chance*


When one has just written sentences like those
On the preceding page *I am with the twigs*
*My most up-to-date mistress thinking she will hoard my*
*Doubt as the pretext for a mill in an*
*In an ancient countryside* (if you can get used to the idea
Of paper and ink in the Chinese empire
At a time more ancient than the
Mill would have been) *I fill the instrument of this wonder*
*With a large number of incentives familiar to my*
*Imagination. Familiar, while the foot is cautious-*
*ly placed on the rim of the bathtub, the left hand*
*Lowering the washcloth toward the folds that are*
*At the level of her stomach.* Etc. Of course; otherwise
Who cares, about greenery or the fountain?
No longer would it matter at all what I had to tell you
When I embraced your legs. Advice in brief: continue
With the next title


5

*Interlude between chances: of vowels and erosion*


"On the 20th I confess to finding my condition that of one
Dead." *Ambrosia of the enchanting poem,* like
Luggage that the innkeeper prepares to remove,
Receives a certain direct glint. Thunder
Hardly came. I reconsider the earth's
Progression (this time abrupt), that which was left
Fallow that by which people died where there remain
Apricot-trees where death but not theirs falls
Impressed in the peas place of arrests grav-
And so forth, speech being nothing.
Could fatigue be only a kind of
Discipline? That might blind me when I
Write. The girls who are your beauty's neighbors
Might laugh over our exchange not seeing
That our hands create ambrosia of the en-
chanting poem.————————————————

6

« *le Passement de Jouy* » ou « *du triomphe* »

Je ne peux trouver plus sûr que l'association
De cette page de garde tendue de toile de Jouy
Avec l'idée agressive de passement dont Littré
Dit que c'est *une cuve pleine d'une liqueur acide*
*dans laquelle le tanneur passe les peaux pour les*
*Faire gonfler.* D'Estrevallières qui, n'en forni-
cant plus, s'était effacée dans son domaine d'Eu,
S'habille en me tournant le dos de sorte que
J'admire à la fois ses flancs et la perspective des
Tilleuls. L'odeur des fleurs jaunes, la sienne
Et les piécettes du tissu ancien manifestement
M'imposent de garder une attitude stricte que le
Dictionnaire, tombant, n'interrompt pas. Qu'en
Fis-je du tout autrement qu'un pas aérien qui
M'amène dans une région désencombrée de la pièce
Où le tissu se trouve arraché la glotte passant
Dans d'autres fleurs, allant et venant, épaissie


7

*Après une exposition prolongée au soleil,*
*Rideau*

Mais ma parole douce, confondante, où pire
Existence *la seconde chope lui affirme que*
*C'est vrai,* sur le penchant de ma ruine, mon
Absolution. Pêcheur modeste, orduriers mots,
Ordurière appellation, seule une musique enchan
Teresse se soutient près de moi. Son trépas
Résolu, la mélodie imaginant ma lente montée
Vers les prés de son existence, la rencontre
Fortuite du mélange de cette vision colorée
(couleurs des cheveux, des pots sur scène)
Et de ma maladie, tout cela rejoint mon pas
Sans audace, l'hyperbole, mon enjambement de
Balcon en balcon vert, en droite ligne je me
Prolonge comme le paysage vers une nouvelle
Fournée mortuaire, vers sa tombe de toute façon.
(Détumescence-sourire)

6

—*"Jouy Lace"* or *"Of the Triumph"*

I can find nothing more certain than the connection
Between this flyleaf mounted on Jouy linen
And the provocative idea of plumping of which Littré
Says that there is a *vat filled with acid solution*
*in which the tanner plumps his skins to*
*Distend them.* D'Estrevallières who, when she abandoned
fornication, withdrew to her property at Had,
dresses with her back toward me so that
I at once admire her flanks and the perspective of
Lime-trees. The smell of yellow blossoms, her own smell,
And the chips of antique cloth plainly
Require that I maintain a strict stance which the
Dictionary, falling, does not break. What
Did I make of it all but an aerial leap that
Brings me to a cleared area of the room
Where the cloth has been torn away my throat proceeding
Among other blossoms, coming and going thickly

7

*After prolonged exposure to the sun, curtain.*

But my tender, confounding speech, where worse
Existence "the second tankard tells him that
It's true," on my ruin's inclination, my
Absolution. Modest angler, words foul,
Designation foul, only a bewitching mus-
ic survives near me. Its decease
Settled, the tune that imagines my slow ascension
Toward the meadows of its being, the chance
Encounter of the medley of this florid vision
(colors of horses, of the jugs on stage)
And my disease, all this overtakes my step
Without presumption, the hyperbola, my straddling
Balcony to green balcony, in a straight line I
Extend myself like the landscape toward a new
Shipment for burial, in any case toward her grave.
(Detumescence-smile)

—HARRY MATHEWS

# ÉNIGME

I

la disponibilité

ne signifie

le même
absence

*Travail pratique: car il faut savoir*

exergue:

des a de c
de la lettre un adjectif ou un nom

Quelle est la compacité du déplacement

(le mouvement)

# Anne-Marie Albiach

1937-

ENIGMA

I

availability

doesn't mean

likewise
absence

*Practical endeavor: for we must know*

epigraph:

   some a from c
      from the letter an adjective or a noun

How compact is the displacement

(the movement)

(sa rébellion
 opaque)


A proche
le souffle-ci des angles
(d'envol)

énigme


     impondérables du désir


l'irradiation
la paroïdale transparence


leur présent deux dimensions
l'éternité quatre


aux choses lourdes perspective de la durée
la crainte devant la vélocité
et sa nudité
             étrangère
le vide du propos

NOUVELLE


     l'autre
le premier
de la trame sa pureté
            une


toutes les évidences lui sont mystère

(its opaque
  rebellion)


near A
breath here of the angles
(of ascent)

enigma


    imponderables of desire


irradiation
the paroidal transparency


their present two-dimensional
eternity four


for heavy things the perspective of duration
fear in the face of speed
and its strange
                nakedness
the subject's vacancy

TALE


    the other
the first
from the plot its purity
        one


all the clues are mystery to him

I I

    Car s'il est un thème qu'il soit dit
cette intrusion de chiffres
non pas naturelle davantage
que sa disparition


la simplicité
nous est-elle donnée le possible de jouir
                pour laquelle
l'arbre sec fait différence


la chute en arête n'existe que dans


le cadre l'absout
le foyer en deçà consume aux lisières de la logique et
les structures n'en demeurent
                c'est l'apaisement de la direction
intermittente à sa recherche et où
            discontinue
valide teneur de notre éloignement sans cesse remis


ce géomètre
où se défait l'assujettissement
de cet accord
labeur d'exigence


elles se contemplent en suspension

la terreur

parmi les mouvements disjoints
ces nécessités
termes de hasard
présences femelles qui troublent les
données
elles arrachent

II

   For if it's a theme state it
this interference of numbers
no more natural
than its disappearance


have we been
given the simplicity power to enjoy
                      which makes
the dry tree matter


the ridged fall exists only in


the outline absolves it
the nearer focus burns at the edges of logic
its structures unremain
                  calming the irregular
direction of his quest and
                discontinued
the valid tenor of our estrangement ceaselessly deferred


geometrician
breaking the bind
of this concord
heavy labor


they regard each other in suspense

terror

among disjointed movements
these necessities
chance terms
female presences that disturb the
data
they upwrench

et la protestation
où tu adictes


dans le mouvement
que tu oses dénommer où l'étonnement
venus pour la fiction
nous ne voyons que nos manies défectrices


I V


EXERGUE

*l'imprécisable*
*l'inépuisable roman*


d'une situation

l a   p l u i e   a   e u   c e t t e   c o u l e u r


le corps qui prend
de savoir
les poses


élucidation


à cet enveloppement


les formes
elles reviennent de leur
plus retenue lenteur
s'appesantissent


l'attention est grossière

and the protest
where you habituate


in the movement
that you dare specify where amazement
here for a fiction
we find only our craze for desertion


IV

EPIGRAPH

the unspecifiable
the inexhaustible novel


of a situation

t h e   r a i n   h a d   t h a t   c o l o r


body caught
by knowing
the exposures


elucidation


to this envelopment


the forms
recover from their
most circumspect slowness
become heavy


attention is crude

(a su veiller en quelque lieu la studieuse
  odiosité
  du faire)


la prétention

          nos censures
pour la nudité blanche de la lettre


Cette maturation

              et pleinement cadence

un trait d'union


« *abaisser la paume sur la luxure des dalles* »


Antécédent:
l'horizontal

dans l'énoncé
à l'horizontal
les énigmes s'énonceraient
n'était-ce la confusion
et cette absence

                  j'ai commis envers toi
                  de par mon insuffisance
                  ce lapsus


I X

et l'emphase
sa destruction
inéluctable
          des métaphores

(managed to stay awake somewhere the studious
  odium
   of doing)


pretence


      our censure
for the white nakedness of the letter


This maturation


          and full cadence


a hyphen


*"to bring the hand down on the lust of sidewalks"*



Antecedent:
the horizontal

in the statement
horizontally
enigmas would be stated
were it not confusing
and this absence


         I have perpetrated on you
         by my incompetence
         this lapsus


I X


and the emphasis
its ineluctable
destruction
     of metaphors

le dénuement de
la nécessité
elle n'obtient pas
          refuse

son hasard
en défection
extrême

DE SA VENUE

      et la simplicité
l'extension sans rapport
par comparaisons
dont nous n'avons critère

lassitude

      de nos

mesures
indiscernables

Vers leur article

se donne

de métaphore

    le plus

incessant relief

à fin d'autres

teneurs
les graphismes

Ainsi l'élan
de convoiter
nous les simulons

the penury of
necessity
she doesn't get
                  refuses

its chance
in defection
extreme

OF HER ARRIVAL

          and the simplicity
extension without relation
by comparisons
for which we have no criterion

weariness

            of our

indistinguishable
measures

Towards their article

metaphor

given

      the most

unceasing contrast

for benefit of other

modes
notations

So the impulse
to covet
we counterfeit them

refuse les syntaxes
                    la justesse


du geste

nous forme infirme

Ainsi pour

          l'insoupçonnable


sa matière


Énigme

      Cette personne
seconde
par laquelle il n'en
est point
si ce n'est
ce
perpétuel

rejects syntaxes
             precision


of the gesture

forms us infirm

So much for

             the above suspicion


its substance


Enigma

        This second
person
through which it
doesn't belong
if not
this
perpetual

—KEITH WALDROP

## LES ESPIONS THRACES
## DORMAIENT PRÈS DES VAISSEAUX

Au pied des Grottes d'Hercule, sur le littoral atlantique, l'archéologue Montalban mettait au jour les vestiges d'un comptoir romain—établissement commercial du premier siècle que les Vandales en leur temps avaient saccagé: les peintures murales avaient été systématiquement martelées et leurs débris, abandonnés à même le sol, peu à peu recouverts par les sables. Quant aux murs qui les avaient supportées, ils avaient pourvu aux besoins en pierre de générations d'autochtones; tout récemment encore Monsieur Doolittle avait trouvé là de quoi édifier le mur d'enceinte de sa villa.

Des semaines durant, chaque journée apporta son lot de fragments colorés d'anciennes fresques, lesquels une fois lavés et disposés sur de longues tables s'avéraient inaptes aux plus patientes tentatives de reconstitution, même partielle, du moindre pan mural.

En revanche, cette irréductibilité du fragment à réintégrer l'ensemble originel amorça, par le biais des lacunes, la disparition du support et la perte définitive du modèle, l'hypothèse d'une nouvelle redistribution du monde, née du hasard de ces éclats auxquels quinze siècles d'ensablement avaient conservé aux couleurs une étonnante fraîcheur, dans le pressentiment d'une rythmique où l'*entre* commençait à engloutir à travers la ville morte la vivante et jusqu'à la mer proche, la saison déjà très avancée avec le risque des grandes marées d'équinoxe . . .

Libérés de l'origine et laissés à leur trop grande évidence propre, il fallut

# Emmanuel Hocquard

## 1940-

### THE THRACIAN SPIES
### LAY SLEEPING BESIDE THE SHIPS

At the base of the Grottoes of Hercules on the Atlantic shore the archeologist Montalban brought to light the vestiges of a Roman counting-house, a first-century commercial establishment that the Vandals had sacked: the murals had been systematically hammered to bits and their remains, left there on the ground, had gradually been obscured by the sands. As for the walls that had supported them, these supplied stone to generations of locals; most recently Monsieur Doolittle had found the materials there for building the wall around his villa.

As the weeks went by, each day offered its share of colored fragments from ancient frescoes. Once cleaned and arranged on long tables these proved resistant to the most patient efforts at even partial reassembly of the smallest section of wall.

In turn this intractibility of the fragments caused the armature's collapse along the rift-line and total loss of the model, and consequently that hypothesis of a novel reorganization of the world generated by the randomness of these shards whose colors fifteen centuries of sand had kept astonishingly fresh, an hypothesis born from the augury of cadenced tremors whereby, from within the dead city, the *interface* was beginning to engulf its living counterpart right to the sea's edge, the season being already well advanced with attendant risk of equinoctial high tides . . .

Freed from their source and left to their own intractable presence, it became

bien, par raison, les rendre aux sables, les fragments, nam quodcumque suis, mutatum finibus exit / Continuo hoc mors est illius quod fuit ante (Lucr.).
C'était en été cinquante trois.


ANNO AETATIS XXXV

*A Claude Royet-Journoud*

— . . . et, quand nous l'appellerons faiseur d'images,
il nous demandera ce que nous appelons image.

— Platon. *Le sophiste,* 239-d.

*Aussi longtemps que la parole maintint l'éloignement, que la métaphore pût doubler le monde de sens, la vie resta en mon pouvoir. Je jouais de ma voix contre l'air, de ma parole sur la pierre, lorsque l'accident eut lieu. Sous le choc, l'enveloppe protectrice se déchira sans bruit et, dans la perte du sens qui s'ensuivit, la distance s'abolit brusquement. La chose écrite (scripta) se mit à faire monde. Et je sus que je périssais emmuré à mon tour dans les choses.*

Il y a la ville. Ce qui figure. L'eau est au premier plan. La pierre est au premier plan. Ce qui est, toujours, devant. Neige ou vent. (Épreuve de la surface.) L'ombre est au-dessus.

Le jour prend la pierre. La date inscrite obscurcit la pierre jusqu'à ce que le nombre, s'inversant, fasse pierre. Renversement du corps dans la pierre. Le corps s'empierre.

Là où était le jardin, l'événement est passé sous silence. La couleur fait toujours défaut. (La couleur fait du blanc ce qui repousse la couleur.) Chute de la couleur dans les feuilles. Déclinaison où la pierre s'excède.

De son amour, il attendait plus que tout. (Que la surface d'une feuille coïncidât avec sa couleur.) Ce qui serait toujours devant. La neige ou les feuilles par terre. Tout fait sol—ou pierre.

Même le travail de l'eau: l'empreinte exacte de ma tête dans la pierre.

necessary to return them to the sands, these fragments, nam quodcumque suis, mutatum finibus exit / Continuo hoc mors est illius quod fuit ante (Lucr.)
  That was in the summer of fifty-three.

—MICHAEL PALMER

## ANNO AETATIS XXXV

*For Claude Royet-Journoud*

. . . and, when we call him a maker of images,
he will ask us what we call an image.

  — Plato, *The Sophist,* 239-d

*As long as the word kept its distance and metaphor could double for the sensible world, life remained in my power. I was playing my voice out against the air, my words across stone, when the accident happened. Upon impact the protective layer noiselessly tore and, in the loss of consciousness which followed, distance abruptly ceased to be. The thing written (the* scripta*) set out to make a world. And I knew that I was dying, walled up (in my turn) among things.*

There is the city. That which embodies. Water at the first level. Stone at the first level. That which always lies before. Snow or wind. (Testing of surface.) Shadow above.

Day seizes the stone. The inscribed date hides the stone until the number, reversing itself, becomes stone. Inversion of the body to stone. The body petrifies.

There where the garden was, the event happened in silence. Color is always absent. (From whiteness color fashions what suppresses color.) Color's fall among leaves. Declination where stone transcends itself.

From his love he expected more than everything. (That the surface of a leaf might coincide with its color.) That which would always lie before. Snow or leaves on the ground. Everything becomes earth—or stone.

Even the working of the water: the precise imprint of my head in stone.

—MICHAEL PALMER

# SUR UNE APHRODITE ANADYOMÈNE

ainsi arrivèrent les pluies (réveil et chants d'oiseaux)
        préfaçant l'hiver

              —profonds jardins
              sombres orangers

. . . . . . . . .

des événements de cette période . . .
des houles, des houles

           . . . pliante, ondoyante tendresse

              —profonds jardins
              sombres palmeraies, etc.

il reste (le hasard opérant un tri)

              des morceaux
              et des précisions d'image

           . . . petites dents mouillées
les formes modifiées entre la pierre et l'eau

              à présent Tso Sseu peut bien
              disposer partout dans sa maison
              du papier et des pinceaux

ici et là
pluie et chants d'oiseaux

              —profonds jardins
              sombre rivière

. . . . . . . . .

           . . . petites dents luisantes
la pierre polie par l'eau de l'estuaire

              l'herbe et la pluie
              lente migration

# OF A SEA-BORN APHRODITE

thus the rains came (waking and bird-song)
                  prefacing winter

                —deep gardens
                dark orange trees


. . .  . . .  . . .
of events then . . .
swellings, swellings
                  . . . soft, rippling tenderness

                —deep gardens
                dark groves of palm, etc.

there remain (with chance arranging things)

                a few fragments
                and focussed images

                . . . moist little teeth
between water and stone the altered forms

                now Tso Sseu can undoubtedly
                lay pen and paper out
                anywhere in his house

here and there
rain and bird-song

                —deep gardens
                dark stream

. . .  . . .  . . .

                . . . little glistening teeth
stone polished by estuary's flow

                grass and rain
                slow drift

ici commence et finit le cocon
avec la mort du ver à soie
ce qui est dit et ce qui ne l'est pas
dans tout ce qui fut dit et qui ne le fut pas

## TROIS LEÇONS DE MORALE

I

Regardons autour de nous.
Tous nos camarades ont un nom;
tous les objets,
tous les animaux de nos gravures
ont un nom pour les désigner.

Toutes les personnes,
tous les animaux,
toutes les choses
ont un nom.

II

Si on vous dit:
dessinez une orange . . .
Vous demandez:
une orange verte, mûre, grosse, petite, ronde?

Pour la dessiner exactement
il faut vous dire comment elle est.
Les mots: verte, mûre, etc.
qu'on ajoute au nom orange
et qui disent ses qualités
bonnes ou mauvaises
sont des adjectifs qualificatifs.

Les mots qui disent comment sont les personnes
les animaux et les choses
sont des adjectifs qualificatifs.

here the cocoon begins and ends
with the silkworm's death
what is said and what is not
in all that was said and was not

—MICHAEL PALMER


## THREE MORAL TALES

I

Let's look around ourselves.
All our companions have a name;
all objects,
all the animals in our engravings
are indicated by a name.

All the people,
all the animals,
all things
have a name.

II

If someone tells you:
draw an orange . . .
You ask what kind:
green, ripe, large, small, round?

To draw it exactly
you must be told what it's like.
The words: green, ripe, etc.
that are added to the name orange
and which tell of its qualities
good or bad
are modifiers.

The words which tell what persons
animals and things are like
are modifiers.

III
Si je dis:
Une hirondelle vole,
on me comprend.

Si je dis:
Une hirondelle rase,
on me demande:
Elle rase quoi?
La rue,
le toit,
le pré?

Il me manque un renseignement.
Par exemple:
Une hirondelle rase le toit.
Il a suffi d'ajouter le complément.

Ainsi, parfois,
le verbe a besoin d'un complément.

III

If I say:
A swallow flies,
I am understood.

If I say:
A swallow skims,
I am asked:
Skims what?
The street,
the rooftop,
the meadow?

I need more information.
For example:
A swallow skims the rooftop.
It was enough to add the complement.

Thus sometimes
the verb needs a complement.

—MICHAEL PALMER

## LE CRI-CERVEAU

crêtes
au-delà du cri
de
nerfs
de neige
et de ciels
suppliciés
par des talons   de ciels
où signe
a pouvoir de négation
d'effacement
mortel

silences   mottes de blancheur

l'autre limite   l'autre partage
et la cage
où neigeaient   forêts
enfouies
sous l'ongle

# Jean Daive

## 1941-

BRAIN-CRY

crests
beyond the cry
of
nerves
of snow
and cries
tortured
by the heels   of skies
where sign
has power of negation
of mortal effacement

silences   clumps of whiteness

the other limit   the other portion
and the cage
where it snowed   forests
buried
under my fingernail

une chaîne de ciels physiques
traversa mon corps
qui courait dans la glace
et grandissait dans un immense
jardin transparent
le dos
s'ouvrit et
l'arbre combla
ma poitrine
du crâne
s'écoula le jardin
en blancheur verticale
l'horizon
se dédoubla

un ciel un sol
noirs de lunes soyeuses
reptiliennes

mobilier numérique

———

allée de jour
sous
les décharges
de l'air et du ciel
béant

l'aube
à feuillage blanchâtre
se retire
sous
la mémoire
et
illumine
le haut
de l'arbe   son regret

puis
un trou d'ombre
parmi les branches

———

a chain of physical skies
crossed my body
that ran in the ice
and grew in an immense
transparent garden
my back
opened and
the tree overwhelmed
my chest
the garden
flowed from my skull
in vertical whiteness
the horizon
split

a sky a ground
black with silky
reptilian moons

numerical chattel

———————

daylight's path
under
the discharges
of the cavernous air
and sky

dawn
dappled white
with foliage
recedes
under memory
and
lights
the top
of the tree   its lament

then
a hole of shadow
among the branches

———————

tout   ciels
qu'il
nommait

      cris ou surdité

      lorsque le nom
répandit l'œuvre
sur le jardin
abandonné

      signes blancs   secondes
s'abattant
sur l'heure
verticale

&#61;&#61;&#61;&#61;&#61;&#61;

ciel expiatoire
foudre   au-delà
qui tombe
en quelque point solaire de l'esprit

(pas de l'ombre et de la morte
scansion du ciel
et du vide
cessation de tout)

        folie

mémoire   (de l'autre
côté
de la   ) trajet
de l'ombre au corps   trajet
du silence
au
signe persécuteur

&#61;&#61;&#61;&#61;&#61;&#61;

partie   ou   champ   aveugle

l'absolu   hors
moi   du cri

all   skies
that he
named

      cries or deafness

      when the name
spread the work
over the abandoned
garden

      white signs   seconds
pouncing
on the vertical
hour

═══════

sky of atonement
thunder   beyond
what falls
into a sun-hole of the mind

(not from the shadow and the dead
scansion of sky
and emptiness
the end of everything)

        madness

memory   (from the other
side
of the   ) journey
of the shadow to the body   journey
of silence
to the
persecuting sign

═══════

fragment   or   field   blind

the absolute   outside
me   from the cry

silence et savoir
qui   pour qui
en soi
compte   tout   un à un
et
oublie ce qu'il a compté

=======

alignements de terres
transparentes
derrière
des ciels
qui fusent et dérivent et s'effritent
sous des fonds phosphorescents

arêtes
lames terreuses
liquides vitreux
suspendus
hauteurs avec les vagues
de feu et de terre
parmi des lunes pétrifiées
mentales parmi des soleils
détruits blancs livres   hauteurs
mondes
dressés
sur le cri sur la rupture
et
le vide et l'heure et
un invisible
mécanisme d'étouffement

=======

j'étais
   porosité
vivante   votre
neigeuse incertitude
votre
neige   aube
et
tombée
entre vos doigts entre

silence and knowledge
which   for which
in itself
counts   everything   one by one
and
forgets what it counted

========

alignments of transparent
lands
behind
skies
that spread and drift and fritter away
under phosphorescent depths

ridges
waves of earth
liquid glass
hovering
heights with the tide
of fire and earth
among petrified
mental moons among demolished
suns white books   heights
worlds
lined up
on the cry on the rift
and
the void and the hour and
an invisible
engine of suffocation

========

I was
   living
porosity   your
snow-ridden doubt
your
snow   dawn
and
what fell
between your fingers between

vos corps
par-dessus vos voix
vos tempes   et
tombée par-dessus vos
bouches
fermées pressées
fendues
comme le temps

blancheur
ô blancheur des années
longues
et
sirènes

blancheur
des
nuits

blancheur
des
langues

blancheur
des voix
qui
hantaient
vos ombres

horizons   corps étendus
seuils brisés   corps enroulés
autour de vos tempes
pleines de terre
et de ciels
solaires noires meurtries

traversant   nom
traversant   cri

puis

traversant   plage
chargée de corps et d'heures
ne

your bodies
over your voices
your skulls   and
what fell over your
mouths
pressed
shut   split
like time

whiteness
o whiteness of long
and
siren-like years

whiteness
of
nights

whiteness
of
tongues

whiteness
of voices
that
haunted
your shadows

horizons   stretched-out bodies
broken sills   bodies wrapped
around your skulls
filled with earth
with black
and battered
solar skies

crossing   name
crossing   cry

then

crossing   beach
loaded with bodies and hours
lifting

soulevant ni ombre
ni
silence

j'enfonçai   langue

talon
dans le néant

—————

de la terre
se répand dans le corps
terrifié
de l'invisible
puis
de l'espace
criblé d'horizons cellulaires et
projetant
au-dessus de la peau
presque noire au-dessus des membres
immobiles
une ombre exténuée
blanche
et
comme un mot-diffraction
orienté
par une flèche de silence
de lumière
du côté
du chiffre de toute négation
ombilical

neither shadow
nor silence

I dug in   tongue

heel
in nothingness

=======

earth
spreads through the body
terrified
of the invisible
then
space
riddled by cellular horizons and
casting
over the almost
black skin over the motionless limbs
a weary white
shadow
and like the fission of a word
guided
by a shaft of silence
of light
from the flank
from the cipher of all
umbilical
negation

—PAUL AUSTER

## LE CERCLE NOMBREUX

### 1

Deux cercles. Le cercle supérieur beaucoup plus petit. De la fumée sans feu et dans chaque vague des femmes en prière. Au centre, adossé aux deux cercles, le Bouddha. Vers le bas comme vers le haut, une tache noire.

### 2

Absence du palais. Arbre rejeté en arrière. Ici passe le cheval couleur d'air. Une gueule de pierre a pour langue unique un homme agressif. Tout le reste est paisible. Un arbre pousse aussi imperceptible (évanescent) que ses feuilles. Plénitude du gris.

### 3

Deux lapins, trois singes imitent l'homme. Laborieuse mer.

### 4

Le loup sort du dormeur. Flamme rose et ascendante. Le vide envahit la montagne. Le vide se déploie.

### 5

Le troisième œil. Celui qui ne s'éteint. Ou encore la main, telle une offrande, un pardon.

### 6

Dague mollement dressée (cri noir). Entre tes jambes agitées de flammes, la gueule fine d'un renard.

# Claude Royet-Journoud
## 1941-

<br>

## THE CROWDED CIRCLE

### 1

Two circles. The upper circle much smaller. Some smoke without fire and in each puff women praying. In the center, back to the two circles, the Buddha. As above, so towards the bottom, a dark splotch.

### 2

Absence of palace. Tree relegated to the background. There goes a horse the color of air. The one tongue of a stony jaw is an aggressive man. The rest is peaceful. A tree grows as imperceptibly (evanescent) as its leaves. A load of gray.

### 3

Two rabbits, three monkeys imitate the man. Sluggish sea.

### 4

The wolf comes out of the sleeping man. Rosy flame rising. The void invades the mountain. The void spreads.

### 5

The third eye. The one that never closes. Or maybe the hand, as an offer, pardon.

### 6

Dagger raised weakly (a black shriek). Between your legs, quick with flames, the narrow muzzle of a fox.

7

Le trait souple des cils. Ta bouche infime, tes quatre regards. Étoffe nouée entre les seins. Tu dors dans le cercle nombreux des couleurs.

8

Une porte, une cible. Mains au repos, le regard échappe.

9

Mains innombrables. L'inconnue du regard répond à tes cils, divise ton visage. Tes seins disparaissent dans la diversité du motif. Le brun est une pâte. Le rouge, une encre.

1 0

C'est le sang. Le sang couvrant l'épaule, faisant croître deux lucarnes aux angles supérieurs de l'image.

1 1

Je prie. Les fesses en arrière, je prie. Colliers, bracelets, je cache mes pouvoirs, pieds nus sur le bois.

1 2

Il pleure. Il ment. Elle ne dit rien. Elle souffre. Un peu.

1 3

Tu ne sais plus. Au loin une tache bleue roule vers ta nuque.

1 4

Vous vous effacez.

1 5

La lumière part de ton dos. Ta peau est fine. Tes paumes potelées. Tes doigts brefs. Le lobe de ton oreille est le côté gauche du visage.

1 6

Derrière les cercles retrouvés tu ignores les processions lointaines du temps.

1 7

Trois hommes dans ton étoffe écarlate. Deux cercles à peine tracés, à peine visibles. Tu fonds tes mains dans la blancheur de ta poitrine.

1 8

Deux courbes à ton ventre. Un marbre vert et apaisé.

7

The supple stroke of eyelashes. Your tiny mouth, your quadruple glances. Cloth knotted between the breasts. You sleep in the crowded circle of the color-wheel.

8

A door, a target. Hands at rest, a glance escapes.

9

Innumerable hands. The unknown quantity of the eyes replies to your lashes, divides your face. Your breasts disappear in the variety of subject-matter. The brown is a paste. The red, an ink.

1 0

Blood. Blood all over the shoulder, enlarging two skylights at the upper angles of the image.

1 1

I pray. Ass in the air, I pray. Necklaces, bracelets, I hide my potential, bare feet on the boards.

1 2

He weeps. He lies. She says nothing. She suffers. A bit.

1 3

You no longer know. In the distance a spot of blue is rolling towards your nape.

1 4

You step aside.

1 5

Light springs from your back. Your skin is first-rate. Your palms fleshy. Your fingers short. Your earlobe is the left side of the face.

1 6

Back of the recovered circles, you are blind to the far-off processions of time.

1 7

Three men in your crimson cloth. Two circles barely traced, barely visible. Your hands merge into the white of your breast.

1 8

Two curves at your belly. A green unruffled marble.

19

Transparence du fruit. Les cercles superposés obéissent. Tu ne regardes pas.

20

En haut et sur la gauche, une tache rouge . . . comme sur ta robe.

21

Nous sommes quatre, peut-être cinq, le crâne chauve, l'œil mal formé. Moi seule qui suis sans coiffe connais le cercle.

22

Je vous écoute. Soyez bref.

23

Nous sommes en prière. Nous sommes armés.

24

Je suis seul. Personne ne me croit.

25

Je suis l'homme noir dans le sang. Je suis le flic géométrique.

26

Arbres coupés d'horizon. Cheval entamé par le temps. On te mène à l'enclos, celui qui n'existe pas. A terre, encore une tache.

27

Nous avons faim. Nour irons dans la mer.

28

Animaux sauvages à l'angle d'un palais près d'une route verte et d'une mer colorée.

29

Entrez! Le chapiteau va s'écrouler. Le marbre se trouble.

30

Nous ne savons plus prier. J'écoute mon voisin.

31

Trois femmes. Triangle. Au-delà du mur un arbre en fleur. Tout est jaune.

1 9

Transparency of fruit. The superimposed circles obey. You do not watch.

2 0

Up and to the left, a red stain . . . like the one on your dress.

2 1

There are four of us, perhaps five, bald, with misshapen eyes. Only I, hatless, am aware of the circle.

2 2

I am listening. Be brief.

2 3

We are at prayers. We are fortified.

2 4

I am alone. No one believes me.

2 5

I am the black man in the blood. I am the projective detective.

2 6

Trees cut by the horizon. A horse broken in by time. You are brought to the enclosure, the one that does not exist. On the ground, another splotch.

2 7

We are hungry. We walk into the sea.

2 8

Wild animals at the corner of a palace near a green path and a varicolored sea.

2 9

Come in! The capital is about to topple. The marble falters.

3 0

We no longer know how to pray. I listen to my neighbour.

3 1

Three women. A triangle. On the other side of the wall, a flowering tree. Everything is yellow.

—KEITH WALDROP

A T É

*cela*                    *bleu*

et qui ne s'éloigne pas

=====

premier passage.
le dehors,
la pensée traversait les rôles

=====

ce qui n'aura jamais lieu

=====

insistance de la doublure
la transparence est un leurre

vers le neutre
lumière dispersée de l'attente

=====

main intarissable
(la description du châtiment)

=====

ensevelissement de la filiation!
masque—

=====

elle s'apaise (elle dort métaphoriquement)

=====

paysage soustrait à l'enveloppement biographique

# A T É

*that*                              *blue*


and unwithdrawing

=====


                              first crossing.
   the outside,
                   thought bridges the roles

=====


which will never take place

=====


insistence of the understudy
transparency is a lure

towards neutrality
scattered light of expectations

=====


unfailing hand
(description of the punishment)

=====


shrouding the relationship!
mask—

=====


she calms down (she sleeps metaphorically)

=====


landscape preserved from biographical wrappings

une théâtralité de l'air
dans l'hors-jeu de la répétition

======

*ce qui est tu*

l'usage dérive
            l'air rebondit sur la pente
où nulle forme ne paraît

– –portrait abandonné– –

les chambres refroidissent dans l'énigme

obsession de l'écart

======

comme plus loin *cette vue dorsale*

======

dans la disposition et
le nombre

a theatricality of air
in the outfield of the rehearsal

══════

*what is hushed*

custom diverts
        the air surges at the gradient
where no form appears

    – –abandoned portrait– –

rooms grow chilly in a riddle

obsession with duration

══════

    as farther along *this dorsal aspect*

══════

    in arrangement and
    number

—KEITH WALDROP

## VERS L'AUTRE . . .

J'ai eu une place au dehors, une place que j'ai voulu retrouver, et ce n'est plus qu'une tache sous la main.

Maintenant que je ne pousse plus, mes gestes effacent toute couleur, toute trace. Il ne me reste plus qu'à rentrer.

———

Pour m'être chauffé un instant dans la place, me voici livré à moi-même, sans corde, sans chaînes. Avec des mains, des pieds, dont j'ignore la forme, qui ne me servent à rien. Et il y a tant de mains, de pieds, au-devant de moi, *de l'autre côté!* J'entends les pas, les coups, sans éprouver la moindre douleur . . . Serais-je déchiré, piétiné, les mots me manqueraient pour l'écrire.

———

Celui qui a frappé le dernier coup m'écrivait dans l'ignorance de la tuerie. Cherchant, à tâtons, à me dégager de la terre, il laissait intacte la masse indistincte (presque de la poussière . . .), avec quoi je ferai corps à la fin, au commencement du récit.

———

*Je* lui adresse la parole, *je* l'implique, comme si nous étions tous deux du même lieu, du même temps. Mais *il* est *de l'autre côté*, là où *je* serai quand vraiment *je* parlerai, tout homme hors d'atteinte, tout terrain perdu.

# Alain Veinstein

## 1942-

## TOWARD THE OTHER . . .

I had a place outside, a place I wanted to find again, and all that is left is a spot under my hand.

Now that I am no longer pushing, my gestures wipe away any color, any trace. All I can do is go back in.

———

Just because I warmed myself for a moment there, in that place, I am now at my own mercy, without rope, without chains. With hands and feet whose shape I do not know, which are of no use. And so many hands, so many feet ahead of me, *on the other side.* I hear steps, blows, without feeling the slightest pain . . . I could get battered or trampled and would have no words to write it down.

———

The man who dealt the last blow wrote me down, unaware of the slaughter. Blindly he tried to get me up from the ground, but left intact the vague mass (dust, almost . . .) with which I shall merge in the end, at the beginning of the story.

———

*I* speak to him, *I* imply him as if we were both of the same place, the same time. But *he* is *on the other side* where *I* shall be once it is really *I* who speak, all human beings out of reach, all ground lost.

====

*Je creuse un trou.* Un rien de terre suffirait pour l'enfermer. Mais mon travail paraît sans fin . . . Me voici, dans ce trou, presque entièrement effacé, et sans autre issue, bientôt, que de m'attaquer à mon corps. Seul mon corps pourra me fournir ce qu'il faut de force pour lutter contre le froid.

====

Aucun bruit n'éclate autour de lui. Il est seul, au bout de son espace, incapable de faire les quelques gestes . . . A chaque instant, il suffirait d'un souffle pour l'emporter. Sa main, pourtant, accentue l'âge, impuissante à chasser les mots. Et il doit s'appuyer entièrement sur cette main pour ne pas être *pris* tout à fait dans la blancheur.

====

Reste la poussière, les résidus d'insecte. Et le personnage immobile, distrait seulement par les craquements de la terre. S'il se tue au travail encore, c'est pour enfouir son visage avant qu'un coup de talon ne lui écrase la tête.

====

Rien ne permet de penser qu'il puisse un jour arriver, descendre jusqu'à moi. Il n'a presque rien dit. Il s'est tapi contre la terre, comme je me suis jeté sur la première phrase. Quand il disparaîtra, ce sera le *milieu:* les travaux pourront commencer.

═════

*I am digging a hole.* The smallest amount of earth would do to close it. But my work seems endless . . . Here I am now in the hole, nearly all wiped out, and soon there will be nothing for it but to tackle my own body. Only my body can give me the strength to fight against the cold.

═════

No sound around him. He is alone at the edge of his space, unable to make the few gestures . . . Any moment a puff of wind could carry him off. His hand, though, betrays his age, powerless to chase after words. And he must depend entirely on this hand in order not to get completely *trapped* in the whiteness.

═════

Remains the dust, the hulls of insects. And the immobile figure distracted only by the cracking in the ground. If he kills himself working it is to bury his face before some kick crushes his skull.

═════

Nothing allows me to think he could arrive some day, come all the way down to me. He has hardly said anything. He is crouching on the ground the way I threw myself on my first sentence. When he vanishes it will be the *mid point:* the work can begin.

—ROSMARIE WALDROP

## LA COLLINE, LA FOLIE

qui ne sait pas parler
qui ouvre le chemin
    le voyage perdu

et la grammaire des étoiles l'appauvrit
si le sentier parfois existe elle le doit
aux tremblements

aux yeux de la montée
quand la lumière devient plus violente et s'éteint

## LOGIQUE

saisons là-bas terreau qu'on tamisait
comme appliquant la carcasse des suites:
par ces fenêtres où le mental nous traîne,
inexplicablement le jour déjà donné

# Alain Delahaye

## 1944-

## THE HILL, THE FRENZY

who cannot speak
who opens up the way
    the lost journey

and the grammar of the stars impoverishes her
if the path is sometimes there she owes it
to the flickerings

to the eyes of ascent
when the light glows fiercer and dies out

—ANTHONY BARNETT

## LOGIC

seasons over there loam sifted
like applying the framework of the consequences:
through these windows where the intellect drags us,
inexplicably the day already given

trouve naissance et sa vraie mort en nous,
se fait parole blanche, souffle et sens:
oui, cela s'accomplit, à la saison d'automne,
parmi des fracas d'outils.

## DEUX PAYSAGES, GRAMMAIRE

avec la terre et tout
ce qui brûla ici longtemps
avec cette caverne de l'encore

et l'œil soudain lisible de la plaine

interruption unique non suivie
de cordes ni de voix

## GRANDE PRAIRIE

l'enfant revient pour ne rien t'enseigner

caresse l'apparence, les clameurs:
le nerf de l'interdit gagne sur la musique

et c'est un autre qui s'en va
vers le non-dit
de terre sèche et sang contre le ciel plombé
trop près de l'horizon

finds birth and its true death in us,
turns into white word, breath and meaning:
yes, this happens in the autumn season,
among the clang of implements.

—ANTHONY BARNETT

# TWO LANDSCAPES, GRAMMAR

with the earth and all
that burned here a long time
with this cavern of the once again

and the suddenly readable eye of the plain

sole interruption followed neither
by strings nor voice

—ANTHONY BARNETT

# BROAD MEADOW

the child returns to teach you nothing

clings to appearance, the clamors:
the nerve of forbidden things overtakes the music

and it is another who goes away
towards the unsaid
of dry earth and blood against the murky sky
too near the horizon

—PAUL AUSTER

## PARCE QU'EN DÉTRUISANT
## IL CRÉE

éboulements comme des doigts

où ton ombre s'achève
commence notre chemin

dans l'ocre de telle œuvre une poussière
encore poursuivie de vent

d'où cette vibration, ces taches
nerveuses déchirant le vide

ces ossements d'espace répandus et simples


## LE PAYSAGE INTENSE

phrases rêvées de feu, puis effacées
pour qu'il y ait le feu

il faudra que la voix
ait le même silence
que la clarté de l'air

être de tout amour
comme le livre existe entier dans la blancheur

# BECAUSE IN DESTROYING
# HE CREATES

landslides like fingers

where your shadow draws to an end
our path begins

in the ochre of this work the wind
still chasing dust

therefore this quivering, these hectic
blots tearing open the emptiness

these scattered and simple bones of space

—PAUL AUSTER

# THE INTENSE LANDSCAPE

words dreamed by fire, then erased
so the fire might begin

the voice must have
the same silence
as the radiant air

being of all love
as the book lives whole in whiteness

—PAUL AUSTER

# TERRE . . .

Terre—comme si j'entrais où un corps
ne peut plus durer

(aveu du jour . . . jusqu'au vent

Leurre d'une étoile bue,
qui aura été unique perplexité
entre le ciel et soi . . .

Place vide, où je rejoins ce corps.

# Philippe Denis

## 1947-

EARTH . . .

Earth—as though I had entered
where no body can live

(daylight confession . . . into the teeth
of the wind

The lure of a drunken star
will have been
the sole enigma
between sky and self . . .

Empty place,
where I merge with this body.

—PAUL AUSTER

## LE MONDE . . .

Le monde est déjà loin derrière—
comme une apparence de chacun de nous.

Hâte de ce qui nous emporte, et qui n'est
qu'avenir.

Véhicule de lenteur
(dans l'oblique du froid)

où une image crie.

## ÉTOILE . . .

Étoile
là—
dans le non vivable
de tout ce qui vit
chassé de la vie.

La douleur
infuse
toute blancheur,
artère
la force du voyage—

(la grande route d'eau

ALREADY . . .

Already, the world is far behind—
like an apparition
of each one of us.

Haste bears us away,
and leads toward nothing
but future.

Vehicle of slowness
(in the sharp slanting of cold)

where an image howls.

—PAUL AUSTER

A STAR . . .

A star,
there—
in the unlivable
heart
of each living thing
driven from life.

Pain
seeps
into whiteness,
pumps blood
into the quick
of the journey

(the vast road of water

—PAUL AUSTER

A L'AMARRE . . .

A l'amarre de ton sang,
le creux
laissé par ton somme,
pour toi,
maintenant, respire—

(le vent entre les dernières étoiles
circule

des lambeaux de coq
crépitent
dans les enclos—

avant que ne grossissent
les routes
—comme les veines
de tes poignets.

A VIVRE . . .

A vivre comme respirer,
à s'avancer
au-devant de sa vie—

ce que nous rejoignons
sort de ce jour
comme le vent,

aveugle
notre respiration.

MOORED . . .

Moored to your blood,
the hollow
left by your sleep,
now breathes
for you—

(the wind
flows between the last stars

rooster
scraps
sputter in the paddock—

before the roads begin
to swell
—like the veins
of your wrists.

—PAUL AUSTER

TO LIVE . . .

To live in the way one breathes,
to move on
in front of one's life—

what we reach
emerges from the day
like the wind,

blinds
our breath.

—PAUL AUSTER

## SUR LES AILES . . .

Sur les ailes du papillon—gravé,
l'équilibre de la poussière
bourgeonne—

L'alphabet
et les fleurs,
           pour toi, annoncent
un nouveau temps de douleur—

(Tandis que la graine du pavot ourle
son écarlate blessure)

## ON THE BUTTERFLY'S . . .

On the butterfly's wings—engraved,
the equilibrium of dust
blooms—

the alphabet
and the flowers
                    herald a new time
of sorrow for you—

(while the poppy seed stitches
its scarlet wound)

—PAUL AUSTER

# Notes on the Poets

ANNE-MARIE ALBIACH

Born 1937. One of the founding editors (with Claude Royet-Journoud and Michel Couturier) of the review *Siècle à mains*. Albiach lived in London for several years during the sixties and has translated work by Louis Zukofsky, Frank O'Hara and other American poets.

Principal collections of poetry: *Flammigère* (1967), *État* (1971), *"H II" linéaires* (1974), *Le Double* (1975), *Césure: le corps* (1975), *Objet* (1976).

GUILLAUME APOLLINAIRE (Wilhelm Apollinaris de Kostrowitzky)

1880–1918. Born in Rome of mixed Polish and Italian parentage. Taken to Monaco as a child, where he received a French education. In 1899 the family settled in Paris; in 1901 Apollinaire worked as a tutor in Germany. Returned to Paris in 1902 and soon thereafter began close association with Picasso, Max Jacob, Alfred Jarry, Marie Laurencin and other young artists and writers of the period. Apollinaire became the hub of the new spirit in art, writing poems, stories, articles, erotica, columns for the daily papers and tirelessly promoting the work of the Cubists. His first book, a collection of stories entitled *L'Hérésiarque et Cie*, appeared in 1910. *Le Bestiaire*, his first book of poetry, was published in 1911, with woodcuts by Raoul Dufy. Later that same year he was mistakenly implicated in the theft of the Mona Lisa from the Louvre and held in prison for six days. In 1913 two of his most important books were published: *Alcools* (poems) and *Les Peintres Cubistes* (a gathering of his writings on Picasso, Braque, Picabia, Léger and other artists). In 1914 he became a French citizen and enlisted in the French army. He was wounded in the head by shell fragments in March 1916, while serving as a lieutenant with the infantry at the front. In 1917 his play, *Les Mamelles de Tirésias*, was performed. In his introduction to that work the word "surrealist" appeared for the first time. Apollinaire died on Armistice Day,

1918, of Spanish influenza brought on by an operation to remove a shell fragment from his skull.

Principal collections of poetry: *Alcools* (1913), *Calligrammes* (1918), *Poèmes à Lou* (posthumous).

Poetry in English: *Selected Writings*, trans. by Roger Shattuck (New Directions, 1948; reprinted 1971); *Alcools*, trans. by William Meredith (Doubleday, 1964); *Alcools*, trans. by Anne Hyde Greet (University of California Press, 1965); *Calligrammes*, trans. by Anne Hyde Greet (University of California Press, 1980).

## LOUIS ARAGON

1897–1982. Mobilized in 1917; met André Breton while studying military medicine during the war. In 1919, along with Breton and Soupault, founded the review *Littérature*. Active participant in the French Dada movement. Later one of the principal members of the Surrealist group. Broke with the Surrealists in 1931 and joined the Communist Party, to which he has remained closely attached. Taken prisoner by the Germans during World War II, escaped to the Unoccupied Zone, and became one of the leading figures in the Resistance. Much of his finest poetry was written during this period. Awarded Lenin Peace Prize in 1954 and for many years served as director of *Les Lettres françaises*. In addition to his abundant output as a poet, Aragon has written novels, essays, a long study of Matisse, a translation of Lewis Carroll and journalism. A good deal of his fiction has been translated into English.

Principal collections of poetry: *Feu de joie* (1920), *Le Mouvement perpétuel* (1925), *La Grande Gaîté* (1929), *Persécuté Persécuteur* (1931), *Hourra l'oural* (1934), *Le Crève-Coeur* (1941), *Cantique à Elsa* (1942), *Les Yeux d'Elsa* (1942), *Le Musée Grévin* (1943), *La Diane française* (1945), *Le Nouveau Crève-Coeur* (1948), *Les Yeux et la mémoire* (1954), *Le Roman inachevé* (1956), *Elsa* (1959), *Les Poètes* (1960), *Le Fou d'Elsa* (1963), *Le Voyage en Hollande* (1964), *Elégie à Pablo Neruda* (1966).

## ANTONIN ARTAUD

1896–1948. Active in Surrealist movement until break with Breton in 1930. Film actor (Dreyer's *La Passion de Jeanne d'Arc*, Gance's *Napoléon*), stage director, philosopher of the theater (*The Theater and Its Double*), and poet. Travels to Mexico in late thirties. Spent many of his last years in confinement at the mental hospital in Rodez. Following his release (1946), he delivered a series of lecture-performances in Paris that had a profound effect on many writers of the younger generation.

All of Artaud's writings have been collected in the multivolumed set, *Oeuvres Complètes*, published by Gallimard.

In English: *Artaud Anthology*, ed. by Jack Hirschmann (City Lights, 1965); *Black Poet and Other Texts*, trans. by Paul Zweig (M. J. Minard, 1966); *Collected Works*, trans. by Victor Corti (Calder & Boyers, 1968); *Selected Writings*, trans. by Helen Weaver (Farrar, Straus & Giroux, 1976).

## YVES BONNEFOY

Born 1923. In addition to the writing of poetry, Bonnefoy has been extremely active as a critic of art and poetry. A member of the editorial board of the review *L'Éphémère*

(with André du Bouchet, Jacques Dupin, Michel Leiris, Louis-René des Fôrets and Paul Celan). Bonnefoy has taught at several universities in the United States and has translated works by Shakespeare, Yeats and Seferis.

Principal collections of poetry: *Du mouvement et de l'immobilité de Douve* (1953), *Hier regnant désert* (1958), *Pierre écrite* (1965), *Dans le leurre du seuil* (1975).

Poetry in English: *On the Motion and Immobility of Douve*, trans. by Galway Kinnell (Ohio University Press, 1968); *Selected Poems*, trans. by Anthony Rudolf (Jonathan Cape, 1968); *Words in Stone*, trans. by Susanna Lang (University of Massachusetts Press, 1976).

## ANDRÉ DU BOUCHET

Born 1924. Went to the United States at the age of seventeen, where he remained for seven years. B.A. from Amherst College; M.A. from Harvard, where he was Teaching Fellow in English and Comparative Literature. Du Bouchet has written an important meditation on the work of Alberto Giacometti and published numerous essays on painting and poetry. A member of the editorial board of the review *L'Éphémère* and translator of works by Shakespeare, Hölderlin, Hopkins, Joyce, Pasternak, Celan and Laura Riding.

Principal collections of poetry: *Dans la chaleur vacante* (1961), *OU LE SOLEIL* (1968), *Air (1950–1953)* (1977), *Laisses* (1979).

Poetry in English: *The Uninhabited*, trans. by Paul Auster (Living Hand, 1976).

## ANDRÉ BRETON

1896–1966. Early medical studies, marked by discovery of Freud's writings. Founded the review *Littérature* with Soupault and Aragon in 1919, the same year in which he collaborated with Soupault on *Les Champs magnétiques*, the first example of automatic writing in France. Participated in Paris Dada activities led by Tzara. Published first manifesto of Surrealism in 1924, which heralded the new movement. From then until his death Breton was the chief organizer, theoretician and "pope" of Surrealism. Second manifesto published in 1930. During the Popular Front period, close contacts with the Communist Party. Definitive break with Communists in 1935. Trip to Mexico in 1938, where he met Diego Rivera and Leon Trotsky. Breton came to New York in 1941 where he founded the magazine *VVV* with Marcel Duchamp, Max Ernst and David Hare. In 1942 he delivered a lecture at Yale University, "Situation du surréalisme entre les deux guerres." Although prolific as a poet, Breton is best known for his prose works: the numerous essays and tracts connected with Surrealism and books such as *Nadja*, *L'Amour fou* and *Arcane 17*.

Principal collections of poetry: *Clair de terre* (1925), *L'union libre* (1931), *Le Revolver à cheveaux blancs* (1932), *L'Air de l'eau* (1934), *Ode à Charles Fourier* (1947), *Poèmes* (1948).

Poetry in English: *Young Cherry Trees Secured Against Hares*, trans. by Edouard Roditi (View, 1946; reprinted 1969 by The University of Michigan Press); *Selected Poems*, trans. by Kenneth White (Jonathan Cape, 1969).

## BLAISE CENDRARS (Frédéric Sauser)

1887–1961. Born in Switzerland. Innumerable travels, jobs and adventures as a young man. Arrived in America in 1911 and worked in New York for six months (as a tailor,

as a pianist for a Bowery movie house, etc.), while spending most of his free time reading in the New York Public Library. First major poem, *Les Pâques à New York*, written there in 1912. Returned to Paris, where he became friends with Apollinaire, Jacob, Reverdy, Robert and Sonia Delaunay, Chagall and Léger. Lost his right arm in World War I (1915). After the war Cendrars worked as an editor for Éditions de la Sirène, publishing his own *Anthologie nègre* and the first edition of Lautréamont's *Maldoror* to appear since the original publication of 1868. Parallel career as film maker, collaborating with Abel Gance on *La Roue* in 1921. Stopped writing poetry in 1924. Between 1924 and 1940, a period of constant travel, mostly to North and South America. Published several novels in the twenties, *L'Or* (1925) and *Dan Yack* (1927) among them, and formed close friendship with Henry Miller. Worked as correspondent attached to British army at the beginning of World War II. Soon thereafter went into isolation in Provence. In 1943 began last stage of career as writer, producing four autobiographical chronicles and several novels. Much of this work has been translated into English.

Principal collections of poetry: All of Cendrars' poetry was collected in two separate volumes published in 1947, *Du monde entier* and *Au coeur du monde*.

Poetry in English: *Panama, or The Adventures of My Seven Uncles*, trans. by John Dos Passos (Harper and Brothers, 1931); *Selected Writings*, ed. by Walter Albert (New Directions, 1966); *Kodak*, trans. by Ron Padgett (Adventures in Poetry, 1976); *At the Heart of the World*, trans. by Annabel Levitt (O Press, 1976); *Selected Poems*, trans. by Peter Hoida (Penguin, 1979); *Complete Postcards from the Americas*, trans. by Monique Chefdor (University of California Press, 1979).

### AIMÉ CÉSAIRE

Born 1913 in Martinique. Educated at the École Normale in Paris, where he became one of the founders of the *négritude* movement. Returned to Martinique in 1939 to teach. In 1941 met André Breton, who became a champion of his work. Elected mayor of Fort-de-France after being invited to run by the Communist Party. After the Hungarian uprising of 1956, Césaire broke with the Communists and formed the Independent Revolutionary Party of Martinique. He has also served as a deputy to the French National Assembly. In addition to poetry, Césaire has written several plays, many essays, and a number of historical studies.

Principal collections of poetry: *Les armes miraculeuses* (1946), *Cahier d'un retour au pays natal* (1956), *Ferrements* (1960), *Cadastre* (1961).

In English: *Return to My Native Land*, trans. by John Berger and Anna Bostock (Penguin, 1969). *Aimé Césaire: The Collected Poetry, 1939–1976*, trans. by Clayton Eshleman and Annette Smith (University of California Press, 1983).

### RENÉ CHAR

Born 1907. Char was an active participant in the Surrealist movement in the early thirties and published a collaborative work with Breton and Éluard (*Ralentir Travaux*). Broke with the Surrealists in 1935. During the war, he joined the *maquis* and became a Resistance leader in the field. In 1944–45 he was attached to Allied Headquarters in Algeria, in charge of parachute missions into France. After the war, he founded the review *Empédocle* with Albert Camus. In addition to poetry and essays, Char has written on the art of Miró and Braque.

Principal collections of poetry: *Le Marteau sans maître* (1935), *Seuls demeurent* (1945), *Feuillets d'Hypnos* (1946), *Fureur et mystère* (1948), *Les Matinaux* (1950), *La Parole en archipel* (1962), *Commune Présence* (1964), *Retour Amont* (1966), *Dans la pluie giboyeuse* (1968).

In English: *Hypnos Waking*, ed. by Jackson Mathews (Random House, 1956); *Poems*, trans. by Mary Ann Caws and Jonathan Griffin (Princeton University Press, 1976).

## JEAN-PAUL DE DADELSEN

1914–1957. Worked as a teacher and journalist. From 1948 until his death he was with the French Service of the BBC in London. He began writing poetry at the age of thirty-eight; he died of brain cancer in June 1957.

Posthumous collection: *Jonas* (1962), with preface by Henri Thomas.

In English: *Jonah*, trans. by Edward Lucie-Smith (Rapp & Carroll, 1967).

## JEAN DAIVE

Born 1941. Founder of the review *Fragment* and translator of Paul Celan.

Principal collections: *Décimale blanche* (1967), *Fût bati* (1973), Υ ≫ (1975), *Le jeu des séries scéniques* (1976), *Le cri-cerveau* (1978).

## RENÉ DAUMAL

1908–1944. Invited by André Breton to join the Surrealist movement, Daumal declined and instead founded his own magazine, *Le Grand Jeu*, in 1928. Daumal wrote two novels, *La Grande beuverie* (1938) and the unfinished *Le Mont Analogue* (published in 1952)—both of which have appeared in English—numerous literary and philosophical essays, and studies of Eastern religions. Translations of Hemingway's *Death in the Afternoon*, D. T. Suzuki's studies of Zen Buddhism and a number of important Hindu texts.

All of Daumal's poetry was collected in a single volume, *Poésie noire, poésie blanche*, published in 1954.

## MICHEL DEGUY

Born 1930. Deguy taught philosophy from 1953 to 1968 and now lectures on French literature at the University of Paris. Director of the magazine *Revue de poésie*. He has written numerous essays as well as a study of Thomas Mann, and has published translations of Hölderlin, Góngora, Pindar and others.

Principal collections of poetry: *Fragments du cadastre* (1960), *Poèmes de la presqu'île* (1961), *Biefs* (1964), *Ouï dire* (1966), *Figurations* (1969), *Tombeau de du Bellay* (1973), *Donnant Donnant* (1981).

## ALAIN DELAHAYE

Born 1944. Extended stays in England and the United States; translations of W. S. Merwin.

Principal collections of poetry: *L'Éveil des traversées* (1971), *L'être perdu* (1977).

**PHILIPPE DENIS**

Born 1947. Denis has taught French literature at the University of Minnesota and Bennington College. In 1979, he edited a special issue of *Sub-Stance* (published by the University of Wisconsin) devoted to contemporary French poetry. Denis has translated the work of several American poets, including Emily Dickinson, Marianne Moore and Sylvia Plath.

Principal collections of poetry: *Cahier d'ombres* (1974), *Les Cendres de la voix* (1975), *Malgré la bouche* (1977), *Revif* (1978), *Carnet d'un aveuglement* (1980), *Surface d'écueil* (1980).

**ROBERT DESNOS**

1900–1945. One of the most important members of the Surrealist group in the twenties, praised by Breton as having played a "necessary, unforgettable role" in the development of the movement. Broke with Breton in 1930. Later worked for French radio, wrote numerous film scenarios, and poems for children. His long poem, *Complainte de Fantômas*, was broadcast in 1933, with accompanying music by Kurt Weill. Desnos was active during the war as a journalist and participated in the Resistance. He was arrested by the Gestapo in February 1944 and sent to Buchenwald in April. He died shortly after the liberation the following year in the German concentration camp in Terezine, Czechoslovakia.

Principal collections of poetry: *Corps et biens: poèmes 1919–1929* (1930), *Fortunes* (1942), *Contrée* (1944). Posthumous collection: *Destinée arbitraire* (1975).

In English: *22 Poems*, trans. by Michael Benedikt (Kayak, 1971).

**JACQUES DUPIN**

Born 1927. Dupin is director of publications for the Galerie Maeght in Paris and was a member of the editorial board of the review *L'Éphémère*. He has published major studies of Miró and Giacometti (both available in English) and has written extensively on contemporary artists.

Principal collections of poetry: *Gravir* (1963), *L'embrasure* (1969), *Debors* (1975).

Poetry in English: *Fits and Starts*, trans. by Paul Auster (Living Hand, 1974).

**PAUL ÉLUARD** (Eugène Grindel)

1895–1952. A participant in the activities of French Dada and later a major presence in the Surrealist movement. A prolific poet, Éluard also published a number of collaborative works (with Breton, Péret, Char, Aragon), as well as several prose collections, including *Donner à voir* (1939). Éluard broke with Surrealism in 1938 and joined the Communist Party. A member of the Resistance during the war, he remained in Paris during the four years of the German Occupation, constantly changing his address to avoid arrest. His clandestine poetry of that period gained him recognition as a national figure.

Principal collections of poetry: *Capitale de la douleur* (1926), *L'Amour la poésie* (1929), *La Vie immédiate* (1932), *La Rose publique* (1934), *Facile* (1935), *Les Yeux fertiles* (1936), *Cours naturel* (1938), *Au Rendez-vous allemand* (1944), *Le dur désir de durer* (1946), *Corps*

*mémorable* (1948). Éluard's complete writings have been published in two volumes by the Éditions de le Pléaide.

In English: *Selected Poems*, trans. by Lloyd Alexander (New Directions, 1946).

### LÉON-PAUL FARGUE

1876–1947. Studied English with Mallarmé at the Lycée Rollin in Paris and later became a regular at Mallarmé's Tuesday evenings in the Rue de Rome. Close friendships with Ravel, Stravinsky, Satie, Debussy, Larbaud, Valéry and Gide. In 1924 he took over the direction of the review *Commerce* with Valéry and Larbaud. Also closely associated with the group that formed around Sylvia Beach and an early supporter of Joyce's work. Fargue was above all a poet of Paris, and he was legendary for his long walks through the city, his late-night café conversation, his solitary, almost reclusive existence. Although a number of his poems were written as early as 1894, his first book was not published until 1911.

Principal collections of poetry: *Tancrède* (1911), *Poèmes, suivi de Pour la musique* (1912), *Banalité* (1928), *Vulturne* (1928), *Sous la lampe* (1930), *Le Piéton de Paris* (1939), *Haute Solitude* (1941), *Refuges* (1942), *Méandres* (1946). Fargue's early books were collected in a single volume, *Poésies*, published in 1963 with a preface by Saint-John Perse.

### JEAN FOLLAIN

1903–1971. Follain studied law, entered the bar in 1928, and in 1951 became a district judge. After his retirement, he traveled extensively. In addition to poetry, Follain wrote several collections of prose poems, as well as a book about Peru and a *Petit Glossaire de l'argot*.

Principal collections of poetry: *Usage de temps* (1943), *Exister* (1947), *Territoires* (1953), *Tout instant* (1957), *Des Heures* (1960), *Appareil de la terre* (1964), *D'Après Tout* (1967).

In English: *Transparence of the World*, trans. by W. S. Merwin (Atheneum, 1968). *D'Après Tout*, trans. by Heather McHugh (Princeton University Press, 1981).

### ANDRÉ FRÉNAUD

Born 1907. Frénaud studied philosophy and law and taught French at the University of Lwów (Poland) in 1930. Became a civil servant in 1937, working for the French Railways until his retirement. Mobilized in 1940, captured that same year. All the poems in his first book were written in captivity. Escaped from German POW camp in 1942 and joined the Resistance.

Principal collections of poetry: *Les Rois Mages* (1943; new and revised edition, 1966), *Il n'y a pas de paradis* (1962), *La Sainte Face* (1968), *Depuis toujours déjà* (1970).

In English: *A Little Round O*, trans. by Keith Bosley (Interim Pres, 1978).

### ROGER GIROUX

1925–1973. Giroux's one book was awarded the Prix Max Jacob. Translator of Yeats, Lawrence Durrell and others.

Collection of poetry: *L'arbre temps* (1964). Posthumous works: *Voici* (1974), *Thé-âtre* (1976), *S* (1977), *L'arbre le Temps suivi de Lieu-Je et de Lettre* (1977).

### EUGÈNE GUILLEVIC

Born 1907. Entered civil service in 1935 and worked in the Ministry of Finance until his retirement. Joined the clandestine Communist Party during the war. Since 1947 has traveled widely: to North Africa, Eastern Europe, the Soviet Union and the United States.

Principal collections of poetry: *Terraqué* (1942), *Exécutoire* (1947), *Gagner* (1949), *Carnac* (1961), *Sphère* (1963), *Avec* (1966), *Euclidiennes* (1967), *Ville* (1969), *Paroi* (1970), *Inclus* (1973), *Du domaine* (1977).

In English: *Selected Poems*, trans. by Denise Levertov (New Directions, 1969); *Selected Poems*, trans. by Teo Savory (Penguin, 1974).

### EMMANUEL HOCQUARD

Born 1940. Spent childhood in Tangiers. Hocquard lives in Paris and is director of Orange Export Ltd., a small press that has published work by both French and American poets.

Principal collections of poetry: *Album d'images de la Villa Harris* (1977), *Les Dernières nouvelles de l'expédition sont datées du 15 février 17 . .* (1978), *Une journée dans le détroit* (1980), *Une ville ou une petite île* (1981).

### EDMOND JABÈS

Born 1912 in Cairo. Jabès studied in Paris in the early thirties, served as an officer in the British army during the war, and formed early literary friendships with Max Jacob and a number of the Surrealists. Forced to leave Egypt during the Suez crisis, he has been living in Paris since 1957.

Principal works: *Je bâtis ma demeure, poèmes 1943–1957* (1959; new edition 1975), *Le Livre des Questions* (1963), *Le Livre de Yukel* (1964), *Le Retour au Livre* (1965), *Yaël* (1967), *Elya* (1969), *Aély* (1972), *. (El, ou le dernier livre)* (1973), *Le Livre des Ressemblances* (1976), *Le Soupçon Le Désert* (1978), *L'Ineffaçable L'Inaperçu* (1980).

In English: *Elya*, trans. by Rosmarie Waldrop (Tree, 1972); *The Book of Questions*, trans. by Rosmarie Waldrop (Wesleyan University Press, 1976); *The Book of Yukel & Return to the Book*, trans. by Rosmarie Waldrop (Wesleyan University Press, 1977); *A Share of Ink*, trans. by Anthony Rudolf (Menard Press, 1979).

### MAX JACOB

1876–1944. Met Picasso in 1901 and for some time shared a studio with him. After-ward, and for many years to follow, he lived three doors away from the artist on the Rue Ravignan. One of the key members of the group that formed around Apollinaire. A painter as well as a poet, Jacob lived in extreme poverty, working at all manner of jobs throughout his life. Although born a Jew, he converted to Catholicism in 1915, six years after having a vision of Christ. In 1921 he moved from Paris to the small village of Saint Benoît-sur-Loire, close to a Benedictine church, where he remained until his

arrest by the Nazis in February 1944. He died the following month in the concentration camp at Drancy.

Principal collections of poetry: *Les Oeuvres Burlesques et Mystiques de Frère Matorel* (1912), *Le cornet à dés* (1917), *La Defense de Tartuffe* (1919), *Le Laboratoire Central* (1921), *Les Pénitants en maillots roses* (1925), *Morceaux choisis* (1937), *Derniers Pòemes* (1945).

In English: *For Max Jacob*, trans. by Andrei Codrescu (Tree, 1974); *The Dice Cup*, ed. by Michael Brownstein (Sun, 1979).


PHILIPPE JACCOTTET

Born 1925 in Switzerland. In addition to poetry, Jaccottet has published prose meditations, notebooks, numerous essays on poets and a study of Rilke. He is well known as the translator of Hölderlin, Musil, Rilke and Ungaretti.

Principal collections of poetry: *L'Effraie* (1953), *L'Ignorant* (1958), *Airs* (1967), *Leçons* (1969), *Chant d'en bas* (1974).

In English: *Breathings*, trans. by Cid Corman (Grossman, 1974); *Seedtime*, poems trans. by Michael Hamburger (New Directions, 1977).


PIERRE JEAN JOUVE

1887–1976. Early work heavily influenced by the Symbolists. During World War I enlisted as civil volunteer in military hospital for contagious diseases. Came into close contact with Romain Rolland and became a follower of "Unanism." Published several collections of poetry between 1912 and 1923. A deep spiritual crisis in 1924 led Jouve to renounce all his early works. After 1925, his output included five novels, seventeen volumes of poetry, several collections of essays and translations of Hölderlin and Shakespeare. He spent World War II in Geneva, working for the Resistance and the Allies.

Principal collections of poetry: *Noces* (1928), *Les Noces* (1931) *Sueur de sang* (1933), *Hélène* (1936), *Matière celeste* (1937), *Kyrie* (1938), *La Vierge de Paris* (1946), *Hymne* (1947), *Diadème* (1949), *Ode* (1951), *Lyrique* (1956), *Mélodrame* (1957), *Inventions* (1958), *Moires* (1962). All of Jouve's poetry has been published in a four-volume edition by Mercure de France.

Poetry in English: *An Idiom of Night*, trans. by Keith Bosley (Rapp & Whiting, 1968).


VALERY LARBAUD

1881–1957. Studied English literature at the Sorbonne. First literary effort was a translation of Coleridge (*The Rime of the Ancient Mariner*). Later translated works by Sir Thomas Browne, Landor, Butler and Whitman. Intimately connected with American writers in Paris in the twenties. Helped support the founding of the bookstore Shakespeare and Company. Translator of *Ulysses* into French and a close friend of Joyce. In addition to poetry, Larbaud wrote stories, novels and numerous essays.

Principal collection of poetry: *Les Poésies de A. O. Barnabooth* (1908, 1913).

Poetry in English: *Poems of a Multi-Millionaire*, trans. by William Jay Smith (Bonacio & Saul with Grove Press, 1955); *The Poems of A. O. Barnabooth*, trans. by Ron Padgett & Bill Zavatsky (Mushinsha, 1977).

ROBERT MARTEAU

Born 1925. In addition to poetry, Marteau has published two novels, a study of Chagall's stained-glass windows, essays on art and translations of the Yugoslav poet Miodrag Pavlovic. He worked as art critic for the review *Esprit* and for the past several years has been living in Montreal.

Principal collections of poetry: *Royaumes* (1962), *Travaux sur la terre* (1966), *Sibylles* (1971), *Atlante* (1976), *Traité du blanc et des teintures* (1978).

Poetry in English: *Salamander*, trans. by Anne Winters (Princeton University Press, 1979).

HENRI MICHAUX

Born 1899 in Belgium. Numerous occupations as a young man, among them sailor, tutor and private secretary to Jules Supervielle. Traveled extensively in the twenties and thirties to North and South America, India, China, Japan, Egypt and Africa. A 1941 article by André Gide helped bring Michaux's work to a larger audience. Michaux is also an artist and has exhibited his paintings and drawings widely. In addition to his imaginative works, he has written books about his travels and his experiments with drugs. He turned down the Grand Prix National des Lettres in 1965 as a protest against the institution of literary prizes.

Principal works: *Qui je fus* (1927), *Ecuador* (1929), *Mes Proprietés* (1929), *Un Certain Plume* (1930), *Un Barbare en Asie* (1933), *La Nuit remue* (1935), *Voyage en Grand Garabagne* (1936), *Plume, précédé de Lointain intérieur* (1937), *Au pays de la magie* (1942), *Épreuves, exorcismes* (1945), *La Vie dans les plis* (1948), *Passages* (1950), *Face au verrous* (1954), *Misérable miracle* (1956), *L'infini turbulent* (1957), *Paix dans les brisements* (1959), *Connaisance par les gouffres* (1961), *Vents et poussières* (1962).

Poetry in English: *Selected Writings*, trans. by Richard Ellmann (New Directions, 1968).

O. V. DE L. MILOSZ (Oscar Vladislas de Lubicz-Milosz)

1877–1939. Lithuanian diplomat in Paris after World War I. Eventually became French citizen. Milosz wrote fiction, drama and essays, as well as collecting Lithuanian folk tales. Exerted great influence on his younger cousin, Czeslaw Milosz, winner of the Nobel Prize for literature in 1980. Largely neglected during his lifetime, Milosz has increasingly come to be considered as an important figure in French poetry.

Principal collections of poetry: *Le Poème des décadences* (1899), *Les Sept Solitudes* (1906), *Les Éléments* (1911), *Poèmes* (1915), *Adramandoni* (1918), *La Confession de Lemuel* (1922), *Poèmes* (1929), *Dix-sept Poèmes de Milosz* (1937). All of Milosz's poetry is available in a two-volume edition published by André Silvaire.

BENJAMIN PÉRET

1899–1959. Earliest poems published in *Littérature*. Active and ardent Surrealist from the beginning of the movement (1924) until his death. Co-founder and first editor of the review *La Révolution Surréaliste*. Published what many consider to be the first Surrealist fiction in 1923, *Au 125 du boulevard Saint-Germain*. Collaborative works

include *152 Proverbes mis au goût du jour* with Paul Éluard and *Au grand jour,* an important Surrealist broadside, with Breton, Éluard and Aragon. Joined Communist Party in 1926, worked as Party organizer in Brazil in 1931, and fought in the Spanish Civil War. Arrested by the Germans in 1940 for "subversive activities," but managed to escape to Mexico. Later works include the editing of a number of anthologies.

Principal collections of poetry: *Le grand jeu* (1928), *De derrière les fagots* (1934), *Je sublime* (1936), *Feu central* (1947), *Air mexicain* (1952). All of Péret's poems have been collected in a two-volume *Oeuvres Complètes,* published by Éditions Losfeld.

In English: *Twenty Poems,* trans. by J. H. Matthews (M. J. Minard, 1965); *Children of the Quadrilateral,* trans. by Jane Barnard (Bitter Oleander, 1977).


MARCELIN PLEYNET

Born 1933. One of the founding editors of the review *Tel Quel,* of which he is the *secrétaire de rédaction.* Pleynet is also widely known as an art critic and has published a study of Lautréamont.

Principal collections of poetry: *Provisoires Amants des nègres* (1962), *Paysages en deux, suivis de Les Lignes de la prose* (1964), *Comme* (1965).


FRANCIS PONGE

Born 1899. Studied law in Paris and literature in Strasbourg. Peripheral contacts with Surrealists in late twenties. Between the wars worked as an editor and journalist. Joined the Communist Party in 1937 and was active during the war in organizing the Resistance movement among journalists. Broke with the Communists in 1947 and spent the following two years in Algeria. From 1952 to 1965 he was a professor at the Alliance Française in Paris. Since then, he has given many lectures abroad. An article by Sartre in the early forties praising his work was instrumental in bringing Ponge to the public's attention. Awarded the *Books Abroad*/Neustadt International Prize for Literature in 1974.

Principal collections: *Le Parti pris des choses* (1942), *Proêmes* (1948), *La Rage de l'expression* (1952), *Pour un Malherbe* (1965), *Le Savon* (1967), *La Fabrique du Pré* (1971). The greater part of Ponge's work has been gathered into *Le Grand Recueil* (3 vols., 1961), *Tome Premier* (1965), and *Le Nouveau Recueil* (1967).

In English: *Soap,* trans. by Lane Dunlop (Jonathan Cape, 1969); *The Voice of Things,* trans. by Beth Archer (McGraw-Hill, 1971); *Things,* trans. by Cid Corman (Grossman, 1971); *The Sun Placed in the Abyss,* trans. by Serge Gavronsky (Sun, 1977); *The Power of Language,* trans. by Serge Gavronsky (University of California Press, 1979).


JACQUES PRÉVERT

1900–1977. Member of the Surrealist movement in the late twenties. Traveled with the theatrical company Groupe Octobre from 1932 to 1936, writing many sketches and often acting in them himself. Throughout the thirties and forties wrote scenarios for a number of films, many of them now classics: *Le Crime de Monsieur Lange* (directed by Jean Renoir); *Drôle de drame, Quai des brumes, Le Jour se lève, Les Visiteurs du soir,* and *Les Enfants du paradis* (all directed by Marcel Carné). Many of Prévert's poems were set to music; as an artist, he exhibited photo-collages.

Principal collections of poetry: *Paroles* (1946), *Spectacle* (1951), *La Pluie et le beau temps* (1955), *Histoires* (1960).

Poetry in English: *Paroles*, trans. by Lawrence Ferlinghetti (City Lights, 1958); *Words for All Seasons*, trans. by Teo Savory (Unicorn Press, 1979).

### RAYMOND QUENEAU

1903–1976. Earned degree in philosophy in 1925. Participated in Surrealist activities in the late twenties; worked as journalist in the thirties. Joined Éditions Gallimard in 1938 and was named *secrétaire général* in 1941. Director of the Éditions Pléïade series and editor of Kojève's lectures on Hegel. Queneau was elected to the Académie Goncourt in 1951, was a member of the Sociéte Mathémathique de France, and a co-founder of the "College of Pataphysics." In addition to his poetry, Queneau's output includes seventeen novels (several of them available in English), short stories and studies of Miró, Vlaminck and other artists.

Principal collections of poetry: *Les Ziaux* (1943), *Bucoliques* (1947), *L'Instant fatal* (1948), *Petite cosmogonie portative* (1950), *Si tu t'imagines* (1952), *Le chien à la mandoline* (1958), *Cent mille milliards de poèmes* (1958), *Courir les rues* (1967), *Battre la campagne* (1968), *Fendre les flots* (1969).

Poetry in English: *Raymond Queneau*, trans. by Teo Savory (Unicorn Press, 1971).

### PIERRE REVERDY

1889–1960. Early friendships with Jacob, Apollinaire and many of the Cubist painters. One of the founders of the review *Nord-Sud* in 1917. Although never a part of the Surrealist movement, Reverdy was declared by Breton to be "the greatest poet of the time" in the first Surrealist Manifesto. Gradually withdrew from Paris literary life in the twenties. By 1926 he had settled in the rural village of Solesmes, near the abbey of Solesmes. He continued this secluded existence—with occasional trips to Paris and abroad—until his death. In addition to his poetry, Reverdy published three volumes of notebooks, two early novels, a collection of stories and a study of Picasso.

Principal collections of poetry: *Poèmes en prose* (1915), *La Lucarne cvale* (1916), *Les Ardoises du toit* (1918), *Les Jockeys camouflés* (1918), *La Guitare endormie* (1919), *Étoiles peintes* (1921), *Cravates de chanvre* (1922), *Grande Nature* (1925), *La Balle au bond* (1928), *Sources du vent* (1929), *Pierres blanches* (1930), *Ferraille* (1937), *Plein Verre* (1940). The majority of Reverdy's poems were gathered into the following two volumes: *Plupart du temps: poèmes 1915–1922* (1945) and *Main d'oeuvre: 1913–1949* (1949).

Poetry in English: *Selected Poems*, trans. by Kenneth Rexroth (New Directions, 1969).

### DENIS ROCHE

Born 1937. Spent early childhood in the Caribbean and South America. Roche has been connected with the review *Tel Quel* since its founding in the early sixties. Active as a translator, he has published French versions of Pound's *Pisan Cantos* and the *ABC of Reading*, as well as translations of works by e e cummings, Charles Olson, Charlotte Brontë and William Blake. Roche has also written a novel (*Louve basse*, 1976) and numerous essays.

Principal collections of poetry: *Récits complets* (1963), *Les Idées centésimales de Miss Elanize* (1964), *Éros énergumène* (1968), *Le Mécrit* (1972).

## JACQUES ROUBAUD

Born 1932. Roubaud is one of the editors of the review *Change*. He has published a volume of free translations from the Japanese and translations of the American poet William Bronk. Roubaud has visited the United States several times and is the editor of the most comprehensive anthology of contemporary American poetry to have appeared in France. He is professor of mathematics at the University of Nanterre.

Principal collections of poetry: *Σ* (1967), *Renga*, with Octavio Paz, Charles Tomlinson and Edoardo Sanguineti (1971), *Autobiographie chapitre dix* (1977).

## CLAUDE ROYET-JOURNOUD

Born 1941. One of the founding editors of the review *Siecle à mains*. Lived in London for several years during the sixties; translations of George Oppen.

Principal collections of poetry: *Le Renversement* (1972), *La Notion d'obstacle* (1978).

In English: *Reversal*, trans. by Keith Waldrop (Hellcoal, 1973); *Até*, trans. by Keith Waldrop (Blue Guitar, 1981).

## SAINT-JOHN PERSE (Alexis Saint-Léger Léger)

1887–1975. Born on a small coral island near Guadeloupe, Saint-Léger-les-Feuilles, which was owned by his family. Went to France in 1899. Joined diplomatic service in 1914. From 1916–1920, Secretary of the French Embassy at Peking. Served in a variety of diplomatic posts in Washington and Paris after 1921. In 1933, appointed Permanent Secretary for Foreign Affairs. Fled to England and from there to Canada and the United States after the fall of France in 1940. In 1941, at the invitation of Archibald MacLeish, was appointed Literary Advisor to the Library of Congress. After the war, he continued to live in Washington. Saint-John Perse was awarded the Nobel Prize for literature in 1960.

Principal collections of poetry: *Éloges* (1911), *Anabase* (1924), *Exil, suivi de Poème à l'étrangère, Pluies, Neiges* (1946), *Vents* (1953), *Chronique* (1960), *L'Ordre des oiseaux* (1962), *Poésie* (1963). All of Saint-John Perse's work is available in a volume published by the Éditions Pléiade.

In English: *Collected Poems*, trans. by several hands (Princeton University Press, 1971).

## VICTOR SEGALEN

1878–1919. Studied medicine at the Naval School in Bordeaux. In 1901 traveled to Tahiti via New York and San Francisco to join his first ship. Three months after Gauguin's death in 1903, Segalen visited the painter's hut on Hiva Hoa and studied his manuscripts. This led to the prose work, *Les Immémoriaux*, published pseudonymously in 1907. In China from 1909 to 1913, he was professor of medicine at Tientsin and personal physician to the Chinese president. Published *Stèles* (1912) in an edition of eighty-one copies. In China again in 1914 as part of an archaeological mission led

by Edouard Chavannes. Literary friendships with Huysmans, Remy de Gourmont, Saint-Pol Roux and Claudel. Segalen also wrote a number of libretti for Debussy. His many publications and reputation are largely posthumous.

Principal collection of poetry: *Stèles* (1912). Posthumous publications of poetry: *Stèles, Peintures, Équipée* (1955), *Ode, suivi de Thibet* (1963).

Poetry in English: *Stelae*, trans. by Nathaniel Tarn (Unicorn Press, 1969).


PHILIPPE SOUPAULT

Born 1897. Founder of the review *Littérature* in 1919 with Breton and Aragon. Co-author with Breton of *Les Champs magnétiques* (1920). Active in French Dada and central figure of Surrealism in its early years, though he eventually drifted away from the movement. Prolific novelist and essayist. Starting in 1925, innumerable travels to all parts of the world. Taught for one semester at Pennsylvania State College in 1929; in 1944 was visiting professor at Swarthmore College. A friend of James Joyce, Soupault participated in the revisions of the translation into French of *Anna Livia Plurabelle*. One of his early novels, *Last Nights of Paris* (1928), was translated into English by William Carlos Williams. Soupault was arrested by the Germans in 1942 and spent six months in prison. He was active as a journalist during the latter part of the war. Soupault has also written pieces for radio and theater, edited one of the first complete editions of Lautréamont (1927) and translated Blake's *Songs of Innocence and Songs of Experience*.

Principal collections of poetry: *Aquarium* (1917), *Rose des vents* (1920), *Westwego* (1922), *Georgia* (1926), *Poésies Complètes 1917–1937* (1937), *L'Arme secrète* (1946). Soupault's complete poems, *Poèmes et Poésies: 1917–1973*, were published in a single volume by Grasset in 1973.


JULES SUPERVIELLE

1884–1960. Born in Montevideo, Uruguay. Supervielle went to France at the age of ten, where he completed his education, and thereafter divided his time between Uruguay and France. Early literary friendships with Gide, Valéry and Jacques Rivière. Meeting with Rilke in 1923, whose work was to exert a great influence on his own. In addition to his poetry, Supervielle wrote a number of novels and collections of stories, as well as several plays.

Principal collections of poetry: *Gravitations* (1925), *Le Forçat innocent* (1930), *Les Amis inconnus* (1934), *La Fable du monde* (1938), *1939–1945* (1946), *Oublieuse Mémoire* (1949), *Naissances* (1951), *L'Escalier* (1956).

Poetry in English: *Selected Writings*, trans. by several hands (New Directions, 1967).


TRISTAN TZARA (Sami Rosenstock)

1896–1963. Born in Rumania. With Hugo Ball and Richard Huelsenbeck, Tzara founded the Dada movement in Zurich in 1916. Arrived in Paris in 1919 and led French Dada activities until 1922 (when the movement was declared officially dead). Serious quarrel with Breton in 1922, which lasted until 1929, when Tzara became a member of the Surrealist group. Left Surrealism in the mid-thirties to join the Communist Party. In Spain during the Civil War as a delegate of the "Association for the Defense

of Culture." Participated in the Resistance during the war. In addition to his poetry, Tzara wrote numerous essays, polemics and manifestoes, particularly during the Dada period, as well as several plays.

Principal collections of poetry: *Vingt-cinq poèmes* (1918), *Cinéma calendrier coeur abstrait maisons* (1920), *De nos oiseaux* (1923), *Indicateur des chemins de coeur* (1928), *L'Homme approximatif* (1931), *Où boivent les loups* (1932), *Midis gagnés* (1939), *Terre sur Terre* (1946), *Phases* (1949), *Parler seul* (1950), *Le temps naissant* (1955), *Le fruit permis* (1956), *Frère bois* (1957).

Poetry in English: *Selected Poems*, trans. by Lee Harwood (Trigram Press, 1975); *Approximate Man and Other Writings*, trans. by Mary Ann Caws (Wayne State, 1973).

ALAIN VEINSTEIN

Born 1942. Veinstein lives in Paris and works for the *France Culture* section of the French national radio.

Principal collections of poetry: *Répétition sur l'amas* (1974), *Recherche des dispositions anciennes* (1977), *Vers l'absence de soutien* (1978).

# Acknowledgments

*Grateful acknowledgment is made to the following for permission to include the poems and translations in this anthology:*

ANNE-MARIE ALBIACH

"Énigme" (I, II, IV, IX) from *État*, © Mercure de France, 1971. Reprinted by permission of Mercure de France.
"Enigma" (I, II, IV, IX), trans. by Keith Waldrop. Printed by permission of Keith Waldrop.

GUILLAUME APOLLINAIRE

"Zone," "Le Pont Mirabeau," "Crépuscule," "Annie," "Automne," "1909," "Automne malade," "Cors de chasse" from *Alcools*, © Éditions Gallimard, 1920; "La petite auto," "Toujours," "La jolie rousse" from *Calligrammes*, © Éditions Gallimard, 1925. Reprinted by permission of Éditions Gallimard.
"Zone," trans. by Samuel Beckett, from *Collected Poems in English & French*, by Samuel Beckett, © Grove Press, 1977. Reprinted by permission of Samuel Beckett and Grove Press. "Mirabeau Bridge," trans. by Richard Wilbur. Printed by permission of Richard Wilbur. "Dusk," trans. by Dudley Fitts. Reprinted by permission of Mrs. Dudley Fitts. "Annie," trans. by William Meredith, from *Alcools*, Doubleday & Co., 1964. Reprinted by permission of William Meredith. "Autumn," trans. by W. S. Merwin. Reprinted by permission of W.S. Merwin. "1909," trans. by Robert Bly. Reprinted by permission of Robert Bly. "Automne Malade" and "Hunting Horns," trans. by Paul Blackburn. Printed by permission of the Estate of Paul Blackburn. "Always," trans. by Roger Shattuck, from *Selected Writings of Guillaume Apollinaire*, New Directions, 1971. Reprinted by permission of New Directions Publishing Corporation. "The Little Car," trans. by Ron Padgett. Printed by permission of Ron Padgett.

"The Pretty Redhead," trans. by James Wright, from *Collected Poems*, by James Wright, Wesleyan University Press, 1971. Reprinted by permission of Mrs. James Wright and Wesleyan University Press.


LOUIS ARAGON

"Poème à crier dans les ruines" from *La Grande Gaîté*, Librairie Gallimard, 1929; de "Valse du Tcheliabtraktrostroi" from *Hourra l'oural*, Éd. Denoël et Steele, 1934; "Les Lilas et les roses," "Tapisserie de la Grande Peur," "Zone libre" from *Le Crève-Coeur*, Librairie Gallimard, 1941.

"Poem to Shout in the Ruins," trans. by Geoffrey Young. Printed by permission of Geoffrey Young. From "Tcheliabtraktrostroi Waltz," trans. by Nancy Cunard. Reprinted by permission of the Estate of Nancy Cunard. "The Lilacs and the Roses," and "The Unoccupied Zone," trans. by Louis MacNeice, from *The Collected Poems of Louis MacNeice*, Oxford University Press, 1966. Reprinted by permission of Oxford University Press. "Tapestry of the Great Fear," trans. by Malcolm Cowley, from *Aragon: Poet of the French Resistance*, ed. by Hannah Josephson & Malcolm Cowley, Duell, Sloan, & Pearce, 1945. Reprinted by permission of Malcolm Cowley.


ANTONIN ARTAUD

"Là où d'autres . . . ," "Description d'un état physique," "Vitres de son", "Il me manque . . ." , "Toute l'écriture . . ." , "Manifeste en langage clair", "Correspondance de la momie" from volume I of *Oeuvres complètes*, © Éditions Gallimard, 1956. Reprinted by permission of Éditions Gallimard and Farrar, Straus, & Giroux, Inc.

"Where others" . . . , "Description of a Physical State," "What I lack" . . . , "All writing" . . . , "Manifesto in Clear Language," trans. by Helen Weaver, from *Antonin Artaud: Selected Writings*, © Farrar, Straus, & Giroux, Inc, 1976. Reprinted by permission of Farrar, Straus, & Giroux, Inc. "The Panes of Sound," and "Correspondence of the Mummy," trans. by Paul Zweig, from *Antonin Artaud: Black Poet and Other Texts*, M. J. Minard, 1966. Reprinted by permission of Paul Zweig.


YVES BONNEFOY

"Vrai nom," "Quelle parole . . . ," "Une Voix," "Tais-toi . . . ," "Lieu de la salamandre" from *Du mouvement et de l'immobilité de Douve*, © Mercure de France, 1953; "L'Imperfection est la cime," "Le Ravin," "La même voix, toujours" from *Hier régnant désert*, © Mercure de France, 1958; "L'Arbre, la lampe" and "Le Sang, la note si" from *Pierre écrite*, © Mercure de France, 1965; "Heure . . ." from *Dans le leurre du seuil*, © Mercure de France, 1975. Reprinted by permission of Mercure de France.

"True Name," "What word springs . . . ," "Place of the Salamander", trans. by Galway Kinnell, from *On the Motion and Immobility of Douve*, Ohio University Press, 1968. Reprinted by permission of Galway Kinnell and Ohio University Press. "A Voice," "Quiet . . . ," "The Same Voice, Still," "Utmost hour . . . ," trans. by Paul Auster. Printed by permission of Paul Auster. "Imperfection Is the Summit," "The Ravine," "The Tree, The Lamp," "Blood, The Note *B*" trans. by Anthony Rudolf, from *Yves Bonnefoy: Selected Poems*, Jonathan Cape, 1968. Reprinted by permission of Anthony Rudolf.

ANDRÉ DU BOUCHET

"Le Moteur blanc" from *Dans la chaleur vacante*, © Mercure de France, 1961; "Ajournement" and "La Lumière de la lame" from *OU LE SOLEIL*, © Mercure de France, 1968. Reprinted by permission of Mercure de France.

"The White Motor," "Postponement," "The Light of the Blade," trans. by Paul Auster, from *The Uninhabited: Selected Poems of André du Bouchet*, Living Hand, 1976. Reprinted by permission of Paul Auster.

ANDRÉ BRETON

"Tournesol", "L'Union libre", "Non-lieu", "Facteur Cheval", "Une Branche d'ortie entre par la fenêtre", "Le grand secours meurtrier", "Le marquis de Sade . . ." from *Clair de terre*, © Éditions Gallimard, 1966; "Sur la route de San Romano" from *Poèmes*, © Éditions Gallimard, 1948. Reprinted by permission of Éditions Gallimard.

"Sunflower", trans. by Edouard Roditi, from *Young Cherry Trees Secured Against Hares*, View, 1946. Reprinted by permission of Edouard Roditi. "Free Union" and "A Branch of Nettle Enters through the Window" trans. by David Antin. Reprinted by permission of David Antin. "No Grounds for Prosecution", trans. by Paul Auster, from *A Little Anthology of Surrealist Poets*, S. B. Press, 1972. Reprinted by permission of Paul Auster. "Postman Cheval", trans. by David Gascoyne, from *Selected Verse Translations*, Oxford University Press, 1970. Reprinted by permission of David Gascoyne and Oxford University Press. "Lethal Relief", trans. by Samuel Beckett. Reprinted by permission of Samuel Beckett. "The Marquis de Sade . . ." trans. by Keith Waldrop. Reprinted by permission of Keith Waldrop. "On the Road to San Romano", trans. by Charles Simic & Michael Benedikt. Reprinted by permission of Charles Simic and Michael Benedikt.

BLAISE CENDRARS

"Crépitements", "Dernière Heure", "Aux 5 coins", "Mee Too Buggi", "La Tête" from *Du monde entier: poésies complètes 1912–1924*, © Éditions Denoël, 1947; "En route pour Dakar", "Orion", "Trouées", "Hommage à Guillaume Apollinaire", "Au coeur du monde" from *Au coeur du monde: poésies complètes 1924–1929*, © Éditions Denoël, 1947. Reprinted by permission of Éditions Denoël.

"Sputterings", "The Head", trans. by Ron Padgett. Reprinted by permission of Ron Padgett. "Stop Press", "At the Five Corners", "Me Too Boogie", "Homage to Guillaume Apollinaire", "In the World's Heart", trans. by Anselm Hollo. Reprinted by permission of Anselm Hollo. "On the Way to Dakar", "Orion", and "Clearings", trans. by John Dos Passos, from *Panama, or The Adventures of My Seven Uncles*, Harper and Brothers, 1931. Reprinted by permission of Mrs. John Dos Passos.

AIMÉ CÉSAIRE

"N'ayez point pitié", "Soleil serpent", "Phrase", "Perdition", "Au delà", "Prophétie", from *Les armes miraculeuses*, © Éditions Gallimard, 1946. Reprinted by permission of Éditions Gallimard.

"Have No Mercy", "Serpent Sun", "Sentence", "Perdition", "Beyond", "Proph-

ecy", trans. by Clayton Eshleman and Annette Smith. Printed by permission of Clayton Eshleman and Annette Smith.

RENÉ CHAR

"Les Seigneurs de Maussane", "Toute vie" . . . , from *Les Matinaux*, © Éditions Gallimard, 1950; "A\*\*\*", from *A une serenité crispée*, © Éditions Gallimard, 1951; "A la santé du serpent", from *Fureur et mystère*, © Éditions Gallimard, 1962; "Vers l'arbre-frère aux jours comptés", "Victoire éclair", "La Chambre dans l'espace", from *La Parole en archipel*, © Éditions Gallimard, 1962; "Lutteurs", "Septentrion", "Faction du Muet", "Convergence des multiples", from *Retour Amont*, © Éditions Gallimard, 1966. Reprinted by permission of Éditions Gallimard.

"The Lords of Maussane" and "Every life . . . ", trans. by James Wright, from *Hypnos Waking: Poems and Prose by René Char*, edited by Jackson Mathews, Random House, 1957. Reprinted by permission of Mrs. James Wright and Random House, Inc. "To the Health of the Serpent", trans. by Jackson Mathews, from *Hypnos Waking*. Reprinted by permission of Random House, Inc. "To . . . ," trans. by Michael Hamburger. Reprinted by permission of Michael Hamburger. "To Friend-Tree of Counted Days", trans. by William Carlos Williams, from *Hypnos Waking*. Reprinted by permission of the Estate of William Carlos Williams and Random House, Inc. "Lightning Victory" and "Room in Space", trans. by W. S. Merwin, from *Hypnos Waking*. Reprinted by permission of W. S. Merwin and Random House, Inc. "Fighters", "Septentrion", "Faction du Muet", "Convergence of the Many", trans. by Thomas Merton. Reprinted by permission of the Estate of Thomas Merton.

JEAN-PAUL DE DADELSEN

"Grand livre", "Peupliers et trembles", "Psaume", "Cantique de Jonas", from *Jonas*, © Éditions Gallimard, 1962. Reprinted by permission of Éditions Gallimard.

"The Great Book", "Poplars and Aspens", "Psalm", "Jonah's Canticle", trans. by Anselm Hollo. Printed by permission of Anselm Hollo.

JEAN DAIVE

"Le cri-cerveau", from *Le cri-cerveau*, © Éditions Gallimard, 1978. Reprinted by permission of Éditions Gallimard.

"Brain-Cry", trans. by Paul Auster. Printed by permission of Paul Auster.

RENÉ DAUMAL

"Triste petit train de vie", "La peau de lumière", "La Révolution en été", "Le Pays des métamorphoses", "Jésus devant Pilate", from *Poésie noire, poésie blanche*, © Éditions Gallimard, 1954; "Le Mot et la mouche", from *Les Pouvoirs de la parole*, © Éditions Gallimard, 1962. Reprinted by permission of Éditions Gallimard.

"The skin of light . . . ", trans. by Michael Benedikt. Reprinted by permission of Michael Benedikt. "Sad Little Round of Life", trans. by Kenneth Rexroth. Reprinted by permission of Kenneth Rexroth. "Revolution in Summertime" and "The Country

of Metamorphoses", trans. by Armand Schwerner. Printed by permission of Armand Schwerner. "Jesus before Pilate", trans. by Katharine Washburn. Printed by permission of Katharine Washburn. "Poetry and Thought", trans. by Michael Wood. Reprinted by permission of Michael Wood.

MICHEL DEGUY

"O la grande apposition . . . ", "Toi", "Les Yeux", from *Poèmes de la presqu'île*, © Éditions Gallimard, 1961; "C'est entre nous . . . ", from *Biefs*, © Éditions Gallimard, 1964; "Alluvion . . . ", "Quand le vent . . . ", from *Ouï dire*, © Éditions Gallimard, 1966; "Le mur . . . ," from *Tombeau de du Bellay*, © Éditions Gallimard, 1973. Reprinted by permission of Éditions Gallimard.
"O great apposition . . . ", "The Eyes", "Alluvium", "When the wind . . . ," "The wall . . . ", trans. by Clayton Eshleman. Printed by permission of Clayton Eshleman. "You", "It's between ourselves . . . ," trans. by Anthony Rudolf. Reprinted by permission of Anthony Rudolf.

ALAIN DELAHAYE

"La colline, la folie", "Logique", "Deux paysages, grammaire", "Grande prairie", "Parce qu'en détruisant il crée", "Le paysage intense", from *L'être perdu*, © Maeght Éditeur, 1977. Reprinted by permission of Maeght Éditeur.
"The Hill, The Frenzy", "Logic", "Two Landscapes, Grammar", trans. by Anthony Barnett. Printed by permission of Anthony Barnett. "Broad Meadow", "Because in Destroying He Creates", "The Intense Landscape", trans. by Paul Auster. Printed by permission of Paul Auster.

PHILIPPE DENIS

"Terre . . . ", "Le monde . . . ", "Étoile . . . ", "A l'amarre . . . ", "A vivre . . . ", from *Cahier d'ombres*, © Mercure de France, 1974. Reprinted by permission of Mercure de France. "Sur les ailes . . . ", from *Revif*, © Maeght Éditeur, 1978. Reprinted by permission of Maeght Éditeur.
"Earth . . . ", "Already . . . ", "A star . . . ", "Moored . . . ", "To live . . . ", "On the butterfly's . . . ", trans. by Paul Auster. Printed by permission of Paul Auster.

ROBERT DESNOS

"J'ai tant rêvé de toi", "Non l'amour n'est pas mort", "La Voix de Robert Desnos", from *Corps et biens*, © Éditions Gallimard, 1953; "Mi-route", "Coucou", from *Fortunes*, © Éditions Gallimard, 1945; "Couchée", from *Destinée arbitraire*, © Éditions Gallimard, 1975; "L'Épitaphe", from *Contrée*, © Éditions Gallimard, 1962. Reprinted by permission of Éditions Gallimard.
"I Have Dreamed of You So Much", trans. by Paul Auster, from *A Little Anthology of Surrealist Poets*, S. B. Press, 1972. Reprinted by permission of Paul Auster. "No Love Is Not Dead", "The Voice of Robert Desnos", "Lying Down", trans. by Bill Zavatsky. Printed by permission of Bill Zavatsky. "Midway", trans. by George Quasha. Reprinted by permission of George Quasha. "Cuckoo," trans. by Armand Schwerner.

Printed by permission of Armand Schwerner. "Epitaph", trans. by Kenneth Rexroth. Reprinted by permission of Kenneth Rexroth.

### JACQUES DUPIN

"Le Règne minéral", "La Soif", "Reste le seul . . . ", "Mon corps . . . ," from *Gravir*, © Éditions Gallimard, 1963. "Ouverte . . . ," "La vague . . . ," "Il m'est interdit . . . ", "Saluons . . . ", "Dans l'attente . . . ", "Sous la frayeur . . . ," from *L'embrasure*, © Éditions Gallimard, 1969. Reprinted by permission of Éditions Gallimard.
"Mineral Kingdom", "Thirst", "The only beating . . .", "My body . . .," "Opened . . .", "The wave . . . ", "I am forbidden . . . ," "Let us salute . . . ," "Waiting . . . ," "Gripped by the dread . . . ," trans. by Paul Auster, from *Fits and Starts: Selected Poems of Jacques Dupin*, Living Hand, 1974. Reprinted by permission of Paul Auster.

### PAUL ÉLUARD

"L'Invention", "L'amoureuse", "Le sourd et l'aveugle", "Seconde nature V", from *Capitale de la douleur*, © Éditions Gallimard, 1926; "Confections", "A perte de vue dans le sens de mon corps", "Chassé", from *La Vie immédiate*, © Éditions Gallimard, 1951; "Liberté", from *Poésie et Vérité*, © 1942; "Du Fond de l'abîme", from *Le dur désir de durer*, © 1946. Reprinted by permission of Éditions Gallimard.
"Lady Love", "Second Nature", "Confections", "Out of Sight in the Direction of My Body", trans. by Samuel Beckett, from *Collected Poems in English & French*, by Samuel Beckett, © Grove Press, 1977. Reprinted by permission of Samuel Beckett and Grove Press. "The Invention", trans. by Samuel Beckett. Reprinted by permission of Samuel Beckett. "The Deaf and Blind", trans. by Paul Auster. Reprinted by permission of Paul Auster. "Hunted", trans. by David Gascoyne, from *Selected Verse Translations*, Oxford University Press, 1970. Reprinted by permission of David Gascoyne and Oxford University Press. "Liberty", trans. by W. S. Merwin. Reprinted by permission of W. S. Merwin. "From the Death of the Abyss", trans. by Stephen Spender & Frances Cornford. Reprinted by permission of Stephen Spender.

### LÉON-PAUL FARGUE

"Dans les villes jaunes . . . ", "Le boulevard . . . ", "Dans un quartier . . . ", "Une odeur nocturne . . . ", "On a trouvé . . . ," "Colère," "Postface", from *Poésies*, © Éditions Gallimard, 1963. Reprinted by permission of Éditions Gallimard.
"In yellow towns . . . ," "The boulevard . . . ", "On the body . . . ," trans. by Lydia Davis. Printed by permission of Lydia Davis. "In a quarter . . . " and "A fragrance of night . . . ", trans. by Wallace Stevens, from *Opus Posthumous*, by Wallace Stevens (Alfred A. Knopf, Inc.), © by Elsie Stevens and Holly Stevens, 1957. Reprinted by permission of Random House, Inc. "Tumult", trans. by Maria Jolas. Reprinted by permission of Maria Jolas. "Nocturne", trans. by Kenneth Rexroth. Reprinted by permission of Kenneth Rexroth.

### JEAN FOLLAIN

"Mutilation volontaire" and "Paysage de l'enfant allant chez le régents", from *La Main chaude*, © Éditions Gallimard, 1933. Reprinted by permission of Éditions Galli-

mard. "Soirs d'encre", from *Ici-Bas*, © Éditions du Journal des Poètes. Reprinted by permission of Madeleine Follain. "Noir d'une enfance", from *Les Poèmes de l'année*, ed. by Alain Bosquet and Pierre Seghers, Ed. Seghers, 1956. Reprinted by permission of Madeleine Follain. "L'Oeuf", "Pensées d'octobre", "Chien aux écoliers", "Vie", from *Territoires*, © Éditions Gallimard, 1953; "Fin de siècle", "Le Costume du soir", from *Des Heures*, © Éditions Gallimard, 1960; "Ève", from *Appareil de la terre*, © Éditions Gallimard, 1964. Reprinted by permission of Éditions Gallimard.

"Voluntary Mutilation", "Landscape of a Child on His Way to the Place of the Regents", "Evenings of Ink", "The Egg", "October Thoughts", "End of a Century", "The Evening Suit", "Eve", trans. by W. S. Merwin, from *Transparence of the World: Poems by Jean Follain* (Atheneum), © by W. S. Merwin, 1968, 1969. Reprinted by permission of W. S. Merwin and Atheneum Publishers. "Child's Blackness", "Dog with Schoolboys", "Life", trans. by Keith Waldrop. Reprinted by permission of Keith Waldrop.


ANDRÉ FRÉNAUD

"Épitaphe" and "Maison à vendre", from *Les Rois Mages: poèmes 1938–1943*, © Éditions Gallimard, 1977; "Il n'y a pas de paradis", "Machine inutile", "Pour boire aux amis", "Haineusement mon amour la poésie", "Je ne t'ai jamais oubliée", from *Il n'y a pas de paradis: poèmes 1943–1960*, © Éditions Gallimard, 1962. Reprinted by permission of Éditions Gallimard.

"Epitaph", "House for Sale", "To Drink to Friends", trans. by Keith Bosley, from *A Little Round O*, Interim Press, 1978. Reprinted by permission of Keith Bosley. "There is No Paradise", "Useless Machine", "Hatefully Poetry My Love", trans. by Serge Gavronsky, from *Poems and Texts*, October House, 1968. Reprinted by permission of Serge Gavronsky. "I Have Never Forgotten You", trans. by Kenneth Rexroth. Reprinted by permission of Kenneth Rexroth.


ROGER GIROUX

"La ligne sinueuse . . . ", "Et peut-être . . . ", "Un oiseau . . . ," "Le centre . . . ", "Le temps . . . ", "Reine d'aller . . . ", "Nue . . . ," "Beauté perdue . . . ," "Visage . . . ," "C'était . . . ," "Sa mémoire . . . ," "loin . . . ," "des lèvres . . . ," from *L'arbre le temps*, © Mercure de France, 1964. Reprinted by permission of Mercure de France.

"Once more . . . ," "Queen of going . . . ," "Naked . . . ," "Lost beauty . . . ," Surface . . . ," "This memory . . . ," "far . . . ," "touched . . . ," trans. by Anthony Barnett. Printed by permission of Anthony Barnett. "The sinuous . . . ," "And perhaps . . . ," "The center . . . ," "It was . . . ," trans. by Paul Auster. Reprinted by permission of Paul Auster. "A bird . . . ," trans. by Jonathan Griffin. Reprinted by permission of Jonathan Griffin.


EUGÈNE GUILLEVIC

"Face," from *Terraqué*, © Éditions Gallimard, 1942; "Que déjà je me lève . . . ," from *Terre à bonheur*, © Éditions Pierre Seghers, 1952; "La mer . . . ," "Soyons justes . . . ," from *Carnac*, © Éditions Gallimard, 1961; "L'éternité . . . ," "Un bahut,"

"La flamme," "Un marteau," from *Sphère*, © Éditions Gallimard, 1963; "Espagne," from *Avec*, © Éditions Gallimard, 1966. Reprinted by permission of Éditions Gallimard.

"Face," "Let me get up early . . . ," "A Cabinet," "The Flame," trans. by Teo Savory, from *Guillevic: Selected Poems*, Penguin Books, 1974. Reprinted by permission of Teo Savory. "Eternity . . . ," "A Hammer," "Spain," trans. by Denise Levertov, from *Guillevic: Selected Poems* (New Directions), © by Denise Levertov Goodman and Eugène Guillevic, 1968, 1969. Reprinted by permission of New Directions Publishing Corporation. "The sea . . ." and "Be fair . . . ," trans. by John Montague. Reprinted by permission of John Montague.

EMMANUEL HOCQUARD

"Les Espions Thraces dormaient près des vaisseaux," "Anno Aetatis XXXV," from *Album d'images de la Villa Harris*, © Librairie Hachette, 1977; "Sur une Aphrodite anadyomène," "Trois Leçons de morale," from *Les Dernières nouvelles de l'expédition sont datées du 15 février 17 . . .* , © Librairie Hachette, 1978. Reprinted by permission of Librairie Hachette.

"The Thracian Spies Lay Sleeping Beside the Ships," "Anno Aetatis XXXV," "Of a Sea-born Aphrodite," "Three Moral Tales," trans. by Michael Palmer. Printed by permission of Michael Palmer.

EDMOND JABÈS

"La chute et l'exil," from *Le Retour au livre*, © Éditions Gallimard, 1965; "Réponse à une lettre," from *Aély*, © Éditions Gallimard, 1972. Reprinted by permission of Éditions Gallimard.

"Fall and Exile," trans. by Rosmarie Waldrop, from *The Book of Yukel & Return to the Book* (Wesleyan University Press), © 1977 by Rosmarie Waldrop. Reprinted by permission of Rosmarie Waldrop and Wesleyan University Press. "Answer to a Letter," trans. by Rosmarie Waldrop. Reprinted by permission of Rosmarie Waldrop.

MAX JACOB

"Poème déclamatoire," "Poème," "La rue Ravignan," "Moeurs littéraires" (I, II), "La Clef," "Les vrais miracles," "La mendiante de Naples," "Au pays des collines," "Le Centaure," "Le Bibliophile," "Ma Vie," "Le Papier de tenture de M. R.K.," "Littérature et poésie," from *Le cornet à dés*, © Éditions Gallimard, 1945. Reprinted by permission of Éditions Gallimard.

From *The Dice Cup*, by Max Jacob, Sun, 1979: "Declamatory Poem," trans. by Michael Brownstein; "The Rue Ravignan," "The Beggar Woman of Naples," "In the Hill Country," "Literature and Poetry," trans. by John Ashbery; "The Key," "The Bibliophile," "My Life," trans. by Ron Padgett. Reprinted by permission of the translators. "Poem," "Literary Manners" (I, II), trans. by Jerome Rothenberg. Reprinted by permission of Jerome Rothenberg. "Miracles Real Miracles," "The Centaur," trans. by Armand Schwerner. Reprinted by permission of Armand Schwerner. "The Wallpaper of Mr. R.K.," trans. by Andrei Codrescu, from *For*

*Max Jacob*, by Andrei Codrescu, Tree Books, 1974. Reprinted by permission of Andrei Codrescu.

PHILIPPE JACCOTTET

"La Veillée funèbre," from *L'Ignorant*, © Éditions Gallimard, 1958; "Une semaison . . . ," "Lune d'hiver," "Là où la terre . . . ," "Je marche . . . ," "La parfaite . . . ," "Poids des pierres . . . ," "Fleurs . . . ," "Aube," from *Airs*, © Éditions Gallimard, 1967; "Cascade noire . . . ," from *La Semaison*, © Éditions Gallimard, 1971. Reprinted by permission of Éditions Gallimard.
"The Vigil," trans. by Anthony Rudolf. Reprinted by permission of Anthony Rudolf. "A sowing of tears . . ." and "Dawn," trans. by W. S. Merwin, from *Selected Translations 1948–1968* (Atheneum), © by W. S. Merwin, 1968. Reprinted by permission of W. S. Merwin and Atheneum Publishers. "Where earth . . . ," "I walk . . . ," "Perfect . . . ," "Weight of stones . . . ," "Flowers . . . ," trans. by Paul Auster. Reprinted by permission of Paul Auster. "Winter Moon," trans. by Charles Tomlinson. Reprinted by permission of Charles Tomlinson. "Black cascade . . . ," trans. by Michael Hamburger, from *Seedtime*, © New Directions, 1977. Reprinted by permission of Michael Hamburger and New Directions Publishing Corporation.

PIERRE JEAN JOUVE

"Après le déluge," from *Les Noces*, © Mercure de France, 1931; "Car la peau blanche . . . ," "Gravida," from *Sueur de Sang*, © Mercure de France, 1933; "Une seule femme endormie," "Blanches hanches," from *Matière céleste*, © Mercure de France, 1937; "Nous avons étonné . . . ," "Lorsque," from *Kyrie*, © Mercure de France, 1938; "A soi-même," from *Diadème*, © Mercure de France, 1949; "Le travail . . . ," from *Moires*, © Mercure de France, 1962; "Promenade," from *Ébauches*, © Mercure de France, 1966. Reprinted by permission of Mercure de France.
"After the Flood" and "Work . . . ," trans. by John Montague. Reprinted by permission of John Montague. "For white skin . . . ," "We have amazed . . . ," "When," "To Himself," "A Walk," trans. by Keith Bosley, from *An Idiom of Night: Poems of Pierre Jean Jouve*, Rapp & Whiting, 1968. Reprinted by permission of Keith Bosley. "Gravida" and "A Lone Woman Asleep," trans. by David Gascoyne, from *Selected Verse Translations*, Oxford University Press, 1970. Reprinted by permission of David Gascoyne and Oxford University Press. "White Haunches," trans. by Kenneth Rexroth. Reprinted by permission of Kenneth Rexroth.

VALERY LARBAUD

"Ode," "Le Masque," "Matin de novembre près d'Abingdon," "Alma Perdida," "Musique après une lecture," "Ma Muse," "Le Don de soi-même," from *Les Poésies de A.O. Barnabooth*, © Éditions Gallimard, 1948. Reprinted by permission of Éditions Gallimard.
"Ode," trans. by William Jay Smith, from *Poems of a Multi-Millionaire*, Grove Press, 1955. Reprinted by permission of William Jay Smith. "The Mask," "November Morning near Abingdon," "Alma Perdida," "Music after Reading," "My Muse," "The Gift of Oneself," trans. by Ron Padgett & Bill Zavatsky, from *The Poems of A.O.*

*Barnabooth*, Mushinsha, 1977. Reprinted by permission of Ron Padgett and Bill Zavatsky.


ROBERT MARTEAU

"Métamorphose des amants," from *Royaumes*, © Éditions du Seuil, 1962; "Là-bas," "Banderilles noires," "Salamandre," from *Travaux sur la terre*, © Éditions du Seuil, 1966. Reprinted by permission of Éditions du Seuil. "Stèle," from *Sibylles*, Éditions Galanis, 1971. Reprinted by permission of Robert Marteau. "Innommé toujours. . . ." Reprinted by permission of Robert Marteau.
"The Metamorphosis of Lovers" and "Down There," trans. by John Montague. Reprinted by permission of John Montague. "Black Banderillas," "Salamander," "Stele," trans. by Anne Winters, from *Salamander: Selected Poems of Robert Marteau*, © Princeton University Press, 1979. Reprinted by permission of Princeton University Press. "Unnamed always . . . ," trans. by Louis Simpson. Reprinted by permission of Louis Simpson.


HENRI MICHAUX

"Mes Occupations," "La Simplicité," "Intervention," from *Mes Proprietés*, © Éditions Gallimard, 1929; "L'Avenir," from *La Nuit remue*, © Éditions Gallimard, 1967; "Repos dans le malheur," from *Plume*, © Éditions Gallimard, 1963; "Je vous écris d'un pays lointain", from *Lointain intérieur*, © Éditions Gallimard, 1938. Reprinted by permission of Éditions Gallimard .
"My Occupations," "Simplicity," "Intervention," "I Am Writing To You from a Far-off Country", trans. by Richard Ellmann, from *Henri Michaux: Selected Writings*, © New Directions Publishing Corporation, 1968. Reprinted by permission of New Directions Publishing Corporation. "Tomorrow," trans. by Armand Schwerner. Reprinted by permission of Armand Schwerner. "Repose in Calamity," trans. by W. S. Merwin, from *Selected Translations 1948–1968* (Atheneum), © W. S. Merwin, 1968. Reprinted by permission of W. S. Merwin and Atheneum Publishers.


O. V. DE L. MILOSZ

"L'Étrangère," "Le roi don Luis . . . ," "Quand elle viendra . . . ," "Symphonie de novembre," "H," from *Poésies I, II*, © Éditions André Silvaire, 1960. Reprinted by permission of Éditions André Silvaire.
"L'Étrangère," "King don Luis," "When She Comes," trans. by John Peck. Reprinted by permission of John Peck. "Strophes," trans. by Ezra Pound, from *Ezra Pound: Translations* (New Directions), © by Ezra Pound, 1963. Reprinted by permission of New Directions Publishing Corporation. "H," trans. by David Gascoyne. Printed by permission of David Gascoyne.


BENJAMIN PÉRET

"Chanson de la sécheresse," "Quatre à quatre," "Faire des pieds et des mains," "Louis XVI s'en va à la guillotine," from *Oeuvres Complètes* I, II, © Éditions Losfeld, 1970, 1971. Reprinted by permission of Éditions Losfeld.

"Song in Time of Drought" trans. by James Laughlin. Reprinted by permission of James Laughlin. "On All Fours," trans. by Charles Simic & Michael Benedikt. Reprinted by permission of Charles Simic and Michael Benedikt. "Making Feet and Hands," trans. by David Gascoyne, from *Selected Verse Translations*, Oxford University Press, 1970. Reprinted by permission of David Gascoyne and Oxford University Press. "Louis XVI Goes to the Guillotine," trans. by Charles Simic. Reprinted by permission of Charles Simic.

MARCELIN PLEYNET

"Noir," "de charbon," "la nouvelle république." Reprinted by permission of Marcelin Pleynet. "ces matinées . . . ," "C'est toujours . . . ," "où la lumière . . . ," from *Comme*, © Éditions du Seuil, 1965. Reprinted by permission of Éditions du Seuil. "It's always . . . ," trans. by Serge Gavronsky, from *Poems and Texts*, October House, 1968. Reprinted by permission of Serge Gavronsky. "Black," "of coal," "the new republic," trans. by John Ashbery. Reprinted by permission of John Ashbery. "these mornings . . . " and "where the light . . . ," trans. by Harry Mathews. Reprinted by permission of Harry Mathews.

FRANCIS PONGE

"Pluie," "La Bougie," "Les Plaisirs de la porte," "Faune et flore," from *Le Parti pris des choses*, © Éditions Gallimard, 1942; "Rhétorique" and "Introduction au galet," from *Proêmes*, © Éditions Gallimard, 1948. Reprinted by permission of Éditions Gallimard.
"Rain," trans. by Peter Riley. Printed by permission of Peter Riley. "The Candle" and "The Pleasures of the Door," trans. by Raymond Federman. Reprinted by permission of Raymond Federman." "Fauna and Flora," trans. by Richard Wilbur. Reprinted by permission of Richard Wilbur. "Rhetoric," trans. by Serge Gavronsky, from *Francis Ponge: The Power of Language*, University of California Press, 1979. Reprinted by permission of Serge Gavronsky. "Introduction to the Pebble," trans. by Paul Bowles, © View, Inc., 1945. Reprinted by permission of Paul Bowles.

JACQUES PRÉVERT

"Pater Noster," "Le Cancre," "La Cène," "Et la fête continue," "Barbara," from *Paroles*, © Éditions Gallimard, 1946. Reprinted by permission of Éditions Gallimard.
"Pater Noster," "The Dunce," "The Last Supper," "And the Fete Continues," "Barbara," trans. by Lawrence Ferlinghetti, from *Paroles*, by Jacques Prévert, © City Lights Books, 1958. Reprinted by permission of City Lights Books.

RAYMOND QUENEAU

"Les Ziaux," from *Les Ziaux*, © Éditions Gallimard, 1943; "Cygnes," "Pauvre type," "Pour un Art Poétique I," "L'Espèce humaine," "Si Tu t'imagines," from *L'Instant fatal*, © Éditions Gallimard, 1948. Reprinted by permission of Éditions Gallimard.

"The Seyes," "Sines," "Poor Fellow," "Toward a Poetic Art I," "The Human Species," trans. by Teo Savory, from *Raymond Queneau*, © Unicorn Press, 1971. Reprinted by permission of Unicorn Press. "If You Imagine," trans. by Michael Benedikt. Reprinted by permission of Michael Benedikt.


PIERRE REVERDY

"Pour le moment," "Auberge," "Mémoire," from *Plupart du temps: poèmes 1915–1922*, © Flammarion, 1967. Reprinted by permission of Flammarion and the Comité Pierre Reverdy. "Clair hiver," "Quai aux Fleurs," "Voyages sans fin," "Perspective," "Encore l'amour," "L'Invasion," "Cascade," "Chair vive," from *Main d'Oeuvre: 1913–1949*, © Mercure de France, 1949. Reprinted by permission of Mercure de France and the Comité Pierre Reverdy.

"Perspective," trans. by David Gascoyne, from *Selected Verse Translations*, Oxford University Press, 1970. Reprinted by permission of David Gascoyne and Oxford University Press. "For the Moment," trans. by Ron Padgett. Printed by permission of Ron Padgett. "Inn," trans. by Eugene Jolas. Reprinted by permission of Maria Jolas. "Memory," "Flower Market," "Live Flesh," trans. by Kenneth Rexroth, from *Pierre Reverdy: Selected Poems* (New Directions), © by Kenneth Rexroth, 1969. Reprinted by permission of New Directions Publishing Corporation. "Clear Winter," "Endless Journeys," "Love Again," "The Invasion," trans. by John Ashbery. Reprinted by permission of John Ashbery. "Waterfall," trans. by Mark Rudman. Printed by permission of Mark Rudman.


DENIS ROCHE

"Théâtre des agissements d'Éros," from *Éros énergumène*, © Éditions du Seuil, 1968. Reprinted by permission of Éditions du Seuil.

"Eros Possessed," trans. by Harry Mathews. Reprinted by permission of Harry Mathews.


JACQUES ROUBAUD

"le mieux serait . . . ," "petit tamis . . . ," "soleil bruit . . . ," "tu es sauf . . . ," "le temps . . . ," "je rêve . . . ," "(noyade)," "Jardin de roses à Oakland," from *Σ* © Éditions Gallimard, 1967. Reprinted by permission of Éditions Gallimard.

"the best thing . . . ," "small sieve . . . ," "Oakland Rose Garden," trans. by Neil Baldwin. Printed by permission of Neil Baldwin. "sun noise . . . ," "you are safe . . . ," "time . . . ," "I dream . . . ," "(drowning)," trans. by Robert Kelly. Printed by permission of Robert Kelly.


CLAUDE ROYET-JOURNOUD

"Le Cercle nombreux," from *Le Renversement*, © Éditions Gallimard, 1972; "Até," from *La Notion d'obstacle*, © Éditions Gallimard, 1978. Reprinted by permission of Éditions Gallimard.

"The Crowded Circle," trans. by Keith Waldrop, from *Reversal*, Hellcoal First Edition Series, 1973. Reprinted by permission of Keith Waldrop. "Até," trans. by Keith

Waldrop, from *Até*, Blue Guitar Books and Imprint Editions, 1981. Reprinted by permission of Keith Waldrop.

### SAINT-JOHN PERSE

"Poème pour Valery Larbaud," "Exil 7," "Neiges 4," "Oiseaux 8," from *Oeuvre Poétique*, © Editions Gallimard, 1960. Reprinted by permission of Madame Alexis Léger. "Anabase VII": Reprinted by permission of Harcourt Brace Jovanovich, Inc. from *Anabasis* by Saint-John Perse, translated by T.S. Eliot, copyright 1938, 1949 by Harcourt Brace Jovanovich, Inc.; renewed 1966, 1977 by Esme Valerie Eliot.

"Exile 7" and "Snows 4," trans. by Denis Devlin; "Birds 8," trans. by Robert Fitzgerald, from *Collected Poems*, © Princeton University Press, 1971. Reprinted by permission of Princeton University Press. "Poem for Valery Larbaud," trans. by Richard Howard. Reprinted by permission of the *Quarterly Review of Literature*.

### VICTOR SEGALEN

"Aux Dix mille années," "A celui-là," "On me dit," "Libation Mongole," "Écrit avec du sang," "Les mauvais artisans," "Nom caché," from *Stèles*, © Librairie Plon, 1929. Reprinted by permission of Librairie Plon.

"To the Ten Thousand Years," "To That Person," "I Am Told," "Mongol Libation," "Written in Blood," "Bad Craftsmen," "Hidden Name," trans. by Nathaniel Tarn, from *Stelae*, Unicorn Press, 1969. Reprinted by permission of Nathaniel Tarn and Unicorn Press.

### PHILIPPE SOUPAULT

"Horizon," "Georgia," "Say It with music," "Le Nageur," "Comrade," "Médaille de sauvetage," "Articles de sport," from *Poèmes et Poésics: 1917–1973*, Bernard Grasset, 1973. Reprinted by permission of Philippe Soupault.

"Horizon," "Life-Saving Medal," "Sporting Goods," trans. by Rosmarie Waldrop. Printed by permission of Rosmarie Waldrop. "Georgia" and "The Swimmer," trans. by Paul Auster, from *A Little Anthology of Surrealist Poets*, S.B. Press, 1972. Reprinted by permission of Paul Auster. "Say It With Music," trans. by Eugene Jolas. Reprinted by permission of Maria Jolas. "Comrade," trans. by Pat Nolan. Reprinted by permission of Pat Nolan.

### JULES SUPERVIELLE

"Que m'importe," from *Débarcadères*, © Éditions Gallimard, 1922; "Pointe de flamme," "Haute mer," "Pont superieur," from *Gravitations*, © Éditions Gallimard, 1925; "Emmêlé . . . ," "La Pluie et les tyrans," from *La Fable du monde*, © Éditions Gallimard, 1938; "Hommage à la vie," "Le Clos," from *1939–1945*, © Éditions Gallimard, 1946; "Je vous rêve . . . ," from *Oublieuse Mémoire*, © Éditions Gallimard, 1949. Reprinted by permission of Éditions Gallimard.

"What do I care . . . ," trans. by William Alwyn. Reprinted by permission of William Alwyn. "Flame Point," trans. by Allen Mandelbaum. Printed by permission of Allen Mandelbaum. "Rain and the Tyrants," trans. by David Gascoyne, from

*Selected Verse Translations,* Oxford University Press, 1970. Reprinted by permission of David Gascoyne and Oxford University Press. "Deep Sea," "A Pot of Earth," trans. by Denise Levertov; "Homage to Life," trans. by Kenneth Rexroth; "Entangled . . . ," "The Enclosure," "I dream you . . . ," trans. by James Kirkup; from *Jules Supervielle: Selected Writings,* © New Directions, 1967. Reprinted by permission of New Directions Publishing Corporation.


TRISTAN TZARA

"Soir," "La Mort de Guillaume Apollinaire," "Voie," "Accès," "Volt," "L'homme approximatif I," "Monsieur AA L'antiphilosophe I," "Poème pour une robe de Mme Sonia Delaunay," from *Oeuvres complètes* (I, II), © Flammarion, 1975, 1979. Reprinted by permission of Flammarion.
"The Death of Guillaume Apollinaire," "Way," "Approach," "Volt," trans. by Lee Harwood, from *Tristan Tzara: Selected Poems,* Trigram Press, 1975. Reprinted by permission of Lee Harwood. "A Poem in Yellow after Tristan Tzara," trans. by Jerome Rothenberg. Printed by permission of Jerome Rothenberg. "Evening," trans. by Charles Simic & Michael Benedikt. Reprinted by permission of Charles Simic and Michael Benedikt. "Approximate Man I," trans. by Paul Auster, from *A Little Anthology of Surrealist Poets,* S.B. Press, 1972. Reprinted by permission of Paul Auster. "Monsieur AA, Antiphilosopher I," trans. by Richard Howard. Reprinted by permission of Richard Howard.


ALAIN VEINSTEIN

"Vers l'autre . . . ," from *Recherche des dispositions anciennes,* © Maeght Éditeur, 1977. Reprinted by permission of Maeght Éditeur.
"Toward the Other . . . ," trans. by Rosmarie Waldrop. Printed by permission of Rosmarie Waldrop.

# Index of Translators